HISTORICAL DICTIONARIES
OF WAR, REVOLUTION, AND CIVIL UNREST
Jon Woronoff, Series Editor

Historical Dictionary of the Holocaust

Second Edition

Jack R. Fischel

Historical Dictionaries of War, Revolution, and Civil Unrest, No. 42

The Scarecrow Press, Inc.
Lanham • Toronto • Plymouth, UK
2010

Published by Scarecrow Press, Inc.
A wholly owned subsidiary of The Rowman & Littlefield Publishing Group, Inc.
4501 Forbes Boulevard, Suite 200, Lanham, Maryland 20706
http://www.scarecrowpress.com

Estover Road, Plymouth PL6 7PY, United Kingdom

British Library Cataloguing in Publication Information Available

Library of Congress Cataloging-in-Publication Data

Fischel, Jack.
  Historical dictionary of the Holocaust / Jack R. Fischel. — 2nd ed.
      p. cm. — (Historical dictionaries of war, revolution, and civil unrest ; No. 42)
  Includes bibliographical references.
  ISBN 978-0-8108-6774-1 (cloth : alk. paper) — ISBN 978-0-8108-7485-5
(ebook)
    1. Holocaust, Jewish (1939-1945)—Dictionaries. 2. Antisemitism—Germany—
Dictionaries. I. Title.
  D804.25.F57 2010
  940.53'1803--dc22
                                                                2010006483

Printed in the United States of America

To my wife Julie

Contents

Editor's Foreword

Among those events that should never be forgotten, lest they be repeated in another form, is the Holocaust. Yet, more than half a century later, there is a tendency to forget—if not to relativize—the Nazi extermination campaign against the Jews. More insidiously, a vicious effort is being made in limited circles to deny the Holocaust. This *Historical Dictionary of the Holocaust* is another reminder of what happened to the Jews and other victims of Nazi Germany's genocidal policies. Even this straightforward account of who did what and when, who did not react and why, and consequently how many persons (Jews and others) died or suffered makes for grisly and painful reading. The dictionary's purpose is to inform, and it covers the subject broadly and objectively. Moreover, it takes into account many of the residual unresolved issues of the Holocaust up to the present and shows that there are still many loose ends, even after all this time.

This is not the only reference work on the Holocaust, but it has many useful features. The background is presented in an extensive introduction, and detailed aspects involving persons, place, events, and organizations are covered in the dictionary entries. The progression of the Holocaust is shown in the chronology. And the book includes a comprehensive bibliography that allows the reader to pursue aspects of the Nazi genocide under specific categories. This second edition builds on an already impressive and well-received first edition by adding to all parts of the book. The introduction and chronology have been brought up-to-date, and there are many new entries in the dictionary section. Some of these make the wartime events more explicit, if not comprehensible, while others demonstrate clearly that this is not an issue that can simply be relegated to the past, that it is necessary to refute spurious claims even today. The bibliography now includes more titles and indicates useful resources on the Web and in cinematic form.

This second edition, like the first, was written by Jack Fischel, who has drawn on decades of experience as a teacher, lecturer, writer, editor, and organizer of conferences relating to the Holocaust. This includes several decades as a professor of history at Millersville University and also as director of its annual conference on the Holocaust. Over this period, he has written two books of his own, *The Holocaust* and *The Holocaust and Its Religious Impact*, edited *The Encyclopedia of Jewish American Popular Culture*, and coedited *Jewish American History and Culture: An Encyclopedia*, as well as coedited the *Holocaust Studies Annual* several times. His extensive and varied experience has been put to good use in this expanded and even more informative second edition of the *Historical Dictionary of the Holocaust.*

Jon Woronoff
Series Editor

Acronyms and Abbreviations

AB	Ausserordentliche Befriedungsaktion (Extraordinary Pacification Action)
AFSC	American Friends Service Committee
CDJ	Comité de Défense des Juifs (Belguim)
COJE	Committee for Special Jewish Affairs (The Netherlands)
Degesh	Deutsche Gesellschaft für Schädlingsbekämpfung (German Vermin Combating Corporation)
DP	Displaced Persons
GEKRAT	Gemeinnützige Kranken-Transport G.m.b.h. (Charitable Society for the Transportation of the Sick)
GESTAPO	Geheime Staatspolizei (Secret State Police)
ICRC	International Committee of the Red Cross
IHR	Institute for Historical Review
IMT	International Military Tribunal
JÄGERSTAB	German Central Planning Board
JDC	American Joint Distribution Committee (The "Joint")
KRIPO	Kriminalpolizei (Criminal Police)
K-Z	Konzentrationlager (concentration camp)
Nazi(s)	Acronym formed from "NAtional and soZIalist." The term refers to Germany between 1933 and 1945 and the National Socialist German Workers' Party (NSDAP)
ORPO	Ordnungspolizei (Order Police)
RSHA	Reichssicherheitshauptamt (Reich Security Main Office)
SA	Sturmabteilung (Storm Troopers or "Brown Shirts")

SD	Sicherheitsdienst (Security Service)
SIPO	Sicherheitspolizei (Security Police)
S.N.B.	Swiss National Bank
SS	Schutzstaffel (Guard Corps)
T-4	Tiergarten Strasse 4 (the Berlin address of the Euthanasia Program)
UGIF	Union Générale des Israélites en France (The Organization of French Jewry)
UNSCOP	United Nations Special Commission on Palestine
WJC	World Jewish Congress
WRB	War Refugee Board
WVHA	Wirtschaft und Verwaltungshauptamt (Economy and Administration Main Office)
YISHUV	The Jewish community in Palestine
ZEGOTA	Rada Pomocy Zydom (Council for Aid to the Jews)
ZOB	Zydowska Organizacja Bojowa (Jewish Combat Organization)

Chronology

1879 Wilhelm Marr, a member of the German Reichstag, coins the term "anti-Semitism" and subsequently organizes the League of Anti-Semitism.

1881 German composer Richard Wagner, in an essay titled "Know Thyself," attacks Jews as the "demon causing mankind's downfall." Karl Eugen Duhring, German economist and philosopher, writes the first in a series of tracts on racial anti-Semitism. He argues that the "Jewish type" presents a biological danger to the German people.

1886 Edouard Drumont publishes *La France Juive*, in which he charges that the Jews control the economic, political, and cultural life of France.

1894 **15 October:** Captain Alfred Dreyfus, an officer on the French general staff, is accused of passing secrets to the Germans and is arrested. **19–22 December:** Dreyfus is court-martialed, found guilty, and sentenced to life imprisonment on Devil's Island off the coast of French Guiana.

1895 Karl Lueger, the head of the anti-Semitic Christian Socialist Party, is elected for the first time as mayor of Vienna, and reelected in 1897.

1896 Theodor Herzl, offended by the virulent anti-Semitism while he attended the Dreyfus trial, writes *The Jewish State*.

1897 **29–31 August:** Theodor Herzl convenes the First Zionist Congress in Basel, Switzerland.

1899 Houston Stewart Chamberlain publishes *The Foundations of the Nineteenth Century*.

1905 *The Protocols of the Elders of Zion* is published in Russia.

1914 **28 June:** The assassination of Archduke Francis Ferdinand at Sarajevo precipitates the events that lead to the outbreak of World War I in August 1914.

1917 **2 November:** The British government issues the Balfour Declaration. **7 November:** The Bolshevik Revolution begins in Russia.

1918 **11 November:** The armistice is signed, bringing World War I to an end.

1919 **5 January:** The German Workers' Party (DAP), the forerunner of the Nazi Party, is founded in Munich by Anton Drexler and Karl Harrar. **16 September:** Adolf Hitler joins the German Workers' Party.

1920 **24 February:** The DAP party platform is written, and a week later the party changes its name to Nationalsozialistische Deutsche Arbeiterpartei, the National Socialist German Workers' Party (NSDAP).

1921 **July:** Hitler becomes chairman of the NSDAP. **November:** Hitler is recognized as party Führer.

1922 **24 June:** Walther Rathenau, a Jewish industrialist and Germany's foreign minister, is assassinated by a reactionary nationalist.

1923 **9 November:** In Munich, the Nazis, led by Hitler, fail to overthrow the government of Bavaria in what becomes known as the Beer Hall Putsch.

1925 Hitler publishes *Mein Kampf* (My Struggle).

1928 **20 May:** The Nazis win 12 seats in the Reichstag elections.

1930 Alfred Rosenberg publishes *The Myth of the Twentieth Century*. **14 September:** The Nazis become the second-largest political party in Germany as they win 107 seats in the Reichstag elections.

1932 **13 March:** President Paul von Hindenburg defeats Adolf Hitler for the presidency of Germany but does not attain a majority, thus forcing a runoff. **April:** In the second election in April, Hindenburg defeats Hitler with a plurality of 6,000,000 out of a total vote of 36,000,000.

1933   30 January: Hitler becomes chancellor of Germany after the Nazi Party receives approximately 33 percent of the vote in the Reichstag election. Archbishop Michael Cardinal von Faulhaber delivers Advent sermons defending Jews against Nazi persecution. **27 February:** The Reichstag building is set afire, and the government declares a national emergency the next day. **2 March:** The first Nazi concentration camp is established at Dachau. **24 March:** The Reichstag passes the Enabling Act, which becomes the basis for Hitler's dictatorship. **1 April:** A one-day nationwide boycott is instituted by the German government against Jewish businesses. **7 April:** Quotas are applied to the number of Jewish students allowed in higher education, and laws are passed prohibiting Jews from working in the government. **10 May:** Books are publicly burned throughout Germany. Thousands of students gathered and put to the torch approximately 20,000 books written by Jews and other "undesirables." The books destroyed included those by such writers as Albert Einstein, Sigmund Freud, Andre Gide, Helen Keller, Jack London, Erich Maria Remarque, H. G. Wells, and Emile Zola. **25 August:** Jewish leaders from Palestine and Nazi authorities sign the Transfer Agreement ("Haavara Agreement"). **22 September:** Jews are removed from literature, music, art, broadcasting, theater, and the press in Germany.

1934   17 May: Julius Streicher publishes a special issue of *Der Stürmer* on the subject of Jewish ritual murder. A storm of international protest results in Hitler ordering the suppression of the issue. **30 June:** Hitler orders the Schutzstaffel (SS), under Heinrich Himmler, to purge the Sturmabteilung (SA) leadership. In what is known as the "Night of the Long Knives," many are murdered, including Ernst Rohm. **2 August:** Paul von Hindenburg, the German president, dies, giving Hitler the opportunity to establish a dictatorship.

1935   15 September: The Nuremberg Laws are decreed, defining who may be a German citizen and banning marriage and other forms of contact between Jews and Germans. **31 December:** Jews are dismissed from the civil service in Germany.

Late 1930s   The Nazis introduce a Euthanasia Program designed for the "mercy killing" of the incurably ill, "asocials," and other categories deemed "life unworthy of living." Ultimately the techniques used in the euthanasia campaign were applied to the death camps. Between 80,000 and 100,000 people died in the euthanasia killing process.

1937   14 March: Pope Pius XI issues "With Burning Concern" ("Mit Brennender Sorge"), a statement against racism and nationalism. **16 July:** A concentration camp is established at Buchenwald.

1938   13 March: In the Anschluss, Germany annexes Austria. **24 April:** The German government announces that all Jewish property must be registered. **26 April:** Orders are issued in Austria for expropriation of Jewish property. **29 May:** The first anti-Jewish law is proclaimed in Hungary, restricting to 20 percent the Jewish share in the economy. **25 June:** German-Jewish physicians are permitted only to treat Jewish patients. **6–15 July:** A conference is held at Evian-les-Bains, attended by representatives from 32 nations, to discuss the refugee problem; little action toward solving the problem is taken. **17 August:** All Jewish men in Germany are required to add "Israel" to their name, and all Jewish women, "Sarah." **26 August:** The Central Bureau for Jewish Emigration (Zentralstelle fur Judische Auswanderung) is organized in Vienna under Adolf Eichmann. **27 September:** Jews are banned from practicing law in Germany. **5 October:** Passports of German Jews are marked with the letter J, for *Jude*. **28 October:** Between 15,000 and 17,000 stateless Jews are expelled from Germany to Poland; most are interned in Zbazyn. **9–10 November:** The Kristallnacht pogrom takes place in Germany and Austria, and 30,000 Jews are interned in concentration camps. **12 November:** In the aftermath of the Kristallnacht pogrom, German Jews are fined 1 billion reichsmarks.

1939   1 January: "The Measures for the Elimination of Jews from the German Economy" are invoked, banning Jews from working with Germans. **2 March:** Cardinal Eugencio Pacelli becomes Pope Pius XII. **17 May:** A British government white paper is issued, severely restricting Jewish immigration to Palestine. **4 July:** The Reichsvereinigung der Juden in Deutschland (Reich Association of Jews in Germany) replaces the Reichsvertretung der Deutschen Juden (Reich Representation of German Jews). **23 August:** The German–Soviet Pact is signed. **1 September:** A curfew is imposed that forbids Jews throughout Germany from being out of doors after 8 p.m. Germany invades Poland. **3 September:** France and Great Britain declare war on Germany. **27 Sep-**

tember: The Reich Security Main Office (Reichssicherheitshauptamt, RSHA) is established. **28 September:** Poland is partitioned between Germany and the Soviet Union; German forces occupy Warsaw. **1 October:** The Polish government-in-exile is formed in France (later it moves to London). **8 October:** The Nazis establish the first ghetto in Piotrkow Trybunalski in Poland. **16 October:** Krakow becomes the capital of the General-Gouvernement. **9 November:** Lodz is annexed to the German Reich. **12 November:** The deportation of Jews from Lodz to other parts of Poland begins. **23 November:** Hans Frank orders that by 1 December Jews in the General-Gouvernement must wear the yellow Star of David badge. **28 November:** Frank issues an order calling for the establishment of Judenräte in the General-Gouvernement.

1940   February: The Lodz ghetto is established. **12 April:** Frank declares that Krakow must be *Judenfrei* ("free of Jews") by November. **27 April:** Himmler orders the establishment of a concentration camp at Auschwitz. **16 May:** Hans Frank issues orders whereby thousands of Polish leaders and intellectuals are killed. **June:** The first prisoners, mostly Poles, are brought to Auschwitz. **22 June:** Germany and France sign an armistice. **16 July:** The expulsion of Jews from Alsace and Lorraine to southern France begins. **19 July:** Telephones are confiscated from Jews in Germany. **6 September:** Michael I becomes the king of Romania, after his father, Carol II, flees the country, and a National Legionary government is set up under Ion Antonescu. **3 October:** The first Statut des Juifs is announced in Vichy France. **7 October:** The Law for the Protection of the Nation is issued in Bulgaria, curbing the rights of Jews. **22 October:** Jewish businesses are registered throughout the Netherlands. **4 November:** Jewish civil servants are dismissed throughout the Netherlands. **15 November:** The Warsaw ghetto is sealed.

1941   21–23 January: The Iron Guard unsuccessfully attempts a coup in Romania, accompanied by riots against the Jews. **5 February:** The Law for the Protection of the State is issued in Romania, making Romanian Jews subject to double the punishment for crimes committed. **13 February:** The Joodse Rand (Jewish Council) meets for the first time in Amsterdam. **22 February:** In Amsterdam, 389 Jewish males from the Jewish quarter are sent to Buchenwald. **25 February:** A general anti-Nazi strike is held in Amsterdam. **March:** By March, 40,000 out of 60,000 Jews have been deported from Krakow. **1 March:** Bulgaria joins the Tripartite Pact. Himmler orders the construction of a camp at Birkenau (Auschwitz II). **15 May:** A law is passed in Romania permitting Jews to be drafted for forced labor. **2 June:** The second Statut des Juifs is promulgated in Vichy France. **6 June:** The Kommissarbefehl (Commissar Order) stating that political officers in the Soviet army must be singled out and killed is issued in preparation for the invasion of the Soviet Union. **22 June:** Operation Barbarossa, the invasion of the Soviet Union, is launched by Germany. **23 June:** The Einsatzgruppen begin their killings in the Soviet Union and submit daily reports of their activities. **24 June:** German forces occupy Vilna. **27 June:** Hungary enters the war on the Axis side. **1 July–31 August:** Einsatzgruppe D, Wehrmacht forces, augmented by Romanian forces, kill between 150,000 and 160,000 Jews in Bessarabia. **4 July:** A Judenrat is established in Vilna. About 5,000 Vilna Jews are killed during the month of July by Einsatzkommando 9 and local collaborators. **21 July:** Hermann Goering signs an order giving Reinhard Heydrich the authority to prepare a "Final Solution" to the "Jewish question" in Europe. **1 August:** The Bialystok ghetto and the Minsk ghetto are established. **17–21 August:** Seventy thousand Jews pass through the Drancy transit camp. **1 September:** The Euthanasia Program is officially ended; between 80,000 and 100,000 people were killed in Germany. **3 September:** The first experimental gassing at Auschwitz is conducted on Soviet prisoners of war. **19 September:** Jews in the Reich are required to wear the yellow badge in public. **19 September:** Kiev is captured by the Germans. 10,000 Jews are killed in Zhitomir. **29–30 September:** At Babi Yar, 33,771 Kiev Jews are killed by Einsatzkommando 4a. **1 October–December 1943:** In *Aktionen* in Vilna, 33,500 Jews are killed. **19 October–28 September 1943:** Luxembourg Jews are deported to Lodz in eight transports. **28 October:** Nine thousand Jews are killed in an *Aktion* outside Kovno at the Ninth Fort; 17,412 Jews remain in the Kovno ghetto. **8 November:** The establishment of a ghetto in Lvov is ordered. **24 November:** The Theresienstadt ghetto is opened by the Germans. **29 November:** The Union Générale des Israélites de France (UGIF), the organization of French Jewry, is formed. **7 December:** Japanese bomb Pearl Harbor; the United States declares war on Japan. **8 December:** The first transport of Jews arrives at the Chelmno death camp; transports continue to arrive until March 1943. **11 December:** Nazi Germany declares war on the United States.

1942   16 January: Deportations from Lodz to Chelmno begin and continue until September 1942. **20 January:** The Wannsee Conference is presided over by Heydrich and attended by top Nazi officials, in order to coordinate the Final Solution. **1 February:** The SS Wirtschafts Verwaltungshauptamt (VHA) (Economy and Administration Main Office) is established under Oswald Pohl. **8 February:** The first transport of Jews from Salonika is sent to Auschwitz. **23 February:** The *Struma*, a ship loaded with Jewish refugees, is refused entry to Palestine and sinks off the coast of Turkey; 768 passengers drown and only one survives. **1 March:** Construction of the Sobibor death camp begins in Poland; Jews are killed there beginning in May. **12 March–20 April:** Thirty thousand Jews are deported from Lublin to Belzec. **17 March:** Killings begin at the Belzec death camp; the first of the Aktion Reinhard camps is put into operation. **27 March:** The first transport of 60,000 Jews from Slovakia are sent by Adolf Eichmann's office to Auschwitz. **28 March:** The first transport of French Jews is sent to Auschwitz. **27 May:** In Belgium, the wearing of the yellow Star of David badge is decreed and goes into effect on 3 June. **7 June:** The Jews in occupied France are required to wear the yellow Star of David badge. **11 June:** Adolf Eichmann's office orders that the deportations of Jews from the Netherlands, Belgium, and France begin in a few weeks. **22 June:** The first transport from the Drancy camp in France leaves for Auschwitz. **26 June:** A transport from Brussels is sent to the Organisation Todt labor camps in northern France. **14 July:** The systematic transfer of Dutch Jewry to Westerbork camp begins. **15 July:** The first transport leaves Westerbork for Auschwitz. **16–17 July:** In Paris, 12,887 Jews are rounded up and sent to Drancy; a total of about 42,500 Jews are sent to Drancy from all over France during this *Aktion*. **19 July:** Himmler orders that the extermination of the Jews of the General-Gouvernement be completed by the end of the year. **22 July:** Construction of the Treblinka extermination center is begun and is completed by August 1943; about 870,000 Jews were eventually killed there. **22 July–12 September:** During mass deportations from Warsaw, some 300,000 Jews are deported, 265,000 of them to Treblinka; about 60,000 Jews remain in the Warsaw ghetto. **23 July:** The head of the Warsaw Judenrat, Adam Czerniakow, commits suicide rather than assist the Nazis in deporting the Warsaw Jews. **6 August–29 December 1943:** Jewish inmates from the Gurs camp in France are deported to Auschwitz and Sobibor.

8 August: In Geneva, Gerhart Riegner cables Rabbi Stephen S. Wise in New York and Sidney Silverman in London about Nazi plans for the extermination of European Jewry. The U.S. Department of State holds up delivery of the message to Wise, who receives it from Silverman on 28 August. **12 August:** Winston Churchill, Joseph Stalin, and Averell Harriman meet in Moscow and affirm their goal of destroying Nazism. **13–20 August:** The majority of Croatian Jews are deported to Auschwitz. **1 November:** The deportation of Jews from the Bialystok district to Treblinka begins. **24 November:** Rabbi Wise releases to the press the news contained in the Riegner cable. **4 December:** The Zegota (Council for Aid to the Jews) is established in Poland. **10 December:** The Polish government-in-exile asks the Allies to retaliate for the Nazi killing of civilians, especially Jews. **17 December:** An Allied declaration is made condemning the Nazis' "bestial policy of cold-blooded extermination."

1943 **14–24 January:** Churchill and Franklin D. Roosevelt meet at Casablanca and proclaim that Germany's unconditional surrender is to be the central war aim. **18–22 January:** Over 5,000 Jews are deported from Warsaw and are killed; the first Warsaw ghetto uprising breaks out. **5–12 February:** In Bialystok, 2,000 Jews are killed and 10,000 deported to Treblinka; Jews offer armed resistance. **26 February:** The first transport of Gypsies reaches Auschwitz, where they are placed in a special section of the camp called Gypsy Camp. **20 March–18 August:** Transports from Salonika arrive at Auschwitz. **13 April:** Mass graves are discovered at Katyn, Poland, the site of a massacre of Polish officers by the Soviets. **19 April–16 May:** The Warsaw ghetto uprising starts; the ghetto is eventually destroyed by the Germans. **8 May:** Mordecai Anielewicz and other leaders of the Warsaw ghetto uprising are killed in a bunker at 18 Milna Street during the fighting. **12 May:** Samuel Arthur Zygielbojm, a Jewish representative of the Polish government-in-exile in London, commits suicide as an expression of solidarity with the Jewish fighters in Warsaw, and in protest against the world's silence regarding the fate of the Jews in Nazi-occupied Europe. **1 June:** The final liquidation of the Lvov ghetto begins. When the Jews resist, 3,000 are killed; 7,000 are sent to Janowska. **5 July:** Himmler orders that Sobibor, an extermination camp, be made a concentration camp. **2 August:** The uprising at Treblinka takes place. **15–20 August:** Nazi forces under Odilo Globocnik surround the Bialystok ghetto, and its 30,000 remaining Jews are ordered to appear for evacuation; a Jewish uprising breaks out in the ghetto. **18–21 August:** The final deportation of Bialystok Jewry takes place. **1 September:** An uprising is attempted in the Vilna ghetto but is aborted. During the rest of September, the fighters escape to the partisans. **23–24 September:** The Vilna ghetto is liquidated; some 3,700 Jews are sent to labor camps in Estonia and 4,000 are deported to Sobibor. **1–2 October:** German police begin rounding up Jews for deportation in Denmark. The Danish population begins the rescue of 7,200 Danish Jews. **2–3 October:** Throughout the Netherlands, families of Jewish men are drafted for forced labor and sent to Westerbork. **14 October:** The Sobibor uprising takes place. **18 October:** In Rome, 1,035 Jews are deported to Auschwitz. **22 October:** The Germans destroy the Minsk ghetto and all those remaining in it.

1944 **13 January:** U.S. Assistant Secretary of the Treasury Josiah Dubois delivers his report titled "Report to the Secretary on the Acquiescence of This Government in the Murder of the Jews" to Treasury Secretary Henry Morgenthau Jr. Later in the month, President Roosevelt establishes the War Refugee Board. **19 March:** Fearful that Hungary would secede from the war and determined to annihilate Hungarian Jews, the German army marches into Hungary. **5 April:** Jews in Hungary begin wearing the yellow badge. **7 April:** Alfred Wetzler and Rudolf Vrba escape from Auschwitz and arrive in Slovakia with detailed information about the killing of Jews in Auschwitz. Their report, which reaches the free world in June, becomes known as the Auschwitz Protocols. **15 May–9 July:** Approximately 437,000 primarily Hungarian Jews are deported to Auschwitz. Most of those sent to Auschwitz are gassed soon after their arrival. **6 June:** D-Day, Allied forces land in Normandy with the largest seaborne force in history. **23 June–14 July:** Transports from Lodz reach Chelmno. **9 July:** Miklos Horthy, Hungarian regent, orders an end to the deportations from Hungary; two days later they cease. **21–25 July:** Children's homes in France operated by the Union Générale des Israélites de France are raided. Three hundred Jewish children, in addition to adult staff, are sent to Drancy and then to Auschwitz. **23 July:** A delegation of the International Committee of the Red Cross (ICRC) visits Theresienstadt. **28 July:** The first major death march begins, with the evacuation of the Gesia Street camps in Warsaw.

Some 3,600 prisoners set out on foot for Kutno; 1,000 are killed on the journey of 81 miles. **6–7 October:** In the Sonderkommando uprising at Auschwitz, one of the gas chambers is destroyed before the uprising is quelled. **8 November:** Deportations from Budapest are resumed.

1945 17 January: The Schutzstaffel (SS) is ordered to evacuate Auschwitz and depart on the following day. Some 66,000 prisoners are marched on foot toward Wodzislaw, to be sent from there to other camps, and 15,000 die on the way. At this time, 48,000 men and 18,000 women are still prisoners in Auschwitz and its satellite camps. **19 January:** Lodz is liberated by the Red Army. **5–6 April:** More than 28,250 inmates are evacuated from Buchenwald, and between 7,000 and 8,000 others are killed. **9 April:** The evacuation of Mauthausen begins. **11 April:** The Buchenwald concentration camp is liberated by American forces. **15 April:** Danish Jews in the Protectorate are transferred to Sweden, with the help of the ICRC. **29 April:** Dachau is liberated by the American Seventh Army. **29–30 April:** Ravensbruck is liberated; in the camp are 3,500 sick women. **30 April:** Adolf Hitler and Eva Braun commit suicide in Hitler's bunker in Berlin. **3 May:** The Nazis hand over Theresienstadt, with 17,247 Jewish inmates, to the ICRC. **7 May:** The Germans surrender to the Allies. **8 May:** Soviet troops liberate Theresienstadt. **18 October–1 October 1946:** The Nuremberg Trials, under an international military tribunal, are held to try and punish those who had planned or waged aggressive war, or acted criminally against humanity. Great Britain, the United States, the USSR, and France act on behalf of the United Nations for the 26 countries who had fought Germany. The evidence taken by the tribunal exposed to the world the genocidal fury that had fueled the Nazi movement. The initial trial of 22 major Nazi war criminals resulted in the following judgments. Sentenced to death: Marin Bormann, Hans Frank, Wilhelm Frick, Hermann Goering, Ernst Kaltenbrunner, Wilhelm Keitel, Alfred Jodl, Joachim von Ribbentrop, Alfred Rosenberg, Fritz Sauckel, Arthur Seyss-Inquart, and Julius Streicher. Sentenced to life imprisonment: Walthur Funk, Rudolph Hess, and Erich Racder. Sentenced to prison terms: Karl Donitz (10 years), Konstantin von Neurath (15 years), Baldur von Shirach (20 years), and Albert Speer (20 years). Acquitted: Hans Fritzche, Franz von Papen, and Hjalmer Schacht.

1946 4 July: In the town of Kielce, the Polish residents instigate a pogrom that results in the murder of 42 Jews.

1947   8 May–30 July 1948: The Nuremberg Tribunal sentences 13 I. G. Farben officials to prison terms ranging from 18 months to eight years for exploiting slave labor. **2 July:** The Polish Parliament creates a museum at the Auschwitz death camp. **July–August:** *Exodus 1947*, a ship bearing 4,550 Jews from displaced persons camps in Germany, is refused entry to Palestine by the British. Subsequently, the passengers are returned to displace persons (DP) camps in Germany. **16 August–31 July 1948:** The Nuremberg Tribunal convicts 12 officials of the Krupp Works to sentences ranging from 6 to 12 years in prison. Alfried Krupp is sentenced to 12 years but his punishment is reduced by clemency to time served and restoration of assets.

1948   14 May: The State of Israel is founded.

1951   September: The West German Bundestag agrees to make amends for Nazi crimes against the Jews in the form of material payments to Israel and compensation for Holocaust survivors.

1952   10 September: Israel and West Germany sign a reparation agreement in which the German Federal Republic agrees to send millions of dollars of goods to Israel and provide individual restitution to victims of Nazi persecution.

1953   18 May: The Israeli Knesset (Parliament) establishes Yad Vashem, the Holocaust Martyrs' and Heroes' Remembrance Authority.

1956   September: A stage adaptation of *The Diary of Anne Frank* is premiered simultaneously in several West German cities to great critical acclaim.

1959   27 March: Pope John XXIII declares that the phrase *pro perfidis Judaeis* ("Let us pray for the unbelieving Jew") be deleted from the Good Friday service.

1960   May: Adolf Eichmann is abducted from Buenos Aires, Argentina, by Israeli agents and flown to Israel to stand trial for crimes against the Jewish people. The televised trial opens in Jerusalem in April and is viewed in many countries, including the United States.

1961   15 December: Eichmann is convicted and sentenced to death.

1962 **31 May:** Adolf Eichmann is executed by hanging following the denial of his appeal.

1964 **26 February:** Rolf Hochhuth's controversial play *The Deputy* opens to mixed reviews. The play indicts Pius XII for his failure to publicly protest the mass murder of the Jews during the Holocaust. **12 October–24 August 1965:** The West German government tries and convicts 10 members of the Schutzstaffel (SS) who served at Treblinka. Among those convicted of war crimes is Kurt Franz, the deputy commandant of the camp, who is sentenced to life in prison. **November:** The Second Vatican Council repudiates the notion of the Jewish people as "rejected, cursed or guilty of deicide."

1970s Marcel Ophul's *The Sorrow and the Pity*, which depicts the general indifference of the French population to the plight of the Jews under the Vichy government, is banned in France and not shown on French TV until 1981. **21 April 1970:** Bruno Kreisky is elected chancellor of Austria. Kreisky, who fled the Nazis in 1938, becomes the first Jew to hold such office. **5–6 September 1972:** During the Munich Summer Olympics, members of the Israeli Olympic team were taken hostage and eventually 11 were murdered by Black September, a militant Palestinian group with ties to Yasser Arafat's Fatah organization. The massacre of the Israeli athletes is followed by criticism of the West German government's rescue efforts. **22 October 1979:** An estimated audience of 20 million West Germans views the TV miniseries *Holocaust*. The film results in a national demand for information about both the Nazi era and the Holocaust.

1983 **April:** President Ronald Reagan announces the transfer of two large buildings in Washington, D.C., for the construction of a Holocaust museum.

1984 Carmelite nuns attempt to establish a convent in a vacant building that borders the Auschwitz death camp. The effort is opposed by Jewish groups, which sets off a bitter controversy between Poles and Jews that is not resolved until the intercession of Pope John Paul II temporarily resolves the conflict.

1985 **5–7 May:** Despite widespread criticism, President Ronald Reagan visits the Bitburg military cemetery in West Germany where 47

Waffen SS men lay buried among the 2,000 German soldiers. **8 May:** Richard von Weizsacker, president of the German Federal Republic, in a speech in the Bundestag commemorating the murder of six million Jews, acknowledges, in regard to the Nazi era, that "everyone who wanted to be informed could not fail to observe that the deportation trains were on their way." **November:** A Vatican document on Christian Jewish relations, "The Common Bond: Christians and Jews; Notes for Preaching and Teaching," for the first time mentions Israel and the Holocaust in a Vatican document. Claude Lanzmann's more than nine-hour documentary *Shoah* opens to worldwide acclaim. The film records the memories of survivors, perpetrators, and bystanders to the Holocaust.

1987   April: The U.S. Justice Department places Kurt Waldheim, the former secretary-general of the United Nations and the current president of Austria, on its Watch List as a suspected war criminal. **July:** Klaus Barbie, a Gestapo official in Lyon, France, who was responsible for the execution of at least 4,000 persons and the deportation of 7,000 Jews to concentration camps, is convicted of war crimes by a French court and sentenced to prison, where he dies on 25 September 1991.

1988   8 February: A six-man international commission of prestigious historians found that Kurt Waldheim was aware of Nazi atrocities and did nothing to stop them, though he did not personally participate in war crimes.

1991   19–21 May: President Lech Walesa of Poland, speaking before Israel's Knesset, apologizes for anti-Semitism in Poland's history.

1993   22 April: The U.S. Holocaust Memorial Museum is opened. **15 December:** Stephen Spielberg's film *Schindler's List* is greeted with universal acclaim.

1994   20 April: Paul Touvier, director of the Milice (a French paramilitary group formed in 1943 to support German occupation and the Vichy government), is convicted of crimes against humanity, which included his responsibility for the deportation of Jews to the death camps from 1943 to 1944. The trial is opposed by French prime minister Francois Mitterrand. Touvier dies of cancer in prison on 17 July 1996.

1996   5 September: David Irving files a libel suit against historian Deborah Lipstadt and her publisher, Penguin Books, for stating in her 1993 book, *Denying the Holocaust*, that Irving was a Holocaust denier, a falsifier of history, and a bigot.

1995–1998   In the mid-1990s the World Jewish Congress demands that Swiss banks account for the unclaimed deposits of Jewish victims of the Holocaust.

1998   16 March: The Catholic Church issues a document, *We Remember: A Reflection on the Shoah*, that acknowledges that centuries of Christian prejudice aimed at the Jews rendered many Christians insensitive to Nazi atrocities against the Jews. The document absolves the church from complicity in the Holocaust and gives credit to Pope Pius XII for saving the lives of several hundred thousand Jews. The document, however, skirts the issue of Pius XII's silence in the face of his knowledge of the Final Solution. **2 April:** Maurice Papon, the secretary-general of the Gironde prefecture in Bordeaux, France, between May 1942 and August 1944, is found guilty by a French court of complicity in Nazi crimes against humanity. **October:** Jewish and Serbian groups protest the action of Pope Paul II, who beatified Alojzije Cardinal Stepinac, the Archbishop of Zagreb, who was imprisoned in 1946 by the government of Joseph Tito of Yugoslavia, as a Nazi collaborator. **11 October:** Pope Paul II pronounced Edith Stein, a Jewish intellectual who became a Carmelite nun and died in Auschwitz, a saint and a martyr for the Roman Catholic faith.

2000   11 April: In *DJC Irving v. Penguin Books LTD and Deborah Lipstadt*, Justice Charles Gray rules against David Irving and finds Professor Lipstadt's claims against Irving in *Denying the Holocaust* (1993) to be true.

2005   20 September: The "Nazi hunter" Simon Wiesenthal, famed Holocaust survivor who dedicated his life to the pursuit of Nazi war criminals, dies.

2006   11 December: The International Conference to Review the Global Vision of the Holocaust opens in Tehran, Iran. The conference is hosted by Iran's President Mahmoud Ahmadinejad and features Holocaust deniers and neo-Nazis.

2007   **19 April:** President George W. Bush speaks at the U.S. Holocaust Memorial Museum on the subject of the importance of Holocaust remembrance and the need for action in preventing genocide in Darfur. **9 September:** President Mahmoud Ahmadinejad speaks at Columbia University and questions those who oppose his right to cast doubt on the Holocaust.

2008   **1 November:** President George W. Bush visits the Yad Vashem Memorial in Israel and notes that the memorial is a sobering reminder that evil must be resisted, and praises the victims for not losing their faith.

2009   **19 April:** Former president Bill Clinton opens the Illinois Holocaust Museum and Education Center in Skokie. **12 May:** John Demjanjuk, the alleged guard at Sobibor who was accused of herding thousands of Jews into the gas chambers, arrives in Germany to stand trial after being extradited from the United States. **5 June:** President Barak Obama, accompanied by Elie Wiesel, visits the Buchenwald Concentration Camp. **10 June:** White Supremacist and neo-Nazi James von Brunn kills a guard at the U.S. Holocaust Memorial Museum. **18 September:** President Ahmadinejad calls the Holocaust a "lie" at an anti-Israel rally in Tehran. **24 September:** Prime Minister Benjamin Netanyahu of Israel, speaking before the United Nations, displays Nazi-era documents on the extermination of the Jews. In his rebuke of Iran's president, Mahmoud Ahmadinejad, the Israeli prime minister brandishes two documents: a copy of the minutes of the Wannsee Conference and the original blueprints of the Auschwitz-Birkenau death camp. **30 November:** The trial of John Demjanjuk opens in Munich, Germany. **18 December:** Thieves steal the sign *"Arbeit Macht Frei"* (Work liberates) from the entrance to the former Auschwitz death camp. **19 December:** Pope Benedict XVI moves Pius XII, whom a number of Jewish groups have accused of remaining publicly silent during the Holocaust, a step closer to sainthood when he confirms his predecessor's "heroic virtues." The announcement was denounced by the American Gathering of Holocaust Survivors as "a disturbing and callous act." **20 December:** Polish police recover the *"Arbeit Macht Frei"* sign that was stolen from the gate of Auschwitz. Five suspects are arrested.

Introduction

Germany, during the years between 1933 and 1945, was a state organized around the principle of race. Rudolph Hess, Hitler's confidant, was not being facetious when he defined National Socialism as applied biology. To the Nazis, paraphrasing Benjamin Disraeli, race was everything. This manifested itself in Nazi ideology that juxtaposed the superiority of the Aryan race with the alleged inferior races of the East. Although Jews were viewed as inferior to the Aryan race, there was a categorical difference implied between the Jews and the other races. Jews were perceived as inferior but powerful because they had attained positions of influence and power throughout the Western world. Specifically, Jews were accused of serving their own interests as Jews rather than as loyal citizens of the German nation. Nazi propaganda emphasized the Jewish domination of international finance as well as their disproportionate numbers in the leadership of the Russian Revolution. The Nazis further charged that the Jews had gained excessive influence over all aspects of German public life, as well as throughout the rest of Europe and the United States.

NAZI ANTI-SEMITISM BETWEEN THE TWO WORLD WARS

In the aftermath of Germany's defeat in World War I, anti-Semitic political parties in Weimar Germany, including the Nazis, blamed the Jews for the nation's loss in the war. This charge was reinforced by the canard that the loyalty of the Jews transcended geographic boundary lines. The allegiance of the Jews, the Nazis argued, was to one another across international boundaries rather than to the nation of their birth, and the Nazis accused "international Jewry" of profiting from Germany's defeat in the war. Similarly, the Nazis believed that the Jews had weakened the moral fabric of Germany through their "bolshevization" of the social and cultural life of the nation. The avant-garde in art, music, and film, and modernism in general, were viewed as Jewish weapons in the fight to permeate German life with a "Jewish sensibility." The achievements of Albert Einstein (the theories of relativity), Sigmund Freud (psychoanalysis), and other Jewish scientists, for example, were attacked as promoting what Josef Goebbels called a "Jew science" that sought to destroy the moral and spiritual vitality of the nation.

Nazi racial ideologists claimed that the Germans originally descended from the Aryan race, an Indo-European language group, and that the reassertion of national greatness necessitated the removal of the Jewish Semites from Germany, if not from all of Europe. This ideology held that the struggle between the Aryans and the Semites was the preeminent theme of world history. Although in antiquity the Aryan races generally prevailed over the Semites in warfare—as, for example, Greece's defeat of Persia and Rome's defeat of Carthage—the Semitic spiritual system, in the form of Christianity, with all of its implications for protecting the weak from the strong, had triumphed throughout Europe. In an age in which the ideas of Social Darwinism and "survival of the fittest" had become a mantra in right-wing circles, Christianity and its derivative moral system were seen as giving succor to the weak and the least fit in society.

Having identified Christianity as a Semitic and, therefore, an alien religion, the Nazis attacked both Jews and Judaism as the progenitor of an unacceptable value system. Mixing both religious and racial categories, the Nazis wasted little time in purging their German churches of Jewish or Semitic influences. But the Nazi critics of the Jews were not content to attack the doctrines of St. Paul, derisively referred to as "Rabbi" Paul, or ritual practices. They also insisted that baptized Jews who served in the churches of Germany be eliminated from their ecclesiastical positions. This demand, however, ran counter to the beliefs of the churches, which taught the redemptive nature of baptism. The reaction in both the Catholic and Protestant churches to the purging of converted Jews was to confront the regime over this matter. The response of the Evangelical German Confessional Church and Pope Pius XI's encyclical, "With Burning Concern" (Mit Brennender Sorge), issued in 1937, condemned the racist practices of the Nazis as being incompatible with Christian teaching. The attitude toward the Nazi persecution of the Jews, however, was one of silence, which may have indicated approval. The Nazis were not the first to legislate anti-Jewish laws; rather, discrimination against Jews was as old as Christianity itself. For example, the Nuremberg Laws (1935), which denationalized the Jews of Germany, had their counterpart in the Middle Ages when Jews were subjected to all sorts of restrictions, including their contacts with the Christian majority.

What was new about the Nazis' treatment of the Jews was their rejection of the efficacy of baptism, which precluded discrimination on the basis of ethnic origin or racial categories. The Catholic Church, in particular, viewed itself as a universal church with a mission to convert nonbelievers to accept Jesus as the Christ. The Catholic Church taught that Jews would one day accept Jesus but, while they remained a "stiff-necked" people because of their unwillingness to accept Christ, their persecution was God's way of punishing the Jews for their stubbornness. Catholic doctrine, therefore, taught the unity of all mankind in Christ, and this applied to Jews once they accepted the Savior. Nazi racial doctrine, on the other hand, stressed the primacy of race as an inherent characteristic that can never be altered. For this reason, Jews could never be Aryans or true Germans regardless of the redemptive nature of baptism. Thus, in the years prior to the outbreak of World War II in September of 1939, two anti-Jewish attitudes came into conflict with one another: the traditional or Christian anti-*Judentum*, and the more modern and "scientific" racial anti-Semitism.

The components of Nazi anti-Semitism, however, were not limited to racial bigotry. Added to the mix of ideas that eventually justified the Nazi genocide of the Jews was the belief in conspiracy theory, whereby the Jews were accused of playing a prominent behind-the-scenes role in shaping the course of modern history in general and Germany's loss in World War I in particular. Specifically, Hitler and his inner coterie of radical anti-Semites were believers in the forgery known as the *Protocols of the Elders of Zion*, which purported to describe the efforts of a cabal of Jews to rule the world. As the Nazis analyzed the post–World War I events in Europe, the message of the *Protocols* reinforced their belief in a Jewish conspiracy. Adolf Hitler, in many of his public speeches during the 1920s, accused the Jews of instigating the communist revolution in Russia and spreading Marxist ideology throughout Germany. For Hitler, "Bolshevism" and world Jewry became synonymous. His reading of the *Protocols* led him to conclude that in the struggle between capitalism and communism, there would be great suffering, but the Jews would emerge triumphant because they were strategically placed in both camps. Thus, the Nazis actively sought to prevent the Jewish cabal from achieving its objectives, as outlined in the *Protocols*, by expelling the Jews from Germany, and when the opportunity subsequently presented itself, to exterminate them.

Nazi ideology also held that the Jews not only were an inferior race but also that the approximately 600,000 Jews, or 1 percent of the German population, were a diseased people who must be separated from the rest of the German nation. Nazi propaganda reinforced this view in all aspects of German public life, including the entertainment industry. Nowhere was the caricature of the diseased Jew more pronounced than in the film *The Eternal Jew* (1940), wherein Jews were equated with rats and the spread of disease. The description of Jews as "parasites" or "bacilli" was commonly used by Nazi propaganda to secure support for anti-Semitic measures, and ultimately for the extermination of the Jews.

ELIMINATING JEWS FROM PUBLIC LIFE

Until World War II commenced in September 1939, Nazi policy toward the Jews was limited first to the Jews of Germany, and after the annexation of Austria and the establishment of the Protectorate of Bohemia and Moravia, to those living in the Greater Reich. During the years between 1933 and 1939, the Nazis enacted laws that drove Jews from public life. When the Nuremberg Laws of 1935 were enacted, the Jews lost their German citizenship. Once a force in all aspects of German life, Jews now found themselves barred from employment in the professions, the universities, and the civil service. The Nuremberg Laws not only defined the different classification of Jews but also effectively segregated them from the rest of the population. A primary objective of the anti-Semitic legislation was to encourage the Jews to leave the country, and if they refused, to accept their inferior status as defined by the anti Jewish laws.

Following the annexation of Austria in February 1938, a large number of German and Austrian Jews attempted to migrate but found that worldwide restrictive immigration laws prevented them from reaching a safe haven in most countries. In July 1938, the United States initiated the Evian Conference, ostensibly to deal with the "refugee crisis," but the conference failed because none of the countries, including the United States, was willing to liberalize its immigration laws. Following the state-organized pogrom known as *Kristallnacht*, which occurred on 9–10 November 1938, an additional number of Jews from Germany and Austria sought refuge but found that, with notable exceptions such as Great Britain until 1939, the nations of the world refused entry to Jewish refugees.

Kristallnacht marked a turning point in Nazi policy toward the Jews. Whereas the policy, prior to *Kristallnacht*, was to make life so difficult for Jews that they would voluntary leave the country, the government now sought to intimidate the Jews to leave Germany. During *Kristallnacht*, Jews were murdered, synagogues burned, Jews' property looted, and thousands of Jews incarcerated in concentration camps. The use of violence also indicated a change of direction as the Nazis discarded the enactment of legislative anti-Semitic decrees as a strategy to rid themselves of the Jews. Inasmuch as the pogrom of 9–10 November 1938 heralded this new policy, it also marked the legitimation of violence as a means of solving Germany's "Jewish problem."

WORLD WAR II AND THE TURN TO GENOCIDE

The year 1939 was a particularly painful one for the Jews of Europe. Because of the imminence of war, Great Britain dramatically reduced the number of refugees allowed to enter Britain, and in order to placate the Arabs, the government issued a white paper that limited the number of immigrant entry to Palestine to 75,000 over a five-year period. Once the war began in September 1939, the rapid defeat of Poland placed millions of Jews under German control, thus necessitating a much broader solution in regard to the future of the Jews. The Nazis quickly realized that the policies that were implemented in the Greater Reich were not applicable for dealing with the millions of captive Polish Jews.

At first, Germany's Jewish policy in Poland took the form of the Lublin Plan and then the Madagascar Plan. Both schemes sought to remove the Jews under its control and move them beyond German-occupied territory. The implementation of either plan, however, would have removed Jews to areas whose economic infrastructure was incapable of absorbing such large numbers. The Nazis were aware of the severity of their solution, but the expectation was that once resettled, the Jews would slowly die of hunger and illness. The failure of both of these schemes to materialize led to the second phase of Nazi policy toward the Jews, which was characterized by the wholesale murder of millions of civilians.

The invasion of the German army into Poland was accompanied by special killing squads or Einsatzgruppen units. Their duties included shooting those civilians deemed a threat to Nazi rule. The introduction of these killing squads in Poland marked the beginning of Germany's willingness to commit acts of genocide under the cover of war. This resulted in the wholesale murder of civilians by the Einsatzgruppen in Poland and subsequently in the Soviet Union.

THE EUTHANASIA PROGRAM

In the aftermath of the Nazi seizure of power in 1933, measures were taken to eliminate the racially unfit. Nazi propaganda sought to stigmatize the chronically ill, the handicapped, the mentally retarded, and other categories deemed as "life unworthy of living." The Nazis established racial hygiene courts, as well as programs of sterilization, which had as their objective the removal of nonproductive elements from the nation and to ensure that they did not reproduce. With the outbreak of war, Adolf Hitler secretly authorized the Euthanasia Program for the purpose of killing those identified as "social undesirables." Despite the efforts at secrecy, however, public knowledge of the euthanasia killings became widely known. Relatives of those who were murdered engaged in protests, and they were quickly joined by members of the German clergy. In August 1941, Hitler, bowing to public outrage, suspended the Euthanasia Program because he realized that widespread knowledge of the killings was creating unrest among the population. The Euthanasia Program, however, continued to operate sub rosa, and by the end of the war more than 200,000 "patients" were legally murdered under the supervision of physicians. The killing process was not only attended by those in the medical profession but also by technicians who became skilled in subterfuge, whereby they disguised the gas chambers as shower stalls, in order to lull the unsuspecting victims to their death. Those involved in the gassing of the "unfit," as well as the machinery and the technical experts who made it operational, were later transferred to the death camps, for the purpose of implementing the Final Solution.

Having engaged in the killing of innocent people, the Germans had fewer scruples about the murder of European Jewry. Given the apparent indifference of the free world to absorbing Jewish refugees, as evidenced by the failure of the Evian Conference in 1938, the German leadership concluded that the democratic world was indifferent to the fate of the Jews. They calculated that a policy of mass murder against the Jews would bring a pro forma reaction, but it would not elicit more than the normal response generated by wartime atrocity stories. Hitler is credited with asking the question, in regard to an earlier historical instance of genocide, "Who remembers the Armenians?" Hitler's belief that the Allies would not expend energy on saving Jewish lives proved correct. Once the war began, Allied policy focused on winning the war rather than on saving Jewish lives in the belief that the former would result in the latter. Having embarked on a policy of genocide, the Germans were determined to keep it a secret. Consequently, they cloaked their plan to exterminate European Jewry in the language of euphemisms. This form of language served two purposes: to disguise from the victims their ultimate fate and to prevent a repetition of the protests that followed the disclosure of the euthanasia killings in Germany.

TOWARD THE FINAL SOLUTION

Holocaust scholars are divided on the question as to whether the plan to exterminate the Jews of Europe was Hitler's intention from the moment he became the leader of the National Socialist party, or whether the Holocaust was a "functional" response to the strategic problem of ruling more than three million Jews in Poland, and millions more following the invasion of the Soviet Union in June 1941. In either event, the genocide of the Jews was not possible before the outbreak of World War II, but once Hitler was in control of about one third of all living Jews, the opportunity presented itself to solve once and forever the "Jewish problem."

Germany's invasion of Poland would not have been possible without the treaty with the Soviet Union in August 1939. The pact resulted in Germany annexing territory in western Poland, and using the central part of the country, which was referred to as the General-Gouvernement, as an area of "resettlement" for Poles and Jews. The Soviets, in turn, occupied eastern Poland and the Baltic states. Germany denied that the invasion of Poland was an act of aggression but hailed it as an act of restoration, whereby Germany would recover land that Poland acquired at its expense as a result of World War I. This policy of *lebensraum* ("living space") envisioned millions of ethnic Germans, living in the east under foreign rule, being resettled on their ancestral homeland in western Poland. As for the Jews and Poles who resided on the conquered territory, they were to be resettled in the General-Gouvernement, where the Poles would be reduced to the status of serfs serving their German overlords. Jews, however, were to be temporarily placed in ghettos until plans were finalized in regard to their future.

One region that Germany "resettled" was the area surrounding the town of Oswiecim, located in Upper Silesia. The Germans claimed that Oswiecim had once been an integral part of Germany, and upon its occupation they changed its name to Auschwitz. The plan, initially, was to resettle ethnic Germans in the area, but it lacked resources to sustain a large population. In an effort to make the Auschwitz location economically viable, Heinrich Himmler, the chief of the Schutzstaffel (SS), invited the I. G. Farben company to build a factory at Auschwitz that would produce vitally needed synthetic rubber. Himmler enticed the company by promising that an unlimited pool of slave laborers would be placed at its disposal. Himmler's promise to supply I. G. Farben with manpower coincided with his establishment of a concentration camp near the town on 27 April 1940. Initially the camp served to hold Polish workers, who were forced to work under the most brutal conditions. But the camp was also used for the punishment of political prisoners, and subsequently the camp acquired the reputation as one of the cruelest of the Nazi concentration camps, where torture and executions became a daily occurrence.

In March 1941, a second camp known as Auschwitz II or Birkenau was constructed. In March 1942, a third camp was added to the Auschwitz complex near the town of Monowitz, and was designated as Auschwitz III. Both Auschwitz I and the camp at Monowitz were primarily designed as labor camps. It was, however, in the Birkenau or Auschwitz II camp that the Nazis employed gas chambers and crematoria in order to kill their enemies. Once Nazi Germany committed to the Final Solution, Birkenau became synonymous with the mass murder of Jews. It is estimated that between 1.1 and 1.5 million Jews, and more than a million non-Jews, including Soviet prisoners of war, were gassed in Birkenau. The Auschwitz-Birkenau death camp, however, was not the only one of its kind. In different areas of the General-Gouvernement, the Nazis constructed the Treblinka, Sobibor, and Belzec extermination camps, whose primary purpose was to murder Jews. Although the death camps were to play a major role in the implementation of the Final Solution, this was not the only method used by the Germans to exterminate the Jews of Europe.

THE INVASION OF THE SOVIET UNION
AND THE FINAL SOLUTION

Following the German invasion of the Soviet Union in June 1941, squads of Einsatzgruppen accompanied the army into the Soviet Union with orders to kill captured Soviet political commissars, communist functionaries of all ranks, and all Jews. The orders derived from Hitler's authority as described in the "Guidelines for the Treatment of Political Commissars" (6 June 1941), also known as the "Commissar Order." The directive not only legitimized the murder of innocent civilians but also abolished the rules of war as established by custom and formulated in international law. For Hitler, the war in the Soviet Union was to be a war of total destruction against the enemy, which included the Jews. Once deployed in Russia, the *Einsatzgruppen* proceeded to murder Jews through mass shootings as well as the use of mobile vans as gas chambers, whereby carbon monoxide was piped into the back of the crowded trucks, thus causing the death of the victims. It is estimated that more than a million Jews were killed in *Einsatzgruppen* operations.

Once Nazi Germany made the decision in mid-to-late 1941 to exterminate the Jews of Europe, it sought methods that were both inexpensive and efficient. Given the large number of Jews targeted for annihilation, the methods employed by the *Einsatzgruppen* in the Soviet Union proved to be too costly and inefficient for a successful resolution of the "Jewish problem." It became apparent that the murder of millions of Jews required the use of techniques not unlike the methods used in industry. Extermination camps such as Auschwitz, Treblinka, Belzec, and Sobibor became factories of death, whereby the methods of industrial engineering were applied to the implementation of the Final Solution. Every aspect of the extermination process—from the loading of the victims into the cattle cars, to disguising the real purpose of the extermination camp, to lulling the unsuspecting victims into the gas chambers—was calculated to make the process function as efficiently as possible. The murder of such a large number of Jews also required the cooperation of all segments of the German bureaucracy, and toward that end a conference was held in January 1942 at Wannsee, a suburb of Berlin.

The Wannsee Conference was organized by Reinhard Heydrich, the head of the Reich Security Main Office (RSHA) and Himmler's closest aide. Those who were invited to attend the conference represented important jurisdictions within the Nazi bureaucratic system. Heydrich's objective in convening the meeting was to impress upon the assembled government functionaries the high priority that the Nazi leadership, including Hitler, placed on the annihilation of the Jews. Subsequently, he asked for and received the promise of their cooperation in all facets of the implementation of the Final Solution.

THE GHETTOS

In the aftermath of the Wannsee Conference, the plan to exterminate Europe's Jews was intensified. The crowded ghettos, which at first served as a temporary location for Jews until they could be removed to the Lublin area or to Madagascar, now became warehouses for a different kind of resettlement. By moving the Jews in German-occupied Europe into the assorted crowded ghettos of Poland, plans for their demise could be made in a systematic and efficient manner. Toward that end, the Germans appointed Jewish Councils (*Judenräte*) in each ghetto not only to maintain law and order but also to fill the daily quotas of Jews who were to be "resettled" in the east, a euphemism for sending them to the death camps. Historians such as Raul Hilberg and Hannah Arendt have accused the Jewish Councils of complicity in the annihilation of

European Jewry because they made the task of filling the daily quota of Jews for deportation to the death camps that much easier for the Germans. Others historians have argued that the councils had little choice, and had they not undertaken this responsibility, the Germans would have made life even more brutal for the Jews trapped in the ghettos.

The ghettos functioned not only as the primary means by which the Germans transported Jews to the death camps but also as a reservoir for slave labor. Until 1943, Himmler believed that "there was no reason not to use the labor potential of Jews as an integral part of the 'Final Solution.'" By January 1943, however, Himmler concluded that Germany would lose the war, and the murder of European Jewry, regardless of their benefit to the Third Reich as a source of slave labor, became an end in itself. Himmler proceeded to expand the killing machinery at Auschwitz by increasing the operating facilities of the crematoria. Although Jewish slave labor continued in the Auschwitz camps, this labor ceased to be important to Himmler. Only the "special squads," which maintained order among those selected to be killed, mattered. These squads consisted primarily of Jews who were responsible for extracting the gold teeth from the victims and cutting the hair of the dead, which the Germans used for commercial purposes. In addition, they were assigned to burn the corpses and to prepare the belongings of the dead for transport to Germany. These squads, however, generally lasted for a short period of time, and after a few months they were also killed.

JEWS AND THE OTHER VICTIMS OF THE NAZI GENOCIDE

The number of Jews killed by the Germans in the Holocaust cannot be precisely calculated. Various historians, however, have provided estimates that range between 4,204,000 and 7,000,000, with the use of the round figure of six million Jews murdered as the best estimate to describe the immensity of the Nazi genocide. The Germans exterminated approximately 54 percent of the Jews within their reach, including almost two million children under the age of 18. Jews, however, were not the only target of the Nazis. During the war, an estimated 10,547,000 Eastern Europeans, including millions of Poles, Ukrainians, Byelorussians, Gypsies, and Soviet POWs, were also killed. These numbers suggest that the Nazi genocide was far-reaching, although the rationale for the murder of the targeted groups varied from one group to another. The Germans had, in fact, created a priority list of groups that were to be eliminated. The Slavic people were considered inferior by the Nazis, and it is probable that in the long run the Slavs would have become victims of genocide. But during the German occupation of Slavic territories, the objective called for the removal of 100 million Poles, Ukrainians, and other Slavic groups from their homes in the annexed German territory, and the resettlement of millions of ethnic Germans in their place. The majority of the Slavs were to be assigned as slave laborers to serve their German masters, their education limited to counting up to 10, and millions of them were to be deported to Siberia once the Soviet Union was defeated. The targeting of Slavic people by the Germans, however, was not driven by the same ideology that called for the annihilation of every last Jewish man, woman, and child.

THE RESPONSE OF JEWS TO THE HOLOCAUST:
THE JUDENRÄTE

From the perspective of more than 60 years since the liberation of the concentration camps in 1945, there still remain some gnawing questions regarding the response of the Allies, and such institutions as the churches and the Red Cross, to the planned extermination of the Jews. Added to the mix is the question of the response of the Jews to their planned demise. Did the Judenräte betray their fellow Jews by cooperating with the Nazis? How correct is the perception that the Jews went like sheep to their slaughter? How do we interpret the "silence" of the Catholic Church in the face of the unimpeachable evidence at its disposal regarding the Final Solution? Finally, how culpable were the Allies in failing to bomb Auschwitz, lest it interfere with their overall military strategy? Would the bombing of Auschwitz have resulted in the saving of Jewish lives or at least slowed down the extermination process by destroying the train tracks that brought Jews to the death camp?

The condition of the Jews in the ghettos of Poland deteriorated following the Nazi invasion of the Soviet Union in June 1941, as they were now rounded up and deported to the death camps. The first use of carbon monoxide gas to exterminate Jews was introduced at Chelmno in December 1941, and by the following summer all of the death camps were operational. In Auschwitz, the Germans introduced Zyklon B gas as the preferred means of exterminating their Jewish victims.

The response of the Jewish Councils to the deportations to the death camps varied from ghetto to ghetto. In the Lodz ghetto, for example, Mordecai Chaim Rumkowski, the head of the Judenräte, displayed great zeal and organizational ability in running the factories and the internal life of the ghetto. Although not aware of the extermination camps, Rumkowski nevertheless tried, in vain, to halt the deportations. Between January and May 1942, 55,000 Jews were deported from the Lodz ghetto to Chelmno, where they were all killed. By and large, Rumkowski was able to make himself useful to the Germans, and as a consequence, they allowed him to run the ghetto with an iron hand. Some historians have viewed Rumkowski as a traitor and a Nazi collaborator, whereas others believe that his policy of cooperation with the Nazis helped extend the life of the ghetto. A megalomaniac, Rumkowski would not tolerate any criticism of his leadership. At one point, he printed postage stamps bearing his likeness.

In Upper Silesia, the ghetto chairman, Moshe Merin, vigorously enforced the German demand for forced labor. Yet he was aware that those deemed unfit for labor by the Germans were killed. Merin reasoned that in order to protect one segment of the ghetto population, he must sacrifice those too weak to work. In Vilna, Jacob Gens promoted the strategy of "work for life," which meant that as long as Jews engaged in productive work they had a chance to survive. His most controversial act was to deliver to the Germans 406 Jews who were old or chronically ill. The Nazis had originally demanded 1,500 children and women who were unemployed, but Gens countered the order and justified his action by claiming that he wanted the women and children to survive for the future of the Jewish people. Efraim Barasz, the head of the Bialystok ghetto, was aware that the deportations were delivering Jews to the death camps. Nevertheless, he had faith that work "would serve as a protective shield and that our main rescue effort has to be based on the establishment of a highly developed industry." Barasz rigidly enforced German directives and warned the ghetto inhabitants against acts of sabotage against the Germans. Like Gens, Barasz believed that as long as Jews engaged in productive labor, he could save the ghetto from total liquidation, and the Jews from certain death. Upon learning that the deportations from the Warsaw ghetto meant death for those being "resettled," Adam Czerniakow, the head of its Jewish Council, committed suicide rather than comply with German orders.

The Jewish Council leaders were often ruthless toward their own people, but they sought to save as many Jewish lives as possible. Hannah Arendt, in *Eichmann in Jerusalem* (1963), wrote that without the help of the ghetto Jewish leadership, there would have been chaos and disorder, and this would have required the Germans to use their own limited manpower to round up and deport Jews to the death camps. She concluded her controversial book with these condemning words: "To a Jew this role of the Jewish leaders in the destruction of their own people is undoubtedly the darkest chapter of the whole dark story." It would appear that any judgment of the Judenräte's response to Nazi demands must consider the unprecedented nature of the moral ambiguity that informed their leadership. With their options limited, the Judenräte found themselves being forced to decide, through the preparation of the quota lists, who should live and who should die. Despite the efforts of the Jewish Councils to prolong the lives of the ghetto inhabitants through a strategy of survival through work, the fate of the Jews was not in their hands but in those of the Germans. Once Nazi Germany committed to the Final Solution, it was the Nazis who decided the fate of the Jews. Formal resistance was rarely possible, but strategies were devised by the ghetto leadership to keep Jews alive, even if it meant the sacrifice of some for the benefit of the many. Ultimately, it mattered little what the Jewish Councils did. The ghettos were eventually liquidated, and their Jewish population, along with the leadership of the Jewish Councils, was deported to the death camps. The argument remains, however, as to whether a more obstructive resistance to Nazi demands would have made any difference in light of the German determination to exterminate European Jewry.

JEWISH RESISTANCE

Resistance to the Nazi atrocities, however, did occur and manifested itself in ghettos such as Warsaw, and in the Auschwitz, Treblinka, and Sobibor extermination camps. In addition, Jews who successfully fled from the ghettos and the camps joined partisan groups where they engaged in all aspects of guerrilla warfare against the Germans. It is a simplification to believe that Jews allowed themselves to be slaughtered like sheep. Although millions of Jews were murdered by the Nazis, it is also true that, where it was possible, Jews resisted the enemy. Sometimes, as was the case in the Warsaw ghetto, the resistance came too late. The Warsaw ghetto uprising occurred when the Germans had already deported most of the ghetto's inhabitants. Yet, when the revolt broke out in April 1943, it took a special German army unit to crush the Jewish rebels, who held out for almost a month against a superior military force.

The revolt in the Warsaw ghetto inspired uprisings in the ghettos of both Lvov and Bialystok. As was the case in Warsaw, the Germans eventually crushed the revolts, liquidated the ghettos, and sent the remaining Jews to the Janowska camp, where they were killed. Jewish resistance, however, was not limited to the ghettos. As stated above, acts of resistance occurred in the major death camps. The best-known example was the formation of the Auschwitz Fighting Group, which had cadres in Birkenau and Monowitz. On 6 October 1944, Jewish "special squads" (Sonderkommandos) launched a revolt with explosives as their only weapon. Nevertheless, they succeeded in blowing up Crematorium 3, thus destroying the installation. Immediately after the revolt, the participants were rounded up and immediately executed. Similar revolts occurred in Treblinka and Sobibor with the same results.

Where Jews were more successful in confronting the Nazis was in the partisan movements. It is estimated that between 20,000 and 30,000 Jews fought in partisan units in the forests of Byelorussia and the western Ukraine. Perhaps the most famous of the Jewish partisan leaders was Alexander Bielski. Joined by his brothers, he led the so-called Bielski Otriad, consisting of 300 fighters engaged in guerrilla warfare in Byelorussia against the German foe. Some of their activities included the derailment of troop trains and the blowing up of bridges and electric power stations.

Between 1942 and 1944, there were 27 Jewish partisan units fighting against the Germans, and about 1,000 who participated in the Warsaw Polish uprising in the summer of 1944. Jewish partisans placed themselves under the command of the national partisan groups that fought the Germans. The inability of the Jews to organize their own guerrilla movement was due, in part, to the lack of support from the surrounding population or the approval of a government-in-exile. Given the prevalent anti-Semitism in Eastern Europe, Jews could never be certain that in approaching a farmer for food or shelter, they would not be betrayed and handed over to the Germans.

It is difficult to assess the difference Jewish resistance made in light of the millions of Jews who died in the Holocaust. Historian Raul Hilberg has concluded that "the reaction pattern of the Jews is characterized by an almost complete lack of resistance. . . . The Jewish victims, caught in the straitjacket of their history, plunged themselves physically and psychologically into catastrophe." Yet this may be an unfair assessment of their resistance at a time when most Jews were ill-fed, sick, and at the mercy of armed Germans and their auxiliary forces. Elie Wiesel has observed, in regard to Jewish resistance, that "the question is not why all Jews did not fight, but how so many did. Tormented, beaten, starved, where did they find the strength—spiritual and physical—to resist?" Jews were simply too few in number to defend themselves against Germany's determination to annihilate them. Furthermore, the Jews were also victims of an endemic anti-Semitism that permeated much of Eastern Europe. Consequently, the Germans were able to enlist the support of Ukrainians, Latvians, Lithuanians, and others in the implementation of the Final Solution. In Western Europe, Jews also participated in the resistance movements but found that anti-Semitism was a factor in their ability to survive. In France, for example, the anti-Semitic leadership of the Vichy government enthusiastically promoted anti-Jewish laws and expedited the deportation of foreign Jews to the death camps.

RIGHTEOUS GENTILES

As bleak as the situation was, there were those Gentiles who risked their lives to help the Jews. At a time when hiding or assisting Jews meant severe punishment, about half of 1 percent of the total non-Jewish population of occupied Europe helped to rescue Jews. Protecting Jews took many forms: Countess Maria von Maltzan hid the Jewish writer Hans Hirschel, along with other Jews, in her Berlin apartment. In the Dutch village of Nieulande, each villager agreed to hide one Jewish family or at least one Jew. The Protestant village of Le Chambon-sur-Lignon, located in southern France, hid many Jews in full view of Vichy government officials. The mass collective effort of the Danish people resulted in the rescue of 7,000 of its 8,000 Jews.

There were also others who for humanitarian reasons risked their lives and careers in behalf of the Jews. Raoul Wallenberg, a Swedish diplomat, saved the lives of approximately 10,000 Jews on the eve of the deportation of Budapest's Jewish community to Auschwitz. Dr. Aristides de Sonza Mendes, a Portuguese diplomat, discarded orders from his government and issued nearly 10,000 travel visas to Jews escaping the Nazi terror. Paul Gruninger, the police chief of the Swiss canton of St. Gallen, helped save 2,000 Jewish refugees who illegally crossed the Swiss border from Germany and Austria in 1938–1939. The Japanese consul in Kaunas, Lithuania, Sempo Sugihara, working in tandem with his Dutch counterpart Jan Zwartendijk, issued thousands of travel visas for Jews attempting to escape the Germans following their invasion of Lithuania in June 1941. For his effort, Sugihara lost his position and was forced to return to Japan in disgrace.

Sugihara is sometimes referred to as the "Japanese Schindler." Oskar Schindler's efforts on behalf of the Jews were celebrated in Steven Spielberg's epic film *Schindler's List*. Schindler was one of several German entrepreneurs, including Julius Madritsch and Raimund Titsch, who aided Jews interned in the Plaszow labor camp. In Schindler's case, he provided Jews with food and shelter and protected them from the brutal whims of Amon Goeth, the camp commandant. Schindler is credited with saving the lives of 1,100 Jews.

THE CATHOLIC CHURCH

Holocaust historian Henry Huttenbach once remarked that the smallest street in the world was the Avenue of the Righteous, located outside Yad Vashem in Jerusalem. He was referring to the fact that although Gentiles came to the aid of Jews, the number of those willing to risk their lives and livelihoods on behalf of the Jews was small. It is possible that many more Jews would have survived the Holocaust had institutions such as the Catholic Church spoken out against the Nazi genocide. The failure, therefore, of organized Christianity to confront the Nazi menace is also a part of the history of the Holocaust. It is true that in various European countries under German occupation, individual Protestant and Catholic clergy denounced the treatment of the Jews. Jews were also hidden in convents and monasteries, and historian Pinchas Lapide estimates that about 800,000 Jews were saved by the Catholic Church, although historians question whether the Vatican can take credit for the deeds of individual Catholics who saved Jews. It may be that in the case of Catholic clergy, their actions in protecting Jews was a result of "signals" that they received from the Vatican that permitted priests and nuns to help Jews.

As the preeminent moral institution in Europe, the Vatican refrained from publicly condemning the extermination of the Jews, although it was among the first to learn of the Nazi genocide. Perhaps Pope Pius XII feared that in confronting the Nazis over the issue of the Jews, he would be risking the lives of Catholic clergy as well as the confiscation of church property. The result was a policy of silence in the face of one of the most horrendous events in world history. The record of the Vatican is further complicated by its involvement in helping leading Nazis, such as Adolf Eichmann and Josef Mengele, to escape to Latin America at the end of World War II. It remains to be answered whether similar "signals," which Catholic clergy received from the Vatican to help the Jews, were also given on behalf of fleeing Nazi war criminals. Regardless of the motives for his silence, Pius XII's ambivalence toward the Jews groups him in the category of those who failed to voice a condemnation of the Nazi genocide.

THE INTERNATIONAL COMMITTEE OF THE RED CROSS

Like the Catholic Church, the International Committee of the Red Cross (ICRC) also failed to use its moral standing to speak out on behalf of the Jews. The start of World War II and the German implementation of the Final Solution created an unprecedented situation for the ICRC. Inasmuch as the Germans attempted to carry out their annihilation of the Jews in secret, the ICRC rarely was privy to the mass deportation of the Jews. Similarly, aside from visits to Buchenwald and Theresienstadt, the ICRC was never permitted to inspect the concentration camps or the death camps. But early on, the ICRC received information about the Final Solution and agonized over the risks involved in extending help to the Jews who were marked for death. Ultimately, the ICRC chose not to use its humanitarian reputation and its neutral standing in the world community to sound the alarm regarding the Nazi genocide. Instead, as in the case of the Vatican, the ICRC engaged in quiet diplomacy and never attempted to arouse public opinion against the Nazi atrocities. In fact, the ICRC rarely alluded to the extermination of the Jews in its correspondence. Rather, the Jews were included in the general category of prisoners, deportees, and hostages whom the organization believed were entitled to the same protection as were military combatants. The ICRC also refused to raise the question of Nazi racial discrimination inasmuch as it violated the tenets of the Geneva conventions. For example, the ICRC did not protest the separation of German Jewish (*Mischlinges*) medical personnel from their Gentile counterparts on the eastern front.

The failure of the International Committee of the Red Cross to use its moral capital on behalf of the Jews may have resulted from its fear that by doing so, it would compromise its work on behalf of millions of prisoners of war on the eastern front, in particular, and the organization's standing as a neutral in general. Yet, where it was possible, the ICRC did intervene in countries where it believed it could aid the Jews. In 1941, the ICRC established the Joint Relief Commission of the Red Cross for the purpose of providing food, clothes, and medicine to the Jews trapped in the ghettos of the General-Gouvernement. These efforts, however, were stymied by the Allies, who refused the ICRC permission to pass through the continental blockade. Ultimately, the operation was limited to providing quantities of food to a number of camps in the east and to refugees in the south of France.

Perhaps the most successful endeavor of the International Committee of the Red Cross on behalf of the Jews was its intervention in Hungary in the spring of 1944. The Red Cross, along with the War Refugee Board, exerted pressure on the Hungarian government to halt the deportation of the Jews, which, for reasons of national self-interest, it agreed to do. During this period, when the deportations were suspended, the ICRC found food and shelter for thousands of Jews.

The most conspicuous failure of the International Committee of the Red Cross, in addition to its reluctance to arouse the world to the nature of the Nazi genocide, was the aborted plan to organize the emigration of Jews from German-occupied territory and move them by ship to

Palestine by way of the Black Sea and Turkey. The ICRC, however, was careful not to violate the provisions of the British White Paper of 1939, which limited Jewish immigration into Palestine. When the German government predictably refused to issue exit permits, the mission failed.

THE ALLIES

A different type of failure is associated with the controversy surrounding the debate over the question as to whether the Allies did all they could to save the Jews from extermination. In early 1942, the Polish government-in-exile residing in London sent Jan Karski, a courier for the exiled government and a member of the Polish underground, on a mission to evaluate the general situation in occupied Poland. Karski twice slipped into the Warsaw ghetto, where he met with Jewish leaders who informed him of the desperate plight of the Jews. In November 1942, Karski reached London via Sweden, where he briefed the Polish government-in-exile, and subsequently met with Prime Minister Winston Churchill regarding the fate of Polish Jewry. Based on Karski's reports, the Polish government-in-exile called on the Allies to take measures to prevent the destruction of the Jews. Karski next went to the United States where he met with President Franklin Roosevelt, to whom he described the terrible plight of the Jews. The president assured Karski that something would be done. In later years, Karski would lament as to how he was given assurances by the two Allied leaders that action on behalf of the Jews would be forthcoming, only to fail to see it materialize. Karski, however, was not the only source of information that the Allies received regarding the murderous activities of the Nazis.

Reports of the mass murder of the Jews also came to the attention of the Allies from the World Jewish Congress (WJC). The organization, which had its headquarters in Switzerland, received information from Eduard Schulte, a German businessman, to the effect that the Germans were engaged in the mass murder of millions of Jews by means of poison gas and other methods. On 8 August 1942, Dr. Gerhart Riegner, the WJC representative in Geneva, cabled Rabbi Stephen S. Wise, the president of the WJC and a friend of President Roosevelt, and Sidney

Silverman, a member of the British Parliament, the information he had received from Schulte.

The U.S. Department of State, which intercepted the mailing, refused to transmit the Riegner cable to Wise because the information was not substantiated. Toward the end of August, however, Wise received the cable from Sidney Silverman. When Wise passed the information on to Undersecretary of State Sumner Welles, he was asked not to make the information public until the contents of the cable were verified. Wise held on to this information, and it was not until November 1942, when it became evident that the Nazi genocide entailed the murder of millions of Jews, that he publicly disclosed the contents of the Riegner cable. At the time, Wise was willing to maintain secrecy regarding the cable because he had confidence that the Roosevelt administration would respond to the destruction of European Jewry with all the resources available to the U.S. government.

Rabbi Wise's faith in President Roosevelt, however, was not justified by the response of the United States to the Holocaust. Following America's entry into the war, after the Japanese attack on Pearl Harbor on 7 December 1941, and Germany's subsequent declaration of war against the United States, the president operated amid pressures that politically prevented him from taking a more forceful stand on behalf of European Jewry. These pressures arose in the form of opinion polls, which showed a high percentage of anti-Semitic feeling throughout the country, both before and after the United States went to war against Germany. Because anti-Semitism was a factor in the political calculations of the president, Roosevelt concluded that the war could not be depicted as one being fought to save the Jews of Europe. As early as his convening of the Evian Conference in 1938, Roosevelt rarely singled out the plight of the Jews but referred instead to the "political refugees crisis." For this reason, the response of the Roosevelt administration to the Nazi genocide, at least until 1944, was one of gesture rather than action, with the objective of appeasing the concerns of his Jewish constituency.

Although the Allies were aware that Jews were being murdered in the millions, it was never mentioned at any of the major conferences held by the Allied leadership in Casablanca, Teheran, or Yalta. When the British government in mid-1942 found itself facing public pressure to do something on behalf of the Jews, the United States joined

Great Britain in a declaration that condemned the "bestial policy of cold-blooded extermination." What the Allied leaders did not do was advocate a concrete strategy against the Nazi genocide. As the position of the Jews deteriorated and the public became aware of the German extermination policy, they demanded more from their leaders than well-meaning platitudes. The result of this pressure was the British convening of the Bermuda Conference in April 1943.

The Germans, by October 1941, had prohibited the emigration of Jews from German-occupied territory. Fearing, perhaps, that millions of Jews finding havens in the Allied countries would increase the manpower of the enemy, the Germans changed the status of the Jews from that of potential emigrants to prisoners of the Reich. Nevertheless, the Bermuda Conference was organized for the purpose of finding a solution to the large number of both Jewish and non-Jewish refugees who sought safe havens in neutral countries. The conference was not designed, however, to deal with the larger and more immediate issue of genocide. Furthermore, the British insisted that the Jewish character of the crisis be played down, and the euphemism "political refugees" be used to disguise the plight of the Jews. As one proposal for rescue after another was rejected by the delegates, it became clear that the real purpose for convening the conference was to assuage public opinion without committing to specific steps to rescue Jews. Despite evidence of the Final Solution, the British insisted that the Jews be treated as one of the many groups victimized by the Nazis. The failure of the Bermuda Conference was widely condemned by American Jews as well as by non-Jews who were concerned about their governments' apparent indifference toward the fate of the Jews. When concrete steps were finally taken, they were almost forced on President Roosevelt.

In the fall of 1942, when news of the Jewish catastrophe in Europe was filtering back to Washington, Henry Morgenthau Jr., the secretary of the Treasury and the highest-ranking Jew in the Roosevelt administration, was informed by his subordinates in the Treasury Department that officials in the State Department were engaged in deliberately withholding information regarding the murder of the Jews. In January 1944, Josiah DuBois Jr., Morgenthau's assistant, handed the secretary his "Report to the Secretary on the Acquiescence of This Government in the Murder of the Jews." The report documented the "willful failure" of the State Department to use its authority to provide aid to the victims of the Nazi extermination campaign. Sensitive to the highly charged nature of the report's title, Morgenthau changed it to "A Personal Report to the President." On 16 January 1944, Morgenthau, along with two other Jewish advisers to Roosevelt, Benjamin V. Cohen and Samuel Rosenman, presented the report to the president. Fearful, perhaps, that should the information become public it would be politically devastating for him in an election year, Roosevelt quickly moved to defuse a potential scandal for his administration. By the end of the month, President Roosevelt by executive order established the War Refugee Board (WRB).

The creation of the War Refugee Board signaled a new policy whereby the Roosevelt administration would take "all measures within its power to rescue the victims of enemy oppression who are in imminent danger of death." Despite the alleged support of the president, the WRB quickly found that not all government agencies were willing to cooperate with the new policy. The War Department was uncooperative, and the State Department remained obstructive in regard to the WRB efforts to save Hungarian Jewry from being shipped to Auschwitz. Ultimately, the WRB was instrumental in pressuring the Hungarian government to stop the deportation of the approximately 230,000 Jews of Budapest. Despite this success, the WRB, already at odds with other government agencies, was additionally handicapped by poor funding and what appeared to be Roosevelt's lack of interest and support.

One of the WRB's most publicized successes was the evacuation of 982 Jewish refugees and a sprinkling of non-Jews from Italy to a safe haven in an unused army camp in Oswego, New York, in August 1944. Fearful that this humanitarian project would be construed as proof that the administration gave a priority to the rescue of Jews, Roosevelt insisted that non-Jewish refugees be included in the rescue operation. Although the WRB sought to organize additional havens in the United States, the president would agree only to the Oswego project. Although the WRB was established after millions of Jews had already been murdered, the agency sought to save the remnant of European Jewry through activities that included the protection of Jews within Axis-occupied Europe by financing underground activities as well as by exerting diplomatic pressure.

The WRB also was indirectly involved in one of the most controversial issues regarding the Allied response to the Nazi genocide, the bombing of Auschwitz. Although not under the purview of the WRB, its members were sympathetic to the rising demand that Auschwitz, or the railway tracks leading to the death camp, be bombed in order to destroy the gas chambers and crematoria or, at the very least, slow down the process whereby thousands of Jews arriving daily by train to the death camp were killed. By the spring of 1944, if not earlier, the Allied governments were aware of the killing operations in Auschwitz. At the same time, the Allied air forces controlled the skies over Europe and were within bombing range of Auschwitz as well as the tracks leading to the death camp. Although appeals were made to the Allied governments that the camp be bombed for humanitarian reasons, the decision was made not to bomb targets that deviated from the overall military strategy. The U.S. War Department argued that such attacks would be an impractical diversion from vital military and industrial targets and would result in heavy air force casualties. The War Department insisted that the most effective way to save the lives of the Jews in Auschwitz, and in other German concentration camps, was through an early defeat of the Axis enemy. Thus, the air force based in Italy bombed German plants that produced synthetic oil and rubber, which were located within 45 miles of Birkenau. On two occasions, American bombers struck the industrial sites of Auschwitz itself, less than five miles from the huge gas chamber installations.

The efforts of the WRB were further stymied by the Allied policy of unconditional surrender, which prohibited negotiating with Germany, bribing Nazi officials on behalf of the Jews, or ransoming of Jewish lives in exchange for goods and commodities that were in short supply in Germany. Given the "silence" of the Christian churches and the unwillingness of the Allies to include the rescue of Jews as a priority in the war effort, the Germans continued unobstructed their genocidal policy toward the Jews. Bereft of aid from the Allied world, the Jews found themselves at the mercy of their German killers.

Historians will continue to argue as to whether the Allies, the churches, or the International Red Cross could have done more in the face of the Nazi genocide against the Jews. Reflecting on the low priority that was given to saving the Jews from annihilation, it must be noted that our judgments are too often shaped by what we know in the present about events that occurred in the past. In the case of the Allied "failure" to adopt a more active policy toward saving the Jews, the strategy can only be understood by examining the options that were considered realistic at the time. From the perspective of the present, the bombing of Auschwitz appears to have been an obvious means of saving Jewish lives. Yet, at the time, even Jewish leaders were divided on the merits of such an action, and many of them subscribed to the strategy that the best way to save the lives of the Jews in the death camps was through a speedy victory over Germany.

We still are unclear about the reasons for the silence of the churches or even how to interpret that silence. It may be that, with the exception of the Quakers, every Christian denomination under German occupation sought to protect its own. It is clear that the law of self-preservation rather than self-sacrifice informed the reaction of the churches to the extermination of the Jews. The failure of organized Christianity to condemn the German extermination of the Jews, therefore, may have had less to do with the traditional anti-Jewish teachings of the church than with a very earthly fear of Nazi retribution.

CONCLUSION

What we can say with certainty is that the Holocaust was perpetrated by the Nazis as a means of eliminating the Jews from the planet. Although a certain amount of greed motivated the Germans in their war against the Jews, it was primarily their racist ideas that justified the gas chambers and crematoria in death camps such as Auschwitz. If there is anything to be learned from the Holocaust, it is that bigotry has deadly consequences. Unfortunately, humankind has absorbed little of this lesson, as evidenced by the recent war in Bosnia and in other acts of genocide in countries such as Rwanda, Zaire, and Darfur.

The primary identification of the Holocaust with the Jews is not meant to minimize the suffering of the other groups who lost millions during the Nazi terror. Rather, the Nazi assault on the Jews was an unprecedented event in history, inasmuch as a nation-state had never before targeted an entire people for extinction. It was Nazi Germany's intentions toward the Jews rather than the numbers murdered that places the Jews at the center of the Holocaust. Having condemned an entire people to death, a precedent for this type of genocide was established in the future. Can we guarantee that the peculiar ideas and laws that first stripped Jews of their rights in Germany and then condemned them to the gas chambers will not occur again? To trivialize or diminish Hitler's war against the Jews by reducing or relativizing the six million Jewish dead to simply one of many targeted victims of the Nazis is to lose sight of the peculiar fusion of anti-Semitism and apocalyptic ideas that made the resolution of the Jewish question central to Nazi ideology. Once the Final Solution to the Jewish question was adopted as state policy, the Germans constructed the death camps, whose primary function was to murder Jews. To miss this aspect of the Holocaust is to invite the possibility that it could happen again, only with another group replacing the Jews as the victim.

THE DICTIONARY

– A –

ADENAUER, KONRAD (1876–1967). Adenauer was the burgomaster of Cologne from 1917 to 1945. During his tenure, he was twice imprisoned by **Adolf Hitler**. As the first chancellor of the German Federal Republic (1949–1963), Adenauer won approval from the Bundestag to make amends for **Nazi** crimes against the Jews. In September 1951, he addressed the Bundestag and acknowledged the "unspeakable crimes that were perpetrated in the name of the German people that oblige us to make moral and material amends." In 1952, Adenauer negotiated a reparation agreement with **Israel** in which **Germany** made **restitution** of $845 million to Israel. Subsequently, the West German parliament enacted a law that compensated **survivors of the Holocaust** for their suffering.

AGREEMENT IN THE NAME OF HUMANITY. In the beginning of 1945, or earlier, **Heinrich Himmler** realized that **Germany** would lose the war. In an effort to escape retribution for his war crimes, Himmler on 12 March 1945 signed the following agreement, which was part of his overall strategy to make a separate peace with the **Allies**:

1. That **concentration camps** will not be blown up.
2. On the approach of Allied troops, a white flag will be hoisted.
3. No more Jews will be killed, and Jews will be treated like other prisoners.
4. **Sweden** will be allowed to send food parcels to individual Jewish prisoners.

AHENENPASS **(ANCESTRY CARD).** Following the passage of the **Nuremberg Laws** in 1935, the **Nazi Party** issued identity cards to

1

all **Schutzstaffel** (SS) members and civilians to enable them to prove their **Aryan** ancestry.

AHMADINEJAD, MAHMOUD (1956–). Elected president of Iran in 2005, Ahmadinejad is widely regarded as an advocate of **Holocaust denial**. On 14 December 2005, soon after his election as Iran's president, he made several controversial statements about the **Holocaust**, including referring to it as a "myth." He also criticized those European countries, such as **Germany**, that made laws against Holocaust denial. In 30 May 2006, in an interview with *Der Spiegel*, Ahmadinejad insisted, in regard to his previous statement that the Holocaust was a myth, "I will only accept something as truth if I'm actually convinced of it." He went on to argue that "most" scholars who recognized the existence of the Holocaust are "politically motivated . . . then there is the group of scholars who represent the opposite position and have therefore been imprisoned for the most part." In August 2006, in a letter to German Chancellor Angela Merkel, Ahmadinejad expressed his belief that the Holocaust may have been invented by the **Allied** powers to embarrass Germany.

On 11 December 2006, he convened an International Conference to Review the Global Vision of the Holocaust. Among the invitees were such well-known Holocaust deniers as David Duke, Gerald Frederick Töben, and **Robert Faurisson**. The press described the meeting as a "Holocaust denial conference." Ahmadinejad stated that the conference was meant to "create an opportunity for thinkers who cannot express their views freely in Europe about the Holocaust." In his September 2007 appearance at Columbia University, Ahmadinejad said, in regard to the Holocaust, that "I'm not saying that it didn't happen at all. This is not a judgment that I'm passing here," and that the Holocaust should be left open to debate and research like any other historical event. At the 18 September 2009 Quds Day ceremony in Tehran, he stated that "the pretext for establishing the Zionist regime is a lie, a lie which relies on an unreliable claim, a mythical claim, [as] the occupation of **Palestine** has nothing to do with the Holocaust." He went on to refer to the Holocaust as a sealed "black box." In regard to the **Israeli**–Palestinian conflict, Ahmadinejad has argued that the Palestinians played "no role" in the Holocaust, implying that the Palestinians were pay-ing the price for the West's support of the State of Israel. *See also* HUSSEINI, MOHAMMAD AMIN AL-, HAJJ.

AKTION. Literally meaning "action." The *Aktion* consisted of sweeps made by the German military in the **ghettos** for the purpose of their liquidation, and to gather Jews for **deportation** to the **death camps**. The liquidation of the **Warsaw ghetto** in April 1943 was referred to as the *Grossaktion* (large action).

AKTION ERNTEFEST (OPERATION HARVEST FESTIVAL). *See* OPERATION ERNTEFEST.

AKTION 1005. The code name for the German attempt to obliterate all traces of the **Final Solution**. The *Aktion* took the form of exhuming and burning bodies at various extermination centers in Eastern Europe. The "action," which began in the summer of 1942, entailed the selection of Jewish prisoners (**Sonderkommandos**) to unearth the bodies, remove them to funeral pyres, and perform other such tasks. Ultimately the Jewish Sonderkommandos themselves were killed. *See also* DENTISTS.

AKTION REINHARD. After the assassination of **Sicherheitsdienst** (SD) head **Reinhard Heydrich** in May 1942, the **Schutzstaffel** (SS) "honored" their fallen chief by using the code name for the annihilation of Polish Jewry. **Belzec** (March 1942), **Sobibor** (March 1942), and **Treblinka** (June 1942) were the Aktion Reinhard camps that were specifically established for the annihilation of the Jews. Approximately two million Jews were exterminated in the three camps during the 20 months of their operation.

AKTION WOLKE Al. *See* AKTION WOLKENBRAND.

AKTION WOLKENBRAND. On the eve of the liberation of **Dachau** in April 1945, there were 67,665 registered prisoners, among them 22,100 Jews. In the days before the arrival of the American Seventh Army, on 29 April 1945, the Germans forced about 7,000 Jews from Dachau to march to the south of **Germany**. During this forced march, many of them were shot or died from hunger or exhaustion. The

Allies later learned of the **Schutzstaffel** (SS) plan, Aktion Wolken-brand, which was intended to poison or to destroy the camp, and to kill by aerial bombing (Aktion Wolke AI) the remaining inmates of Dachau. *See also* DEATH MARCHES.

ALIYA BET. As the situation worsened for Jews in **Germany** during the 1930s, the **Jewish Agency** executive in **Palestine**, together with the Revisionist Zionists, organized illegal immigration into Palestine under the code name Aliya Bet. Although the Jews who arrived in Palestine without entry certificates were considered illegal immigrants by the British, the Jewish Agency referred to the immigrants as having made *aliya* or legal immigration. *See also STRUMA* AFFAIR; TRANSFER AGREEMENT; YISHUV.

ALLIANZ AG. **Germany**'s largest insurance company worked closely with the **Nazi** government. Prior to the Nazi seizure of power in 1933, executives of Allianz, through cash contributions, openly courted the **Nazi Party**. During the period of the **Third Reich**, an executive of Allianz, Kurt Schmitt, became **Adolf Hitler's** first minister of economics and wore the **Schutzstaffel** (SS) uniform. Another, Eduard Hilgard, worked both as an executive of Allianz AG and as the head of the **Reich** agency that oversaw the insurance companies.

In 1933, the German government legislated a law that permitted the confiscation of the Jewish-owned property of those who had migrated from the country. This same law was later applied to Jews who were deported to the **death camps**. Under these circumstances, insurance companies, like Allianz AG, profited through their cooperation with the government. As a result of Nazi persecution, thousands of Jews **emigrated** from Germany, whereupon the insurance companies seized their insurance policies and handed them over to the government. Perhaps the most significant example of the cooperation of Allianz AG with the Nazis occurred in the aftermath of **Kristallnacht**. Against the background of the vast destruction of Jewish property, Allianz AG limited claims made by Jews to only three cents on a dollar. The money, however, was paid to the Reich treasury, rather than to the victims of the state-sponsored **pogrom**.

In German-occupied Europe, the assets of the local insurance companies were taken over by companies such as Allianz AG.

After the war, **survivors of the Holocaust** and relatives of the victims placed claims against Allianz AG, which the company denied because the claimants lacked death certificates, policy numbers, or other documentation. Furthermore, Allianz AG contended that all survivors who were entitled to benefits were already compensated by the German government. Attorneys for the claimants responded by calling the Allianz AG argument preposterous, and in 1997 filed a lawsuit on behalf of the survivors, which demanded not only equitable compensation for the victims but also that Allianz AG open the files of their transactions during the Third Reich. In May 1998, a New York State Senate committee revealed that German insurance companies, such as Allianz AG, had colluded with the Nazi government in the widespread theft of the insurance assets of European Jews. *See also* SWISS BANKS; SWITZERLAND; WORLD JEWISH CONGRESS.

ALLIED CONTROL COUNCIL LAW NUMBER 10 OF 10 DECEMBER 1945. This law was the basis for the punishment of persons guilty of war and crimes, against the peace, and against humanity. **United States** military tribunals presided over 12 subsequent trials of high-ranking members of the **Nazi Party**, government, military, business leaders, physicians, lawyers, and **Einsatzgruppen** leaders. *See also* CRIMINAL ORGANIZATIONS.

ALLIED DECLARATION, 17 DECEMBER 1942. The **Allies** solemnly condemned the extermination of the Jews and promised to punish the perpetrators. Pressure from members of the British Parliament, from Jewish groups in England, from the Anglican Church, from the British press, and from the Polish government-in-exile persuaded the Allied governments to publish their first official recognition of atrocities in **Poland**. The Allied nations—**Great Britain, United States, Soviet Union, Belgium, Czechoslovakia, Greece, Luxembourg**, the **Netherlands, Norway, Poland, Yugoslavia**, and the French National Committee—officially condemned the **Nazis'** "bestial policy of cold-blooded extermination." They vowed to punish those responsible. The notable exception to the declaration was the refusal of Pope **Pius XII** to join with the Allies to condemn the Nazi atrocities.

Agreeing with the U.S. government's position that the Jews being massacred by the Germans could be helped only by a total and unconditional Allied victory over **Germany**, most of the American press, including the Jewish-owned *New York Times*, continued to treat the **Holocaust** as just another war story, and was unwilling to discuss the systematic annihilation of the Jews. Given the Allied governments' knowledge of the Holocaust at this time, waiting until the Allied armed forces had achieved a total victory over the Germans before acting to prevent the ongoing Nazi **genocide** indicates that the Allied governments had accepted the possibility that the majority of European Jews would be killed before the Germans could be stopped.

ALLIES. The term refers to the coalition of countries that fought against **Germany** during World War II. The major Allied nations were the **United States**, **Great Britain**, and the **Soviet Union**, as well as **resistance** groups throughout German-occupied Europe. The **French** and the **Polish** governments-in-exile had their headquarters in Great Britain. *See also* LIBERATION.

ALTERSGETTO **(ELDERS GHETTO). Nazi euphemism** for the **Theresienstadt ghetto.** Initially the German government announced that the **ghetto** was to house elderly Jews, but subsequently it included Jews of all ages, including children. German and Czech Jews were eventually deported to **Auschwitz.** *See also BRUNDIBAR.*

AMERICAN FRIENDS SERVICE COMMITTEE (AFSC). *See* RIGHTEOUS GENTILES.

AMERICAN JOINT DISTRIBUTION COMMITTEE (JDC, "THE JOINT"). The American Jewish relief agency was founded in 1914 and was active in overseas relief and rehabilitation programs. Prior to America's entry into World War II, its offices in **Nazi**-occupied Europe often became the center of underground activities. The Joint was also active in providing food and money to Polish Jewry and was involved in the evacuation of several thousand Jews from Lithuania, who found sanctuary in East Asia. Perhaps, its most notable achievement was in the **Warsaw ghetto**, where the organization dispensed funds for children centers, hospitals, and organized social, cultural, and educational centers for the Jewish inhabitants. The JDC also supplied funds for armed **resistance** in both the Warsaw and **Bialystok ghettos**. Following the **United States'** entry into the war in December 1941, the JDC found its ability to help the beleaguered Jews of Europe stymied by **Allied** policy, which forbade the transfer of funds to Europe. Nevertheless, where possible, the Joint remained active in the various efforts to ransom Jews from being sent to the death camps.

Perhaps more than any Jewish organization, the JDC was responsible for the survival of thousands of Jewish lives. In **Hungary**, the JDC supplied funds to **Raoul Wallenberg** and Carl Lutz, the Swiss vice-consul in Budapest, for the purpose of establishing shelters for Jewish children (which later were placed under international protection). Through one of its agents, Sally Mayer (1882–1950), efforts were made to raise funds for the aborted **Europa Plan**, in **Slovakia**, and Mayer's work in Hungary in an effort to ransom the Jews from **deportation** (**Blood for Goods**), although the Joint did not support him in this effort. Following the war, the JDC was active in the **displaced persons** camps. Working together with other Jewish organizations, the Joint became the primary **Jewish agency** that supported survivors in the displaced persons camps in **Germany**, **Poland**, **Italy**, Hungary, **Romania**, and elsewhere. *See also* WEISSMANDEL, MICHAEL DOV.

ANCESTRY CARD. *See AHENENPASS.*

ANGEL OF DEATH. The nickname used by **survivors** of **Auschwitz** for **Josef Mengele**, the chief medical doctor at the **death camp** from 1943 to 1945. Mengele often showed kindness to his victims before dispatching them to their death. *See also* MEDICAL EXPERIMENTS.

ANGRIFF, DER (**THE ATTACK**). A major **Nazi** newspaper edited by **Joseph Goebbels** from 1927 to 1945. Goebbels used the paper as a means of Nazi propaganda against the Jews.

ANIELEWICZ, MORDECAI (1919–1943). Anielewicz was the commander of the **Warsaw ghetto uprising** in April 1943. Born into a poor family in the Warsaw slum, he joined a **Zionist** youth group where he excelled as an organizer and youth leader. Following the German invasion of **Poland** in September 1939, he made his way to Soviet-occupied Poland for the purpose of reaching **Romania** so he could establish an escape route for Jewish youth to reach **Palestine**. Arrested by Soviet troops, Anielewicz was sent to jail and upon his release returned to German-occupied Warsaw. By January 1940, Anielewicz had become an underground leader in the **Warsaw ghetto**, with the objective of setting up cells among his Zionist followers.

After receiving a report of the mass murder of Jews following **Germany**'s invasion of the **Soviet Union**, he focused his energy on creating a defense force in the ghetto. Anielewicz attempted to forge an alliance with Polish **resistance** movements that were loyal to the Polish government-in-exile in London but his efforts failed. After the mass deportation of Jews from Warsaw in the summer of 1942, Anielewicz organized his Zionist comrades into an armed resistance movement, the **Jewish Combat Organization** (ZOB). The ZOB, however, lacked arms and its membership was depleted as a result of **deportations**. By the end of 1942, the ghetto was reduced in size with only 60,000 of its original 350,000 Jews still left. Anielewicz proceeded to merge other existing ghetto underground groups with the ZOB, and he was appointed commander. On 18 January 1943, the Germans embarked on a new round of deportations from the ghetto that took the ZOB leadership by surprise. Unable to fully mobilize the various groups that constituted the ZOB for action, Anielewicz decided to take his faction and do battle against the Germans. The fighters deliberately joined the assembled deportees to the **death camps**, and at an agreed-on signal attacked the German troops. Most of his men were killed in battle, but Anielewicz was saved by his men.

Following the clash, the deportations were halted, and from January to April 1943, the ZOB prepared for the expected decisive test that was certain to come. On 19 April 1943, on the eve of Passover, the Germans entered the ghetto for the final deportation of its Jews. This action marked the signal for the Warsaw ghetto uprising, which continued for four weeks of brutal fighting in which the large German force suffered unexpected large casualties. Under Anielewicz's command, the resistance fighters eventually were forced to retreat into a bunker at **18 Mila** Street, and when the bunker fell on 18 May, the main force of the ZOB, including Anielewicz, was killed. In his last letter sent on 23 April 1943 to a member of the ZOB, Anielewicz wrote, "Farewell, my friend. Perhaps we shall meet again. The most important thing is that my life's dream has come true. I have lived to see Jewish resistance in the ghetto in all its greatness and glory." *See also* EDELMAN, MAREK.

ANNUS MUNDI. Latin colloquial term for **Auschwitz** that translates as "asshole of the world."

ANSCHLUSS. This was the German annexation of **Austria** on 13 March 1938, and its incorporation as a province (Ostmark) of the **Third Reich**. Although the annexation was imposed by **Germany** and resisted by some of the population, most Austrians welcomed the Anschluss as evidenced by its overwhelming approval in a subsequent plebiscite.

There were approximately 220,000 Jews living in Austria at the time of the Anschluss. Following Germany's annexation of Austria, it introduced its racial laws and anti-Jewish acts of violence intensified, resulting in the efforts of Jews to **emigrate** from Austria. *See also* EVIAN CONFERENCE; GERMAN-AUSTRIAN JEWISH POPULATION.

ANTI-SEMITIC CONFERENCES. The German government convened two conferences that dealt with solutions to the **"Jewish question."** The first was held in Frankfurt in March 1941 and included leading **Nazi collaborators** in countries under German occupation. Among those participating in the "scholarly" conference were Walter Gross, **Alfred Rosenberg**, Vidkun Quisling, and Sano Mach. The second international anti-Semitic conference was held in Krakow in July 1944, and was organized by Alfred Rosenberg. The participants included many in the hierarchy of the **Third Reich**, among them **Heinrich Himmler**, **Joseph Goebbels**, **Hans Frank**, Martin Bormann, and **Ernst Kaltenbrunner**. Also attending the conference was the exiled pro-Nazi Grand Mufti of Jerusalem, **Hajj Amin al-Husseini**.

ANTI-SEMITISM. The first use of the term is attributed to Wilhelm Marr, a member of the German Reichstag, in 1879. The term reflects the currents of racism and **Social Darwinism** that had permeated much of Western Europe and the **United States** at the end of the 19th century. In his use of the term, Marr intended to distinguish between traditional anti-Jewish attitudes, which were based on **Christianity**'s aversion to the Jews, and repugnance toward Jews based on race. Marr argued that Jews were of the Semitic race and were not a religious fellowship.

Inasmuch as racial theory was widespread in the German universities, it is not surprising that the term "anti-Semitism" caught on among *Volkisch* and other German nationalists at the end of the century. Increasingly, Jews found themselves defined as Semites as juxtaposed to the true German "**Aryans**." The significance of this definition, for Jewish converts to Christianity, was that it negated the assimilative benefits of baptism. Until **Adolf Hitler** made anti-Semitism the primary focus of **Nazi ideology**, most German Jews continued to believe that the racial definition, which held that racial characteristics were fixed in the "blood," was the rhetoric of a radical fringe group and not a threat to their place in German life. *See also* CHAMBERLAIN, HOUSTON STEWART.

APPELL **(ROLL CALL).** The most feared parts of the day in the **concentration camps** were the roll calls that took place at least twice daily. The inmates were forced to stand for hours at attention while they were counted and inspected for illness. Sometimes prisoners were assembled to witness executions and punishments. *See also APPLEMACHER; APPELLPLATZ.*

APPELLMACHER. The term refers to a **concentration camp** inmate assigned to count the assembled prisoners during the roll calls. *See also APPELL; APPELLPLATZ.*

APPELLPLATZ. The term refers to the central square in all **concentration camps** where daily roll calls took place. The roll calls generally took place in the morning and in the evening. The area was also the site where punishments, ranging from whippings to running the gauntlet, took place. Prisoners were also herded to the *Appelplatz* to witness hangings or executions by firing squads. *See also APPELL; APPLEMACHER.*

APRIL BOYCOTT. Following the **Nazi** "seizure of power" in January 1933, the **Sturmabteilung** (SA) intensified its violence against the Jews of **Germany**. As the news reached Jewish communities outside of Germany about the physical violence and the arbitrary incarceration of Jews in the **"wild camps,"** concern was raised about the safety of German Jewry. In the **United States**, leaders of the American Jewish Congress, in conjunction with other concerned Jewish and non-Jewish groups, attempted to organize a boycott of German goods in retaliation for the Nazi excesses. *See* WORLD JEWISH CONGRESS.

In response to the threat, the Nazis organized a boycott of Jewish establishments on 1 April 1933. The boycott lasted one day because the government feared that to prolong it would harm Germany's image in the international community as well as its economy. Overall, the German public displayed little enthusiasm for the boycott and patronized Jewish business establishments despite the presence of SA **storm troopers** guarding the entrance to the stores.

ARBEIT MACHT FREI (**WORK LIBERATES**). Words found atop the gate at the entrance to **Auschwitz** and **Dachau**.

ARENDT, HANNAH (1906–1975). Hannah Arendt was born on 14 October 1906, in Hanover, in Wilhelmine, **Germany**. After graduating from high school in Koenigsberg in 1924, Arendt began to study theology at the University of Marburg, where she became a student of the young philosopher Martin Heidegger, whose lectures would form the basis of *Being and Time* (1927), a classic work of 20th-century philosophy. Her brief but passionate affair with Heidegger, a married man and a father, began in 1925 but ended when she went on to study at the University of Heidelberg with Karl Jaspers. A psychiatrist who had converted to philosophy, Jaspers became her mentor. However, the rising **anti-Semitism** afflicting the German polity distracted her from metaphysics and compelled her to face the historical dilemma of German Jews.

As the **National Socialists** grasped power, Arendt became a political activist and, beginning in 1933, helped the German **Zionist** Organization to publicize the plight of the victims of Nazism. She also did research on anti-Semitic propaganda, for which she was arrested by the **Gestapo**. But when she won the sympathy of a Berlin jailer, she was released and escaped to Paris, where she remained for the rest of the decade. Working especially with Youth **Aliyah**, Arendt helped rescue Jewish children from the **Third Reich** and bring them to **Palestine**.

When the **Wehrmacht** (German army) invaded **France** less than half a year later, she was separated and interned in southern France along with other stateless Germans. Arendt was sent to Gurs, from which she escaped. She soon managed to reach neutral America, where her mother was able to reunite with her. While living in New York during the rest of World War II, Arendt envisioned the book that became *The Origins of Totalitarianism*. It was published in 1951, exactly a decade after she arrived in the United States and the same year she secured her citizenship. *The Origins of Totalitarianism* described the steps toward the distinctive 20th-century tyrannies of **Adolf Hitler** and **Joseph Stalin**, and demonstrated how embedded racism was in Central and Western European societies by the end of the 19th century. The book detailed how imperialism experimented with the possibilities of unspeakable cruelty and mass murder, and she proceeded to expose the operations of "radical evil," arguing that the huge number of prisoners in the **death camps** marked a horrifying discontinuity in European history itself.

In 1963, Arendt published what proved to be the most controversial work of her career, *Eichmann in Jerusalem*. In 1960, Israeli security forces had captured **Schutzstaffel** (SS) Lieutenant-Colonel **Adolf Eichmann**, who had been responsible for **deporting** Jews to the death camps. The following year, he was tried in **Israel**, where Arendt covered the trial as a correspondent for the *New Yorker*. Her articles were then revised and expanded for Eichmann in Jerusalem. Her portrayal of a bureaucrat who did his duty, a "**desk murderer**" who followed orders, rather than a fanatical ideologue animated by demonic **anti-Semitism**, was strikingly original. Far from embodying "radical evil," Eichmann exemplified the "**the banality of evil**," and, Arendt argued, his crimes could not be confined to the political peculiarities of the Third Reich.

Arendt also argued that fewer than six million Jews would have died if the **Jewish Councils** (Judenräte) had not collaborated to various degrees with **Nazis** like Eichmann. Even anarchy and noncooperation would have been better, she stated, than the effort to act as though the occupiers were traditional anti-Semites who might somehow be bribed or appeased. Her attribution of some responsibility for the catastrophe to the councils not only met sharp criticism but also provoked a considerable historical literature that investigated the behavior of Jewish communities under Nazi occupation. She drew criticism because she held the victims of the **Final Solution** accountable for inadequate and ill-conceived political action, and offered the perpetrators a measure of empathy in an effort to understand the "why" of the crimes they perpetrated, lest the horrors be repeated under different historical conditions. According to Arendt, then, Eichmann did not commit crimes because of a sadistic will to do so, nor because he had been deeply infected by the bacillus of anti-Semitism, but because he failed to think through what he was doing (his thoughtlessness). *See also* MILGRAM, STANLEY.

ART AND THE HOLOCAUST. The response of artists to the **anti-Semitic** policies of **Nazi Germany** began in the early 1930s and continued throughout the **Holocaust.** Many of these responses by artists to **Nazi** persecution were those works produced by **concentration camp** inmates and Jews confined in the **ghettos.** Working under impossible conditions, the artists were determined to provide through their art an eyewitness account of what they observed, from the cattle cars to the *Selektion* process, through the brutality of the **Forced labor** camps, to the **gas chambers, and the stack of dead** left unburied by the Nazis. A second motivation of inmate art was to resist dehumanization and bring some sense of their person in the drawings that were penciled on paper that was difficult to obtain. These works of art were, therefore, an affirmation of life and the only way to maintain their dignity.

Among works of art that survived the Holocaust, for example, were those of the underground artists of **Theresienstadt,** Felix Bloch, Friedl Dicker-Brandeis, Karel Fleischmann, Bedřich Fritta (his art sketches were intercepted by camp guards and subsequently Fritta was executed in 1944), Leo Haas, **Alfred Kantor,** and Otto Unger. Their work exposed the pretense of the so-called model **ghetto,** and their drawings revealed the starvation and death that existed daily in the camp.

In **Auschwitz** a number of artists through their drawings recreated the horror of the **death camps**. These included Alfred Kantor (who was transferred from Theresienstadt to Auschwitz and sketched daily life in the death camp), Diana Gottliebova (whose life was saved because Josef Mengele chose her to sketch pictures of **Gypsy** women for purposes of his **medical experiments**), and Karl Stojka (a Roma artist whose drawings recorded the brutal treatment of Gypsy life in the death camp).

There were also the drawings of **Simon Wiesenthal**, who was a **survivor** of five concentration camps. An architect by training, and better known as a "Nazi hunter," Wiesenthal was also a sketch artist. He drew numerous sketches of the horrors he encountered in the concentration camps and he was able to salvage many of them when he was liberated from **Mauthausen** on 5 May 1945.

Common to many artists whose work centered on the concentration camps or their ghetto memories was their representations of the Holocaust through the use of symbols, such as a chimney or barbed wire, to express their experiences. Samuel Bak, for example, who at an early age survived the destruction of the Vilna Ghetto, uses the chimney as a stand-in for the camps. Friedensreich Hundertwasser, the Austrian painter and architect whose mother was Jewish, drew on his Holocaust past by juxtaposing three symbols: the crematorium chimney, a garden of blood, and his personal symbol of hiding, the labyrinth. Even Buky Schwartz's "Pillar of Heroism" at **Yad Vashem** is perceived from the distance as a chimney.

Barbed wire was used in the abstract art of Igael Tumarkin to give a specific Holocaust meaning to his work. Chaim Gross and Marc Klonsky are other artists who used barbed wire as symbols of the **Shoah**. Biblical symbols were also used to oppose Nazism, such as the image of David killing Goliath, found in the works of Jacques Lipchitz. The use of Hebrew Testament imagery is also found in the art of Mordechai Ardon, Frederick Terna, and Nathan Rapaport. In Lipchitz's art, he sought to convey to non-Jews that Nazism was a threat to everyone and not only to Jews. These artists used Hebrew Testament images to convey to God their despair, using the traditional image of the sacrifice of Isaac in a Holocaust context. In Rapaport's "Job," he places a number on Job's arm to symbolize his faith despite everything.

The crucified Jewish Jesus, often wearing a prayer shawl, is also a frequently invoked symbol of the Holocaust. Artists who have invoked this symbol include both Christian and Jews alike, including Christians such as Otto Panokok, or Jews such as Marc Chagall, who use their art to address the Holocaust to the Christian world. Many of the artists who used this imagery, such as Giacomo Manzù, Ernst Fuchs, and Mauricio Lasansky, used their art to denounce the church for not doing enough to save the Jews.

The influence of camp and ghetto art will continue to attracts future artists, inasmuch as not only does the cache of the sketches and drawings found in the postwar years provide evidence of the barbarity of the Nazi perpetrators, but also the art serves as a commitment to Holocaust memory. *See also* FILM AND THE HOLOCAUST; LITERATURE AND THE HOLOCAUST; THEATER AND THE HOLOCAUST.

ARYAN. The **Nazis** claimed that the German people and other people from Northern and Western Europe were descendent from the Aryan race. The term "Aryan" refers to an Indo-European group whose spoken and written language was Sanskrit. The Nazis viewed the Aryan race as superior to all other racial groups and viewed history as a struggle for supremacy between the Aryans and the Semitic races. *See also* CHAMBERLAIN, HOUSTON STEWART; EUGENICS.

ARYAN PARAGRAPH. In its attempt to purge the German churches of any Hebrew influences, the **Nazi** government removed all Christian pastors with Jewish ancestry from their posts. This action was opposed by both the Catholic Church and the German Evangelical **Confessing churches.**

ARYANIZATION. The forcible expropriation of Jewish property and businesses in **Germany** and in much of German-occupied Europe during World War II. The Aryanization process was enacted through a set of government decrees. Examples of laws that ensured the Aryanization of Jewish property in Germany include the decree of 22 April 1938 that made it a crime for a German to disguise the fact that a business was owned by a Jew. The decree of 29 April 1938 required Jews to report the value of their property, except for personal goods, in excess of 5,000 reichsmarks. The decree of 14 June 1938 defined what the government meant by a Jewish-owned business. The decree of 6 July 1938 ordered that in accordance with the law of 14 June 1938 those businesses defined by the government as Jewish must cease operations by 30 December 1938. In the aftermath of **Kristallnacht** on 9–10 November 1938, the German government required the Aryanization and/or liquidation of German-Jewish owned retail businesses. This was followed in December 1938 by a decree that required the Aryanization and/or liquidation of German-owned industrial enterprises. The decrees, which enacted the Aryanization of Jewish property into law, subsequently became models for countries that fell under German influence or occupation. Following the **Anschluss** in March 1938, the **Nazis** Aryanized Jewish property in **Austria**. The process of Aryanization continued in German-occupied **Belgium**, **Bohemia and Moravia**, **France**, **Greece**, **Hungary**, the **Netherlands**, and **Serbia**, and was referred to as "Romanianization" in **Romania**.

AUSCHWITZ (POLISH, OSWIECIM). The largest of the **death camps**, located in Upper Silesia. Auschwitz consisted of three camps: Auschwitz I, the main Auschwitz camp; Auschwitz II, Birkenau, the extermination camp; and Auschwitz III, **Buna works**, the **forced labor** camp where I. G. Farben produced synthetic rubber for the German war effort. The **ideology** that made Auschwitz-Birkenau synonymous with the gassing of between 1.1 and 1.5 million Jews was at cross-purposes with the requirements of forced labor that prevailed at the Buna-Monowitz camp. **Heinrich Himmler** came to terms with the contradiction of utilizing Jews as forced labor and, at the same time, implementing the **Final Solution**.

Himmler adopted a strategy of working to death those Jews who were fit for labor and immediately gassing the others. The decision to use slave labor at the Buna camp was made reluctantly, but he viewed this as a temporary situation that was to be aborted at the first opportunity. The strategy, therefore, was to murder all the Jews arriving in Auschwitz in the long run, regardless of their value to German industry, but in the short run, to encourage them to work as a means of survival. This illusion was cynically reinforced in the sign that stood above the gate that "greeted" the newly arrived victims: *Arbeit*

Macht Frei (Work liberates). Because of the large number of Jews and others who were exterminated at Auschwitz, the death camp has become synonymous with the **Holocaust** and has come to symbolize the **genocidal** policies of **Nazi Germany**.

AUSCHWITZ, BEAST OF. The striking blue-eyed blonde Erma Grese, the "Beast of **Auschwitz**," was also dubbed by prisoners in Auschwitz as the "Beautiful Beast." Grese was the most notorious **Schutzstaffel** (SS) guard in the history of Auschwitz, where witnesses at her trial testified that she set dogs on bound prisoners, chose who went to the **gas chambers**, and was accused by **survivors** of the **death camp** of ordering the skinning of three inmates, from which she subsequently made into lamp shades. She ended the war at **Bergen-Belsen** where she was captured by British soldiers on 17 April 1945. Grese was one of a relatively small number of women who had worked in the concentration camps and were hanged for war crimes by the **Allies**.

AUSCHWITZ PROTOCOL (VRBA-WETZLER REPORT). Alfred Wetzler and Walter Rosenberg (Rudolph Vrba) both escaped from **Auschwitz** in April 1944. Eventually, they reached Bratislava (**Slovakia**), where they presented a detailed report of the installations, methods of killing, and maps of the **gas chamber** in Auschwitz. By June 1944, the report reached the **Allies**. Inasmuch as the maps indicated the location of the killing facilities in Auschwitz as well as the rail hubs leading to the camp, Rabbi **Michael Dov Weissmandel** and others in the Working Group urged the Allies to act on this information and bomb the Auschwitz complex, including the rail tracks leading to the camp. The Allies ignored the exhortation.

AUSPEITSCHTISCH. In their "work camps" in **Poland**, the Germans engaged in whipping (*auspeitschen*) of inmates. They set up special tables (*Auspeitschtisch*) where whippings were administered.

AUSSERORDENTLICHE BEFRIEDUNGSAKTION (AB) (EX-TRAORDINARY PACIFICATION ACTION). The **genocidal Nazi** policy in German-occupied **Poland**, as implemented by **Hans Frank**, the governor-general of the **General-Gouvernement**. Its purpose was to liquidate the Polish intelligentsia, which included teachers, clergy, doctors, dentists, war veterans, officers, ranking bureaucrats, merchants, big landowners, writers, and journalists, as well as Poles who had university or high school diplomas.

AUSTRIA. The Austrian republic was founded in November 1918 following the defeat of the Austro-Hungarian Empire in World War I. The population of Austria numbered 6,725,000 inhabitants, including some 220,000 Jews. Austria's Jewish population was proportionately three and a half times as numerous as **Germany**'s Jewish community. During the 1920s, over 200,000 Jews lived in Vienna, the sixth-largest Jewish city in the world, following New York, Warsaw, Chicago, Philadelphia, and Budapest.

Jews made a significant contribution to Austria's cultural and economic life, and included Sigmund Freud, Theodor Herzl, Karl Kraus, Gustav Mahler, Arthur Schnitzler, Arnold Schoenberg, and Ludwig Wittgenstein among the country's more prominent personalities. Austria, however, also suffered from an endemic **anti-Semitism** that manifested itself politically. The three major political parties were hostile to either Jews or Judaism. The anticlerical Social Democratic Party viewed Judaism as a relic of the bourgeoisies. The clerical Christian Socialist Party expressed traditional Christian contempt for Jews and Judaism, and the Austrian pan-Germans espoused the racial forms of anti-Semitism. In fact, **Adolf Hitler**, in his autobiography *Mein Kampf* (My Struggle), writes that it was in Vienna that he became an anti-Semite.

On the eve of the German annexation of Austria (**Anschluss**) on 13 March 1938, anti-Semitism was a widespread ideology in the First Austrian Republic. Although Austria would later claim that it was the first victim of **Nazi** aggression, the reality was that the Austrians welcomed annexation to the Greater **Reich**. Following the Anschluss, anti-Semitic rioting spread throughout Austria. The violence directed toward the Jews by Austrian Nazis exceeded the brutality shown by their counterparts in Germany. This was followed by the expulsion of Jews from the country's economic and social life within weeks after the annexation. In March 1938, Germany set up **Gestapo** offices throughout Austria. One of the first actions taken by the Gestapo was to shut down the offices of the Jewish community organizations and the **Zionist** organizations in Vienna. Jewish leaders were subsequently arrested and placed in jail. This was followed by the looting of Jewish apartments and the confiscation of artworks and other valuables. Shortly thereafter, Jewish ritual slaughtering practices were forbidden and synagogues were desecrated. Torture was also used against Jews until they signed a document stating that they had voluntarily given up their property.

The seizure of Jewish property was followed by the **Aryanization** of Jewish businesses. By the beginning of June 1938, about 26,000 Jewish-owned enterprises had been taken over by the Austrians. The confiscation of Jewish property and wealth was also joined by the German effort to force Austria's Jews to emigrate. Toward that end, the Germans in August 1938 opened the **Central Bureau for Jewish Emigration** in Vienna. The office was headed by **Adolf Eichmann**, who was instrumental in forcing the **emigration** of Jews from Austria to **Switzerland** or **Italy**, before it became difficult for Jews to find a place of refuge. Prior to **Kristallnacht**, about 7,000 Jews emigrated from Austria.

Following Kristallnacht on 9–10 November 1938, Jews were rounded up and placed in **concentration camps** and were not released until they had made arrangements to leave the country. On the eve of the German invasion of **Poland**, 126,445 Jews emigrated from Austria. Those who remained were eventually deported to the **ghettos** and the **death camps**. About 65,000 Austrian Jews died in either the ghettos or the death camps in Poland. Although Austria constituted only 8.5 percent of the population of the Greater Reich, half the crimes committed against Jews during the **Holocaust** were committed by Austrians.

AXIS. The Axis consisted of **Germany** and its partners during World War II. The states that sided with Germany during the course of the war included **Italy, Japan, Hungary**, and other satellites in Eastern Europe under German control.

– B –

BABI YAR (GRANDMOTHER'S RAVINE). Following the invasion of the **Soviet Union** in June 1941, the Germans, along with the support of **Ukrainian** auxiliary forces, shot and buried over 33,771

Jews in a mass grave outside Kiev on 29–30 September 1941. *See also* EINSATZGRUPPEN.

BADGE, JEWISH. *See* YELLOW STAR OF DAVID BADGE.

BALFOUR DECLARATION. *See* GREAT BRITAIN; PALESTINE; ZIONISM.

BALTIC STATES. *See* ESTONIA; FINLAND; LATVIA; LITHU-ANIA.

BANALITY OF EVIL. The "banality of evil" is the controversial phrase coined by **Hannah Arendt** when she incorporated the term as the subtitle of her 1963 book, *Eichmann in Jerusalem: The Banality of Evil*. It describes her argument that the **Holocaust** was not perpetrated by fanatics or sociopaths but rather by ordinary people, like **Adolf Eichmann**, who accepted the premises of their state and therefore participated in mass murder with the view that their actions were normal. *See also* DESK MURDERER.

BARASZ, EFRAIM (1892–1943). *See* BIALYSTOK.

BARBIE, KLAUS (1905–1987). The infamous "butcher of Lyon" was a **Gestapo** official in Lyon, **France**, where he was responsible for the execution of at least 4,000 persons, including Jean Moulin, the head of the French **resistance**. In addition, he ordered the **deportation** of 7,000 Jews to **concentration camps** and in April 1944 gave the order for the arrest and deportation of 44 children at a Jewish orphanage in the French village of Izieu.

Following the war, he was able to avoid arrest because American intelligence officials believed he would be a valuable asset in the cold war against the **Soviet Union**. When it became apparent in 1950 that the French were intent on putting him on trial for war crimes, American intelligence agents provided him with false documents and a Bolivian visa. For the next 32 years, Barbie and his family enjoyed a new life in Bolivia under the assumed name of Klaus Altmann. In 1972, Barbie was located by **Nazi** hunters **Serge and Beate Klarsfeld**, but it was not until 1987 that he was extradited to France, where he was tried and convicted of war crimes. Barbie died in prison in 1987.

BARRY. The name of a dog in the **Treblinka death camp**. Barry was especially trained to attack the genitals of naked victims awaiting their deaths at the entrance to the **gas chambers**.

BAUM GROUP. The largest Jewish **resistance** group in **Nazi Germany**, named after its leaders, Herbert and Marianne Baum. The two Berlin communists were also active in Jewish Youth groups so as to move them ideologically in support of the **Soviet Union**. The Baum Group, although small in number, began their resistance to the **Nazis** in 1936 when they began to distribute anti-Nazi leaflets and wrote anti-**Hitler** slogans on walls in Berlin. The group, which never totaled more than 150 individuals, attempted to set fire to an anti-Soviet exhibition, "The Soviet Paradise," in May 1942, and although they did little damage, the group was arrested. In retaliation for the attack, the Nazis arrested 500 Berlin Jews and subsequently shot almost half of them. The rest were sent first to the **Sachsenhausen concentration camp**, and later **deported** to **Auschwitz**. Among those executed were Herbert and Marianne Baum.

BEER HALL PUTSCH. The Munich putsch was **Adolf Hitler**'s failed takeover of the Bavarian government on 9 November 1923. Hitler's objective was to use the military forces of Bavaria and march to Berlin as a prelude to an overthrow of the **Weimar Republic** and the establishment of a dictatorial government. Hitler announced the revolution in the Burgerbraukeller in Munich, hence the term "beer hall putsch." Hitler was subsequently arrested on April 1924 and sentenced to five years in prison with the possibility of parole after six months. It was during his incarceration in Landsberg prison that he wrote *Mein Kampf*.

"BEHIND THE ENEMY POWERS: THE JEWS" (*DAHINTER DIE FEINDMACHT: DIE JUDEN*). The caption of a German wall poster following **Adolf Hitler**'s declaration of war against the **United States**. By depicting the **Allied** war effort as a cover for an international Jewish conspiracy, **Nazi** propaganda presented mass murder of Jews as a defense of **Germany**.

BELARUSSIA. Belarussia, now called Belarus, is a landlocked country bordered by Russia to the north and the east, **Ukraine** to the south, **Poland** to the west, and **Lithuania** and **Latvia** to the north. In 1939, Belarussia encompassed a substantial Polish and Jewish population that was annexed by the **Soviet Union** and was subsequently transformed into the Belarussian Soviet Socialist Republic. Following **Germany**'s attack on the Soviet Union in June 1941, the **Nazis** commenced to starve Soviet prisoners of war, shoot and gas Jews, and kill civilians in antipartisan actions. Half of the population of Soviet Belarussia was either killed or displaced by the Nazis, thus making it one of the deadliest centers of **genocide** in Europe. According to historian Tim Snyder, "Nothing of the kind can be said of any other European country."

BELGIUM. Germany defeated Belgium in May 1940. At the time, there were approximately 90,000 Jews living in the country, who constituted 1 percent of the population. About an eighth of the Jews were refugees from Germany, **Austria**, and Eastern Europe. Most of Belgium's Jews lived in Antwerp and Brussels, where they were accepted by the overall population. However, **anti-Semitism** in Belgium manifested itself in the pro-**Nazi** Rexist party, which, on the eve of the German invasion, was rejected at the polls. During the six months following the German occupation of Belgium, life rapidly deteriorated for its Jews. The Germans promulgated decrees that defined Jews along racial lines and barred them from the civil service and the professions. Jewish businessmen were required to register their business concerns as a prelude to the **Aryanization** of their property. Within a year of the German occupation, the affluent Jewish community of Belgium was reduced to penury as it was driven from the economy. During the fall of 1941, Jews were subjected to a curfew, prohibited from travel, and forbidden from utilizing parks and other public accommodations. In December, Jewish children were forbidden from attending public schools, and in a slap at the Orthodox Jewish community, the Germans forbade *shehita*, or the ritual practice that enables Jews to eat kosher meat and poultry. By early

1942, Jews were compelled to serve in **forced labor** brigades, and by June 1942, they were required to wear the **yellow Star of David badge** so as to facilitate their deportation to the **death camps**. Not all the citizens of Belgium supported the Nazi legislation. There were displays of solidarity with the Jews, whereby the people of Belgium donned badges similar to the yellow badges in an exhibition of unity with their Jewish countrymen.

In November 1941, the Germans established a **Judenrat** (Jewish Council) that was made responsible for implementing the decrees that affected the status of the Jews of Belgium. Although the Jews were circumscribed in their ability to function under the German occupation, this did not prevent some Jews from establishing a Jewish underground organization, the Comité de Defense des Juifs (CDJ), which was affiliated with the Belgian **resistance** movement. In the summer of 1942, members of the CDJ assaulted an official of the Jewish Council who was responsible for compiling lists for the **deportations**. Its most prominent achievement, however, was in April 1943 when the CDJ attacked a transport from the Mechelen transit camp that was headed for **Auschwitz**, the only instance during the **Holocaust** of an armed attack on a train taking Jews to an extermination camp.

Jews were also included in the various Belgian resistance movements, and with the help of large numbers of the population, including churches, about 25,000 Jews were hidden from the Germans. Despite the support of the population, the deportations began in August 1942 and continued for over a year, culminating in **Operation Iltis**, whereby Jews of Belgian nationality, who had previously been deferred, were now deported to the east. Most of the Jews of Belgium were sent to Auschwitz, with a smaller number sent to **Buchenwald**, Ravensbruck, and **Bergen-Belsen**. The deportations proceeded despite the sympathetic support of the population. About 25,400 Jews were deported to Auschwitz from the Belgian transit camp at Malines from mid-1942 through mid-1944. Others died in Belgian labor camps of hunger and disease. Of the 90,000 Jews who resided in Belgium at the time of the German occupation in 1940, about 40,000 perished.

BELSEN. *See* BERGEN-BELSEN.

BELZEC. The first of the **Aktion Reinhard death camps** was situated in the southeastern part of the Lublin district near the Belzec railroad station. Construction of the camp began in November 1941, and it became operational in March 1942. Belzec was utilized as an exterminating center for the Jews arriving from the **ghettos of Poland**. Under the supervision of **Christian Wirth**, Jews were gassed with **carbon monoxide** from the exhaust fumes of an internal combustion engine. The engine was installed in a shed outside the **gas chamber** from which gas was piped into the enclosed space. Wirth camouflaged the killing process in a manner that caught the prisoners unaware that they were being sent to their death. His intention was to convey to the victims the impression that they had arrived at a work or transit camp. Wirth's strategy of deception entailed speeding up every step of the process, so that the victims would have no chance to grasp the precarious situation that they found themselves in. The objective was to mentally paralyze the victims so as to minimize the possibility of escape or acts of **resistance**.

Wirth's deceptive practices were also applied to the incoming convoys, whose "passengers" were exterminated on arrival. The train depot was composed of a railroad ramp, which had room for 20 freight cars, and two barracks for the arrivals. The victims were brought to the first barrack to undress, and their clothes and other personal items were stored in the second barrack. From this area of the camp, the victims were sent to the extermination sector of Belzec, which consisted of the gas chambers and the mass graves. A path known as "the tube" (*Schlauch*) was fenced in with barbed wire and partitioned off by a wooden fence that separated the reception area from the extermination sector. Estimates of Jews exterminated at Belzec range from a low figure of 500,000 to a high estimate of 600,000.

BERGEN-BELSEN. The **concentration camp**, which was located in Lower Saxony, was constructed in April 1943 as a detention camp designed to exchange German prisoners for German nationals in **Allied** countries whom the **Reich** wanted to repatriate. At the time Bergen-Belsen became a concentration camp in March 1944, it consisted of a main camp and five satellites, which included four that held large numbers of Jewish prisoners. Conditions at Bergen-Belsen were horrific. Prisoners received no medical attention and inadequate food rations. Thousands died from chronic illnesses as a result of the terrible conditions. In the last weeks of the war, tens of thousands of Jews were evacuated from the extermination camps in **Poland** and force-marched to Bergen-Belsen. The evacuation included 20,000 women from **Auschwitz**. The camp, however, was unprepared for the influx of so many people, and as a result conditions at the camp deteriorated. The camp administration did nothing to house the large number of Jews who streamed into the camp. Because of a lack of shelter and shortages of food and water, the camp inmates were subjected to an outbreak of **typhus**, which in March 1945 had already claimed the lives of more than 18,000 prisoners, including **Anne Frank** and her sister, Margot.

The total number of those who died in Bergen-Belsen between January and April 1945 was 35,000. When the British Second Army, 11th Armored Division, along with Canadian units liberated Bergen-Belsen on 15 April 1945, there were 60,000 prisoners in the camp who were chronically ill. There were also thousands of unburied bodies strewn all over the camp, a scene vividly captured on film by the British, who were horrified by what they encountered. In the days following the **liberation** of Bergen-Belsen, an additional 14,000 persons died, and thousands of others perished in the following weeks. *See also* DEATH MARCHES.

BERGSON GROUP. Hillel Kook, whose alias was Peter Bergson, was the nephew of Rabbi Abraham Kook, the famous Ashkenazic chief rabbi of Jerusalem. As one of the leaders of the Revisionist **Zionist** movement, he opposed many of the policies of the **Jewish Agency** executive in **Palestine**. Between 1940 and 1948, Bergson and his group, which included members of the Palestine underground group Irgun Tseva'i Le'ummi (Etsel), arrived in the **United States** where they attempted to mobilize public opinion on behalf of a more forceful policy toward **Nazi Germany**. Their objectives included agitation for the creation of an independent Jewish army that would fight against Germany. Toward this end, the Bergson group formed the Committee for a Jewish Army of Stateless and Palestinian Jews. Following the failed **Bermuda Conference**, they organized the Emergency Committee to Save the Jewish people of Europe, which urged the **Allies** for immediate action on behalf of the Jews and called on neutral countries to open their doors to offer temporary asylum to Jewish refugees. The activities of the Bergson Group, however, brought it into conflict with the mainstream Jewish leadership as exemplified by Rabbi **Stephen S. Wise** and the American Jewish Congress. *See* WORLD JEWISH CONGRESS.

The Bergson Group also attracted a great many journalists and intellectuals such as Max Lerner, Billy Rose, and Ben Hecht. The latter, a Hollywood screenwriter as well as playwright, wrote the pageant "We Will Never Die," which was initially performed on 9 March 1943, in a packed Madison Square Garden. Hecht wrote the pageant in memory of the two million Jews who had been murdered up to that time. From New York, the play then toured other cities throughout the United States.

The committee also organized a campaign to obtain a million signatures on a petition, which was to be presented to Congress and President **Franklin D. Roosevelt**, calling for the creation of a government body that would deal specifically with the rescue of Jews. In this endeavor it won the backing of such public figures as William Randolph Hearst, Secretary of the Interior Harold Ickes, former president Herbert Hoover, Mayor Fiorello LaGuardia of New York, and Will Rogers, Democratic congressman from California. In all, 34 senators and 37 American admirals and generals supported the group.

Although many of its objectives resulted in failure, there was also a notable achievement. The Bergson Group did gain the support of Democratic senator Guy Gillette from Iowa and Congressman Will Rogers, as well as Republican congressman Joseph Baldwin from New York, to introduce identical resolutions in both the House of Representatives and the Senate that called on the president to establish a government commission for the rescue of Europe's Jews.

Together with the pressure exerted on President Roosevelt from the Department of the Treasury, led by **Henry Morgenthau Jr.**, the president issued an executive order on 22 January 1944 that established the **War Refugee Board**.

Although the Bergson Group played no role in either rescue or aid operations in behalf of European Jewry, its contributions were, nevertheless, important. Its signal achievements were to bring to the attention of the American people the **Nazi** extermination of the Jews and to pressure high-level government officials to search for means of rescuing the remaining Jews of Europe.

BERMUDA CONFERENCE. The second of two conferences initiated by the **Allies** to deal with the wartime refugee crisis (the **Evian Conference** in 1938 was the other) was convened by the **United States** and **Great Britain** on 19 April 1943. Although the ostensible purpose of the conference was to find some form of relief for victims of **Nazi** persecution, in reality the conference was organized to defuse public protest over revelations that the Germans had embarked on a program of systematically liquidating the Jews of Europe. Great Britain insisted that it would not participate in the conference should the issue of **Palestine**, as a refuge for Europe's Jews, be placed on the agenda. The meeting resulted in failure inasmuch as none of the participating countries was willing to liberalize its immigration laws to take in refugees. In addition, the Jewish character of the crisis was minimized through the use of a **euphemism** that referred to them as "political refugees."

"BETTER HITLER THAN BLUM." The refrain of **anti-Semitic** French fascists during the 1930s, when Leon Blum, a Socialist and a Jew, became premier of **France**.

BIALYSTOK GHETTO. Located in northeastern **Poland**, Jews constituted half the 100,000 population of prewar Bialystok. **Germany** occupied the city in September 1939 following its conquest of Poland, but it was handed over to the **Soviet Union** as part of the pact between both countries in August 1939. In June 1941, in the wake of the **Nazi** invasion of the Soviet Union, the **Wehrmacht** (German army) reoccupied the city and forced its Jews into a **ghetto**. As was the case of other ghettos established by the Nazis, a **Judenrat** was formed with Efraim Barasz as its head. Unlike the **Lodz ghetto**, however, Barasz formed a personal relationship with the Jewish **resistance** organization led by Mordecai Tenebaum although, like **Rumkowski** in Lodz, he was confident that by providing their labor, the Jews would become indispensible to the German war effort. Confident that he could avoid having to deport Jews to **Treblinka**, Barasz was lulled into a false sense of security about the ghetto's future. He convinced the Jewish population that "salvation through work" was their best chance for survival.

   Their trust in Barasz's leadership accounts for the ghetto's lack of support for the Jewish resistance, and when the Nazis turned to the **deportation** of Bialystok's Jews, it was too late to mobilize the ghetto population, although Tenebaum and his small group of fighters attempted to battle the Germans for the sake of Jewish honor, but it was too late. The ghetto was liquidated on 16 August 1943 followed by the failed uprising, and approximately 30,000 Jews were deported to Treblinka and **Majdanek**. The Judenräte leadership, including Barasz, subsequently were deported to Majdanek. No precise details are available concerning the circumstances or month of Barasz's death in late 1943.

BIELSKI OTRIAD. Otriad refers to **partisan** brigades that fought the **Nazis** in **Belarussia**. The best known of the Jewish partisan brigades was the Bielski Otriad, which was organized in the summer of 1942 with Tuvia Bielski as the commander. Along with his brothers Zus and Asael, Tuvia Bielski from the beginning saw as his mission to save as many Jews as possible, which included sending his men into nearby **ghettos** to encourage them to leave and join the partisans in the forest. Despite internal opposition from some in his group who thought that too large a number of Jews would endanger the Otriad, Tuvia never abandoned his policy of welcoming and protecting Jews from their Nazi tormentors. In all, the Bielski Otriad is credited with saving 1,200 Jewish lives. In 2008, the Bielski partisans were the subject of the film *Defiance*. *See also* FILM AND THE HOLOCAUST.

BIRKENAU. *See* AUSCHWITZ.

BITBURG. During the week of 5–7 May 1985, President Ronald Reagan planned to observe the 40th anniversary of the end of World War II. The president saw an opportunity to demonstrate the friendship between the **United States** and its former German foe, and German Chancellor Helmut Kohl suggested that they both visit the nearby cemetery at Bitburg, thus symbolizing the reconciliation of both countries. The controversy that ensued resulted from the disclosure that the cemetery included the graves of **Waffen-Schutzstaffel** (SS). The protest that followed included the impassioned plea made by **Elie Wiesel**, a survivor of **Auschwitz**, who, directing his remarks to the president, told him, "That place, Mr. President, is not your place." Subsequently 53 senators (including 11 Republicans) signed a letter asking the president to cancel, and 257 members of the House of Representatives (including 84 Republicans) signed a letter urging Chancellor Kohl to withdraw the invitation.

As relations between both countries became strained, President Reagan defended his decision to visit Bitburg by saying, " These [SS troops] were villains, as we know, that conducted the persecutions. . . . But there are 2,000 graves there, and most of those, the average age is about 18. . . . There is nothing wrong with visiting that cemetery where those young men are victims of Nazism also, even though they were fighting in German uniforms . . . drafted into service to carry out the hateful wishes of the **Nazis**. They were victims, just as surely as the victims in the **concentration camps**." Reagan was criticized for this statement by opponents because he equated Nazi soldiers with **Holocaust** victims. Rabbi Alexander Schindler, president of the Union of American Hebrew Congregations, chastised the president by calling his statement "a callous offense for the Jewish people." To try and contain the political uproar, on Sunday, 5 May, Reagan and Kohl appeared at the **Bergen-Belsen** concentration camp. The president's speech there, according to *Time*, was a "skillful exercise in both the art of eulogy and political damage control." *See also* GERMANY.

BLACK BOOK OF SOVIET JEWRY. *The Black Book* was compiled by Soviet Jewish writers Ilya Ehrenburg and Vasily Grossman, along with additional Soviet writers and poets, who collected testimonies and documents concerning crimes against Soviet Jews by **Nazi Germany** following its invasion of the **Soviet Union** in 1941. One of the projects initiated by the **Jewish Anti-Fascist Committee** was to take testimonies from Jewish **survivors** and non-Jewish witnesses beginning in 1942. The first version was completed by the end of 1944. Subsequently, *The Black Book* was published in English in 1981. At the end of 1987, the material in the Ehrenburg archive was opened to the public at **Yad Vashem** in **Israel** and included an almost complete handwritten manuscript of *The Black Book*.

BLACK MARKET. Following the German occupation of **Poland**, the black market became a source of huge profits for those who engaged in this nefarious practice. This was especially true in regard to the availability of food supplies. Food shortages manifested themselves soon after the German invasion, exacerbated by the burning of crops by the retreating Polish army, which resulted in huge queues outside food stores across occupied Poland. In the **General-Gouvernment**, the situation became critical in the first few months of 1940 as the German administration was forced to bring grain in from **Germany** to feed a near-starving population.

The distribution of the food, however, was based on criteria established by the German government; the bulk of the supplies went to the occupiers, as well as to Poles working on key installations like the railways, **Ukrainians** and ordinary Poles were next, and Jews at the bottom of the list. As food became ever more scarce by 1941, the rations for the Poles in Warsaw were reduced to 669 calories a day as opposed to 2,613 for the Germans and 184 calories for the Jews. Under these conditions, a black market thrived for those who could afford to pay for food. As more Jews were concentrated in **ghettos**, the food situation grew progressively worse, and exorbitant prices were paid by those who still had the means to purchase food. But as the food became scarcer, death by starvation became commonplace. *See also* TYPHUS.

BLACK PEARLS. One of the most precious commodities in the **ghettos** was fuel. Families would descend on vacant buildings and tear them apart looking for any substance that would keep them warm. Coal was the most sought after of the fuel commodities and scarce enough in the ghetto to be referred to as "black pearls."

BLOCK 10. Area at **Auschwitz** designated for **medical experiments** on women.

BLOCK 11. This was the area in **Auschwitz** where punishments were meted out to prisoners. It was also in Block 11 that the Germans first tested **Zyklon B** gas. The tests were conducted on 600 Soviet prisoners of war and approximately 200 hospital patients. The area was also known as the "**cellar**."

BLOOD AND SOIL (*BLUT UND BODEN*). **Nazi** racial **ideology** held that the German community derived its strength from the purity of blood and its roots in the soil. This definition precluded Jews from ever becoming Germans because they lacked pure blood and roots in the soil because of their Semitic origins. Using the metaphor of the parasite, the Nazis depicted the Jews as a foreign element that insidiously attacked the nation's immune system. Nazi propaganda warned that if the nation (*Volk*) was ever to become healthy, it must purge itself of this foreign substance.

BLOOD FOR GOODS. On the eve of the **deportation** of the Jews of **Hungary** in mid-1944, Joel Brand, a member of the Relief and Rescue Committee of Budapest (Va'ada), which had been established in January 1943 to help Jewish refugees who had escaped from **Slovakia** and **Poland**, was summoned by **Adolf Eichmann** on 25 April 1944 for the purpose of offering his "blood for goods" deal. Approved by **Heinrich Himmler**, the arrangement would have exchanged one million Jews for goods outside of Hungary. This would have included 10,000 trucks that, Eichmann assured Brand, would be used for civilian purposes, or on the eastern front. The exchange would have allowed Jews to leave Hungary and find refuge in any Allied-controlled part of the world save **Palestine**, where the Germans had promised **Hajj Amin al-Husseini**, the mufti of Jerusalem, that Jews would not be permitted to enter.

Brand was allowed to go abroad and establish contact with representatives of world Jewry and the **Allies**. Receiving his travel papers on 15 May, the day the deportations began in Hungary, Brand set out for Turkey but was eventually detained by the British in Cairo. His offer, however, did reach the Allies, who considered and rejected it. On 13 July 1944, the British government's Committee for Refugee Affairs concurred with the **Soviet Union** that the trucks would be used against the Soviets and voted against making the exchange. The trade would also have violated the Allied principle of "**unconditional surrender**," which eschewed the possibility of negotiating with the enemy. Eichmann who had committed to suspend the deportations until a reply was received, reneged on his promise and continued without interruption the transport of Jews to **Auschwitz**.

BLOOD LIBEL. The canard that Jews murder and then use the blood of Christian children for the purpose of baking unleavened bread on Passover has its origin in Christian Europe in 12th-century England (although the first accusation is acknowledged to be that of Apion in the first century) and then flooded Europe during the following centuries. The blood-libel charge was frequently used in **Nazi Germany** by **Julius Streicher** in his **anti-Semitic** weekly *Der Stürmer* (The Stormer) as both a caricature and propaganda to incite the German people against Jews. *See also* POGROMS IN POLAND.

BLUE BADGE. *See* YELLOW STAR OF DAVID BADGE.

BLOBEL, PAUL (1894–1951). Blobel was the head of the **Einsatzgruppe** unit in **Ukraine** responsible for the massacre at **Babi Yar** in September 1941. He was later assigned to **Aktion 1005**, whose purpose was to destroy the evidence of mass murder in Eastern Europe. Convicted of war crimes in 1948, he was executed in 1951.

BOHEMIA AND MORAVIA. *See* CZECHOSLOVAKIA.

BOLSHEVISM. The term is synonymous with Soviet communism and refers to the dictatorship established by Lenin in Russia in October 1917. The **Nazis** claimed that the Bolshevik Revolution was both fomented and led by the Jews who were determined to spread communism throughout Europe. **Adolf Hitler** believed that it was necessary to destroy Jewish Bolshevism in order both to realize Germany's expansionist policies in the East and to prevent the spread of communism in the West. *See also* IDEOLOGY; *LEBENSRAUM*.

BOOK BURNING. Following **Adolf Hitler**'s appointment as chancellor of **Germany** in January 1933, the **Nazis** removed all traces of "Jewish culture" from German public life. In May 1933, under the direction of Nazi propaganda minister **Joseph Goebbels**, books written by Jews and by non-Jews identified as enemies of the **Reich** were publicly burned in bonfires that were lit on university campuses and in front of churches as well as other prominent buildings throughout Germany.

BOTHMANN SECTION. The term refers to Hans Bothmann, who headed the **Schutzstaffel** (SS) killing squad at the **Chelmno** extermination camp. The Bothmann Section was a **euphemism** for the killing squad.

BOXHEIM PAPERS. In 1931, the German police in Frankfurt uncovered documents that detailed **Nazi** objectives should they come to power. The documents describe the "ruthless measures" the party would take against its enemies and included plans for barring Jews from economic activities and for slowly starving them to death.

BOYCOTT, ANTI-JEWISH. On 1 April 1933, the **Nazis** authorized a boycott of Jewish enterprises in **Germany**. The boycott was ostensibly in retaliation against American Jewish leaders who urged a boycott of German goods because of the Nazi persecution of the Jews in Germany. The boycott lasted only one day because the government feared that if it were to continue, it would hurt Germany's economic position in the world community. Although the **Sturmabteilung** (SA) "discouraged" customers from patronizing Jewish businesses, the boycott does not appear to have had the support of the German people. *See also* WORLD JEWISH CONGRESS.

BRAND, JOEL (1907–1964). *See* BLOOD FOR GOODS.

BREAD AND MARMALADE. As the process of **deportation** intensified in the **ghettos**, the Germans would on occasion entice starving Jews to volunteer for deportation with the promise of bread and marmalade or jam.

BROWN FOLDER. The *Reichssicherheitshauptamt*, the **Reich Security Main Office Bureau** (RSHA) code name for the instructions contained in a brown folder from **Alfred Rosenberg** in regard to the treatment of Jews following the German invasion of the **Soviet Union**. Rosenberg, a Baltic German from **Estonia**, gave instructions that the peoples of the occupied territory be encouraged to incite **pogroms** against the Jews. *See also* EINSATZGRUPPEN.

BROWN SHIRTS. The Brown Shirts was another name for the **storm troopers** of the **Sturmabteilungen** (SA). The term refers to the color of their uniforms.

BRUNDIBAR. A children's opera by Jewish Czech composer Hans Krasa with a libretto by Adolf Hoffmeister, *Brundibar* was originally performed by the children of the **Theresienstadt ghetto**. A special performance was staged in 1944 for the **International Committee of the Red Cross**, who were invited by the **Nazis** to visit the ghetto to silence the negative propaganda about the their treatment of the Jews. Excerpts from the opera were later used in a Nazi propaganda film, *Der Führer Gibt den Juden eine Stadt* (The Führer Gives a City to the Jews), that attempted to show the world the benevolence of the Nazi treatment of the Jews. Many of the children filmed were subsequently **deported** to **Auschwitz**.

BUCHENWALD. Located north of **Weimar**, Buchenwald was founded in July 1937. The camp was initially used to incarcerate political prisoners, but subsequently the **Nazis** added "asocials" to the camp mix. Following **Kristallnacht** on 9–10 November 1938, about 10,000 Jews were incarcerated, but most were released by the end of the month. Buchenwald was used by the Germans, prior to the outbreak of the war in September 1939, to terrorize Jews into leaving the country. In October 1942, the incarcerated Jews in Buchenwald were transferred to **Auschwitz**. When the Germans commenced the dismantlement of Auschwitz in January 1945, thousands of Jews were moved to Buchenwald, where many of them were used in **medical experiments**.

The Germans began to evacuate the camp in April 1945, but of the 28,250 prisoners designated for removal from the main camp, between 7,000 and 8,000 were either killed or died by some other means. On April 11, approximately 21,000 prisoners, including 4,000 Jews, were **liberated** by American forces. *See also* CONCENTRATION CAMPS; DEATH MARCHES.

BULBUTZYE. Between the two world wars, areas of present day **Ukraine** were part of Polish territory. Following the **Nazi** invasion of the **Soviet Union**, the **Wehrmacht** occupied the former Soviet zone in the eastern part of **Poland**. In the areas inhabited by Ukrainians, roving bands of Ukrainian nationalist called "Bulbutzye," named after the fictional Cossack warrior Taras Bulba, with ties to the Orthodox Church felt an affinity with **Adolf Hitler**, who they thought would reward them with Ukrainian statehood. They fought Soviet

partisans, assaulted ethnic Poles, and hunted down Jews who had escaped into the nearby forests. Many Jewish **survivors** who hid in the forests viewed the Bulbutzye as more threatening than the Germans. *See also* OPERATION ZEPPELIN.

BULGARIA. The Jewish population in Bulgaria at the outbreak of World War II was approximately 50,000, which constituted less than 1 percent of its six million people. At first, Bulgaria remained neutral during the war. This changed, however, in March 1941, when **Germany** recognized Bulgaria's annexation of western Thrace from **Greece** and Serbian Macedonia from **Yugoslavia,** thus realizing its dream of a "Greater Bulgaria." Germany also became Bulgaria's principal trading partner, and paramilitary groups appeared throughout the country. Although **anti-Semitism** existed in Bulgaria, it was not until Bulgaria became a partner of the **Axis** that it was faced with a Jewish problem.

Restrictions on Bulgaria's Jews preceded its alliance with Germany, but its ties with the **Nazis** brought about heightened pressure for the enactment of anti-Jewish legislation. Germany demanded that Bulgaria decree additional anti-Jewish laws, which was in accord with the sentiments of Bulgaria's anti-Semitic prime minister, Bogdan Filov. As early as December 1940, the Bulgarian parliament passed the Law for the Protection of the Nation, which closely copied the racial categories found in the German **Nuremberg Laws** of 1935. The Bulgarian government, however, exempted Jewish converts to **Christianity** from the racial definition, which led to an increase in mixed marriages and hundreds of "mercy baptisms." Other categories of Jews exempted by the racial laws were Jews wounded in the war or who were decorated war veterans.

A partial list of the restrictions resulting from the laws included barring Jews from certain types of employment, prohibiting them from owning real estate in rural communities, and requiring Jews to register their property with the government. Jews were also subjected to a curfew and prohibited from owning telephones and radios. In September 1943, spurred on by its German partner, the government enacted legislation that required all Jews to wear the **yellow Star of David badge.** The law was also applied to the 14,000 Jews residing in Thrace and the territory taken from Yugoslavia.

In August 1942, the Bulgarian government established a Commissariat for Jewish Affairs with the objective of expelling the Jews of Bulgaria and confiscating their property. The ultimate aim of the commissariat, however, was not only for the Jews to finance the cost of implementing the Law for the Protection of the Nation but also to prepare them for shouldering the cost of **deportation** to the **death camps** in **Poland**.

Alexander Belev, the head of the commissariat, secretly agreed to hand over to **Adolf Eichmann**'s representative in Bulgaria the Jews in Bulgaria proper and in the newly acquired territories. In March 1943, the Bulgarian government approved the agreement, and two days later, approximately 12,000 Jews from Thrace and Macedonia were placed in **concentration camps**, and an additional 11,384 Jews were deported to **Treblinka**. News of the deportations, however, outraged the Bulgarian population, which reacted with a determination to protect the Jews of Bulgaria proper. As the Germans continued to pressure the government to deport the Jews, public opinion, now joined by the Bulgarian Orthodox Church, forced the government to withdraw its cooperation with the deportations. Although Bulgarian anti-Semitism continued to manifest itself in subsequent decrees promulgated by the government, the threat of deportation to the death camps was removed.

In the fall of 1943, Germany realized the futility of forcing its policy on an unsupportive Bulgarian population and halted its pressure regarding deportations. By the middle of 1944, all anti-Jewish legislation was nullified. Factors that may explain the Bulgarian people's opposition to the deportations include the presence of Armenians, Greeks, **Gypsies**, and other ethnic groups within its borders; as a consequence, Bulgarians shared no particular prejudice against Jews, as did other European countries. An additional consideration was Bulgaria's decision to surrender to the **Allies** as the Red Army approached Bulgarian soil and subsequently declared war on the country in September 1945.

BUNA WORKS (AUSCHWITZ III). The camp was built by I. G. Farben for the purpose of producing synthetic rubber for the war effort. The name *Buna* derives from the molecule butadiene and the element sodium (Na).

BUTZ, ARTHUR R. (1933–). Butz is a **Holocaust denier**, who is also an associate professor of electrical engineering at Northwestern University. His 1976 book, *The Hoax of the Twentieth Century*, was one of the first major works of Holocaust denial in the English language. Along with other deniers, such as **David Irving**, Butz played a role in the **Holocaust** denial movement by writing articles for the now-defunct *Journal of Historical Review* (on whose editorial advisory board he served from 1980 through 2001) and by occasionally speaking at Holocaust denial conferences.

– C –

CANADA. The term is sometimes spelled as "Kanada" and refers to the area in **Auschwitz** where the Germans stored the clothes, baggage, and other personal property of their Jewish victims before it was shipped to **Germany**. "Canada" was thought to be a country of great wealth, and the warehouse, where Jewish property was stored, contained valuable possessions.

CARBIDE TOWER. The tower stood in the center of **Auschwitz-Buna** and was referred to by prisoners as *Babelturm* (Tower of Babel) because it was built on the backs of angry and resentful **forced labor**. *See also* BUNA WORKS.

CARBON MONOXIDE. The poisonous gas was used in the **Aktion Reinhard death camps** as the primary means of exterminating the Jews. *See also* CHELMNO; SOBIBOR; TREBLINKA; WIRTH, CHRISTIAN.

CASE WHITE. The code name for the decision by **Nazi Germany** to wage war against **Poland** that **Adolf Hitler** signed on 11 April 1939.

CATCHER (*GREIFER*). About 6,800 Jews lived an underground existence in **Germany** during the war. These hidden Jews or *U-Boote* were hunted down by the **Gestapo** with the aid of paid Jewish informers known as *Greifer* (catchers), who were responsible for the **deportation** of hundreds of Berlin's Jews to the extermination camps. At the end of the war, only 28,000 Jews as defined by **Nazi** racial laws remained in Germany and **Austria**.

CELLAR. The term refers to the underground cellar in **Auschwitz I** where punishment was meted out to the prisoners. The cellar is also known as **Block 11**, where the first experiments with **Zyklon B** gas were performed in the underground area.

CENTRAL BUREAU FOR JEWISH EMIGRATION (ZENTRAL-STELLE FUR JIUDISCHE AUSWANDERUNG). This government agency was initially created in Vienna by the **Nazis** following the **Anschluss** on 13 March 1938. The agency was placed under the supervision of **Adolf Eichmann**, whose primary task was to encourage Jews to leave **Austria**. Eichmann was so successful in this endeavor that a similar bureau was created in **Germany**.

CENTRAL MUSEUM OF THE EXTINGUISHED JEWISH RACE. An aborted **Nazi** plan, the intent was to construct a museum in **Czechoslovakia** celebrating their destruction of the Jewish people.

CHAMBERLAIN, HOUSTON STEWART (1855–1927). Adolf Hitler was greatly influenced by Chamberlain's *The Foundations of the Nineteenth Century* (1899), a seminal work that synthesized German nationalism, Nordic racist theory, and **anti-Semitism** to explain how the Jews threatened **Aryan** superiority. Much of what Chamberlain wrote was subsequently incorporated into **Nazi ideology**. *See also VOLK; VOLKISCH.*

CHAMBON-SUR-LIGNON. *See* RIGHTEOUS GENTILES.

CHELMNO. Located in the Polish village of Chelmno some 47 miles west of Lodz, the Kulmhof castle was the first German facility in which stationary **gas trucks** were used to kill Jews. Kulmhof (the German word for the village of Chelmno) was established in late 1941 for the purpose of exterminating the Jewish population of the Polish provinces of Poznen (**Posen**) and Lodz. Shortly after **Germany**'s conquest of **Poland**, the two provinces were incorporated into the **Reich** and renamed the **Warthegau**. In addition to Polish Jews who were the Germans' primary target, thousands of Germans, **Austrians**, and Jews from **Czechoslovakia** were transported and killed in Chelmno, as well as 5,000 **Gypsies**. The first transport of Jews arrived on 7 December 1941 and the camp began operations on the following day under SS-Hauptsturmfuhrer (roughly equivalent to a first lieutenant) Herbert Lange. The actual killings took place in the Kulmhof castle, the former residence of a local lord, located outside of the village of Kulmhof. Historians number the Jews killed at Chelmno from a low estimate of 152,000 to a high of 310,000, and over 4,000 Gypsies. *See also* LANGE SONDERKOMMANDO.

CHILDREN'S TRANSPORT (*KINDERTRANSPORT*). During the 1930s, when it still was possible for Jews to **emigrate** from **Germany**, preference was given by German Jewish organizations to children and young men and women. As a consequence, various *Kindertransporten* were organized to expedite the migration of children from Germany to temporary or permanent shelters. Many of the youngsters from **Zionist** groups were sent in these transports to **Palestine**. The transports also had a more sinister connotation when they refer to the **deportation** of children, who were placed in trains or trucks whose destination was the **death camps**.

CHRISTIANITY. Christianity played an important role in forming the attitudes of generations of Europeans toward Jews. Indeed, the roots of Christianity are found within Judaism; Jesus and his disciples were Jews who belonged to a sect that preached salvation in the context of Jewish tradition. The break between Christianity and Judaism was fostered by Paul (Saul of Tarsus), a Jew, who preached Jesus' messiahship to the Gentiles. When most of Roman-occupied Europe converted to Christianity in the fourth century, it led to the imposition of a Semitic religion on the peoples of Europe, who previously had worshiped pagan gods. Some 1,600 years later, the **Nazis** would remind their followers of Christianity's Semitic roots and argue that it was responsible for the destruction of the indigenous beliefs of the German people.

Once Christianity became the state religion of the Roman Empire, it commenced to persecute Jews. Primarily this was a reaction to the refusal of Jews to accept Jesus as the Christ or Messiah. What was fundamental to Christians, the Crucifixion and the Resurrection, was for Jews an erroneous understanding of the Hebrew Scriptures. The adamant refusal of the Jews to accept what, for Christians, was so obviously foretold in the Hebrew Bible led to a bitter estrangement between the two religions. From the fourth century on, Jews were often segregated from Christian communities and demonized by Church theologians. From Saint John of Chrysostem in the fifth century, to Saint Augustine in the seventh century, to **Martin Luther** in the 16th century, a trail of invectives against Jews and Judaism can be documented; Jews were accused of killing Christ, of awaiting the anti-Christ as their Messiah, of serving the devil, of ritual murder, and of poisoning the well water during the Great Plague of 1350, which caused the death of almost half the population of Europe, including many Jews.

The early church fathers argued that the suffering of the Jews and the exile from their homeland was divine punishment for their failure to accept Christ. God had chosen for Jews to suffer but not to be killed because eventually they would see the errors of their ways and convert to Christianity. This argument resulted in not only a tradition of persecution, aided and abetted by the church, but also one of protecting Jews from the violence of the mobs. The average illiterate Christian, however, often did not comprehend the nuance of church policy toward the Jews. During the First Crusade in 1096, unsanctioned violence toward the Jews was initiated by agitators such as Peter the Hermit, who urged mobs to murder Jews. In **Germany**, tens of thousands of Jews were killed by crusaders who thought it foolish to wait until they arrived in the Holy Land to spill the blood of the "infidel" when there were so many close at home.

During the Middle Ages, the papacy restricted the number of occupations permitted to Jews. Jews were prohibited from owning property, joining guilds, and serving in the army. They were also generally prevented from engaging in agricultural occupations. Jews were allowed to enter those endeavors that Christians avoided or held in low esteem. Thus Jews gravitated to commerce, and in particular, lending capital (often without receiving any collateral), and engaging in usury, at a time when the church prohibited interest on loans. In Eastern Europe, Jews served as rent collectors and as intermediaries between the Polish nobility and the peasantry. They were also allowed to own taverns and inns. Jews were also prohibited from employing Christian servants and engaging in sexual unions with Christian women. There was little in the **Nuremberg Laws** of 1935 that did not have a precedent in the church prohibitions against Jews during the Middle Ages. The final indignity, however, was their expulsion from England in 1290, **France** in 1306, **Spain** in 1492, and **Portugal** in 1496.

The Protestant Reformation, despite a seemingly benign attitude toward Jews on the part of some Calvinist denominations, changed little in regard to the perception of Jews among the European Christian population. In Germany, dehumanizing stereotypes of Jews were exacerbated by Martin Luther, who in a series of essays vilified them and called for the burning of their synagogues. The Catholic Counter-Reformation of the 16th century created the first **ghetto** in Venice, **Italy**, in 1516, and the institution quickly spread to Germany, where Jews were confined to ghettos in such cities as Frankfurt.

From the 19th century on, negative Christian attitudes toward Jews remained part of the culture of Germany. At the end of the 19th century, however, traditional anti-*Judentum* was joined by the new racial **anti-Semitism** of the *Volkisch* nationalist movement. The difference between the two anti-Jewish groups, however, was greater than what they shared in common. Christian clergymen believed in the salvational effects of baptism over the primacy of racial characteristics. Therefore, Jews who converted to Christianity were welcomed as full members of the church, whereas for the anti-Semite baptism did not change the status of the Jew. This difference would continue on into the Nazi era and split the Lutheran Church in Germany during the years of the **Third Reich**.

Once the Nazis assumed power in Germany in 1933, they immediately attempted to transform the German churches by eliminating their Jewish roots and influences. In particular, the Nazi version of the Bible held that Jesus was an **Aryan** who had attempted to confront Judaism, not reform it, and that it was Paul who eliminated from the liturgy the authentic teachings of Jesus. The Nazis insisted on the removal of all Jewish elements from the liturgy and Christian practice. Once in power, they sought to control what was taught in the churches and eschewed the significance of the Hebrew Testament for the advent of Christianity. Lutheran clergy, supportive of the Nazi objective to cleanse the church of "Rabbi" Paul's Jewish influence on Christianity, supported the abandonment of the Hebrew scriptures as a source of revelation. In the church elections of July 1933, the radical wing of German Lutheranism, which enthusiastically supported **Hitler** and the Nazi attempt to create a "Positive Christianity," emerged victorious and promptly began to synthesize Christian doctrine with Nazi racial anti-Semitism. Consequently, the so-called German Christian movement supported the expulsion of converted Jews from church offices as well as the church itself. These excesses were condemned by the rival conservative Confessing Church (Bekennende Kirche), which fought all efforts of the Nazis to control the German churches. In particular, pastors such as **Martin Niemoller** and Otto Dibelius challenged the expulsion of converts from the churches. But these same clergy still maintained the traditional Lutheran antipathy toward the Jews and were therefore silent as the persecution of the Jews intensified in the 1930s. The persecution of the Jews was ignored by many in the Confessing Church because they shared the anti-Semitic outlook of most Protestant ministers in Germany.

During the **Weimar Republic**, between 70 and 80 percent of Protestant pastors had allied themselves with anti-Semitic political parties. An almost minuscule number of Protestant pastors protested the Nuremberg Laws of 1935, and they were mostly silent following the excesses of **Kristallnacht**. One can conclude, therefore, that the opposition of the Confessing Church to the Nazi effort to control the churches was motivated by parochial concerns, as they defended church autonomy and resisted efforts to expel Jewish converts. The persecution of the Jews was not part of their agenda until they understood the true nature of the Nazi regime, but, by that point, it was too late. On the eve of World War II in September 1939, many of the pastors who opposed Adolf Hitler, such as Martin Niemoller, were already in **concentration camps** or too intimidated by the regime to protest its policies.

In 1933, the Roman Catholic Church signed a **concordat** with **Nazi Germany** in the hope that the government would not interfere in the internal affairs of the church. This understanding did not last, as the German government began to subvert the influence of the

Catholic Church in Germany from the moment the concordat was signed. When **Pope Pius XI** issued the encyclical, **"With Burning Concern"** (Mit Brennender Sorge) in 1937, he invited retaliation from the government inasmuch as the encyclical condemned the Nazi treatment of the church.

Subsequently, the Nazis arrested monks and nuns who were falsely accused of charges ranging from financial malfeasance to sexual aberrations. Once convicted, hundreds of Catholic priests and nuns were sent to concentration camps. The attempt of the government to intimidate the Catholic Church in Germany, however, did not prevent its hierarchy from joining Protestant clergy in the successful protest against the **Euthanasia Program**.

The Nazi effort to coerce the Catholic Church coincided with the government's attempt to drive Jews from all aspects of German life. Thus, any bid on the part of the Catholic Church to protest the treatment of the Jews was certain to bring about a further deterioration in its relationship with the government. But it is also true that traditional negative beliefs about Jews were deeply ingrained among many Catholics in Germany, which mirrored the religious convictions of the Roman Catholic Church in general. For example, the Oberammergau passion play, which depicted Jews as Christ killers, was one of the official church-sanctioned events that reflected the pervasive anti-Semitism found among many German Christians. Before his death in 1939, **Pope Pius XI** authorized the preparation of a draft that would have condemned anti-Semitism. The draft of the encyclical, "Humani Generis Unitas," included a condemnation of the Nuremberg Laws and rebuked the Nazis for excluding Jews from the nation because of race. But the priests assigned by the pope to work on the draft of the encyclical were themselves still captives of traditional Church anti-Jewish attitudes. The document called for the quarantine of Jews from Christians, "lest their profaneness infect good Christians. . . . The church has always recognized the historic mission of the Jewish people, and its ardent prayers for their conversion, do not make it lose sight of the spiritual dangers to which contact with Jews can expose souls." It is conceivable that had his health not failed him, Pius XI might have moderated the language of the draft in regard to the Jews. Yet the unpublished encyclical, which was not discovered until 1972, indicates that even among

Catholic clergy willing to condemn anti-Semitism, traditional forms of anti-*Judentum* continued to exist in the Vatican.

Upon his death in 1939, Pius XI was succeeded by Cardinal Eugenio Pacelli (1876–1958), who became **Pope Pius XII**. His papacy encompassed the period of the **Holocaust**, and his silence in response to the murder of European Jewry has become a subject of controversy among historians. Much of the criticism of Pius XII emanates from his failure to publicly condemn the murderous campaign against the Jews and his failure to voice moral outrage against the Nazi **genocide**. Rather, Pius XII attempted to protect Catholic interests in Germany, and in other countries where the church was under attack. Where the matter of the Jews did not conflict with church interests, the papacy was active on behalf of the Jews. Sometimes this policy worked and at other times it failed. In **Hungary**, **Romania**, and **Slovakia**, for example, where the church had some leverage, the Vatican opposed anti-Semitic legislation and strongly objected to the deportation of the Jews, which resulted in small numbers of Jews being saved from the **death camps**.

In the **Netherlands**, the Germans retaliated against the church when it interfered in the matter of the Jews. When the Catholic archbishop, Johannes de Jong, condemned the deportation of the Jews from his pulpit, it resulted in the arrest of 201 Jewish converts to Catholicism, including priests and nuns, who were deported to **Auschwitz**. In other parts of Europe, the Vatican gave its silent support to individual priests who aided Jews.

Any assessment of the role of Pius XII during the Holocaust must account for the pope's style of diplomacy. He believed in the efficacy of diplomacy and sought to retain the church's traditional role as Europe's mediator. To be effective, however, the papacy refused to publicly condemn the Nazis, lest it risk forfeiting its neutral position. It is difficult, however, to believe that the Vatican was unaware of the unfolding genocide being perpetrated against the Jews, inasmuch as its clergy, especially in **Poland**, must have made the papacy among the first to receive information about the **Final Solution**. It is also possible that the papacy learned about the ongoing genocide from Catholic priests in Germany who listened to the confession of **Wehrmacht** soldiers returning from Poland and other areas where the Germans engaged in atrocities.

The Vatican also refused to publicly denounce the Nazis because it feared placing German Catholics in danger, as well as providing the government with a provocation that would result in the confiscation of its property in Germany. How else are we to explain the refusal of the Vatican to intervene in Spain to protect refugees in jeopardy of being returned to Germany or its refusal, ostensibly because of the pope's reservations about **Zionism**, to endorse a plan that would have transferred approximately 6,000 Jewish children from **Bulgaria** to **Palestine**? Neither did the Vatican object to **Vichy France**'s anti-Jewish laws. Instead, it made the distinction that although the church repudiated racism, it did not object to every measure against the Jews.

The overall record of the Vatican is a mixed one. Although Pius XII was publicly silent in regard to the fate of the Jews, where it was possible and did not place the church in danger, the Catholic Church did act on behalf of the Jews. For example, in Italy Jews were hidden in monasteries and churches and, therefore, saved from **deportation**. In Hungary, there is evidence that the pope intervened with the regent, Miklos Horthy, to halt the deportation of Jews to Auschwitz. In Romania, the papal nuncio, Archbishop Andrea Cassulo, was instrumental in moving Ion Antonescu, the head of government, to cancel his agreement with the Germans to deport Romania's remaining 292,000 Jews to **Belzec**. In Poland, where the Germans repressed the church, the Catholic Church engaged in rescue attempts to save Jews. Historian Pinchas Lapide credits the Catholic Church with saving approximately 800,000 Jews who were hidden by Catholic clergy who opened their monasteries and convent doors for this purpose. We are less certain, however, as to whether the Jews being sheltered was a product of individual acts of conscience on behalf of Catholic clergy or of "signals" that emanated from the pope that such risks would not be opposed by the Vatican.

The Catholic Church's acts on behalf of Jews, however, were mitigated by Pius XII's failure to exert moral leadership in a time of acute crisis for the Jewish people and others who were victims of Nazi Germany. The papacy's record is also tarnished by its involvement in helping leading Nazis, such as **Adolf Eichmann** and **Josef Mengele**, to escape to South America at the end of the war. It remains to be answered whether the same "signals" that gave permission for Catholic priests and nuns to hide Jews during the war were similarly given on behalf of fleeing Nazi war criminals.

The Catholic Church in March 1998 attempted to clarify its role during the Holocaust when it issued the document **We Remember: A Reflection on the Shoah**. Although the Vatican admitted that centuries of teaching contempt for Jews had contributed to the indifference displayed by most Christians to the persecution of the Jews, it nevertheless insisted that the Nazis represented a pagan movement, thereby denying a link between Christian anti-*Judentum* and the Holocaust. The document also defended the role of Pope Pius XII during the Holocaust, citing the number of Jews saved by the Catholic Church but refrained from commenting on his refusal to condemn the Nazi genocide against the Jews. *See also* "ON THE JEWS AND THEIR LIES."

CHURBAN. The Hebrew word literally means destruction. Through the centuries, Jews used the word to describe the destruction of the second temple by the Romans in 70 C.E. Because a similar catastrophe befell the Jews at the hands of **Nazi Germany**, the word *churban* is used primarily by Orthodox Jews to denote the **Holocaust**. *See also* SHOAH.

CHURCHILL, WINSTON SPENCER (1874–1965). When Winston Churchill became prime minister of **Great Britain** in May 1940, he delegated the responsibility for creating a rescue policy for the Jews to the Foreign Office. Early on in the war, the Foreign Office was guided by three policy principles in regard to the Jews trapped in **Nazi**-occupied Europe: no aid to the Jews that might involve breaking the economic blockade that Britain imposed on the European continent; no negotiations that would lead to a separate peace or to peace terms with the Nazis other than the **unconditional surrender** of **Germany**; and no large-scale movement of Jews out of Europe, either to **Palestine** or to Britain or to its colonies. In essence, the Foreign Office was determined not to single out the Jews of Europe for any special rescue measures. They justified their policy by contending that the best relief for the Jews of Europe was for the **Allies** to win the war as quickly as possible. Although aware of the **genocidal** intentions of the Nazis, the policy refused to single out the Jews from other groups suffering at the hands of the Nazis lest it give credence to Nazi propaganda and other **anti-Semites** that the war was being waged in behalf of the Jews. It was within these constraints that Churchill's response to the **Holocaust** has to be understood.

Within the prescribed limitations, however, there were occasions when Churchill opposed the policy preventing Jewish refugees from reaching Palestine when, at one point, he informed the Colonial office that the government had "to be guided by sentiments of humanity towards those fleeing from the cruelest forms of persecution." On a separate occasion when Churchill was alerted to the imminent **deportation** to Mauritius of 793 illegal Jewish refugees intercepted off Palestine, he immediately instructed his officials to allow them to remain there. But his interventions were infrequent and were the exception to the policy, as Great Britain continued to rigorously enforce the **White Paper of 1939**.

News of the German invasion of the **Soviet Union** in June 1941, with the accompanied murder of thousands of Jews, reached Churchill through his intelligence services, and he responded with a strong reference to these killings in a radio broadcast to his countrymen on 14 November 1941. When the deportations from **France** to **Auschwitz** began in the summer of 1942 (their destination was unknown at the time), and reports reached Churchill that 4,000 Jewish children had been deported, he castigated the Nazi regime in the House of Commons as "the most bestial, the most squalid and the most senseless of all their offences, namely, the mass deportation of Jews from France, with the pitiful horrors attendant upon the calculated and final scattering of families. This tragedy fills me with astonishment as well as with indignation, and it illustrates as nothing else can the utter degradation of the Nazi nature and theme, and degradation of all who lend themselves to its unnatural and perverted passions."

Thus, within the restraints of British policy, Churchill was determined to help those Jews who could get out of Europe to be allowed a safe haven. As Churchill biographer Martin Gilbert records, learning in December 1942 of the successful rescue of 4,500 Jewish children and 50 accompanying adults from the Balkans, a plan which he himself had earlier approved, Churchill wrote "Bravo!" In February 1943, while he was in Algiers, Churchill discovered that the **Vichy** laws against Algerian Jews were still in force there. He insisted they be repealed. In April 1943, he opposed the Spanish closure of the French frontier to Jewish refugees, telling the Spanish ambassador that if his government "went to the length of preventing these unfortunate people seeking safety from the horrors of Nazi domination, and if they went farther and committed the offence of actually handing them back to the German authorities, that was a thing which could never be forgotten and would poison the relations between the Spanish and British peoples."

In seeking a means of halting German atrocities, Churchill told his War Cabinet that issuing a warning to the Germans from Britain, the **United States**, and the Soviet Union "that a number of German officers or members of the **Nazi Party**, equal to those put to death by the Germans in the various countries, and . . . all those responsible for, or having taken a consenting part in atrocities, massacres and executions, were to be sent back to the countries in which their abominable deeds were done in order that they might be judged and punished according to the laws of those liberated countries . . . would have a salutary effect on their further actions." On 1 November 1943, the Allies issued the **Moscow Declaration**, which followed almost exactly the wording of Churchill's proposal, "The Allies would pursue the ranks of the guilty to the uttermost ends of the earth and would deliver them to their accusers in order that justice may be done." To help surviving Jewish refugees, in March 1944, Churchill bypassed the prewar British government's restrictions on Jewish immigration to Palestine. The new rules made it possible for any Jewish refugee who reached Istanbul to be sent on by train to Palestine, irrespective of the quota. Thousands of Jews benefited by this agreement. It was also in March 1944 that Churchill addressed the matter of German-occupied **Hungary**, where three quarters of a million Hungarian Jews were at risk. According to Gilbert, Churchill asked Marshall Tito to protect any Jews who escaped from Hungary to **partisan**-held **Yugoslavia**.

That July, Jewish leaders brought Churchill a horrific account of Auschwitz. It had been smuggled out by two escapees and revealed for the first time the lethal use of the **gas chambers**. Asked to bomb the railway lines to Auschwitz, Churchill instructed Eden: "Get anything out of the Air Force you can, and invoke me if necessary." A few days later, when it was learned that the deportations from Hungary had stopped, the Jewish request changed from bombing to issuing protective documents that would allow Jews safe passage to leave Hungary. Reading in July 1944 of the first detailed account of Auschwitz, Churchill wrote: 'There is no doubt this is the most horrible crime ever committed in the whole history of the world, and it has been done by scientific machinery by nominally civilized men in the name of a great State and one of the leading races of Europe. It is quite clear that all concerned in this crime who may fall into our hands, including the people who only obeyed orders by carrying out the butcheries, should be put to death after their association with the murders has been proved."

The record indicates that from the first to the last day of the war, the fate of the Jews was something to which Churchill took immediate and positive action whenever he was asked to do so. However, the defeat of **Nazi Germany** was his top priority, and so despite his sympathy for the plight of European Jewry, Churchill rarely deviated from the policies that would have rescued large numbers of Jews, such as emphatically urging the revocation of the White Paper of 1939 that would have allowed hundreds of thousands of Jewish refugees a permanent sanctuary.

CLAIMS CONFERENCE. *See* RESTITUTION FOR HOLOCAUST SURVIVORS.

COLLABORATION. During World War II, **Nazi Germany** received the support of people residing in countries under German occupation. Those who collaborated with the **Nazis** were sympathetic not only to **Germany**'s wartime objectives but also to its plan to annihilate the Jews of Europe. The following examples of political organizations that collaborated with the Germans is by no means a complete one but includes the General Commission on Jewish Affairs, established by the **Vichy** regime in March 1941. The organization played an important role in writing the anti-Jewish Statute on the Jews (Statut des Juifs). In **Latvia**, the "Thunder Cross," a paramilitary unit headed by Major Victor Arajs (Kommando Arajs), joined with the **Einsatzgruppen** to spread terror against the Jews of Latvia. In the **Netherlands**, the collaborationist group was the Brandenbergs. In **Hungary**, the Hungarian Dejewification Unit aided **Adolf Eichmann** in the **deportation** of Hungarian Jewry to

Auschwitz. In **Poland,** the "Blue Police" were active in monitoring daily police tasks in the **ghettos,** and in **Ukraine,** the "Expeditionary Forces" aided the Germans in the roundup and killing of Jews. In **Norway,** the name of Vidkun Quisling became synonymous with collaboration. Pro-Nazi collaborationist political groups were active in almost every country under German occupation. *See also* ROMANIA.

COMMISSAR ORDER (*KOMMISSARBEFEHL*). On the eve of the German invasion of the **Soviet Union** in June 1941, **Adolf Hitler** issued a set of instructions in regard to the coming war. He ordered the elimination of the "Bolshevist-Jewish" intelligentsia and authorized **Heinrich Himmler** to undertake "special tasks" in the areas independent of the **Wehrmacht** (German army). Two weeks before the invasion, Hitler ordered a ruthless war against the Bolsheviks and drew up guidelines to that effect. Issued on 6 June 1941, the Commissar Order required the Wehrmacht to hand over captured communist officials to the **Einsatzgruppen,** or if that did not prove feasible, the Wehrmacht was to kill without mercy all political commissars who fell into their hands. The order also called for "merciless intervention" against Jews, Bolshevik agitators, guerrillas, and saboteurs.

Because Hitler equated Jews with **Bolshevism,** his order resulted in a large number of Jews being murdered by Einsatzgruppen, as well as by the army and German auxiliary units. The Commissar Order was a violation of international law regarding the treatment of prisoners of war and civilians, and it is an example of the **genocidal** warfare that **Germany** waged in the Soviet Union.

COMMITTEE FOR HEREDITARY HEALTH MEASURES. Toward the end of 1936 and the beginning of 1937, this committee was established to draw up legislation for a **Reich** Hereditary Health court. Historian Richard Evans suggests that as early as the establishment of this committee, "serious preparations for the killing of the handicapped began. . . . It only needed the imminent prospect of war to put them into effect." *See also* EUTHANASIA.

CONCENTRATION CAMPS. These camps are distinguished from the **death camps,** which had as their primary purpose the murder of Jews and other targeted victims of the **Nazis**. The concentration camps were originally organized to incarcerate political opponents of the Nazi government for the purpose of political rehabilitation. **Dachau**, which was established in 1933 under the supervision of **Theodor Eicke**, marked a transition from the original "**wild camps**," which served as a temporary instrument of repression, to a permanent facility for the preventive detention of anyone whom the government considered an opponent.

Under Eicke, Dachau's system was formalized, and a certain degree of standardization was applied to the detention system. The "Dachau model" was applied to other camps, such as **Buchenwald**, **Sachsenhausen**, and **Mauthausen**, which quickly became known for their brutality, and where murder and torture were everyday occurrences. The **Gestapo** engaged in a policy of arrest calculated to strike terror and intimidate the population. Throughout the whole of **Germany**, individuals would disappear and resurface in the concentration camps. Those who returned after their incarceration brought back tales of the horrors that befell them. The effect of these personal experiences was to create a climate of fear throughout Germany. The Nazis made little effort to keep the brutality of the concentration camps a secret. Quite to the contrary; the release of a relatively high number of persons from custody was calculated to intimidate the population for the purpose of consolidating the regime's grip on the nation.

After 1936, the concentration camps added new groups to the list of those to be incarcerated. The Nazis now included those deemed noxious or socially undesirable. This included Jews, **Gypsies**, habitual offenders, and dangerous sexual offenders, which included **homosexuals**. The concentration camps also became a dumping ground for all types of "asocial" persons, which included beggars, vagrants, prostitutes, carriers of venereal disease, alcoholics, "psychopaths," and anyone who had fallen out of favor with the regime. In this new phase, the **Schutzstaffel** (SS) constructed new concentration camps throughout Germany to meet the growing numbers who were incarcerated: Sachsenhausen in 1936, Buchenwald in 1937, **Flossenbürg** in 1938, Mauthausen in 1939, and Ravensbruck during the same year. In early 1937, the population of the camps numbered 70,000 prisoners. After **Kristallnacht**, 9–10 November 1938, an additional

3,600 Jews were placed in concentration camps. However, those Jews who agreed to **emigrate** and signed a document consenting to the **Aryanization** of their assets were generally released after several weeks. Until 1939, therefore, the concentration camp system served primarily to eliminate political opponents, incarcerate "asocials," and terrorize the population, with labor deployment of secondary importance.

With the outbreak of war, economic considerations became paramount, and camp inmates became an important resource in providing materials for the war effort. The model for this was the establishment of the **Buna works** in **Auschwitz**, which used **forced labor** for the production of synthetic rubber. The conversion of the concentration camp system to meet the demands of labor deployment was carried out by the creation of a new agency in 1942 called the Wirschafts und Vervaltungshauptamt (WVHA) (Economy and Administration Main Office) under the leadership of **Oswald Pohl**.

Only toward the end of the war did the camps change their mission. As the war front collapsed, the Nazis attempted to dismantle the death camps in the east and hide as much evidence of the **Final Solution** as possible. Subsequently, they forced the remaining inmates on **death marches** to the west. Those who survived the forced marches were crowded into the concentration camps in Germany, thus transforming them into sites of mass death. The Germans created more than 10,000 labor and concentration camps across Europe, with 645 labor camps in Berlin alone. In **Poland**, in addition to the death camps, about 5,800 camps were established.

CONCORDAT. On 20 July 1933, the German government negotiated a concordat or agreement with the Vatican. **Adolf Hitler** assured Cardinal Eugenio Pacelli, the future **Pius XII**, who negotiated the concordat, that as long as the Catholic Church kept to otherworldly and metaphysical matters, he would not interfere in church matters. It was soon clear, however, that Hitler would not tolerate the influence of any organization in Germany besides the **Nazi Party**. It was not long after the signing of the concordat that the **Nazi** regime began to subvert the Roman Catholic Church in Germany. Despite protests by German Catholic clergy, a strained relationship between the church and the Nazis emerged that culminated in **Pope Pius XI**'s encyclical

"**With Burning Concern**" (Mit Brennender Sorge) in 1937. Subsequently, the Nazi regime mounted a campaign of terror against the German Catholic clergy that ultimately reduced the influence of the church in Germany. *See also* CHRISTIANITY.

CONDOLENCE LETTER (*TROSTBRIEF*). The secretive nature of the **Nazi Euthanasia Program** required that the relatives of the murdered patients be informed that their loved ones had died of natural causes. This took the form of a condolence letter that was sent by the staff of the killing center to the relatives of the deceased. The reality was that most of the patients were gassed upon arrival. Using subterfuge, the administration of the euthanasia center would backdate letters that indicated the patient had arrived safely and was in good care. About 10 days after the patient's death, the staff mailed the so-called condolence letter, which informed the relative that the patient had died unexpectedly of complications.

CONFESSING CHURCH. *See* CHRISTIANITY.

COUGHLIN, CHARLES E. (1891–1979). Father Charles Edward Coughlin was a Canadian-born Roman Catholic priest at the National Shrine of the Little Flower Church in Royal Oak, Michigan. He was one of the first political leaders to use radio to reach a mass audience, as more than 10 million people tuned in to his weekly broadcasts during the 1930s. Early in his career Coughlin was a vocal supporter of **Franklin D. Roosevelt** and his early New Deal proposals, before he became a harsh critic of Roosevelt. In the mid-1930s, Coughlin began to use his radio program to broadcast **anti-Semitic** commentary, extolling the policies of **Adolf Hitler** and **Benito Mussolini**. In 1936, he established his weekly newspaper, *Social Justice*, and subsequently joined forces with the anti-Semitic demagogue Gerald L. K. Smith and Francis E. Townsend to support the presidential candidacy of William Lemke of the newly formed Union Party in the 1936 election.

Following the election, Coughlin intensified his attacks against Jews and the New Deal. He serialized the **Protocols of the Elders of Zion** in *Social Justice*, reprinted **Nazi** propaganda from **Joseph Goebbels**, and continued to attack bankers and New Dealers of

Jewish descent. He charged that Jews were responsible for Freemasonry, the French and Russian revolutions, world communism, and attacks on **Christian** civilization. When World War II broke out, Coughlin railed against the "British-Jewish-Roosevelt conspiracy," and after Pearl Harbor, when the government warned Archbishop Edward Mooney of Detroit that Coughlin would face sedition charges for his pro-**Axis** activities, the Catholic Church moved to silence him, although he remained the pastor of his parish at Royal Oak until his retirement in 1966.

CREMATORIA. The crematoria were ovens built by engineers associated with the Krupp company and I. G. Farben for the purpose of burning the dead murdered at **Auschwitz, Buchenwald, Dachau,** and **Sachsenhausen.**

CRIMINAL ORGANIZATIONS. Soon after the **Allied** victory over the **Nazi** government, a series of military tribunals were convened in 1945 for the purpose of trying the Nazi leadership for war crimes. The so-called **Nuremberg Trials** condemned the **Schutzstaffel** (SS), **Gestapo,** and the **Sicherheitsdienst** (SD) as criminal organizations. The Gestapo and SD were identified as having been responsible for "the persecution and extermination of the Jews, brutalities and killings in **concentration camps,** excesses in the administration of occupied territories, the administration of the **slave labor** program and the mistreatment and murder of prisoners of war."

CROATIA. Croatia was created by the Germans and the Italians on 10 April 1941, from the dismembered **Yugoslavia.** The new state, which was under the influence of **Germany,** installed Ante Pavelic, the leader of the **anti-Semitic** and pro-**Nazi Ustasa,** as its head of government. Once established, the Croatian government wasted little time in confronting the 30,000 Jews who lived primarily in Bosnia and Herzegovina. The Ustasa, which modeled itself after the **Schutzstaffel** (SS), launched violent attacks against Jews in Sarajevo, and in August 1941 completed the construction of the Jasenovac **concentration camp,** where it interned Jews whom it had arrested. As was the case in most of German-occupied Europe, anti-Jewish legislation was introduced that defined Jews in racial terms. Subsequently, Jews were required to register their property, as well as wear the **yellow Star of David badge**.

Legislation, however, also allowed for the head of state to grant "Honorary **Aryan**" status to those Jews who had made significant contributions to the state prior to 10 April 1941. Additional laws forbade Jews to intermarry or employ Aryan servants under the age of 45, thus emulating the German **Nuremberg Laws** of 1935. By mid-1941, most Jewish enterprises were taken over or "**Aryanized**" by the state, and shortly thereafter, Jews were sent to labor camps. By the end of 1941, two thirds of Croatia's 40,000 Jews had been sent to one of the eight camps constructed by the Croatian government, where upon arrival they were immediately killed or they died soon after.

Ante Pavelic in late 1941 declared that "the Jews will be liquidated within a very short time." Pavelic was true to his word. With German encouragement, and later with their help, the process of annihilating Croatian Jewry began in January 1942. By the spring of 1942, Jews were **deported** primarily to **Auschwitz**. Figures for the total number of Jews deported from Croatia are inconclusive, although the number is estimated to have been about 5,000. The Germans succeeded in ridding Croatia of its Jews except for three categories: the Jews recognized as honorary Aryans, Jews in mixed marriages, and **Mischlinges** or half-Jews.

CZECHOSLOVAKIA. The republic of Czechoslovakia was established on 28 October 1918. The territory of the new republic consisted of Bohemia and Moravia, parts of Silesia, **Slovakia**, Ruthenia, and the Sudetenland. The state included many ethnic groups, including Czechs and Slovaks, **Ukrainians**, **Hungarians**, and a majority of ethnic Germans in the Sudetenland. It was **Germany**'s demand to incorporate the German population of the Sudetenland that precipitated the Munich Conference on 28–29 September 1938, which led to the incorporation of the area into the **Reich** and subsequently the invasion of the whole country in March 1939. On 16 March 1939, **Adolf Hitler** proclaimed the establishment of the Protectorate of Bohemia and Moravia, and although Emil Hacha remained president of the "autonomous" Czech government, in reality it was subject to the interests of Germany. Following the dismemberment of Czechoslovakia, the Germans created Slovakia as an independent state.

On the eve of the German occupation of dismembered Czechoslovakia, there were 136 Jewish religious congregations in Bohemia and Moravia, with a total Jewish population of approximately 93,000. Following the German occupation, **anti-Semitism** intensified throughout the territory, with synagogues burned to the ground and Jews subjected to violence. In June 1939 **Adolf Eichmann** arrived in Prague to deal with the city's Jewish population of 56,000, and immediately set up his **Central Bureau for Jewish Emigration**. Like its counterpart in **Austria**, the office was successful in inducing Jews to leave the country. By October 1941, when Jews were forbidden to **emigrate** from German-occupied territory, an estimated 26,600 Jews had left the former Czechoslovakia. About 2,500 made their way to **Palestine** under the **Transfer Agreement** as a result of negotiations between the Czech Ministry of Finance and the **Jewish Agency**.

In June 1939 Jews in the protectorate were ordered to register and sell their gold and other precious jewels as part of the "**Aryanization**" program. Once the war began in September 1939, Jews were dismissed from their jobs and expelled from the schools, and many were shipped off to the **Lublin ghetto**. The bulk of Bohemia-Moravia's 73,000 Jews were sent to the **Theresienstadt ghetto** and subsequently were **deported** to the **death camps**. It is estimated that the total number of Jews in prewar Czechoslovakia (including Slovakia) totaled 350,000, and that an estimated 200,000 to 300,000 Czech Jews were killed in death camps such as **Auschwitz**, **Belzec**, **Chelmno**, **Majdanek**, and **Treblinka**.

CZERNIAKOW, ADAM (1880–1942). *See* WARSAW GHETTO.

– D –

DACHAU. Dachau was the first of the **Nazi concentration camps** and was located about 10 miles from Munich. The camp, which had the capacity to hold 5,000 prisoners, was opened on 20 March 1933. In June 1933 **Theodor Eicke** was appointed camp commandant and immediately gave it a structure, in the form of his brutal rules and regulations that were applied to the other concentration camps that the Germans constructed throughout the **Reich**. Dachau was founded as a "political camp" with the objective of "rehabilitating" those who opposed the regime. Under Eicke, Dachau's reputation struck fear among the German population. In the early years, those imprisoned in Dachau were not primarily Jews but also included communists, Social Democrats, **Jehovah's Witnesses, Gypsies, homosexuals**, and anyone suspected of disparaging the regime. *See also* LIBERA-TION.

DANNECKER, THEODOR (1913–1945). Dannecker was a key aide to **Adolf Eichmann** in the **deportation** of Jews from **France** and **Italy** and the failed effort to send native Bulgarian Jews to **Auschwitz**. Dannecker, a lawyer by training, operated out of the Berlin office of the **Reich Security Main Office** that dealt with Jewish matters. Sent to France, he supervised the preparation of the list of French Jews who were arrested and deported to Auschwitz. A fanatical **Nazi**, Dannecker consistently urged the **Vichy** government to take more active measures against the Jews. Xavier Vallet, the first French commissioner for Jewish Affairs, described Dannecker as a "fanatical Nazi who went into a trance every time the word Jew is mentioned." From France, Dannecker was reassigned to **Bulgaria** where he concluded an agreement with Alexander Belev, the head of Bulgaria's Commissariat for the Jewish Problem, to deport 20,000 Jews to Auschwitz.

Eventually, 11,000 Jews from Macedonia and Thrace were sent to Auschwitz, but the Bulgarian government reneged on their agreement to deport Jews from Bulgaria proper. In March 1944, Eichmann sent Dannecker to **Hungary** to organize the deportation of the country's 800,000 Jews. Subsequently, approximately 400,000 Jews were deported from Hungary and perished in Auschwitz. Dannecker's next assignment occurred in October 1944 when Eichmann appointed him Jewish commissioner in Italy. He remained in Italy until the end of the war. Captured by American troops in 1945, Dannecker committed suicide in an American prison in Bad Tolz on 10 December 1945.

DEATH CAMPS. The extermination or death camps were constructed in **Poland** for the primary purpose of killing Jews and other targets of **Nazi Germany**. The camps built for this purpose were **Auschwitz**-Birkenau, **Belzec, Chelmno, Majdanek, Sobibor**, and **Treblinka**. Toward the end of the war, additional camps, such as **Mauthausen**

in **Austria,** were used as death camps in order to complete the objectives of the **Final Solution.** *See also* AKTION REINHARD; DEATH MARCHES.

DEATH MARCHES. As the **Third Reich** faced defeat at the hands of the **Allies,** the Germans attempted to hide all evidence of the murder of the Jews and other victims. Toward this end, they dismantled the **death camps** and forced surviving inmates to march from **Poland** to **concentration camps** in **Germany.** Those forced to endure the marches, which entailed much cruelty and many deaths, primarily were Jews.

DENAZIFICATION. In **Germany** immediately after World War II, **Allied** forces and the new German government attempted to prevent the creation of new **Nazi** movements through a process known as "Denazification." The Allied effort to rid German and **Austrian** society of any remnants of the **Hitler** regime specifically included removing those involved with Nazi affiliations from positions of influence and disbanding or rendering impotent organizations associated with the **Third Reich.** Although the program of Denazification was designed to purge Germany of Nazi followers, it was not successful because of the size of the problem and the bureaucratic shortcomings of the program. This failure was reflected primarily in the fact that ex-members and sympathizers of the **Nazi Party** did not change their beliefs. Over 500,000 registered Nazis, for example, were allowed to vote in the 1949 general election. Furthermore, a considerable number of ex-Nazis were reinstated as civil servants, teachers, professors, lawyers, and police officers. There was also a decline in the prosecutions of Nazi war criminals.

DENMARK. In April 1940, the Germans invaded Denmark; in return for the Danes' surrender, **Germany** promised to respect their political independence. The Danes agreed, and King Christian X was allowed to retain his throne, and the Danish army, navy, and police were allowed to function. Danish foreign policy, however, was directed by Germany. This political arrangement between Denmark and Germany was subject to an agreement that no harmful actions would befall Denmark's Jewish population.

At the time of the German occupation of Denmark, there were about 8,000 Jews, who constituted 0.2 percent of the population. The small number of Jews included about 1,500 refugees from Germany, **Austria**, and **Bohemia and Moravia**. Jews were totally integrated into all aspects of Danish political, economic, and social life. Although a Danish **Nazi Party** attempted to stir up agitation against the Jews, **anti-Semitism** did not gain a foothold in Denmark. Despite the agreement with the Danes, **Heinrich Himmler** exerted pressure on the Danes to legislate anti-Jewish measures, but the Danish government resisted any coercion on the issue of the Jews. As a consequence, neither anti-Jewish legislation nor efforts to **Aryanize** Jewish property were attempted by the Germans. At the **Wannsee Conference** in January 1942, the refusal of the Danes to cooperate on the Jewish question was discussed, and the **Final Solution** of Danish Jewry was deferred until the end of the war. This decision, however, was reversed in the spring of 1943 when Werner Best was appointed **Reich** commissioner for occupied Denmark.

During Best's tenure, the Danish **resistance** emerged as a force in opposition to the German occupation. The resistance engaged in raids and acts of sabotage that resulted in Best declaring martial law in Denmark. In declaring a state of emergency, Best also seized the opportunity to introduce the Final Solution in Denmark. In October 1943, the Germans commenced arresting Jews, which, in turn, aroused the ire of the Danish population. They alerted the Jews to their imminent danger and proceeded to find places for them to hide. In cooperation with the Swedish government, nearly the entire Jewish population of Denmark was first hidden and then ferried across to **Sweden**. Initially an act of spontaneous behavior on the part of the Danes, this quickly was given direction by the Danish resistance. The confrontation with the Germans was joined by King Christian X as well as the heads of the Danish churches, who urged their congregations to help the Jews. Sweden also let it be known that it was prepared to absorb all of Denmark's Jewish population. Subsequently, all but 400 Danish Jews were able to escape the Germans. Those who were rounded up were sent to **Theresienstadt**, but the Danish people did not forget them. They sent food parcels and insisted that the Danish government be permitted to inspect the camp.

Although most of the Jews sent to Theresienstadt eventually were deported to **Auschwitz**, this was not the case with the Danish Jews. Because of the agitation of the Danish people, the Jews were eventually transferred to a camp in Sweden in the spring of 1945. At the end of the war, a total of 51 Danish Jews had perished, all of them a result of natural causes at Theresienstadt. *See also* YELLOW STAR OF DAVID BADGE.

DENTISTS. The term refers to a special team of Jewish prisoners at **Sobibor** who were ordered to extract gold from the teeth of those killed in the **gas chambers** before they were thrown into the burial pits.

DEPORTATIONS. The word refers to the movement of Jews in German-occupied Europe to the **death camps** in **Poland**. The German conquest of Poland marked the beginning of the deportation of the Jews of Poland. Initially, the plan for resettling Jews under German occupation focused on relocating them in the Nisko transit camp (**Nisko Plan**) located in the Lublin district. The first deportation of Jews outside of Poland was organized by **Adolf Eichmann** in 1939, when he **resettled** Jews from Germany, **Austria**, and the **Protectorate of Bohemia and Moravia** in the Nisko camp. When plans for the Jewish reservation in the Lublin district were aborted, the **Madagascar Plan** quickly followed in 1940. Because of wartime considerations, this plan also failed to materialize, and the result was that Jews were herded into **ghettos** in the **General-Gouvernement**. By March 1941, approximately 380,000 Jews were deported to the area.

By the spring and summer of 1942, the death camps in Poland were operative, and full-scale deportations from German-occupied Europe proceeded in accordance with the plan for the **Final Solution** of the **Jewish question**. The first deportations of Jews to the death camps began in 1942 and consisted of Jews from **Slovakia**. By July 1942, there were mass deportations from **France** and the **Netherlands**, which were followed in August by Jews from **Croatia** and **Norway**. In May 1943, most of the Greek Jews from **Salonika** were deported to **Auschwitz**.

The last major deportation of Jews occurred in 1944, when it was already apparent that the war was lost. Nevertheless, Eichmann was determined to deport the 437,000 Jews of **Hungary** to Auschwitz, where eventually 400,000 were exterminated. *See also* REICHS-BAHN.

DESK MURDERER. The term "desk murderer" originated with **Hannah Arendt** who, in her articles for the *New Yorker* magazine on the **Adolf Eichmann** trial in Jerusalem in 1961 referred to him as this type of perpetrator of the **Holocaust**. The organizers of the Holocaust, such as **Heinrich Himmler, Reinhard Heydrich**, and Adolf Eichmann, gave the orders, negotiated with industry to supply the **carbon monoxide** and **Zyklon B** poison gasses that were used in the **gas chambers**, and yet they personally killed no one. According to Arendt, they were the paradigmatic "desk murderers," what she labeled as embodying the "**banality of evil**."

DEUTSCHE GESELLSCHAFT FUR SCHADLINGSBEKAMP-FUNG M13H (DEGESH) (GERMAN VERMIN-COMBATTING CORPORATION). The German company that distributed the **Zyklon B** gas that was used to exterminate Jews at **Auschwitz** was a subsidiary of I. G. Farben and the Tesch and Stebenow Company in Hamburg.

"DEUTSCHLAND ERWACHE" (GERMANY AWAKE). The slogan used by the **Nazis** in the 1920s to gain support for their **anti-Semitic** program. The Nazis combined the slogan along with "Judah Verrecke" (Judah perish). The **Nazi Party** paper, the *Volkischer Beobachter*, featured both mottos in its pages as a source of agitation against the Jews.

DIARY OF ANNE FRANK, THE. The diary is **Anne Frank**'s record of her thoughts and comments on everyday existence and adolescent teenage angst, hidden in the "secret annex" on 263 Prisengracht in Amsterdam, Holland, along with her father, Otto; her mother, Edith; her sister, Margot; and the Van Pels—Hermann, Otto's business associate; Auguste, Hermann's wife; and their son, Peter. The eighth member of the group was Fritz Pfeffer, a Jewish dentist who shared the room with the 13-year-old Anne. The group lived in close quarters for two years and one month with constant fear of discovery by the

Nazis. In August 1944, an informer disclosed their hiding place and the **Gestapo** arrested Anne, her family, and the others who shared the annex with them. The diary was found and hidden by one of the Frank's sympathetic former employees, Miep Gies, who helped them survive until their betrayal. Anne and her sister Margot were first sent to **Auschwitz** and then **Bergen-Belsen**, where both sisters died of **typhus**. The diary, whose entries conclude shortly before their arrest, has sold tens of millions of copies and is required reading in schools throughout much of the world. Subsequently, the diary was adapted for the stage, where it was awarded a Pulitzer Prize, and then a highly successful **film**. *See also HET ACHTERHUIS*; SILBERBAUER, KARL.

"*DIE JUDEN SIND UNSER UNGLUCK*" (THE JEWS ARE OUR MISFORTUNE). In 1879, German historian, university professor, and **anti-Semite** Heinrich von Treitschke used this phrase to describe his feelings about the presence of Jews in public life in **Germany**. The **Nazis** adopted the slogan and used it in their propaganda campaign against the Jews. The phrase was prominently displayed on the masthead of Julius Streicher's anti-Semitic publication *Der Stürmer*.

DISPLACED PERSONS (DPs). Of the eight million Europeans who had been driven from their countries during World War II, two million were unable to be repatriated and were placed in displaced persons camps that were administered by the United Nations Relief and Rehabilitation Administration (UNRRA). Among the DPs were approximately 50,000 Jews who had been **liberated** from the **concentration camps** and found themselves in areas under American control. The Jewish DPs came from all parts of German-occupied Europe, and for many of them, there was no place to which they could return. During the **Holocaust**, entire towns and villages had been destroyed by the Germans, and many of the DPs were **survivors** of large families that had been murdered by the **Nazis**.

The camps for the displaced Jews were generally overcrowded, and on occasion the Jewish internees were objects of **anti-Semitic** taunts from their **Allied** liberators. The DPs were aided, however, by the relief efforts of the **American Joint Distribution Committee**. In

August 1945, President **Harry S. Truman** appointed Earl Harrison as his special envoy to inquire into the conditions of the Jews in the DP camps in the American zone in Germany. Harrison was appalled by what he saw, and his report was a devastating indictment of Allied military policy toward the surviving Jews. His report concluded with the observation that "we appear to be treating the Jews as the Nazis treated them, except that we do not exterminate them." Based on the report's findings, President Truman requested the British to grant 100,000 visas to Jewish refugees to enter **Palestine**. The British, however, still guided by the provisions of the **White Paper of 1939**, were willing to grant only 6,000 visas.

Subsequently, 40,000 refugee Jews, including 30,000 who were residents of the DP camps, were illegally smuggled into Palestine by **Zionist** groups in the **Yishuv**. *See also* ALIYA BET.

DRANCY INTERNMENT CAMP. The Drancy internment camp in Paris, **France**, was used to hold Jews who were later **deported** to the extermination camps. On 22 June 1942, the first transport, consisting of 1,000 Jews, left Drancy for **Auschwitz**, and the last transport left Drancy on 31 July 1944. Between these two dates, a total of 64 transports with 64,759 Jews, including children, were sent to their deaths. Of these, 61 transports with 61,000 Jews were sent to Auschwitz, and three transports with 3,753 persons were sent to **Sobibor**. Of the 65,000 Jews who were deported from Drancy, more than 20,000 were French, 15,000 were Polish, and 6,000 were German nationals. Drancy was under the control of the French police until 1943 when administration was taken over by the **Schutzstaffel** (SS).

DÜHRING, EUGEN (1833–1921). German philosopher and economist whose **anti-Semitic** work, *Die Judenfrage als Frage der Rassenschaedlichkeit* (The Parties and the Jewish Question, 1881), foreshadowed the racist policies of the **Third Reich**. In his views on the **Jewish question**, Dühring contended that the Jews were "not a religion but a racial tribe," whose true nature was "hidden to some extent by the admixture of religion." He argued that the Jewish question would have existed even if "all Jews had turned their back on their religion and had gone over to one of the leading churches among us." Dühring stated that baptized Jews used their conversion to enter into areas of public life that had been closed to them as Jews. The result was "the spread of racial Jewry through the seams and crevices of our national structures." Sooner or later, he warned, there would be a backlash against Jews as Germans came to realize "how irreconcilable with our best impulses is the infusion of the qualities of the Jewish race into our national environment." Historian Theodore S. Hamerow notes that "Half a century later, these views would serve as a justification for an official policy of racial extermination." *See also* ARYAN PARAGRAPH.

– E –

ECKART, DIETRICH (1868–1923). Adolf Hitler's mentor, Eckart was the first editor-in-chief of the **Nazi** publication *Volkischer Beobachter*. He served as young Hitler's mentor in racial **anti-Semitic** politics, and Hitler belatedly paid tribute to Eckart when he dedicated *Mein Kampf* to his memory. Eckart also helped to finance the fledgling **Nazi Party** and contributed ideas to its political program. *See also* THULE SOCIETY.

EDELMAN, MAREK (1919 or 1922–2009). During the **Nazi** occupation of **Poland**, Edelman, second in command of the **Jewish Combat Organization** (ZOB), fought in the 1943 **Warsaw ghetto uprising**, becoming its head after the death of **Mordechai Anielewicz**, and its only **surviving** leader. Edelman also took part in the citywide 1944 Warsaw uprising. After the war, he remained in **Poland** and became a noted cardiologist. A member of the Solidarity movement, in the 1970s, he collaborated with the Workers' Defense Committee and other political groups opposing Poland's communist regime.

EICHMANN, ADOLF (1906–1962). Because of his trial in **Israel** in 1961, Eichmann has become, perhaps, the most widely known Nazi perpetrator of the **Holocaust**. Eichmann moved to **Germany** after the Austrian **Nazi Party** was banned in 1933. In Germany, he enlisted in the Austrian unit of the **Schutzstaffel** (SS) in 1934 and volunteered to work in the central office of the **Sicherheitsdienst** (SD) where, in 1935, he was placed in charge of the "**Jewish question**." Unlike

Joseph Goebbels, Heinrich Himmler, or Reinhard Heydrich, Eichmann was not a fanatic, although he was to devote his political life to the implementation of the Final Solution.

During the 1930s, he was one of those charged with devising a plan to rid Germany of its Jewish population. In 1937, he visited Palestine and met with Zionist groups that were involved in Aliya Bet, the Yishuv-sponsored operation to illegally smuggle Jewish refugees into the future Jewish state. Following the German annexation of Austria in 1938, Eichmann was sent by Heydrich to organize the emigration of its Jews. Eichmann set up the Central Bureau for Jewish Emigration (Zentralstelle fur Judische Auswanderung) in Vienna, which proved so successful that he subsequently was ordered to organize a similar office in Germany. In 1939, he was assigned to the Jewish section of the Reich Security Main Office Bureau (RSHA), where he worked on the proposed resettlement plans for the Jews in the Lublin region and the aborted Madagascar Plan.

Eichmann's reputation, as the leading "expert" on the Jewish question, was enhanced by his participation in the Wannsee Conference in January 1942. Heydrich subsequently placed him in charge of implementing the Final Solution. Eichmann approached his task with zeal and immersed himself in every aspect of the killing process. He enthusiastically monitored the gassing techniques in the extermination camps, as well as organizing the deportations to the death camps. Eichmann approached his responsibilities with bureaucratic efficiency and was determined to implement the murder of European Jewry in an impersonal and efficient manner.

Hannah Arendt has argued that Eichmann personified the "desk murderer," ordering the murder of millions without leaving his office. But in Budapest in March 1944, Eichmann left his desk and actively participated in directing the deportation of Hungary's 437,000 Jews to Auschwitz. After the war, Eichmann was able to escape to Argentina, where he lived under an assumed name until Israeli agents kidnapped him and put him on trial in 1961. Having been found guilty, he was sentenced and executed in 1962.

EICKE, THEODOR (1892–1943). Eicke was the inspector of the concentration camps during the Nazi period. Having been awarded the Iron Cross (Second Class) during World War I, he joined the police administration of Thuringia following the war. During the 1920s, he lost various jobs because of his anti-**Weimar** politics but joined the **Nazi Party** in 1928. In March 1932, he was sentenced to two years penal servitude for terrorist acts.

Described as a "dangerous lunatic" by the Nazi *Gauleiter* of the Rhine-Palatinate, Eicke, nevertheless, was appointed the new commandant of **Dachau** in 1933. Under Eicke, the prisoners in Dachau were shown no mercy and were treated with great severity. This included the shooting of inmates who were considered to be agitators, beatings, and solitary confinement for the slightest infraction of his rules. Under Eicke, Dachau became the model for the German concentration camp system.

Eicke also played a prominent role in the purge of the **Sturmabteilung** (SA), when he personally murdered the SA chief, Ernest Rohm. Following this deed, Eicke's star rose dramatically among the party leadership. A brutal and coarse person who warned his **Schutzstaffel** (SS) guards against displaying any softness toward the prisoners, Eicke soon won promotions. Subsequently, he was placed in charge of the SS Death's Head Formation, which saw action in **Poland**. At the time of his death in a plane crash on the eastern front in 1943, he had advanced to the rank of SS general and general of the **Waffen-Schutzstaffel** (SS).

Eicke's attitude toward the Jews is best understood in a speech he gave to the commandants of the concentration camps at the beginning of the war. He argued that the obligation to destroy an internal enemy of the state (the Jews) was in no way different from the obligation to kill your enemies on the battlefield.

EINGEARBEITET. The term refers to the use of brutal beatings administered with whips that had small iron balls attached. The "punishments" took place in the labor camps and were one of the many forms of brutality administered by the Germans in **Poland**.

EINSATZGRUPPEN. The Einsatzgruppen were special killing units of the **Sicherheitsdienst** (SD), and therefore under the jurisdiction of the **Reich Security Main Office Bureau** (RSHA), which was headed by **Reinhard Heydrich**. The special attack units made their first appearance during the **Anschluss**, and then the invasion of **Czechoslovakia**, where they functioned as mobile units of the SD and **Sicherheitspolizei** (SIPO). During the German invasion of **Poland** in September 1939, they engaged in the mass shootings of civilians. Following the German invasion of the **Soviet Union** in June 1941, four Einsatzgruppen units were deployed under commanding officers personally chosen by **Heinrich Himmler**.

Einsatzgruppe A was led by Dr. Franz Stahlecker and consisted of about 1,000 men. Their base of operations was in the **Baltic States**. Einsatzgruppe B was commanded by **Arthur Nebe** and consisted of 655 men. Nebe's unit was responsible for operations in **Belarussia** and the Smolensk region, up to the outskirts of Moscow. **Paul Blobel** commanded Einsatzguppe C, which operated in the area around Kiev in **Ukraine**, and it was his **Sonderkommando** 4a, attached to his Einsatzgruppe, which perpetrated the infamous massacre of Jews at **Babi Yar** in late September 1941 that resulted in the murder of 33,771 Jews in a two-day period. Einsatzgruppe D under **Otto Ohlendorf** was responsible for southern Ukraine, the Crimea, and Ciscaucasia.

The approximately 3,000 Einsatzgruppen, which accompanied the **Wehrmacht** (German army) in the invasion of the Soviet Union, along with regular German police units, the **Ordnungspolizei** (ORPO) (Order Police), and auxiliaries from the Baltic states and Ukraine, had the murder of the Jews as their primary aim. This objective was included in Heydrich's written instructions to the Einsatzgruppen commanders on 2 July 1941 in which he specifically singled out the Jews for execution. By the winter of 1941–1942, almost a half million Jews had been liquidated by the killing squads and their auxiliaries.

EINSATZKOMMANDOS. *See* EINSATZGRUPPEN.

EINSATZSTAB ROSENBERG (OPERATIONAL STAFF ROSENBERG). Organized by **Alfred Rosenberg**, the Einsatzstab Rosenberg had as its objective the plunder of the cultural and artistic property owned by Jews. Its first "success" was in **France** where it looted the artwork of such families as the Rothschilds. Between 1940 and 1944, more than 22,000 items—paintings, furniture, and antiques—were transferred to **Germany** from France.

In the **Netherlands** and **Belgium**, the Einsatzstab Rosenberg confiscated furniture from tens of thousands of apartments of Jews who had **emigrated** or were **deported** to Eastern Europe. In October 1942, Rosenberg reported to **Adolf Hitler** that more than 40,000 tons of furniture had been transferred to Germany. In Eastern Europe, Rosenberg's organization plundered not only artworks but also ritual articles. In all of German-occupied Europe, Jewish libraries were looted, including the ancient Hebrew books of the Netherlands and **Salonika**.

EINZELAKTION. In the aftermath of the **Nazi** seizure of power in January 1933, and before the first **anti-Semitic** laws were passed in April 1933, "individual acts of violence" (*Einzelaktion*) were directed against the Jews of **Germany**. These took the form of boycotting Jewish shops, random arrests of Jews, and the beating of Jews by Nazi **storm troopers**.

EISENHOWER, DWIGHT DAVID (1890–1969). As Supreme Commander of the Allied Expeditionary Forces in World War II, General Eisenhower, the future 34th president of the **United States**, had been given information about the **Nazi concentration camp** system well before he led the invasion to **liberate** Western Europe (June 1944). Reports on the massive **genocide** inflicted on Jews, **Gypsies**, political prisoners, **homosexuals**, dissidents, and other groups by the **Schutzstaffel** (SS) had been circulated among all the **Allied** leaders.

Very few of the Allied commanders, however, had an accurate conception of what is now known to the world as the **Holocaust** until their troops began to encounter the **death camps** as they marched into western Germany. On 4 April 1945, elements of the U.S. Army's 89th Infantry Division and the Fourth Armored Division captured the Ohrdruf concentration camp outside the town of Gotha in south-central Germany. Although the Americans did not know it at the time, Ohrdruf was one of several subcamps serving the **Buchenwald** extermination camp, which was close to the city of Weimar several miles north of Gotha. Ohrdruf was a holding facility for over 11,000 prisoners on their way to the **gas chambers** and **crematoria** at Buchenwald. A few days before the Americans arrived to liberate Ohrdruf, the SS guards had assembled all of the inmates who could walk and marched them off to Buchenwald. They left in the subcamp more than a thousand bodies of prisoners who had died of bullet wounds, starvation, abuse, and disease.

The scene was an indescribable horror even to the combat-hardened troops who captured the camp. Bodies were piled throughout the camp. There was evidence everywhere of systematic butchery. Many of the mounds of dead bodies were still smoldering from failed attempts by the departing SS guards to burn them. The stench was horrible.

When General Eisenhower learned about the camp, he immediately arranged to meet Generals Omar Bradley and George Patton at Ohrdruf on the morning of 12 April. By that time, Buchenwald itself had been captured. Consequently, Eisenhower decided to extend the group's visit to include a tour of the Buchenwald extermination camp the next day. He also ordered every American soldier in the area who was not on the front lines to visit Ohrdruf and Buchenwald. He wanted them to see for themselves what they were fighting against. During the camp inspections with his top commanders, Eisenhower said that the atrocities were "beyond the American mind to comprehend." He ordered that every citizen of the town of Gotha personally tour the camp and, after having done so, the mayor and his wife went home and hanged themselves. Later on Ike wrote to his wife, Mamie, "I never dreamed that such cruelty, bestiality, and savagery could really exist in this world."

He cabled General George Marshall to suggest that he come to **Germany** and see these camps for himself. He encouraged Marshall to bring congressmen and journalists with him. Still it would be many months before the world would know the full scope of the Holocaust, and that the Nazi murder apparatus had slaughtered millions of innocent people. General Eisenhower himself understood that many people would be unable to comprehend the full scope of this horror. He also realized that any human deeds that were so utterly evil might eventually be challenged or even denied as being literally unbelievable. For these reasons, he ordered that all the civilian news media and military combat camera units be required to visit the camps and record their observations in print, pictures, and **film**. As he explained to General Marshall, "I made the visit deliberately, in order to be in a position to give first-hand evidence of these things if ever, in the future, there develops a tendency to charge these allegations merely to 'propaganda.'" *See also* HOLOCAUST DENIAL.

EMIGRATION. Prior to October 1941, Jews living in areas under German occupation could still emigrate. From 1933 to 1938, the **Nazis** encouraged Jewish emigration from **Germany**. Nazi policy toward Jewish emigration changed after **Kristallnacht**, when a policy of intimidating Jews to leave Germany through violence and the confiscation of property was promoted by the government. Prior to 1939, some Germans Jews emigrated to **Palestine**, but others found restrictive immigration quotas barring their entry into countries such as the **United States**. Once **Nazi Germany** turned to the implementation the **Final Solution**, following the invasion of the **Soviet Union** in June 1941, it became increasingly difficult for Jews to leave Europe. By October 1941, Jews were not permitted to leave those areas under German occupation. *See also* BERMUDA CONFERENCE; EVIAN CONFERENCE.

ENDLAGER. See EUPHEMISMS.

ENDLOSUNG. See EUPHEMISMS; FINAL SOLUTION.

ENDZIEL. See EUPHEMISMS.

ESTONIA. Following the pact between **Nazi Germany** and the **Soviet Union** in August 1939, the **Baltic states** of **Estonia, Finland, Latvia**, and **Lithuania** became part of the Soviet sphere of influence in the region. In August 1940, Estonia was annexed as a Soviet republic. Following its invasion of the Soviet Union in June 1941, Estonia was occupied by the Germans. During its three years under **Nazi** rule, Estonia was granted self-rule but again became a Soviet republic following the Red Army's return in 1944. On the eve of World War II, there were approximately 4,500 Jews in Estonia, which constituted about 0.4 percent of the population. Despite their small numbers, Jews were the objects of **anti-Semitic** attacks from the Omakaitse, the anti-Soviet nationalist political movement.

During July 1941, the Germans occupied Estonia and in the first few weeks of their occupation subjected the Jews to many anti-Jewish measures; forcing them to wear the **yellow Star of David**, prohibiting them to walk on sidewalks or use public transportation, and confiscating their property. As was the case throughout the Baltic states under German occupation, the Estonian Jewish community was targeted for death by **Einsatzgruppe** A, which was assisted by the Omakaitse. By January 1942, Einsatzgruppe A reported that 936 Jews had been killed. Thousands of the more fortunate Jews were able to escape to the Soviet Union, where they remained until the end of the war.

ETHNIC CLEANSING. Although the term is usually associated with the Bosnian war in the 1990s, it also describes **Nazi Germany**'s objectives following its defeat of **Poland** in September 1939. Major shifts of population occurred, resulting in the brutal removal of large numbers of Poles from the annexed **Warthegau** (western Poland), which became part of the **Third Reich**, and **resettling** German minorities living in other areas of Poland as well as those Germans who lived under the control of the **Soviet Union**, as a part of the understanding between the Soviets and Nazi Germany following the signing of their treaty in August 1939. The Poles were relocated to the **General-Gouvernement**, which served as a "dumping" ground for Poles and Jews. The **Nazi** policy of ethnic cleansing was also implemented after the fall of **France** in 1940 when thousands of French people, in particular Jews, were **deported** to the unoccupied part of France.

ETHNIC GERMAN SELF-PROTECTION MILITIA. At the very outset of the German invasion of **Poland**, **Adolf Hitler** ordered the establishment of this ethnic German militia whose purpose can best be summarized in the words of **Heinrich Himmler**'s adjutant, Ludolf von Alvensleben, "You are the master race here. . . . Don't be soft, be merciless, and clear out everything that is not German and could hinder us in the work of construction." The militia engaged in the mass shooting of Polish civilians, which they justified as revenge for supposed atrocities committed by Poles against ethnic Germans.

EUGENICS. The **ideological** foundation of **Nazi** doctrine rested on its objective of producing a master race of blond, blue-eyed **Aryans**.

Because the Nazis believed that race was the primary determinant of national greatness, they sought to improve their racial stock through eugenic measures. Toward this end, the Nazis were aided by prominent racial scientists who were concerned that the population of **Germany** was being overwhelmed by racial inferiors, which included not only Jews and **Gypsies** but also the weak, the poor, the insane, the handicapped, and the asocials. Many of Germany's most prominent racial hygienists, including biologists and geneticists, gravitated to the Kaiser Wilhelm Institute for Anthropology, Human Genetics, and Eugenics, which was headed by Eugen Fischer, who professed a dogmatic belief in the importance of racially perfecting the German people.

During the 1920s and 1930s, the eugenics movement was popular on both sides of the Atlantic, and during the Weimar decade, there was a body of shared information between American and German eugenicists. In fact, the Rockefeller Foundation was a prime source for the funding of genetic research both in the **United States** and in the **Weimar Republic**. The Rockefeller Foundation continued to support German eugenicists even after the Nazis had gained control over German science. There is evidence to suggest that American eugenicists, in fact, influenced the most important figures of the Nazi regime, including **Adolf Hitler**. In 1934, Hitler wrote to Leon Whitney of the American Eugenics Society for a copy of his book, *The Case for Sterilization*, and shortly thereafter the author received a personal letter of thanks from the **Führer**. The correspondence between Whitney and Hitler is indicative of the close ties between American and Nazi racial scientists.

Throughout the 1930s, eugenicists in the United States were the strongest foreign supporters of Nazi racial policy. It was not, therefore, a flippant remark when Rudolph Hess defined **National Socialism** as "applied racial science." *See also* EUTHANASIA PROGRAM.

EUPHEMISMS. Following the German invasion of the **Soviet Union** in June 1941, the decision was made by the **Nazis** to implement the **Final Solution**. The **Schutzstaffel** (SS), headed by **Heinrich Himmler**, was the **Reich** agency responsible for making German-occupied Europe *Judenrein* (free of Jews). **Reinhard Heydrich**, the head of the **Reich Security Main Office** (RSHA), was placed in charge of coordinating the genocidal project. One of his early decisions was to disguise **genocide** by referring to the mass murder of the Jews with euphemisms as expressed in orders, memos, letters, and other forms of written communication. Heydrich placed a high premium on secrecy and cautioned German soldiers returning from the east not to talk about the atrocities they had witnessed or participated in. Thus, words were used that in themselves appeared harmless but were deadly in their consequences. Several samples of these euphemisms follow: "Cargo" referred to Jews who were crowded into the back of trucks, where they were murdered by **carbon monoxide** gas piped into the back of the vehicle. The term was also used to refer to the trainloads of Jews being deported to the **death camps**. "Deloused" refers to the Nazi ruse whereby the victims, upon arrival in the death camps, were told to undress and shower in order to rid themselves of lice. Moments later they were gassed to death.

Final Solution (*Endlosung*) was the Nazi euphemism for the extermination of European Jewry, or the **Holocaust**. Final Goal (*Endziel*) was the term used before the decision was made to implement the "Final Solution of the **Jewish Question**." Reinhard Heydrich used this term in correspondence with Nazi officials to describe the pending physical annihilation of Polish Jewry.

"Resettlement" referred to the **deportation** of the Jews to the death camps. The victims were led to believe that they were being resettled on Jewish reservations in the east. "Special Handling" (*Sonderbehandlung*) referred to the extermination of European Jews. The term was used in **Einsatzgruppen** reports describing the liquidation of Jews in a specific area. A report of a particular atrocity would be sent to Berlin with the information that a targeted group of Jews "had been dealt with." Both "Russian east" and "final camp" (*Endlager*) were the Nazi euphemisms for the death camps (**Auschwitz** was an *Endlager* but not **Theresienstadt**). "Special action" was the code name for an Einsatzgruppen killing operation against Jews. Following the invasion of **Poland** in September 1939, Heydrich predicted a "political housecleaning," by which he meant the elimination of the Polish clergy, intelligentsia, aristocracy, and the Jews.

"Evacuation" was a Nazi euphemism that came into use at the end of October 1941, when Heinrich Himmler formally ended Jewish

emigration from areas under German control. The word refers to Heydrich's plan for the deportation of all Polish Jews to the east in huge labor columns. The expectation was that the great majority would die on the journey; the **survivors** would be "treated accordingly," that is, worked to death or exterminated. "Final evacuation" was the term used by the RSHA to describe plans for the mass murder of the Jews in Poland. The term "re-Germanization" referred to the German plan to expel Jews and Poles from their homes in the annexed part of Poland and resettle ethnic Germans from Eastern Europe in their place.

"Usefully employed" referred to the use of **forced labor**. Those who were arrested by the **Gestapo** and sent to **concentration camps** were said to be in "protective custody." *See also* PASSING THROUGH; ROAD TO HEAVEN; SPECIAL TRAINS; WAY TO HEAVEN.

EUROPA PLAN. *See* SLOVAKIA; WEISSMANDEL, MICHAEL DOV.

EUTHANASIA PROGRAM. Taken from the Greek meaning "helping to die." The **Nazi** turn to **genocide** did not begin with the Jews or Poles but with its own citizens in the Euthanasia Program. The Nazis believed that three groups threatened the racial hygiene of the nation: those deemed unfit by virtue of a handicap, the **Gypsies,** and the Jews. During the 1930s, the handicapped were initially sterilized, but at the start of the war, the policy shifted to one of "mercy" killing. **Nazi Germany** commenced its policy toward the unfit in July 1933 with the Law for the Prevention of Hereditarily Diseased Offspring. In line with eugenic theory, which was current on both sides of the Atlantic, the German law allowed for the sterilization of persons suffering from such acute problems as epilepsy, chronic alcoholism, manic-depressive psychosis, and other maladies thought to be incurable hereditary illnesses. By 1937, 200,000 people had been sterilized. In 1935, a law prohibited marriage between partners who had serious infectious diseases or hereditary illnesses. Nazi propaganda, through film and textbooks, depicted the mentally ill and the physically deformed as threats to the **Reich**, as well as an expense for the nation. Prior to the outbreak of war in September 1939, **Adolf Hitler** authorized the Euthanasia Program, with the intention of killing **"life unworthy of life."** By spring of 1939, the program focused on the killing of the mentally deficient and physically deformed children. Approximately 5,000 "racially valueless" children were killed as a result.

The Euthanasia Program was intensified following the invasion of **Poland** in September 1939. Hitler authorized physicians and medical aides to participate in the process, which resulted in the murder of their incurably ill patients. The operation, known as the **T-4** program (T-4 refers to the street address, 4 Tiergarten Strasse, where the facilities of the Euthanasia Program were located), gassed its victims in rooms camouflaged as shower stalls. The bodies were then cremated. The estimate is that more than 100,000 people were killed in this manner. Many of those who were part of the T-4 operation were members of the **Schutzstaffel** (SS) and subsequently were assigned to the **death camps,** where their experience in the operation of the **gas chambers** and **crematoria** was put to use in the murder of the Jews and other victims of Nazi Germany.

The medical personnel involved did not appear particularly disturbed by their participation in the Euthanasia Program. Rather, they appeared to believe that by eliminating "life unworthy of life," they were cleansing the nation of disease much as a surgeon removes a cancer. The Euthanasia Program ostensibly was halted in September 1941, when relatives of the deceased protested the deaths of their loved ones. The protest was joined by the churches, and as a consequence, **Hitler** promised to terminate the program but the killings continued under a more effective disguise until the end of the war. *See also* CONDOLENCE LETTER.

"EVENT REPORT NUMBER 128." On 1 August 1941, the **Reich Security Main Office** sent **Adolf Hitler** reports it was receiving from its **Einsatzgruppen** units in the **Soviet Union.** The "Event Report number 128" issued on 3 November 1941 contained the report of Einsatzgruppen killing operations from July to October 1941. The information was widely distributed to **Nazi Party** and government officials. The reports confirm that not only Hitler but also many in the senior ranks of the **Third Reich** were fully informed of the massacres carried out by the **Schutzstaffel** (SS) Einsatzgruppen forces in the East.

EVIAN CONFERENCE. The conference was convened by the **United States**, at the suggestion of President **Franklin D. Roosevelt**, in July 1938 in Evian-les-Bains, **France**, for the purpose of dealing with the problem of Jewish **refugees** that was precipitated by their persecution in **Austria** following the **Anschluss**. The conference hoped to draw attention to the plight of all refugees, but without special reference to the Jews. The nations represented at the conference hoped that in condemning the German government's mistreatment of its nationals, it would force **Germany** to back down. Many at Evian, however, feared that should they come to the rescue of the victims of **Nazi** persecution by creating havens in their countries, this would establish a precedent whereby nations would engage in persecution in order to drive out unwanted minorities. This argument was certainly a factor in the reluctance of the assembled nations to liberalize their immigration laws, as the plight of the Jews worsened in areas under German control.

The fear was also expressed at Evian that the influx of large numbers of Jews in countries still grappling with the depression would lead to an **anti-Semitic** backlash. This concern is best exemplified by the comments made by Colonel Thomas White, Australia's delegate to the Evian Conference: "Under the circumstances, Australia cannot do more, for . . . undue privileges cannot be given to one particular case of non-British subject without injustices for others. It will no doubt be appreciated also that, as we have no real racial problems, we are not desirous of importing one by encouraging any scheme of large-scale foreign migration."

EXEMPTION STAMPS. During the German occupation of the **Netherlands**, there was a pool of approximately 140,000 Jews targeted for **deportation**. Because trains were unavailable on a daily basis to carry Jews to the **death camps**, the Germans prioritized the list of Jews scheduled for deportation. This plan was implemented through the distribution of stamps that "guaranteed" exemptions from deportations. Exemption stamps were issued for every category of Jew found in the Netherlands, including stamps for baptized Jews, Jews working in the military industries, Jews in mixed marriages, Jews working for the Jewish Council (Joodse Raud), and so on. About one of six Jews was a recipient of the stamps as a result of their association with the Jewish Council. The system of allocating stamps, however, often turned on the influence one had with the Jewish Council or a connection with an important German official. The result was a desperate competition to gain recognition that one was an "indispensable Jew" and therefore worthy of the exemption stamp.

EXTERMINATION THROUGH LABOR. At the **Wannsee Conference** on 30 January 1942, a discussion was held concerning the labor shortage that the German war economy was increasingly enduring. Using Jewish workers was, therefore, unavoidable but not a substitute for killing them, simply a different method of doing it. The **euphemism** "extermination through labor" was understood to mean that the Jews who survived **forced labor** would eventually be killed.

– F –

FAURISSON, ROBERT (1929–). A French **Holocaust denier** who was formerly a professor of literature at the University of Lyon, Faurisson generated controversy with a number of articles, published in the *Journal of Historical Review* and elsewhere, which denied various aspects of the **Holocaust**, including the existence of **gas chambers** in **Nazi concentration camps**, the systematic killing of European Jews by gas during World War II, the authenticity of *The Diary of Anne Frank*, and the veracity of **Elie Wiesel's** accounts of his wartime suffering. Faurisson was fined for defamation by a French court in 1983, for the maliciousness of his revisionist writings, which were found to violate hate speech laws. Shortly after the passing of the Gayssot Law in 1990 in **France**, Faurisson was convicted of Holocaust denial.

FILMS AND THE HOLOCAUST. It is unlikely that the public would seek out primary source material or archival footage for their knowledge of the **Holocaust**. Between fictionalized versions of the Holocaust as portrayed in film and works of popular fiction, it is probable that in the future unmediated forms of knowledge about **Nazi Germany** will become more frequently used as sources of "knowledge" about the **Nazi genocide** of the Jews than scholarly volumes on the subject. To date, cinema in particular has played a role in our understanding of the **Shoah**, but those who know little about the history surrounding the mass murder of the Jews, may find it difficult to distinguish films that attempts to illuminate the history of the Holocaust from those that are produced to exploit the destruction of European Jews for commercial rewards.

The films mentioned here were produced not only to entertain but also to inform viewers of the murderous crimes of the **Third Reich**. Film audiences were exposed to issues arising from the Holocaust as early as *The Juggler* (1953), the first American film shot entirely in **Israel** and the first film to deal with the traumatic effects of the Holocaust on **survivors**. Perhaps the most widely viewed film in the first two decades following World War II was *The Diary of Anne Frank* (1959), which was directed by George Stevens, and went on to win three Academy Award Oscars. The film, based on the stage play, however, avoided any mention of the **concentration camps** and certainly provides no hint of what later happened to Anne both in **Auschwitz** and then in **Bergen-Belsen**. In contrast, Stanley Kramer's *Judgement at Nuremberg* (1961) approached the Holocaust by presenting the full range of Nazi crimes, including **medical experiments** on camp prisoners. Jews, however, as a group are not mentioned, but footage of the concentration camps is shown as part of the trial of the Nazi war criminals. Sidney Lumet directed the independently produced film *The Pawnbroker* (1965), based on the novel by Edward Lewis Wallant. The main character is a German-Jewish survivor haunted by his memories of the concentration camps, and the film depicts the camps with harrowing reality. Also produced in the 1960s was *Ship of Fools* (1965), a film that uses the theme of virulent **anti-Semitism** to set the stage for the Holocaust.

The 1970s continued to provide films dealing with the Holocaust, although many of these films used the Shoah as a background for thrillers. Nevertheless, two commercial films in particular stand apart in this genre: *Cabaret* (1975), which deals with the rise of the Nazis in **Germany** in the 1920s, and *The Man in the Glass Booth* (1975), loosely based on the trial of **Adolf Eichmann**. Both were film versions of Broadway stage plays. However, the most important Holocaust film of the 1970s was not a film in the strict sense of its meaning and certainly not viewed in the commercial cinemas but a movie made for television. Gerald Green's *Holocaust* (1978), produced as a NBC miniseries, sought to put faces on the Holocaust by telling the story of the Weiss family from their comfortable existence in Germany before the Nazis came to power, through the events of the Holocaust. The television series was criticized by Holocaust scholars, as well as by **Elie Wiesel**, as a soap opera. *Holocaust*, nevertheless, was one of the most successful programs in television history and had a major impact in West Germany among the post-Holocaust generation.

The 1980s into the 21st century witnessed a number of important Holocaust films produced both in the **United States** and in Europe. The most significant of these films, judging from its impact on audiences, was Steven Spielberg's *Schindler's List* (1984). The film won seven Academy Awards, including Best Picture. The film chronicled the story of **Oskar Schindler**, a Nazi businessman who saved the lives of hundreds of Jews during the Holocaust. Although the film has detractors, it remains the definitive representation of the Holocaust in American commercial cinema. Other Holocaust films of note include Alan J. Pakula's *Sophie's Choice* (1982); Peter Kassovitz's *Jakob the Liar* (1999), a remake of the Czech production; and Tim Blake Nelson's *The Grey Zone* (2001), which depicts the painful labor of the **Sonderkommandos**, the special squads of Jews who processed the corpses from the **crematoria** at the **Auschwitz**-Birkenau **death camp**.

A different kind of Holocaust film, which became the subject of controversy, was Roberto Benigni's *Life Is Beautiful* (1997). The film is a dark comedy that depicts a Jewish father trying to shield his son from the horrors of a death camp by convincing him that all that was happening was a game. The film won three Academy Award Oscars (Best Foreign Language Film, Best Director, and Best Actor). Another foreign film that won awards was Roman Polanski's *The Pianist* (2002), which gave many Jewish viewers what they did not receive from *Schindler's List*: a Jewish hero, the famed Polish pianist Wladyslaw Szpilman, a survivor of the Krakow **ghetto**. Other notable award-winning films touching on the Holocaust include Caroline Link's *Nowhere in Africa* (2003) and *The Counterfeiters* (2007), directed by Stefan Ruzowitzky. The **Bielski Otriad** was the subject of Edward Zwick's *Defiance* (2008), one of the very few films that showed the manner in which Jewish **partisans** fought back against the Nazis. *See also* ART AND THE HOLOCAUST; LITERATURE AND THE HOLOCAUST; THEATER AND THE HOLOCAUST.

FILM IN NAZI GERMANY. The German film industry made approximately 1,100 films between 1933 and 1944. Most of the films were made for the purpose of entertaining the German public, but 96 of these were made under the supervision of **Joseph Goebbels'** Propaganda Ministry. Few of the propaganda films, however, were **anti-Semitic.** Nevertheless, the few films that did cast Jews in a dehumanized manner were popular and prepared the public for what later occurred in the **death camps.** Perhaps the most important anti-Semitic film was *Jew Suss*, which was the most popular feature of the 1939–1940 season. The story, which the **Nazis** insisted was based on fact, depicted the manipulation of Joseph Suss Oppenheimer, the court Jew to the Duke of Wurttemberg in Stuttgart. He is depicted as a swindler, manipulator, and rapist and is executed in the film's climax. The film's projection of anti-Semitism was so powerful that before 1945, it was shown to **Schutzstaffel** (SS) **Einsatzgruppen** before they carried out their missions against the Jews in the east. Fritz Hippler's film documentary *The Eternal Jew* (1940) depicted Jews as **Germany**'s greatest enemy. In one memorable scene, he equates large numbers of rats emerging from sewers with Jews. The film's narrator informs the audience that "they bring ruin, by destroying mankind's goods and foodstuffs. They spread disease and plague. . . . They are cunning, cowardly, and cruel." Other incendiary anti-Semitic films made by the Nazis include *Linen from Ireland* (1939), which depicted Jewish profiteers, and *The Rothschilds* (1940), which accused the Jewish bankers of bringing about an international stock market crisis that results in a great profit for their banking house.

FINAL GOAL (*ENDZIEL*). *See* EUPHEMISMS.

FINAL SOLUTION (*ENDLOSUNG*). This was **Nazi Germany**'s euphemism for the decision to annihilate the Jews of Europe. In a letter dated 31 July 1941, which actually was written by **Reinhard Heydrich, Hermann Goering** authorized Heydrich to "send me, as soon as possible, a draft setting up details of the preliminary measures taken in organizational, technical, and material needs for the achievement of the 'final solution' which we seek." **Heinrich Himmler,** who was directly responsible for implementing the Final Solution, invoked **Adolf Hitler** as the source of his authority for the murder of European Jewry.

FINAL SOLUTION OF THE GYPSY QUESTION. As early as December 1938, **Heinrich Himmler** had spoken of "the **Final Solution** of the **Gypsy** question." Toward resolving this objective, **Reinhard Heydrich** in September 1939 informed his subordinates that along with the Jews, the Gypsies would also be **deported** from **Germany** to the east of **Poland.**

FINLAND. Approximately 2,000 Jews lived in Finland at the outbreak of World War II in September 1939. In November 1939, the **Soviet Union** invaded Finland, which led it to cede land to its attackers. When the Germans attacked the Soviet Union in June 1941, the Finns joined the invasion and allowed **Germany** to use their territory as a base of operations. Although **anti-Semitism** was practically nonexistent in Finland, the Germans sought to spread its anti-Jewish **ideology** throughout the country. In July 1942, **Heinrich Himmler** urged the Finns to **deport** its Jews but found the government unresponsive to its appeal. Much of this reaction was due to the outstanding record of Finland's Jewish soldiers in the war against the Soviet Union, in which their casualty rate was disproportionately higher than the rest of the population. Speaking at a synagogue in Helsinki in 1944, Field Marshall Carl Mannerheim praised the contribution of Jewish fighting men in defense of the nation. Needing the Finns as an ally on the eastern front, Himmler discontinued his pressure on the government to deport its Jews. Finland's Jews, for the most part, escaped from the clutches of the Germans, although eight Jewish refugees were handed over by the Finnish police to the Germans in Tallinin on 6 November 1942. Of the eight, only one survived the war.

FLOSSENBÜRG CONCENTRATION CAMP. The German town of Flossenbürg is located in Bavaria and borders on the **Czech Republic** in the east. During World War II, the Flossenbürg **concentration camp** was located here. Built in May 1938 by the **Schutzstaffel**

(SS) Economic-Administrative Main Office, the camp between 1938 and **liberation** in April 1945, held more than 96,000 prisoners, of which about 30,000 died. During World War II, most of the inmates sent to Flossenbürg, or to one of about 100 subcamps, came from the German-occupied eastern territories. The inmates in Flossenbürg were housed in 16 huge wooden barracks. Its **crematorium** was built in a valley straight outside the camp. In September 1939, the SS transferred 1,000 political prisoners to Flossenbürg from **Dachau**. In 1941–1942, about 1,500 Polish prisoners, mostly members of the Polish **resistance**, were **deported** to Flossenbürg. Between February and September 1941, the SS executed about one third of the Polish political prisoners deported to Flossenbürg.

During the war in the **Soviet Union**, the **Wehrmacht** turned tens of thousands of Soviet prisoners over to the SS for execution. More than 1,000 Soviet prisoners of war were executed in Flossenbürg by the end of 1941. There were over 4,000 prisoners in the main camp of Flossenbürg in February 1943. More than half of these prisoners were political prisoners. Almost 800 were German criminals, more than 100 were **homosexuals**, and seven were **Jehovah's Witnesses**. With time the camp expanded, so that by war's end approximately 94,000 prisoners, including 16,000 females, were imprisoned there or in its numerous subcamps. In addition to German prisoners, inmates included Russian, Polish, French Czech, Italian, Greek, Danish, Norwegian, British, Canadian, and American nationals, and some **Allied** prisoners of war (POWs), deserters from the German Armed Forces, and common criminals.

Before 1944, relatively few Jews were prisoners in Flossenbürg, probably no more than 100. In mid-October 1942, the SS deported the surviving 12 Jews to **Auschwitz** in accordance with general SS orders concerning Jews in German concentration camps. Between 4 August 1944 and the middle of January 1945, at least 10,000 Jews, mostly Hungarian and Polish Jews, arrived in Flossenbürg and its subcamps. Some 13,000 more came in the winter months of 1945, as the SS evacuated other camps to the east and west.

Initially, the SS staff deployed the prisoners in the construction of the concentration camp itself and in the nearby granite quarry. Until mid-1943, the quarry occupied the labor of about half of the prisoner population. In accordance with SS efforts to provide **forced labor** for the German armaments industry, the Messerschmidt Company established a plant in February 1943 in which prisoners produced parts for ME-109 fighter planes. After Allied bombers seriously damaged the central Messerschmidt plant in Regensburg in August 1943, the company's managers moved surviving production facilities to various locations, among them concentration camps, including Flossenbürg and its subcamps. The production of aircraft parts thus dominated labor deployment in the Flossenbürg system by 1944.

The conditions under which the camp authorities forced the prisoners to work and the absence of even rudimentary medical care facilitated the spread of disease, including dysentery and **typhus**. In addition to the dreadful living conditions, the prisoners suffered beatings and arbitrary punishments. SS overseers and prisoner functionaries (the camp and block elders and the **kapos**) abused and killed prisoners according to whim, in addition to the typical "official" punishments of prisoners (solitary confinement, standing at attention for hours, whipping, hanging from posts, and transfer to penal labor details).

On 9 April 1945, shortly before American forces liberated Flossenbürg, the SS executed Admiral Wilhelm Canaris, General Hans Oster, Pastor Dietrich Bonhoeffer, and other conspirators associated with the German resistance groups or implicated in the July 1944 attempt to assassinate **Adolf Hitler**.

FLUGHAFENLAGER (AIRPORT CAMP). The camp, located in Lublin, was opened in the fall of 1941. The camp's primary purpose was to sort out the booty taken from the Jews who perished in **Aktion Reinhard**. A secondary economic activity was the production of brushes, but the camp was notorious for turning its "workers" into corpses. Part of the camp was known as the "clothing works" whereby the camp population, made up exclusively of Jews, was exploited by the Germans for economic production and profit.

FORCED LABOR. Jews and others who were not immediately gassed in the **death camps** were used as slave laborers for producing vital materials for the German war effort. Examples of this include the production of synthetic rubber in **Buna Auschwitz** and work on the V-I and V-2 rockets, as was the case in Dora, located in a gigantic underground complex near the Nordhausen **concentration camp** in the central German state of Thuringia. Conditions for the workers were horrific, as they suffered from little if any medical attention, a starvation diet, and deplorable working conditions. Under Albert Speer, **Adolf Hitler**'s armaments minister, the forced labor system was turned into a brutal slave empire employing at least seven million people. Speer and some German industrialists, including Alfried Krupp, were sentenced at the **Nuremberg Trials** for using forced labor.

FRANC-TIREURS. A term frequently found in German **Wehrmacht** reports following the occupation of **Poland**. The term is a linguistic creation borrowed from the War of 1871 between **France** and Prussia when French militia engaged in guerrilla warfare against German troops. One example of its use appears in a diary from the German General Quartermaster Eduard Wagner who notes in his 5 September 1939 entry that "the difficulties in rear-area Poland continue to increase. Terrible battles with gangs and franc-tireurs; uncertainty everywhere. The troops have taken drastic measures." In a letter to the heads of the **Einsatzgruppen** in Poland on 21 September 1939, **Reinhard Heydrich** wrote that "Jews had been crucial participants in attacks by franc-tireurs and in plundering operations" and gave explicit instructions that they be arrested and concentrated in **ghettos**.

FRANCE. Following its victory over France in June 1940, **Germany** and **Italy** divided the country into a military occupied zone and an autonomous government at **Vichy** under the leadership of Marshal Philippe Petain. In theory, the Vichy regime had jurisdiction throughout France, but the reality was that its independence was subject to German policy. In May 1941, Petain pledged cooperation with the German government, and nowhere was this better exemplified than in the Vichy regime's response to the **Jewish question**.

In June 1940, there were approximately 350,000 Jews living in France, of whom more than half were not French citizens. Many of them were refugees from Germany, **Belgium**, the **Netherlands**, and **Luxembourg** and who came to France to escape **Nazi** persecution. There were also about 20,000 Jewish refugees from Eastern Europe who had sought refuge for similar reasons. The presence of Jewish refugees in Vichy was in accord with German policy, which sought to dump the Jews under its control into unoccupied France. The **anti-Semitic** Vichy government, however, without prodding from the Germans, enacted its own version of the Nazi racial laws against the Jews. Inspired by the **Nuremberg Laws** of 1935, the Vichy government in October 1940 passed into law its definition of a Jew. The law defined Jews as those with two or more Jewish grandparents, as well as those who belonged to the Jewish religion. Based on this definition, Jews were excluded from public office or serving in the military, and were banned from most middle-class professions. The legislation was also used to intern Vichy's foreign Jewish population.

In March 1941, the Vichy government established the Commissariat for Jewish Affairs and appointed Xavier Vallet as its head. The ostensible purpose of the agency was to coordinate anti-Jewish measures throughout the country, but its primary function was to **"Aryanize"** Jewish property. Toward the end of 1941, the Vichy government created the Union Générale des Israélites de France (UGIF), France's version of the **Judenräte** (Jewish Councils). The function of the UGIF was to represent France's Jewish community in its dealings with the Vichy government. A similar organization was established by the Germans in the occupied zone. Following the **Wannsee Conference** in January 1942, **Adolf Eichmann** and his Jewish "experts" made plans to deport the Jews of France, Belgium, and the Netherlands to the **death camps** in the east. In March 1942, the first transports of Western European Jews were sent to **Auschwitz**. In June 1942, Eichmann finalized the technical plans that would deport 100,000 French Jews, divided equally from both zones. In the occupied zone, the position of the Jews had deteriorated even earlier under the German occupation.

Jews suffered from the same racial laws in the occupied zone as did those living in Vichy, but the **deportations** began earlier. In May 1941, the Germans deported 3,200 Polish Jewish refugees to the east. In August 1941, the **Drancy** transit camp was established in a suburb of Paris. During the same month, an additional 4,300 Jews, including 1,300 native French Jews, were interned at the Drancy transit camp in preparation for deportation to **Auschwitz**. About 70,000 Jews passed through the camp from its beginning in August 1941 to **Liberation** Day in August 1944. The camp was initially run by

Vichy officials but taken over by the Germans in July 1943, when a concentrated effort was made to deport as many Jews as possible to Auschwitz. The total number of Jews sent to their deaths from the Drancy camp was about 65,000, including women and children. Among those who were deported from France to the extermination camps were 20,000 French Jewish citizens, 15,000 Polish Jews, and 6,000 German Jews.

Prior to the deportations, Jews were required to wear the **yellow Star of David badge** for purposes of identification. In the occupied zone, the UGIF coordinated relief services to the Jews, as well as caring for the children whose parents had been sent to Drancy. When the Germans sent 12,000 foreign Jews, including 4,000 children, to the Velodrome d'Hiver sports stadium in July 1942, in preparation for their deportation to the extermination camps, the UGIF provided assistance to ameliorate the horrible conditions faced by those who would soon die in Auschwitz. The UGIF officials, however, balked when they were ordered to encourage Jews to voluntarily join their relatives in the Drancy camp. For this "insubordination," several UGIF leaders were arrested and sent to Drancy.

In July 1942, the Vichy regime decided that French Jews would remain under its control, but that foreign Jews would be handed over to the Germans. In November 1942, the UGIF encouraged Jews to flee to the Italian occupation zone in southeastern France, where anti-Jewish measures were not in effect. Approximately 30,000 Jews found refuge in the Italian zone until September 1943, when the Germans occupied the area following **Italy**'s surrender to the **Allies**. With the assistance of French **collaborators**, the Germans hunted down thousands of Jews, who were subsequently deported to Auschwitz. All told, the number of Jews who were deported from France, executed by the Germans, or died in the transit camps was approximately 90,000.

FRANK, ANNE (1929–1944). The efforts of Dutch Jews to escape **deportation** to the **death camps** included a number of Jews who went into hiding. The best-known example of "diving under," as the expression was used to describe those who hid from the Germans, was the Frank family. Anne Frank and her family went into hiding on 9 July 1942 but not before Otto Frank, her father, had planned the move. Having few illusions about the **Nazis**, Otto Frank, who had

emigrated to the **Netherlands** from Germany, began the preparations almost immediately after the German occupation of the country.
In an incremental but methodical manner, the Franks moved their
possessions to the vacant annex located at the top of a house on
Prinsengracht 263.

They remained there until 4 August 1944, when the **Sicherheitsdienst** (SD) in Amsterdam received an anonymous phone call that
disclosed the Franks' hiding place. When the police arrived and
arrested the Franks, they also searched for money and jewelry. In
the process of searching for valuables, a policeman inadvertently
emptied an attaché case that contained Anne Frank's diary. After the
police departed, Miep Gies, one of Otto Frank's employees, returned
to the annex and found the diary, which has since become a classic
in the literature of the **Holocaust**.

The Franks were sent to the Westerbork camp and then deported
to **Auschwitz**, where Anne's mother, Edith, perished. Anne and her
sister Margot were sent to **Bergen-Belsen** at the end of October
1944, where both died of **typhus**. Otto Frank was the only surviving
member of the family.

FRANK, HANS (1900–1946). Frank was the governor-general of the
General-Gouvernement in German-occupied **Poland** from 1939
to 1945. During the 1920s he received both his doctorate and law
degree from the University of Kiel. A militant nationalist, Frank
joined the **Sturmabteilungen** (SA) in 1923 in time to participate in
Adolf Hitler's **beer hall putsch**, his ill-fated attempt in Munich to
overthrow the Bavarian government. Until the **Nazi** seizure of power
in 1933, Frank was the **Nazi Party**'s chief attorney and Hitler's personal lawyer. From 1934 to 1941, he served as the president of the
Academy for German Law, and he was appointed to his position as
head of the General-Gouvernement in Poland following the German
occupation in September 1939.

Frank has been described as an ambitious but insecure person with
a penchant for brutality. His cruelty was displayed toward the Poles,
whom he treated as slaves of the **Reich**. Frank was even more hostile
toward the Jews. In a speech that he gave in December 1941, Frank
called for the extermination of the Jews. Frank's ambition, however,
tempered his enthusiasm for mass murder. He desired to rule over
a modern crusader kingdom in the General-Gouvernement, which

would emulate the medieval order of Teutonic Knights. In this scenario, Frank saw both the Poles and the Jews performing the same role as that of the medieval serfs who served the nobility. But Frank's jurisdictional rivalry with **Heinrich Himmler** over the fate of the Jews in the General-Gouvernement prevented him from accomplishing his objective.

Although Frank approved of the policy of extermination in principle, the need for **forced labor** outweighed his preference and brought him into conflict with Himmler and the proponents of the **Final Solution**. Frank had written to Hitler that "you should not slaughter the cow you want to milk," but Hitler viewed Frank's "kingdom" as a racial dumping ground and an area in which the Final Solution would eventually take place. Thus, Frank vacillated between advocating the rational exploitation of the **ghetto** economies and the policy that encouraged the starvation and mass murder of the Jews. Ultimately he lost his battle against Himmler, and in March 1942, he was stripped of all jurisdiction over racial and police matters in the General-Gouvernement. Frank was tried as a war criminal at the **Nuremberg Trials** and hanged in October 1946.

FRY, VARIAN (1907–1967). Varian Fry, a New York writer and humanitarian, was employed by the American-based Emergency Rescue Committee for the purpose of smuggling selected **refugees**, mostly intellectuals, out of World War II **France**. Based in the Hotel Splendide in Marseilles, Fry established a team of relief workers who boldly proceeded to find refuge for Jews and political refugees. Despite obstacles from the American State Department as well as **Vichy** bureaucrats, Fry was able to get some 1,800 people to safety.

Although the Emergency Rescue Committee had provided Fry with a precise list of noted intellectuals who were to be smuggled out of France, Fry expanded his work to include as many refugees as possible. The list of those saved by Fry included British soldiers and pilots as well as some of Europe's leading intellectuals: **Hannah Arendt**, Andre Breton, Marc Chagall, Max Ernst, Wanda Landowska, Jacques Lipchitz, Hans Sahl, and many others. In September 1941, the Vichy government, suspicious of Fry's activities, forced him to leave the country. Varian Fry is the only American honored as a **"Righteous Gentile"** at **Yad Vashem**.

FUGU PLAN. *See* JAPAN.

FÜHRER. In 1934, following the death of President Paul von Hindenburg, **Adolf Hitler** combined the office of chancellor and president
of **Nazi Germany** with the title of "Führer," or "leader."

FUHRERPRINZIP (**LEADERSHIP PRINCIPLE).** This was based
on the belief in **Nazi Germany** that **Adolf Hitler** was answerable
to the people through plebiscitarian measures, and that all authority emanated from the Führer. In **Nazi** Germany, Hitler delegated
authority to his subordinates, who were expected to unquestioningly
carry out his orders. The **Final Solution** was implemented in the
name of the **Führer**, and although a written order to exterminate the
Jews of Europe has not been uncovered, Hitler's verbal order would
have had the same authority as a document.

FUNCTIONALISTS. This is the school of historians who argue that
the **Holocaust** was not planned in advance of the German invasion of
the **Soviet Union** in June 1941 but was a functional response to the
presence of millions of Jews in German-occupied territories. This opportunity was not lost on radical **Nazis**, who found the circumstances
favorable to the extermination of every man, woman, and child of
Jewish extraction.

Primarily centered in the **United States**, historians who represent
the functional approach to our understanding of the Holocaust include Christopher Browning (*Fateful Months: Essays on the Emergence of the Holocaust*, 1985), Raul Hilberg (*The Destruction of the
European Jews*, 1985), and Karl Schleunes (*The Twisted Road to
Auschwitz: Nazi Policy toward German Jews, 1933–1939*, 1990). *See
also* INTENTIONALISTS.

– G –

GAREL NETWORK. The underground organization in **France**
named after its leader, Georges Garel. Garel was a member of the
Children's Aid Society, a worldwide Jewish organization committed
to health care and the welfare of children. In the summer of 1942,

the agency organized the Garel network with the objective of placing Jewish children with **Christian** families or with religious institutions involved in saving Jews. The Garel network, with the support of the Catholic and Protestant hierarchy, was responsible for saving the lives of thousands of Jewish children, as well as transferring a thousand more to **Switzerland**.

GAS CHAMBERS. Following **Nazi Germany**'s invasion of **Poland** in September 1939, inmates from psychiatric hospitals in **Posen** were sent and crammed into a sealed room in the local headquarters of the **Gestapo**. Here they were forced to inhale **carbon monoxide** gas released from canisters. This was the first time in history that a gas chamber had been used for mass killing. The decision to introduce the gas chambers and the **crematorium** as the most efficient means of murder marks the unprecedented characteristic of the **Holocaust**. The technology, the chemicals, and the willingness of the **Nazis** to use both in behalf of their ideological objectives were soon introduced in **Germany** where gas chambers, using carbon monoxide gas, were one method of killing in its **Euthanasia Program**. The technicians who supervised the gas chambers in the Euthanasia Program, such as **Christian Wirth** and **Franz Stangl**, were subsequently transferred to the **Aktion Reinhard death camps** of **Belzec**, **Sobibor**, and **Treblinka**, where they employed the use of carbon monoxide in the gas chambers, as opposed to **Zyklon B**, which was the gas used in the gas chambers in **Auschwitz**.

GASSING TRUCKS. With the invasion of the **Soviet Union** in June 1941, the **Einsatzgruppen**, in addition to mass shootings of Jews and others, also experimented with another form of killing: the use of hoses connected to the exhaust pipe of a truck, locking in their victims, and feeding exhaust fumes into the back of the vehicle for several minutes, thus killing their "merchandise." The "success" of these experiments led to the introduction of mobile instruments of murder or gassing trucks, vehicles with a lockable container into which the exhaust fumes could be pumped. The gassing trucks were altered to specifications for the killing process by the Saurer trucking firm in Germany. *See also* EUPHEMISMS.

GEKRAT (Acronym for Gemeinnutzige Kranken-Transport G.m.b.H.) (Charitable Society for the Transportation of the Sick). The German government agency, which had its headquarters in Berlin, was responsible for routing the gray buses and other vehicles that transported patients to the killing centers that implemented the **Euthanasia Program**. After patients were evaluated, the transportation section compiled the list of names of those who were designated for extermination.

Despite efforts by the German government, it became impossible to keep the operation secret inasmuch as violence was often used to get patients into the buses. Onlookers witnessed these scenes, and soon rumors spread among the population as to the real function of the Gekrat.

Increasingly the population took notice of the gray Gekrat buses, with their windows curtained or painted, traveling en route to the "euthanasia" facilities. The population referred to the Gekrat buses as "killing crates."

GENERAL-GOUVERNEMENT. Following its occupation of **Poland** in September 1939, the Germans attached the western territory to the **Reich** and created an administrative unit in the unannexed part of the country. The area in central Poland called the General-Gouvernement included the districts of Galicia, Krakow, Lublin, Radom, and Warsaw. Initially, the area was to be used to intern Jews until they were resettled in the Lublin district (Lublin Plan). Toward this objective, the Germans established **ghettos** in Polish cities in the General-Gouvernement as temporary areas of Jewish settlement. Once the decision was made to implement the **Final Solution**, the ghettos became centers for the **deportation** of Jews to the **death camps**. The General-Gouvernement was administered by its governor-general, **Hans Frank**.

GENERAL PLAN FOR THE EAST. Initially written on 15 July 1941 and finalized in May 1942, the General Plan for the East became the official policy of the **Third Reich**. The plan envisioned the removal of 80 to 85 percent of the Polish population, 64 percent of the Ukrainian, and 75 percent of the Belarussian and transporting them farther east, thus causing them to perish from disease and malnutrition. The plan, not counting the Jewish population, anticipated the forcible up-rooting of at least 31 million people from their homes. The invasion of the **Soviet Union** extended the plan to a vastly larger area for its brutal and murderous policies *See also* BELARUSSIA; HUNGER PLAN; POLAND; UKRAINE.

GENGHIS KHAN (1162–1227). On the eve of **Nazi Germany**'s inva-sion of **Poland** in September 1939, **Adolf Hitler** told his leading gen-erals, "Our strength lies in our speed and our brutality. Genghis Khan hunted millions of women and children to their deaths, consciously and with a joy in his heart. History sees in him only the great founder of a state." Both Hitler and **Heinrich Himmler** admired the ruthless-ness of Genghis Khan, and the founder of the Mongol Empire may have been the model for the subsequent ruthless **Nazi** campaign in both Poland and the **Soviet Union**. *See also* EINSATZGRUPPEN.

GENOCIDE. The term is generally credited to **Raphael Lemkin**, who in his 1944 book *Axis Rule in Occupied Europe, Laws of Occupa-tion-Analysis of Government, Propositions for Redress*, coined the term, which refers to the deliberate policy of a state to murder an entire racial, political, or cultural group of people. Inasmuch as the Germans deliberately targeted the entire Jewish people for extinction, the **Holocaust** marks the most extreme form of genocide.

The war against the Jews, however, was not the only act of geno-cide perpetrated by the **Nazis** during World War II. The Germans attempted to exterminate the entire **Polish** ruling, political, and intel-lectual leadership, as well much of the **Gypsy** population that fell under its control.

The precedent for the Nazi genocide was conducted against its own people when **Adolf Hitler** signed the order that authorized the **Euthanasia Program** in **Germany** following the start of the war in September 1939. Despite the evidence culled from the Nazi archives, the eyewitness accounts of survivors of the Holocaust, the photos taken by the **Allies** when they **liberated** the **concentration camps**, and the volumes of evidence presented at the **Nuremberg Trials** and the subsequent trials of Nazi war criminals and their collaborators, **neo-Nazis** both in the **United States** and in Europe continue to either negate the **Holocaust**, or insist that the number of Jews murdered by the Nazis is highly exaggerated. In the **United States**, the **Institute for Historical Review** publishes periodicals and sponsors conferences dealing with **Holocaust denial**.

Notwithstanding the lessons of the Holocaust, the world has witnessed in recent years a genocidal war in Rwanda between the Hutus and the Tutsis, acts of mass extermination in Zaire, and "**ethnic cleansing**" in wars in Bosnia and Darfur. Responses of the international community to these acts of genocide have been as slow as during the Holocaust.

GERMAN-AUSTRIAN JEWISH POPULATION. When **Adolf Hitler** became chancellor of **Germany** in January 1933, the Jewish population was approximately 1 percent or about 564,000 in a nation of 60 million. By 1940, the Jewish population, as a result of **emigration**, was about 240,000. The **Nazis** murdered approximately 130,000 German Jews. At the end of the war about 22,000 German Jews remained alive; about 5,000 survived in hiding, approximately 5,000 survived the camps, and the remaining 12,000 survived because they were married to non-Jews. Because Nazi policy with regard to Gentile–Jewish marriages was unclear, the survival rate for these Jews was relatively high.

At the time of the **Anschluss** in 1938, there were approximately 6,725,000 people in **Austria**, with Jews numbering about 220,000. Because of Nazi persecutions that followed Germany's annexation of Austria, approximately 126,000 Jews emigrated to **Great Britain**, **Palestine**, **Shanghai**, and North and South America. Some 15,000 Austrian Jews who sought refuge in other European countries that were soon conquered by the Germans were eventually arrested and deported to the extermination camps. Following **Kristallnacht**, the number of Jews in Austria was reduced to 60,000. All the remaining Austrian Jews were eventually killed by the Nazis in the **Holocaust**.

GERMANY. The precipitating circumstance that led to **Adolf Hitler**'s "seizure of power" in January 1933 was the inability of the **Weimar Republic** to solve the dire economic problems, highlighted by the chronic unemployment, resulting from the Great Depression of 1929. The Weimar Republic, established in the wake of Germany's defeat in World War I, was forced to sign the Treaty of Versailles, which called for Germany to accept sole responsibility for causing the war (the "War Guilt" clause), the forfeiture of German territory in the east, the payment of war reparations, and limiting its army to 100,000 men. The treaty was unpopular in Germany, causing shame and resentment among the population. Because of the threat of communist revolution in Germany, the Social Democratic government of the Weimar Republic formed an alliance with the German military and ignored the right-wing groups and their private militias (*Freikorps*) that engaged the communists in ever-occurring battles.

Among the right-wing groups was the National Socialist German Workers' Party (**Nazis**), which by 1921 was led by Adolf Hitler. Hitler promoted the idea that Germany during the war was betrayed from within ("**stab in the back**") by leftists and, specifically, the Jews. He identified Jews with **Bolshevism** and promised that should he come to power, he would do something about Germany's small but influential Jewish population. In 1923, against the background of high inflation and the French occupation of the Ruhr, Hitler attempted a "putsch" against the state government of Munich with the objective of marching on Berlin to overthrow the Weimar Republic. In the aftermath of the failure of the **beer-hall putsch**, Hitler was arrested and brought to trial, where he was found guilty and sentenced to prison. Serving only months of his five-year sentence, he was released and decided that he would turn to politics rather than using armed force to attain power.

Between 1925 and 1928, Germany recovered from its perilous economic situation, thanks to the initiative of the American Dawes Plan, and Hitler spent the years solidifying his leadership over his party. From 1925 to the 1930s, however, the German government evolved from a democracy to a de facto conservative-nationalist authoritarian state under the former war hero Paul von Hindenburg, who was elected president of the Weimar Republic following the death of Friedrich Ebert. Hindenburg was a conservative who opposed the liberal democratic nature of the Weimar Republic and wanted to find a way to turn Germany into an authoritarian state. When the worldwide depression occurred in 1929, the government, led by Hindenburg, found itself unable to find a solution to the economic crisis. As unemployment increased, both the communists and the Nazis increased their political representation in the Reichstag. The Nazis vowed to bring a bright new future for Germany in lieu of the seemingly incapable democratic government, and promised the restoration of civil order, the elimination of unemployment, the restoration of national pride (principally through the repudiation of the Treaty of Versailles), and racial cleansing by actively removing the influence of Jews in German life. The Nazis also promoted military rearmament, repudiated the reparation payments, and promised the restoration of territory lost after the war.

Nazi propaganda continued to endorse the "stab in the back" canard whereby Hitler accused the Jews of Germany's surrender to the **Allies** and the humiliating aftermath as exemplified in the provisions of the Treaty of Versailles. He referred to the Jews as the traitorous "November criminals," whose goal was to subvert and poison the German blood. Increasingly after 1929, radical German nationalists were attracted to the revolutionary nature of the Nazis and joined them in confronting the communists as the German economy floundered. As unemployment intensified, the middle-class parties lost support as the German electorate polarized around the left and right wings, thus making majority government in a parliamentary system even more difficult.

In the elections of 1928, when economic conditions had improved following the end of the hyperinflation of 1922–1923, the Nazis gained a meager 12 seats. In 1930, months after the stock market crash, they won an astonishing 107 seats, going from a splinter group that ranked ninth in the Reichstag to the second-largest parliamentary party. After the July elections of 1932, the Nazis were the largest party in the Reichstag with 230 seats. Hitler expected to be appointed chancellor by Hindenburg, but the president was reluctant to appoint him. After Hindenburg had gone through a number of chancellors who were not able to solve the country's economic and political crisis, former chancellor Franz von Papen convinced Hindenburg to appoint Hitler chancellor, convincing the president that the more conservative politicians, like himself, would be able to moderate Hitler's extremism. On 30 January 1933, Hindenburg appointed Hitler chancellor of Germany.

Even though the Nazis had gained the largest share of the popular vote in the two Reichstag general elections of 1932, they did not hold a majority of the seats in the Reichstag. Consequently, the Nazis formed a coalition with former Chancellor Franz von Papen, leader of the Catholic Center Party, whose politics were dictated in part by his desire to combat communism and who believed he could restrain the excesses of the Nazis. On the night of 27 February 1933, the Reichstag building was set on fire and a Dutch communist, Marinus van der Lubbe, was found inside the building. He was arrested and charged with starting the blaze. The event had an immediate effect on thousands of anarchists, socialists, and communists throughout the **Reich,** many of whom were arrested and sent to the newly constructed **Dachau concentration camp.** The unnerved public worried that the fire had been a signal meant to initiate the communist revolution, and the Nazis found the event to be of immeasurable value in getting rid of potential political opponents. The event was quickly followed by the Enabling Act rescinding habeas corpus and other civil liberties. The Enabling Act was passed in March 1933 and, together with Article 48 of the Constitution of the Weimar Republic, which allowed the president, under certain circumstances, to take "emergency measures" (including the promulgation of legislative decrees) without the prior consent of the Reichstag, was immediately implemented by Hitler to establish a dictatorship—thus, ending the Weimar Republic and ushering in the **Third Reich.** During the next year, the Nazis ruthlessly eliminated all opposition. The Communist Party had already been banned before the passage of the Enabling Act, and the Social Democrats, despite efforts to appease Hitler, were banned in June 1933. The Catholic Center Party, at Papen's urging, disbanded itself on 5 July 1933 after guarantees that protected Catholic education and youth groups. On 14 July 1933, Germany was officially declared a one-party state.

Symbols of the Weimar Republic, including the black-red-gold flag (now the present-day flag of Germany), were abolished by the new regime, which adopted both new and old imperial symbolism to represent the dual nature of the imperial Nazi regime of 1933. The old imperial black-white-red tricolor, almost completely abandoned during the Weimar Republic, was restored as one of Germany's two officially legal national flags. The other official national flag was the **swastika** flag of the **Nazi Party.** It became the sole national flag in 1935. The national anthem continued to be "Deutschland über Alles" (also known as the "Deutschlandlied") except that the Nazis customarily used just the first verse and appended to it the "Horst-Wessel-Lied" accompanied by the so-called Hitler salute. When President Hindenburg died on 2 August 1934, Hitler declared the office of president vacant, combined the office of president and chancellor, and took on the title of **"Führer"** or "leader."

With Hitler now firmly in charge, the National Socialist movement turned its attention to Germany's Jews. By the early months of 1933, it had already taken its first step in the process of removing them from German society when it called for the boycott of Jewish businesses on 1 April 1933. This was followed by the Law for the Restoration of the Professional Civil Service on 7 April 1933, which barred anyone not of **Aryan** descent from public employment and established the principle of racial difference between Jews and Germans. Subsequently, numerous laws would be passed between 1933 and the outbreak of World War II in September 1939, including the **Nuremberg Laws** on 15 September 1935, and after **Kristallnacht** (9–10 November 1938) on 19 September 1939, German Jews were required to wear the **yellow Star of David badge** on their clothing, as just a few examples. The intention of these laws was to prod Jews to leave Germany and, short of that, remove them from all facets of German life. Once the decision to exterminate the Jews of Europe was decided in mid-summer 1941, it was only a matter of time before the Jews of Germany would be targeted for **deportation**. On 10 December 1942, the first group of German Jews was deported to **Auschwitz**, where, along with most of Europe's millions of Jews, they perished in the **Holocaust**.

Following the Allies' defeat of Germany in April 1945, a series of military tribunals were convened from October 1945 to October 1946. The court's legal designation was the International Military Tribunal (IMT) or better known as the **Nuremberg Trials**, which consisted of prosecutors from **France**, **Great Britain**, the **Soviet Union**, and the **United States**. The first of these trials tried 22 major Nazi war criminals who were accused of war crimes against humanity and peace. The Nazi leaders tried at Nuremberg were found guilty of crimes against humanity and having engaged in a criminal conspiracy by virtue of their membership in the Nazi Party. Of the 22 defendants, 12 were sentenced to death, 3 were sentenced to life imprisonment, and the rest to lesser sentences. Subsequent Nuremberg proceedings were enacted in a series of trials that continued from 1946 to 1948, and included physicians who performed **medical experiments** in the concentration camps (1946), the trial of I. G. Farben (1947), the Krupp case (1947), and the trial of the **Einsatzgruppen** (1947).

In September 1951, **Konrad Adenauer**, the first chancellor of the German Federal Republic, addressed the Bundestag (Parliament) and acknowledged "unspeakable crimes that were perpetrated in the name of the German people that oblige us to make moral and material amends." In 1952, Germany made monetary **restitution** to **Israel**, and the West German parliament subsequently enacted a law that compensated Holocaust **survivors**.

In the decades following the end of the Second World War, a phenomena known as **Holocaust denial** made its appearance in much of the Western world and in the last few decades has spread to the Middle East. Claiming that the Holocaust did not happen or that the Nazi government did not have a policy of deliberately targeting Jews for extermination or that six million Jews were murdered, Holocaust deniers also insisted that the Nazis did not use **gas chambers** to kill Jews or any other targeted people. In short, they insist that the Holocaust was a hoax. In 1985, Germany's parliament passed legislation making it a crime to deny the extermination of the Jews. In 1994, the law was tightened. Now, anyone who publicly endorses, denies, or plays down the **genocide** against the Jews faces a maximum penalty of five years in jail and no less than the imposition of a fine. *See also* LAWS AGAINST HOLOCAUST DENIAL; NAZI GERMANY.

GESTAPO (GEHEIME STAATSPOLIZEI). The Gestapo evolved from the Prussian police section known as the **Sicherheitspolizei** (SIPO) or "security police." When **Heinrich Himmler** placed all of the police forces in **Germany** under his jurisdiction in 1933–1934, he also became the head of the Gestapo. Under Himmler, with **Reinhard Heydrich** as his chief administrator, the Gestapo was transformed into a police agency that became synonymous with terror. The Gestapo was responsible for identifying and arresting enemies of the state and placing them in "**protective custody**," which generally led to imprisonment or incarceration in a **concentration camp**. In its mission to protect the state from its enemies, the Gestapo was exempt from any control by constituted legal authorities, and consequently used whatever means it deemed necessary to extract information, including torture.

GHETTO. The first ghetto was established in Venice in 1516 near an iron foundry (Geto). The Jews were forced to live in the area segregated from the rest of the population. Subsequently, the use of ghettos spread to other Italian cities, then made its appearance in southern **France, Germany, Bohemia and Moravia,** and some **Polish** cities. Over time, the word "ghetto" became a general European term to describe the segregated and enclosed quarters of the Jews. The last ghetto to exist in Europe, prior to its reestablishment by **Nazi Germany,** was the one in Rome, which was terminated in 1870. The ghettos were reintroduced in the towns and cities of Eastern Europe following the German occupation of the area. Unlike the earlier ghettos, which were used to segregate the Jews from the non-Jewish population, the Germans used the ghettos as a transitional phase in the process that led to the **Final Solution** of the **Jewish question.** *See also* KOVNO GHETTO; LODZ GHETTO; LUBLIN GHETTO; WARSAW GHETTO.

GLEICHSCHALTUNG (COORDINATION). The term relates to the process by which the **Nazis** synchronized the institutions of German life to conform to the policies of **National Socialism.** In practice, *Gleichschaltung* not only Nazified all sectors of German public life but was also used to eliminate the regime's opponents, such as political parties, the press, unions, and so on.

GLOBOCNIK, ODILO (1904–1945). Globocnik was head of the **Aktion Reinhard** camps as well as the **Majdanek death camp.** Born in Trieste, Globocnik joined the Austrian **Nazi Party** in 1931 and became the liaison between his party and its German counterpart. In 1938 he became the *Gauleiter* (party district leader) of Vienna, but shortly thereafter he was relieved of his position because of illegal currency dealings. In late 1939, **Heinrich Himmler** pardoned him and subsequently he was appointed SS and police chief for the Lublin district. Himmler placed Globocnik, a virulent **anti-Semite,** in charge of a special **Schutzstaffel** (SS) unit for the purpose of exterminating

Jews in the Aktion Reinhard camps. Globocnik carried out his duties with brutal efficiency that resulted not only in the murder of more than two million Jews but also the seizure of their personal property down to their spectacles and the gold fillings from their teeth. Ultimately, Globocnik was relieved of his duties in August 1943 for stealing his victims' valuables and was reassigned to Trieste.

GOEBBELS, JOSEPH (1897–1945). Goebbels came from a poor but pious working-class Catholic family. He was educated in Catholic schools and subsequently went on to attain a doctorate in history and literature at the University of Heidelberg. Born with a club foot, he was rejected for military service during World War I. His angry persona, which may be attributed to his birth defect, did not prevent him from joining the **Nazi Party** in 1924. Goebbels compensated for his un-**Aryan**-like physical appearance with his ideological zeal and fanatical **anti-Semitism**.

In 1926, Goebbels was appointed *Gauleiter* (party district leader) of Berlin and subsequently he was elected to the Reichstag in 1928. Among the inner coterie of **Adolf Hitler**'s advisers, Goebbels was considered radical with regard to the future of the Jews in **Germany**. As editor of the **Nazi** newspaper *Der Angriff*, he called for a **pogrom** against the Jews. Written in 1932, his articles on the Jewish question would foreshadow his later role as the instigator of **Kristallnacht**. In a diary entry dated 17 October 1939, Goebbels wrote "This Jewry must be annihilated." Prior to his diary entry, Goebbels had ordered the production of a documentary that would reflect the reasons for Germany's anti-Jewish policies. Directed by Fritz Hippler, *The Eternal Jew* (1940) depicted Jews and Jewish ritual practices in the worst possible light. The film equated Jews with rats and distorted Jewish ritual practices, such as the slaughtering of animals for the purpose of fulfilling the laws of *Kashruth* (kosher). Goebbels' motivation was to convince German opinion that Jewish ritual slaughtering practices were cruel to animals.

With Adolf Hitler's accession to power, Goebbels became head of the party's propaganda network, which involved responsibility for all aspects of the media and the release of public information. In this role, he helped to create the myth of an infallible Hitler whose charge was to save Germany from the Jews and their sympathizers. Toward filling this objective, Goebbels organized the public burning of books on 10 May 1923, whereby the works of Jewish authors, Marxists, and other enemies of the state were set afire in huge bonfires throughout Germany.

The list of anti-Jewish confrontations organized by Goebbels includes the 1 April 1933 **boycott of Jewish stores** in Germany, the Kristallnacht pogrom of 9–10 November 1938, and curtailing the movement and activities of Jews in areas under his jurisdiction. Following the Nazi occupation of **Poland** in September 1939, Goebbels organized the first **deportations** from Berlin in keeping with objective to make the city *Judenrein* (cleansed of Jews). It was also Goebbels who urged that Jews wear the **yellow Star of David badges** for purposes of easily identifying them.

Along with **Heinrich Himmler** and other Nazi radicals on the **Jewish question**, Goebbels strongly urged that there be no retreat from the **Final Solution**. He called for a total war of extermination against the Jews but avoided propaganda material that disclosed the methods by which this would be accomplished. In implementing the policy of annihilating the Jews of Europe, the Nazis realized that they had passed the point of no return, and it was Goebbels who counseled Hitler that every effort be made to finish the task.

With the Soviet army approaching Berlin in 1945 and his realization that the war would shortly be over, Hitler committed suicide in his Berlin bunker. In death he was joined by Eva Braun, his mistress, who had married him hours before his death, and the entire Goebbels family, which included his wife and six children. Goebbels committed suicide on 1 May 1945, but not before he had become Hitler's most trusted follower. In fact, in his last days, Hitler, alienated from Goering, appointed Goebbels as his successor, but sensing the end and the humiliation that would attend Germany's surrender, he instead chose to take his life. *See also* BOOK BURNING; FILM. IN NAZI GERMANY.

GOERING, HERMANN (1893–1946). The decorated World War I fighter pilot became involved with the **Nazi Party** in its formative years. A veteran of the failed Munich **beer hall putsch** in 1923, when **Adolf Hitler** attempted to overthrow the government of Bavaria, Goering went on to become the second-most powerful political figure in the **Third Reich**. Goering was instrumental, along with **Heinrich Himmler**, in the organization of the first **concentration camps** in 1933. In 1934, he played a major role in the purge of the **Sturmabteilung** (SA), and shortly thereafter, Hitler appointed him commander-in-chief of the German air force. In January 1935, he was promoted to the position of *Reichsmarschall*, and in 1936 he was appointed head of Germany's Four-Year Plan, which gave him almost dictatorial control over the entire economy. In 1937, as head of the German economy, he established the Hermann Goering Works, which employed about 700,000 workers.

Following the **pogrom** of 9–10 November 1938, which Goering derisively referred to as **Kristallnacht** (crystal night), Goering fined the Jewish community a billion reichsmarks and ordered the elimination of the Jews from the German economy. In September 1939, Hitler appointed him as his successor, as well as placing him in charge of the **Jewish question**. Not as fanatical as Hitler, Goering nevertheless was an **anti-Semite** who, after the invasion of **Poland**, was responsible for the expulsion of the Jews from the western part of Poland. During the same year, he set up the Main Trusteeship Office East, which administered confiscated Jewish property. In May 1941, Goering banned the **emigration** of Jews from all German-occupied territories, and in July 1941 he authorized the implementation of the **Final Solution**. Following the war, he was one of the 22 major **Nazi** war criminals who were tried in Nuremberg in 1945–1946. Goering committed suicide rather than allow himself to be executed by the **Allies**. *See also* NUREMBERG TRIALS.

GREAT BRITAIN. The response of Great Britain to the German Jewish **refugee crisis** was a mixed one. Initially, it admitted few refugees from Germany, limiting the number to approximately 2,000 to 3,000, most of whom were professionals such as scientists and academics. In the aftermath of **Kristallnacht**, however, Great Britain became one of the few islands of sanctuary for Jews, but with the proviso that they would not seek employment or public assistance in the United Kingdom. Somewhere between 50,000 and 80,000 Jewish refugees were given shelter there. Because of fears of alienating the Arab world should war occur, Great Britain, beginning in 1937, restricted immigration into **Palestine**, a policy that reached its climax with the

White Paper of 1939, which limited Jewish immigration into Palestine to 75,000 people over a five-year period.

With the outbreak of war in September 1939, all immigration into Great Britain and the British Empire ceased. Young adult Jewish immigrants were interned and sent to British overseas territories together with German nationals. During the war, along with its ally the **United States**, Great Britain adopted the policy of "**unconditional surrender**," which eschewed any negotiations with **Nazi Germany** and prohibited bartering with German officials in exchange for Jewish lives. British policymakers also refused to revise the strategy, which held that the best way to save the Jews of Europe was to win the war. This strategy precluded the possibility of special air force missions that would have resulted in the bombing of **Auschwitz** or the railroad tracks leading to the **death camp**. *See also* CHURCHILL, WINSTON SPENCER.

GREECE. The Jews of Greece on the eve of World War II numbered about 76,000 or 0.9 percent of the population. They lived primarily in Salonika, where the Sephardic Jews constituted a majority in the city. Many of the Sephardim were engaged in commerce and trade. Although Jews were generally accepted in Greece, this changed after World War I. Between 1924 and 1935, a militant **anti-Semitism** spread throughout the country. But under the military dictatorship of General Ioannis Metaxes, all forms of political agitation were suppressed, including anti-Semitism. Following Metaxes' death in January 1941, and the German invasion in April, the position of the Jews deteriorated. Jews were publicly humiliated by the Germans, and evicted from their homes. In July 1942, 9,000 Jews of Salonika, between the ages of 18 and 45, were arrested and sent to German organized labor battalions in Greece. The Jewish community of Salonika attempted to ransom the laborers but failed to raise the required sum, whereupon the Germans pillaged the Jewish cemetery of Salonika to make up the difference and then proceeded to destroy the gravesites. The first Jews from Salonika were deported to **Auschwitz** on 23 February 1942.

In Greece proper, representatives from **Adolf Eichmann**'s office directed the Greek Jewish Council (**Judenrat**) to implement the **deportation** quota to the **death camps**. Prior to the commencement of the deportations, the Germans ordered all Jews to wear the **yellow Star of David badge** and then forced them into three **ghettos** located near Salonika. Between March and April 1943, 48,000 additional Jews were deported from Salonika to **Auschwitz**, where 37,000 were gassed on arrival and the other 11,000 were selected for **forced labor**. In October 1943, the Germans ordered that all Jews report for registration. Those who failed to appear within five days of the order were to be shot. Similarly, the Greek population was warned that anyone who gave shelter to Jews would be executed without trial. In the beginning of 1944, the deportation of Jews from Athens commenced, and approximately 800 were sent to Auschwitz. In Corfu, 1,800 Jews were sent to Auschwitz in June 1944, where all but 200 were gassed.

Subsequently, the Greek Jews from Rhodes, Canea, Crete, and elsewhere were deported to Auschwitz. Altogether about 54,533 Greek Jews were sent to Auschwitz, where 41,776 were gassed upon arrival. It is estimated that a total of 60,000 Greek Jews were murdered by the Germans, with the bulk of them meeting their deaths at Auschwitz and **Bergen-Belsen**. The **Nazi** destruction of Salonika's Jewish community, the largest and strongest of all the Sephardic communities in Europe, marked the demise of a rich religious and cultural tradition that had been preserved since the Jewish expulsion from **Spain** in 1492. The tragedy of the Greek Jewish community also points to the lack of attention paid by historians to the destruction of the Sephardim Jewry.

GREIFER. *See* CATCHER.

GYPSIES. The Gypsies, or Roma, entered Europe during the Middle Ages from Northern India. The fact that the Roma had migrated to Europe from the ostensible home of the "**Aryan** race" did not prevent the **Nazis** from portraying them as an inferior people because of their lack of roots. Having chosen a nomadic existence, Gypsies by the 15th century were no longer a homogeneous people but divided between the Sinti and Lalleri tribes. Although most of the Roma resided in Eastern Europe and Russia, the Roma were also scattered throughout the rest of Europe. In German-occupied Europe, Nazi **ideology** characterized the Gypsies as parasites who lived off the host nations that allowed them to reside within their borders.

Consequently, when the opportunity presented itself, the Germans attempted to purge the Gypsies from the territories under their control. For the most part, the Germans had assistance in this objective, inasmuch as most Europeans were suspicious of the Gypsies, believing them to be idolatrous, if not practitioners of witchcraft. Only in the Balkan states was there some toleration for the Roma as their stereotype as thieves and kidnappers of little children spread throughout the rest of Europe. In both **Germany** and **Austria**, numerous laws limited their movements and rights. Although population data on the Gypsies is difficult to assess, many scholars estimate that about 1.5 million Roma lived in Europe on the eve of World War II.

The Nazi persecution of the Roma mirrored that of the Jews. In September 1933, Gypsies were arrested throughout Germany in accordance with the Law against Habitual Criminals. The **Nuremberg Laws** of 1935, which defined the status of the Jews in Germany, also included regulations regarding the Gypsies. For example, marriages between Gypsies and Germans were forbidden. The Reich Research Office for Race Hygiene and Population declared that 90 percent of the approximately 28,000 German Roma were **Mischlinges** and therefore non-Aryans. Gypsies were designated as "asocials" and a threat to public health.

Accordingly, most of the **Reich**'s Gypsies were sent to **Dachau**, where many underwent forced **sterilization**. During the summer of 1938, the government proclaimed "Gypsy Clean-Up Week," whereby hundreds of Gypsies in Germany and Austria were rounded up, beaten, and imprisoned. Germany, however, was not alone in its response to the presence of Gypsies. The following are representative examples of the treatment of Gypsies in Europe during World War II.

In **Bulgaria** in early 1941, King Boris put into force the Law for the Protection of the Nation, which was modeled after the German Nuremberg Laws of 1935. Although the Roma were not mentioned specifically in the law, the Nazi-inspired legislation placed the Gypsies in the same racially inferior category as the Jews. Subsequent legislation outlawed marriages between the Roma and Bulgarians. In 1943, when King Boris agreed to surrender the Jews of Macedonia and Thrace for **deportation** to the **death camps**, the Gypsies, themselves fearful of similar treatment, tried to help the Jews. In 1943, when the Bulgarians refused to cooperate with the Germans in the deportation of native Bulgarian Jews, the same rejection was applied to the Gypsies. The Roma also benefited from subsequent legislation that eased anti-Jewish measures in Bulgaria. Gypsies credited King Boris with saving Gypsies who were Bulgarian citizens from the death camps, although the Germans had pressed for the deportation of the Roma, as they had in the matter of the Jews.

Following the German dismemberment of **Czechoslovakia** in 1939, the Czech Gypsies fled to rump **Slovakia** and the Protectorate of Bohemia and Moravia. The estimate is that between 60,000 and 100,000 Roma were able to survive the war in the more tolerant atmosphere of Slovakia, although Gypsies were randomly killed by roving bands of Slovakian Nazis. Nevertheless, the government refused to hand over the Gypsies to the Germans for the purpose of deporting them to the death camps. Germany realized that exerting pressure on Father Josef Tiso would jeopardize the important contribution Slovakia was making to the German war effort. In the protectorate, however, the status of the Gypsies mirrored that of the Jews. Between August 1942 and April 1943, 7,980 Gypsies were sent to **forced labor** camps, and thousands of others were deported to **Auschwitz** beginning in March 1943, and continuing through late 1944. The majority of the 6,000 to 8,000 Czech Gypsies who died in the *Porajmos* (Gypsy Holocaust) met their fate in Auschwitz.

Hungary's decision to join Germany in the invasion of the **Soviet Union** in June 1941 brought an increase in German pressure for Hungary to deal with its Jewish and Gypsy populations. According to the 1941 census figures, there were 57,372 Roma (as defined by language) and 76,209 Roma by nationality in Hungary. The Arrow Cross slogan "After the Jews the Gypsies" led to the deportation of Hungarian Gypsies to Auschwitz beginning in March 1943. Because German officials in Hungary were preoccupied with the roundup of the Jews, they did not begin to deal with the Gypsies in earnest until the fall of 1944. Approximately 28,000 Roma were deported from Hungary to Auschwitz, and only 3,000 survived the war. Specialists estimate that 32,000 Hungarian Gypsies died during the *Porajmos*.

In **Romania**, followers of Ion Antonescu declared that the Gypsy question was as important as the Jewish one. They denied that the Gypsies were part of the Romanian nation and bemoaned the fact that because of mixed marriages there were about 600,000 "half-castes" in the country. To protect Romania from the Gypsies, one newspaper called for the Roma to be eliminated from any part of the civic life of the state, and this was subsequently accomplished when they were placed in labor camps. Under Ion Antonescu, tens of thousands of defenseless Gypsies were deported to Transnistria, where more than half of them died from **typhus**. Approximately 36,000 Gypsies fell victim to Antonescu's anti-Gypsy policy.

Following the start of World War II, the removal of more than 30,000 Gypsies from Germany became a priority for **Reinhard Heydrich**, head of the **Reich Security Main Office** (RSHA) bureau. In the fall of 1941, Austrian Gypsies were sent to the **Lodz ghetto**, where they were segregated from the Jewish population. The great bulk of the Lodz Gypsies were eventually sent to the **Chelmno** extermination camp, where all of them perished.

Unlike the Jews, the Nazis made distinctions among the Gypsy population. Although the bulk of the Gypsies in both Germany and Austria were considered non-Aryan, there were Roma whom the Nazis classified as "pure" Gypsies. In October 1942, **Heinrich Himmler** issued a decree that distinguished between Mischlinge Gypsies and those considered of pure blood. Ultimately Himmler's order exempted some 13,000 Sinti and 1,017 Lalleri from the fate that awaited the great majority of Gypsies. In December 1942, Himmler ordered the **Final Solution** of the Gypsy problem, whereby most Gypsies were deported to Auschwitz-Birkenau, where they were exterminated. Exceptions to the deportations were made for the "socially adapted" Roma, former **Wehrmacht** soldiers, and those necessary for wartime labor.

The first transport of Gypsies from Germany and Austria arrived in Auschwitz in February 1943. They suffered extreme hardships, and many died of starvation and disease. Others were used in **medical experiments**, such as those performed by **Dr. Josef Mengele**, and the rest gassed. According to historian Yehuda Bauer, the total number of Gypsies from the Reich deported to Auschwitz was about 13,000. He also calculated that about 14,000 Sinti and Lalleri, defined by Himmler as pure Gypsies, were spared. The total number of Gypsies killed in the *Porajmos* is difficult to determine, but Bauer estimated the figure as more than 200,000.

– H –

HAAVARA AGREEMENT. *See* TRANSFER AGREEMENT.

HALF-JEWS. Under the **Nuremberg Laws** of 1935, half-Jews were defined as persons who were born to parents of mixed marriages but possessed at least two Jewish grandparents, regardless of their religious affiliation. *See also* MISCHLINGE.

HAYMAKING. The **Nazi** code name for the kidnapping of Polish and Russian children of Nordic or **Aryan** appearance, and their placement in **Schutzstaffel** (SS) maternity homes in **Germany**, where they were adopted by German families. This was a part of the operation of the *Lebensborn* organization created by **Heinrich Himmler** in 1935 for the purpose of increasing the racial stock of the German nation.

HEAVENLY ROAD. The **Nazi** expression for the tube-like (*Schlauch*) path to the **gas chambers** in the extermination camps. The German captors used whips, dogs, and clubs to coerce their victims down the "heavenly road," at the end of which they were killed. *See also* BARRY; DEATH CAMPS.

HERRENVOLK **(MASTER RACE).** The **Nazis'** racial definition of the **Aryan** German people. Nazi **ideology** emphasized the belief that the German people by virtue of their Aryan "blood" deserved to rule over non-Aryan or inferior peoples. *See also* UNTERMENSCH.

HET ACHTERHUIS **(The Rear Annex).** *The Rear Annex* was the original title of *The Diary of Anne Frank*, which was published in the **United States** in 1952 by Doubleday after a series of rejections by publishers. Alfred A. Knopf, for example, found the diary "very dull," dismissing it as a "dreary record of typical family bickering, petty annoyances and adolescent emotions." *See also* FRANK, ANNE.

HEYDRICH, REINHARD (1904–1942). Before his assassination in 1942, Heydrich was **Heinrich Himmler's** second-in-command in regard to the implementation of the **Final Solution**. As head of the **Reich Security Main Office** (RSHA), Heydrich issued the directives that mobilized the bureaucratic machinery in the war against the Jews. In his youth, Heydrich was strongly influenced by racial **anti-Semitism**, and after leaving the navy in 1931, he was attracted to the ideas of the **Nazi Party**. He joined the party that year and quickly attracted Himmler's attention. Tall, blond-haired, and with blue eyes, Heydrich epitomized the **Aryan** ideal, although throughout his life rumors circulated that he had Jewish ancestry.

Heydrich was a ruthless and calculating bureaucrat who made himself indispensable to Himmler. Nicknamed the "Blond Beast," Heydrich acquired a reputation for his use of extortion and terror against his political opponents. In 1938, he acquired authority over Jewish affairs in his capacity as head of the RSHA. Following the annexation of **Austria** in 1938, he dispatched his second-in command, **Adolf Eichmann**, to Vienna to organize the **Central Bureau for Jewish Emigration**, and he was so pleased with Eichmann's work that he created a similar office in Berlin.

Following **Germany**'s conquest of **Poland** in September 1939, Heydrich became involved in all aspects of Germany's Jewish policy. From the organization of the **ghettos** and the creation of the **Judenräte** (Jewish Councils) to the mass **deportation** of Jews from the annexed part of Poland, Heydrich was deeply involved in the strategic planning of Germany's Jewish policy. It was Heydrich's use of **Einsatzgruppen** in Poland, and more extensively in the **Soviet Union**, however, that was responsible for the murder of more than a half million Jews. It was also Heydrich who wrote the letter that was signed by **Hermann Goering** that authorized the plan to carry out the Final Solution.

In January 1942, Heydrich convened the **Wannsee Conference** for the purpose of coordinating the bureaucratic agencies that were necessary for implementing the annihilation of European Jewry. Following his assassination on 27 May 1942 by two **Czech** patriots, he was succeeded by **Ernst Kaltenbrunner** as head of the RSHA.

HIMMLER, HEINRICH (1900–1945). Himmler, as head of the **Schutzstaffel** (SS) and chief of the **Gestapo**, was responsible for constructing the **Nazi** terror state. A veteran of the failed Hitler **beer**

hall putsch in 1923, Himmler joined the SS in 1925, and became its head in 1929. In 1933, Himmler established the first **concentration camp** at **Dachau**, which served to incarcerate political opponents of the government. Himmler was obsessed with race and the occult and believed in the racial superiority of the **Aryan** people. It was this concern with racial purity that motivated him to found the *Lebensborn* organization. It was also his belief in racial superiority that moved him to implement **Adolf Hitler**'s war against the Jews, Slavs, and other groups that he deemed inferior. As the architect of the **Holocaust**, it was Himmler who was responsible for the construction of the German concentration camp system as well as the building of the **death camps** in **Poland**. In **Auschwitz**, Himmler authorized **medical experiments** on Jews, **Gypsies**, and asocial camp prisoners. Himmler was also responsible for using the camps to exploit Jews and other prisoners for **slave labor**.

The **Final Solution**, however, was for Himmler the culmination of his life's work. He viewed the Jews as the primary obstacle to **Nazi Germany**'s objective of attaining racial hegemony over the "inferior" peoples of Europe. For Himmler the Final Solution represented a racial Armageddon whereby the destruction of the Jews was a precondition for the triumph of the Aryan race. In planning the Final Solution, he approached his task with efficiency and dispatch, and rarely departed from the objective of annihilating Europe's Jews. Himmler, in his selection of **Reinhard Heydrich** as his second-in-command, chose someone who shared his views about Jews and the necessity of implementing the Final Solution. Toward the end of the war, and after failing to negotiate with the **Allies** for a separate peace, a disguised Himmler was captured by Allied soldiers. Before he could be tried at the **Nuremberg Trials**, however, he committed suicide.

HISTORIKERSTREIT (HISTORIANS' CONFLICT). In **Germany** a controversy, which has come to be known as the *Historikerstreit* (historians' conflict), questioned whether the **Nazi** crimes were unique or comparable to other national atrocities, such as those perpetrated in the **Soviet Union**. This revisionist view holds that, as appalling as **Auschwitz** was, it was only one form of **genocide** among other massacres that occurred in the 20th century. Ernst Nolte, a leading historian of the revisionist school, suggests that Auschwitz resulted from the Nazi fear of the Soviets and accuses critics of **Nazism** of ignoring what other nations have done in similar situations "with the sole exception of the gassing procedures."

HITLER, ADOLF (1889–1945). Adolf Hitler was born on 20 April 1889 in the Austrian town of Braunau, close to the German border. His father, Alois, was a civil servant who provided his son with the opportunity to acquire a good education, but young Adolf never reached his potential as a student and left school because of poor grades. His failure in school was the first of many failures that would turn Hitler into an embittered person who never accepted personal responsibility for his actions. His adolescent years were filled with contempt for people with advanced education, and in particular those with doctorates and law degrees. Architecture and painting were his two areas of interest, and he vowed that one day he would rebuild the city of Linz, where his mother had lived following his father's death. It appears that Alois had an uneven relationship with his son. Alois was hard and short-tempered, and may have frequently physically punished his son. Adolf was closer to his mother, who died of cancer in 1907. The family doctor, Eduard Bloch, was a Jew, and this fact has produced speculation that Hitler's later **anti-Semitism** was a response to his mother's death, which he blamed on the Jewish physician. This interpretation, however, fails to note that Hitler remained in touch with Bloch and later made possible his safe passage to **Switzerland** in 1938.

The origins of Hitler's anti-Semitism cannot be conclusively determined. In his autobiography, *Mein Kampf* (1925), Hitler wrote that he discovered his hatred of Jews in his Vienna years (1909–1913), when for the first time he encountered ultra-Orthodox Jews with their black caftans and long curly sideburns. This encounter, he wrote, repelled him and led to his conclusion that Jews and people like himself could never be part of the same nation. Another theory suggests that Hitler's fear of Jewish ancestry was one that lingered with him until he became chancellor of **Germany**. At that point he had the **Schutzstaffel** (SS) investigate his family history, which produced no evidence of any Jewish "blood."

In fact, Hitler's genealogy remains unclear, but this much is known: In 1837 Maria Anna Schicklgruber gave birth to an illegitimate child who was named Alois. In 1842, Maria was married to Johann Georg Hiedler, who did not bother to change Alois's surname. As a consequence, Alois continued to be known by his mother's maiden name. In 1876, Johann Nepomuk Hiedler, Alois's uncle, who had actually raised the child, took steps to legitimize Alois. From 1877 on, Alois called himself Hiedler or Hitler. Young Adolf was unaware of any other surname until his political opponents in the 1920s resurrected the long-forgotten story of his father's illegitimate birth and insinuated that Adolf Hitler's real grandfather was a Jew.

In *Mein Kampf,* Hitler denies that his father instilled in him feelings of contempt for Jews. Yet Alois was a follower of George Ritter von Schonerer's anti-Semitic pan-German movement and presumably participated in the growing hostility toward Jews that characterized Vienna at the end of the 19th century. According to August Kubizek, who was young Adolf's friend during their teens, Hitler's anti-Semitism was fully developed by the age of 16. Kubizek writes that Hitler was fond of one of his history teachers at the technical school he attended, who was also a nationalist and an anti-Semite. Hitler was also exposed to teachers who openly expressed their hatred of Jews in front of their pupils.

It appears that when Hitler arrived in Vienna in 1909, he was already receptive to the racist literature that permeated the right-wing circles of the *Volkisch* nationalist movement. Hitler's Vienna years only strengthened his anti-Semitism, which was useful as an excuse to justify his personal failures. Most notably, Hitler was frustrated by his inability to pass the drawing examination at the Academy of Applied Arts in 1909. Young Hitler was devastated that his opportunity to pursue a career as an architect had been denied him. Later, Hitler would refer to the news as an "abrupt blow." Soon anger replaced disappointment as he blamed his failure on the four of the seven examiners who were Jewish who graded his drawings. In a letter he sent to the academy, Hitler threatened that "the Jews will pay for this."

When Hitler enlisted in the German army in August 1914, he was already a confirmed racial anti-Semite. He had fled Vienna in May 1913 to avoid serving in the Austro-Hungarian army because of his refusal to serve in a country that tolerated racial groups such as the Jews. Military service, however, ended Hitler's aimless life when he joined the List Regiment, where he found acceptance by his comrades, although he still remained a loner. As a front-line soldier, Hitler discovered unknown qualities about himself, such as self-discipline and personal bravery. Ironically, despite the fact that his anti-Semitism remained unabated, his Jewish regimental adjutant, Hugo Gutmann, recommended him for one of the two Iron Crosses that he received for bravery under fire.

Following the war, Hitler was sent by his regimental commander to gather information about one of the many paramilitary organizations that appeared at the end of the hostilities. Hitler, however, quickly identified with the objectives of the **National Socialist German Workers' Party** (NSDAP) and joined it in 1919. During this period, Hitler's anti-Semitism was fortified by the short-lived Munich Soviet Republic, which ruled the city following the collapse of Germany in November 1918. The appearance of Jews in leadership positions in the Soviet-oriented party reinforced Hitler's belief in the ties that bound Jews to **Bolshevism**. In 1921 he became chairman of the NSDAP and made anti-Semitism central to its party platform. Following the abortive Munich **beer hall putsch** in 1924, when Hitler attempted to overthrow the government of Bavaria, Hitler spent nine months in the Landsberg prison, where he wrote *Mein Kampf* (My Struggle).

After Hitler's release from prison in 1925, he reorganized the NSDAP. From this point until the **Nazi** "seizure of power" in 1933, Hitler eschewed violence as an option in the overthrow of the **Weimar Republic**. Rather, he focused on constitutional means to attain his objectives, which came to fruition on 30 January 1933, when he was appointed chancellor of Germany by President Paul von Hindenburg. Following the Reichstag fire of 27 February 1933, a national emergency was declared. Hitler then suspended the basic civil rights of the German people, and after elections were held on 5 March, parliamentary rule was virtually suspended with the passage of the Enabling Act. By the end of March 1933, Hitler had established a dictatorship in Germany.

Hitler was an unusual executive. He encouraged his underlings to win his approval by pitting one against the other. Those who were most successful in the fight for bureaucratic survival, like **Hermann Goering** and **Heinrich Himmler**, found themselves presiding over vast political structures,. Hitler, however, was always atop the bureaucratic hierarchy and saw himself as the arbiter among the many jurisdictional disputes that he was asked to adjudicate. It is with this in mind that we can understand Hitler's relationship to the **Final Solution**. Ultimately, he "signaled" the course of action in regard to the **Jewish question**, but gave responsibility to subordinates, such as Himmler and **Hans Frank**, to implement the policy. When jurisdictional rivalry arose over Jewish policy, such as occurred between the Schutzstaffel (SS) and Frank in **Poland**, appeals were made to Hitler to settle the dispute.

Although no document is extant with Hitler's signature authorizing the Final Solution, our understanding of his administrative style suggests that such an order could have been signaled by one of Hitler's speeches or conversations with his subordinates. For example, in his speech to the Reichstag on 30 January 1939, Hitler made the following prophecy: "[I]f international Jewish financiers in and outside Europe succeed in plunging the nations once more into world war, then the result will not be the victory of Jewry, but the annihilation of the Jewish race in Europe." This type of circumstantial evidence has led historians to agree that regardless of the form in which the order was communicated, the **Holocaust** was not possible without Hitler's knowledge and consent.

As the war turned against Germany, Hitler retreated to an underground bunker in Berlin in January 1945. When the Soviets advanced on the city, Hitler wrote his last will and testament, in which he blamed the Jews for Germany's defeat, and exhorted the nation to keep its blood pure. He then married his mistress, Eva Braun, and committed suicide with her on 30 April 1945.

HLINKA GUARD. The **anti-Semitic** and pro-**Nazi** violent armed militia of the **Slovak** People's Party, which was supported by the **Schutzstaffel** (SS). Its founder, Father Andre Hlinka, was a Roman Catholic priest who died in August 1938. Following his death, the guard came under the influence of the Nazis. The Hlinka Guard were distinguished by their uniforms and their armbands, which were blue with a white double cross on a red cotton armband. The double cross symbol was a modification of the Slovakian national emblem, which honors the patron apostles of the Slavs, Saints Methodius and Cyril. Their black uniforms were modeled after those of the SS.

HOLOCAUST. The word derives from Greek and Latin and is translated as "something wholly burnt up" and, in its broader meaning, "a total destruction." The Holocaust refers to the **Nazi** objective of annihilating every Jewish man, woman, and child who fell under their control. By the end of World War II, approximately six million Jews had been murdered by the Nazis and their collaborators. **Elie Wiesel** is generally credited with associating the word "Holocaust" with the murder of six million Jews, although the term appears to have been used on the cover of the 3 October 1941 issue of *The American Hebrew*. In this issue there appeared a photograph of a large partly open gate, upon which is a Star of David, that shows two men, a French army officer or policeman and a man dressed in prayer attire, carrying a Torah scroll from a synagogue in northern **France**. The caption below the photograph reads in large print, "Before the Holocaust." Although Wiesel used the term in the 1950s, its general usage entered the mainstream during the late 1960s.

The term today has stirred controversy because other victims of the Nazi terror, such as the **Gypsies** and people of Slavic ancestry from Eastern Europe, claim that they were as much victims in the Holocaust as were the Jews. To differentiate between the more inclusive use of the word "Holocaust" and its special meaning within the Jewish community, many Jews have substituted the Hebrew word **Shoah** or *Churban* for the Nazi **genocide**.

HOLOCAUST DENIAL, This is the claim that the **genocide** of the Jews during World War II did not occur at all or that the **Holocaust** did not happen in the way historians have recorded it. Holocaust deniers reject the claim that **Nazi Germany** had a deliberate policy to exterminate the Jews of Europe or that mechanisms of mass killing, such as **gas chambers** or **death camps**, ever existed. Rather, Holocaust deniers claim that the **Nazi** concept of the **Final Solution** meant only the **emigration** of the Jews, not their annihilation. Referring to the Holocaust as a hoax, they deny that six million Jews were killed during the war, and claim that the **Diary of Anne Frank** is a forgery. Holocaust deniers view the Holocaust as part of a Jewish conspiracy to advance the interest of Jews, such as using the Holocaust to justify the creation of a Jewish state in the Middle

East, and **Israel**'s treatment of the Palestinians. For this reason, Holocaust denial is generally considered to be **anti-Semitic**. The motivation for Holocaust denial may be to rehabilitate the image of **Adolf Hitler** and his ideology of **Aryan** superiority. To prove that the Holocaust was a fabrication would restore not only Hitler to his rightful place in history but also racial theory as a legitimate subject for public discourse.

In the **United States**, Willis Carto was a leading figure in the then-postwar Holocaust denial movement. In 1969, he founded **Noontide Press**, which published *The Myth of the Six Million* by David Hoggan, the first major book stating that the Holocaust was a lie promoted by a Jewish-led conspiracy. Noontide Press soon became the major publisher of anti-Semitic, Holocaust denial, and racist literature in the United States. Professional historians criticize the methodology of the Holocaust deniers as being based on a predetermined conclusion that ignores extensive historical evidence to the contrary. *See also* AHMADINEJAD, MAHMOUD; BUTZ, ARTHUR R.; FAURISSON, ROBERT; INSTITUTE FOR HISTORICAL REVIEW; IRVING, DAVID; LAWS AGAINST HOLOCAUST DENIAL; NEO-NAZISM.

HOMOSEXUALS. Despite the presence of homosexuals in the **National Socialist** movement, the **Nazis** persecuted them both in **Germany** and in **Austria**. The Nazis viewed homosexuality as a danger to the future of Germany, as well as a threat to public morality. In 1935, the government rewrote the 1871 law that made it a crime to engage in a homosexual act, and those convicted of the offense were sent to **concentration camps**. Oddly, lesbians were not considered a danger to the nation and, therefore, few were arrested. The Nazis also ignored the presence of homosexuals in German-occupied countries.

Between 1933 and 1945, approximately 100,000 homosexuals were arrested under the 1935 law, with the courts convicting about half of the defendants. About 15,000 were sent to the concentration camps, where they were subjected to brutal conditions. In addition, they were required to wear a pink **triangle** patch on their clothing as a means of identification. Approximately 60 percent died in the camps from severe privations and abuse. Homosexuals, however, were not targets for annihilation as were the Jews and the **Gypsies**.

HÖSS, RUDOLF (1900–1947). The commandant of **Auschwitz** between 1940 and 1943. Höss had been a war hero during World War I and joined the **Nazi Party** in 1923. After having served time in prison for a brutal murder, he was released in July 1928, and for the next few years served in various capacities in Nazi Party service groups. In 1934, **Heinrich Himmler** urged him to join the **Schutzstaffel** (SS), and he was subsequently assigned to **Dachau**, where he served under **Theodor Eicke**. In 1938, along with his promotion to the rank of SS captain, he was assigned to the **Sachsenhausen concentration camp.**

In 1940, Höss was promoted to commandant of Auschwitz. In his administration of the **death camp**, Höss proved to be a tireless worker and an efficient bureaucrat in the implementation of the extermination camp. Höss, however, made it a practice to not personally attend the *Selektions* for the **gas chambers** or executions. Rather, he saw to it that the killing process ran smoothly. From all accounts, Höss does not appear to have been a sadist or even a radical **anti-Semite**. He was a family man who attended church, loved animals, and approached the killing process in a purely administrative manner. Höss's concerns dealt with the practical problems of adhering to timetables, the size of transports, the type of ovens that were to be used, and the methods of gassing.

Unlike **Christian Wirth**, Höss was an advocate of **Zyklon B** because he found the gas more efficient in dispatching the victims. Likewise, Höss found the gas safer, inasmuch as the operator was protected by a gas mask and had only to open the tin and scatter the contents through a grill on the roof of the chamber. Within minutes, the victims were dead. Höss would later write that the gassing process had a calming effect on him, because he always had a horror of the shooting process, "thinking of the number of people, the women and children. I was relieved that we were all spared these bloodbaths."

HUNGARY. The last phase of the **Final Solution** occurred in Hungary between 15 May and 9 July 1944. During these months, the Germans deported 437,402 Jews to the **death camps**. The number of Jews in Hungary at the time of the **deportations** numbered some 762,000, with an additional 100,000 converts to **Christianity**, who were considered Jews according to **Nazi** racial criteria.

Although integrated into the social and cultural life of Hungary, Jews became targets of **anti-Semitism** after World War I when they were associated with the short-lived communist dictatorship of Bela Kun in 1919. Following the war, Hungary suffered territorial losses that were accompanied by severe economic hardships. Under these circumstances Admiral Miklos Horthy became the regent of Hungary in 1920. In the decades that followed, anti-Semitism was legitimized by the Horthy regime. During the 1930s, Hungary and **Nazi Germany** drew closer because the latter sought to expand its influence in east-central Europe, and the Horthy regime sought markets for Hungary's agricultural products at a time when it was suffering from the worldwide depression.

Economic cooperation between the two regimes was joined by a political alliance as Hungary tied its political fortunes to **Germany** in hopes of reacquiring territory it had lost during World War I. Following the Munich agreement in November 1938, Hungary received part of its former territory at the expense of dismembered **Czechoslovakia**. As a result of its territorial acquisitions, Hungary added 250,000 Jews to the 400,000 who already resided in Hungary proper. Not all of Hungary's politicians, however, were enthralled with the German relationship. Some feared that a strong Germany would compromise Hungary's political independence, and others saw cooperation with Germany leading to the acquisition of additional territory.

The result was a cautious policy toward Germany. Hungary did not participate in the invasion of **Poland** and, in fact, allowed more than 100,000 Polish **refugees** to find shelter in Hungary. One of its territorial objectives, however, was the recovery of northern Transylvania from **Romania**, but the price for German support for this objective was the recognition of the Nazi *Volkesbund*, the spokesmen for the ethnic Germans residing in Hungary. Following Hungary's acceptance of the German demand, it became a partner in the Tripartite Pact that joined Germany, **Italy**, and **Japan** in a military alliance. By early 1941, Hungary was in a military alliance with Germany and would, in conjunction with its ally, declare war on the **United States** in December 1941.

The alliance with Germany led to the legitimation of the Arrow Cross Party, a pro-Nazi and vehemently anti-Semitic paramilitary group. The Hungarians also joined in the German invasion of **Yu-**

goslavia and the **Soviet Union**. Following the German defeat at Stalingrad, which included heavy Hungarian losses, the government sought to extricate itself from its ally. In late 1943, the Hungarians sent peace feelers to the West, which the Germans did not attempt to stop as long as Hungary maintained its economic agreements. Horthy also called for the withdrawal of his troops from the Soviet Union. It became apparent to Germany, at this point, that Hungary was moving closer to changing sides.

With the Red Army nearing the Carpathian Mountains, **Adolf Hitler** sent for Horthy in March 1944 and informed him of plans to occupy Hungary. Fearing that if Hungary resisted the Germans, the Romanians would take advantage of the situation and occupy Hungarian territory, Horthy capitulated to Hitler's demands, and on 19 March 1944, German troops occupied Hungary. In addition to troops, the Germans also sent their Jewish "experts" to plan the deportation of the country's Jews.

Among the experts were **Adolf Eichmann** and members of the Jewish Section of the **Reich Security Main Office** (RSHA), whose mission was to implement the Final Solution in Hungary. Although the first deportations began in 1944, daily life for Hungarian Jewry had deteriorated much earlier. The first anti-Jewish laws were promulgated by the Horthy government in May 1938, whereby quotas were placed on the number of Jews permitted in private business. In 1939, a more sweeping law defined the status of Jews and barred them from positions in the media as well as placing a quota on the number of Jews allowed in the professions. The laws also enabled the government to expropriate Jewish real property with compensation.

Following the annexation of territories in Ruthenia, the Hungarians rounded up some 17,000 stateless Jews and dumped them into German-occupied **Ukraine**. When Germany objected to the Hungarian action, 6,000 Jews were returned and used as slave labor; the other 11,000 were killed by **Einsatzgruppen** units. From 1942 to the German occupation in 1944, Jews continued to be subjected to **forced labor** but were not handed over to the Germans. The Hungarian government, in fact, refused the German demand that the Jews wear the **yellow Star of David badge** and be deported to Poland. In May 1943, Prime Minister Miklos Kallay rejected the **resettlement** of the Jews as a Final Solution as long as the Germans refused to satisfactorily respond as to their ultimate destination.

The German occupation of Hungary in March 1944 led to the deposal of Kallay and end of whatever protection Hungary's Jews had from being deported. Under the German occupation, Jews were now forced to wear the yellow badge, and with Eichmann's urging, the Hungarians issued decrees that further isolated Hungarian Jewry. Jews were limited in their ability to travel, their telephones and radios were confiscated, and they became ever increasingly targets for the violence of the Arrow Cross gangs. Next came the expropriations of Jewish property as the Jews found that their bank accounts, jewelry, and other valuables were subject to confiscation. Jewish enterprises and financial establishments were prepared for the Hungarian version of **Aryanization** as the government engaged in the wholesale confiscation of the economic wealth of Hungarian Jewry. Hungarians quickly learned that anti-Semitism was a profitable enterprise as they profited from plundered Jewish property.

Jews were concentrated in **ghettos** on 28 April 1944. For this purpose, Hungary was divided into five sections that included 55 ghettos and three **concentration camps**. The objective was to intern Hungary's 427,000 Jews and then deport them to the death camps. Toward this end, Eichmann ordered the establishment of a **Judenrat** (Jewish Council) for the purpose of carrying out the German decrees. From 15 May to 24 May 1944, a total of 116,000 Jews were deported to **Auschwitz**. By the end of July, a total of over 437,000 Jews had been deported to the death camp.

Fearing retribution from the **Allies** in a war that Germany appeared to be losing, Horthy halted the deportations, but his order was a case of "too little and too late." Most of Hungary's Jews, except for those in Budapest, had already been exterminated. Eichmann was taken aback by Horthy's action but continued to round up Jews for deportation. Between August and October of 1944, the situation of Hungary's remaining Jews improved, as Horthy was determined to remove his country from the war and halt the deportation of Jews. But, aided by the Germans, a coup against the government took place on 15–16 October 1944, which was led by Ferenc Szalasi, the leader of the Arrow Cross.

Szalasi became the new prime minister and immediately resumed the deportations. Auschwitz, however, was in the process of being dismantled, and instead of transports leaving the country for the extermination camp, Jews were placed in labor camps in Hungary. By the end of 1944, about 160,000 Jews were left in Budapest, where life was made miserable by Arrow Cross gangs. The winter only added to the suffering as cold and hunger pervaded their existence. By the end of winter, when the Russians occupied Budapest in February 1945, an additional 20,000 Jews had died. In a relatively short period of time, the Final Solution in Hungary had led to the death of over 450,000, or 70 percent, of the Jews of Greater Hungary. About 140,000 survived in Budapest and 50,000 to 60,000 survived in the provinces. *See also* BLOOD FOR GOODS; KASZTNER TRAIN; WALLENBERG, RAOUL.

HUNGER PLAN. One of the objectives of **Nazi Germany**, following the invasion of the **Soviet Union** in June 1941, was to reduce the Slavic population by 30 million. On 1 November 1941, **Hermann Goering** told **Italian** Foreign Minister Galeazzo Ciano, "This year, 20–30 million people in Russia will starve." The so-called hunger plan sought to starve Soviet cities out of existence, to use the entire food production of the conquered areas to feed the German armies, and to maintain nutritional standards at home. **Adolf Hitler** believed that one cause for Germany's defeat in World War I was the collapse of the home front because of malnutrition and starvation. He was determined that this would not occur in this war. The "hunger plan" was developed by Herbert Backe, in the Ministry of Agriculture; in meetings with high-ranking army generals, it was agreed that the armed forces would have to live off the resources of the conquered lands in the east, and concluded that "without doubt, umpteen million people will starve if what is necessary for us is taken out of the country." *See also* GENERAL PLAN FOR THE EAST.

HUSSEINI, MOHAMMAD AMIN AL-, HAJJ (1895–1974). The grand mufti of Jerusalem was the leader of Arab **Palestine** during the period of **Adolf Hitler**'s dictatorship in **Germany**. Husseini was among the first to greet Hitler's rise to power in Germany and informed the German consul in Jerusalem that "Muslims . . . welcome the new regime of Germany and hope for the extension of the fascist anti-democratic, governmental system to other countries." An admirer of Hitler, Husseini organized the "**Nazi** Scouts," based on the Hitler Youth, and the **swastika** became a symbol among many Arabs in Palestine. During the late 1930s, the mufti led the Arab effort to curtail Jewish immigration into Palestine and also orchestrated violence against Jews living in the **Yishuv**. The mufti's campaign against the Jews was aided by the Nazi government, which sent both monetary and logistical support as the violence intensified and which soon included the bombing of British offices in Palestine.

With the outbreak of war, the British sought to have him arrested, whereupon the mufti fled to Berlin where he served as a consultant on Jewish affairs, transmitted anti-Jewish radio broadcasts to the Middle East, and expressed support for the mass murder of European Jews. Having been taken on tour of **Auschwitz** by **Heinrich Himmler**, Husseini expressed the desire to "solve the problems of the Jewish element in Palestine and other Arab countries" by employing the same method being used in "the **Axis** countries." In his memoirs, the mufti wrote, "Our fundamental condition for cooperating with Germany was a free hand to eradicate every last Jew from Palestine and the Arab world. I asked Hitler for an explicit undertaking to allow us to solve the Jewish problem in a manner befitting our national and racial aspirations . . . according to the scientific methods innovated by Germany in the handling of its Jews. The answer I got was: 'The Jews are yours.'" Husseini helped to organize thousands of Muslims in the Balkans into military units known as Handselar divisions that carried out atrocities against **Yugoslav** Jews, **Serbs**, and **Gypsies**.

Following the war, Husseini was declared a Nazi war criminal at the **Nuremberg Trials** and sought by Yugoslavia as a war criminal. He subsequently escaped to Egypt, where he was given asylum and helped to organize former Nazis against **Israel**. Husseini's pro-Nazi sympathies were widespread among his Arab followers in Palestine, who regarded him as a hero even after the disclosure of his role in Nazi atrocities. *See also* WHITE PAPER OF 1939.

– I –

I ACCUSE. Protest against the **Nazi Euthanasia Program** spurred a response by the government. In August 1941, a Nazi propaganda film

I Accuse was released that justified the merits of involuntary euthanasia, including a lecture from a university professor endorsing the program. Reportedly, 18 million people saw the film.

IDEOLOGY. **Nazi** ideology sought to create a German nation that would incorporate the borders of **Germany** as it existed in the Middle Ages. For **Heinrich Himmler**, the boundaries of the old Germany reached as far east as Livonia, an area that encompasses present-day **Latvia** and **Estonia**. The policy of *Lebensraum* or "living space" required the conquest of these areas in the east, and the repatriation of ethnic Germans, living in the **Baltic states** and elsewhere, to the newly annexed German soil. The doctrine of **Blood and Soil** (*Blut und Boden*) also demanded that both the Slavic peoples and the Jews be removed from all areas under German control, allowing only a person of German or cognate ancestry to own land.

Nazi ideology also taught that much of history involved the struggle for supremacy between the "**Aryan**" people and the Jews or Semites. Drawing on examples, such as the wars between Rome and Carthage, and the Greek wars against the Persians, Nazi ideology insisted that the defeat of the Semitic peoples (Jews) was the necessary precondition for the restoration of Germany's greatness, which would last 1,000 years ("**Thousand-Year Reich**"). Germany's weakness as a nation was attributed to the mixing of the races that led to the diminution of German "blood" and the nation's decline. The ideology also contended that although the Aryan race was stronger than the Semites, the Jews had been victorious in one important area: religion.

Christianity was viewed as a Semitic import imposed on Germany and its pagan religions. The objective was to either destroy Christianity and restore the German gods of antiquity or to turn Jesus into an Aryan. Nazi ideology refused to accept the belief that Jesus was a Jew, and therefore set about to Nazify the German churches by purging them of all their traces of Jewish origins, including the primacy of the Hebrew Testament.

The **Holocaust** was the culmination of this conflict. It is an error to believe that Nazi ideology held the Jews as an inferior people. Rather, the Nazis viewed the Jews as bent on the nation's conquest through intermarriage, their control of the press, finance, industry,

Marxism, and the overall world of high culture. Jews, therefore, became the primary enemy in a struggle for the soul of Germany, whereby there was no room for half measures. From the **Reich** Hereditary Farm Law of September 1933 to the **Nuremberg Laws** of 1935 to the **death camps**, Nazi ideology fostered the belief that the biological survival of the Aryan race was predicated on the elimination of the Jews from Europe.

INSTITUTE FOR HISTORICAL REVIEW (IHR). The **Holocaust denial** organization, which was founded in 1978, describes itself as a "public-interest educational, research and publishing center dedicated to promoting greater public awareness of history." Historians have accused it of being an **anti-Semitic** "pseudo-scholarly body" with links to **neo-Nazi** organizations, and assert that its primary focus is to deny key facts of **Nazism** and the **Holocaust**. It has been described as the "world's leading Holocaust denial organization." The IHR publishes the *Journal of Historical Review*, which commenced publication in the spring of 1980 as a quarterly periodical. Publication was suspended in 1986–1987, resumed printing until 2002, and the journal is now again suspended. However, back issues continue to be distributed and sold by its associated organization, the **Noontide Press**.

INTENTIONALISTS. A school of **Holocaust** historians who argue that the path to the murder of millions of Jews was a straight one. From the beginning of the **Nazi** movement in the 1920s, radical **anti-Semites**, like **Adolf Hitler**, **Joseph Goebbels**, and **Heinrich Himmler**, used the language of extermination as one of many options in solving the **Jewish question**. In their objective of **genocide**, the Nazis were supported by large segments of the German population whose hatred of Jews was characterized by a virulent eliminationist anti-Semitism.

In support of their argument, the intentionalists cite Hitler's threat to exterminate the Jews in *Mein Kampf*, and his speech before the Reichstag on 30 January 1939, where he predicted that "if international Jewish financiers in and outside of Europe succeed in plunging the nations once more into world war, then the result will not be the victory of Jewry, but the annihilation of the Jewish race in Europe." The intentionalist argument contends that the murder of European

Jewry was always uppermost in Hitler's mind, and that World War II provided the opportunity to implement the **Final Solution**.

Historians associated with the intentionalist school include Lucy Dawidowicz (*The War against the Jews*, 1975), Gerald Fleming (*Hitler and the Final Solution*, 1984), and Daniel Jonah Goldhagen (*Hitler's Willing Executioner's: Ordinary Germans and the Holocaust*, 1996). *See also* FUNCTIONALISTS.

INTERNATIONAL COMMITTEE OF THE RED CROSS (ICRC).
The nonpartisan organization based in **Switzerland** was founded in 1863 as a private humanitarian organization. The essential responsibilities of the organization included the protection of wounded soldiers; monitoring the treatment of prisoners of war; providing prisoners of war with parcels such as food, clothes, and medicine; and gathering information concerning the fate of detained persons. The international community twice ratified conventions (1864, 1929) that recognized the ICRC's right to intervene in matters that fell under its mandate. Germany was one of 50 nations that ratified the convention in Geneva in 1929.

Following the organization of the **Nazi concentration camp** system in the mid-1930s, the ICRC visited the camps in **Nazi Germany** but relied on its German branch to monitor the treatment of the internees. As Nazi Germany moved from incarcerating Jews and others in the concentration camps to their **deportation** to the **death camps**, the victims looked to the ICRC for help. Despite its humanitarian mission, however, the response of the Red Cross to the **Holocaust** has become a controversial one. The position taken by the ICRC was to reaffirm its traditional mission of providing relief to persecuted groups without distinctions of race or creed. This meant that the ICRC would not make exceptions for Jews inasmuch as it did not regard their plight any differently than it did that of other victims of Nazi persecution. Although officials of the organization were aware of the deportations, they neither insisted on visiting nor were allowed to visit the death camps until the end of the war. This may be explained by their understanding that they lacked an internationally recognized basis for intervention.

From the beginning of Nazi rule in **Germany** in 1933 until the end of the war in 1945, the Red Cross inspected two concentration camps,

Buchenwald and **Theresienstadt**, where it was convinced that nothing extraordinary threatened the prisoners. In May 1944, **Heinrich Himmler** granted the ICRC permission to inspect the Theresienstadt camp and the so-called Familienlager (family camp) for **Czech** Jews at **Auschwitz**-Birkenau. In June 1944, an ICRC team consisting of representatives from **Denmark, Sweden,** and Germany visited the Theresienstadt camp, which Himmler had disguised not unlike a "Potemkin village" in order to impress the Red Cross delegation. The result was a 15-page ICRC report that was positive in its impressions of the camp, and the delegation concluded that there was no need for an inspection of Auschwitz-Birkenau. Less than three weeks later, the Familienlager was liquidated by the Germans.

The ICRC, however, did engage in quiet diplomacy but never appealed to public opinion in regard to the Nazi atrocities. Remarkably, despite knowledge of the carnage directed toward Jews, the ICRC never singled out Jews in its correspondence. This may have resulted from its fear that too much insistence on the fate of the Jews would endanger the ICRC's already limited relations with Nazi Germany. Jews, therefore, were placed in the general category of prisoners, deportees, and hostages whom the organization sought to protect in the same manner as military combatants. It is also possible that the silence of the ICRC was due to its fear that by publicly voicing its horror regarding the extermination of the Jews, it would compromise its ability to protect the millions of prisoners of war on the eastern front.

The ICRC, however, was willing to take risks on behalf of Jews in those countries where it believed it could make a difference. For example, it was instrumental in organizing the **emigration** of Jews from **Romania** to **Palestine** in 1944. In this enterprise, the ICRC was aided by the Romanian Red Cross as well as the **War Refugee Board**, although it was careful not to violate the British **White Paper of 1939**, which limited immigration into Palestine. Perhaps its most successful achievement on behalf of the Jews was in **Hungary**. Working with **Raoul Wallenberg** and the Swiss diplomat Carl Lutz, the ICRC found shelter for thousands of Jews in Budapest. Toward the end of the war, in March 1945, the ICRC negotiated with the **Schutzstaffel** (SS) about permitting the organization to enter the concentration camps to monitor the processing of the internees. The arrangement, however, was less than successful inasmuch as the Germans would permit the ICRC to inspect only **Mauthausen** and Theresienstadt, where only a few hundred victims survived.

Thus, although its record was a mixed one in regard to its response to the Nazi **genocide**, perhaps the ICRC's greatest failure was that it did not use its moral authority on behalf of the victims of the Holocaust.

IRON GUARD. Founded in 1927, the **Romanian** fascist Iron Guard was characterized by extreme **anti-Semitism** matched only by that of the Nazi **Schutzstaffel** (SS). Meshing **Christian** mysticism with a cult of death, the Iron Guard appealed to the country's peasantry, which constituted 80 percent of Romania's population. A primary objective of the fascist group was to exclude Jews from all aspects of Romanian life as well as to deprive them of their civil rights. Iron Guard propaganda blamed Jews for all of the ills that afflicted Romania, and during the 1930s, the Iron Guard forged ties with the **Nazis**. Seeking to exploit the Iron Guard for their own political purposes, various Romanian governments invariably underestimated the movement's appeal.

In 1938, King Carol II dissolved Romania's political parties in order to stymie the growing power of the Iron Guard and to maintain Romania's neutrality as tensions intensified between **Germany** and **Great Britain** and **France**. Following **Poland**'s defeat at the hands of Germany in September 1939, Romania tilted toward the **Third Reich**. At the beginning of World War II, King Carol II found himself forced to appoint Ion Antonescu as prime minister and Horia Sima, the leader of the Iron Guard, to an important government position. Subsequently, the Iron Guard became the country's only legal party and celebrated its accession to power two months later, when it commenced a campaign of terror against Romania's Jewish population.

The excesses of the Iron Guard brought a prompt response from **Adolf Hitler**, who required a stable and disciplined Romania in preparation for his attack against the **Soviet Union** in June 1941. Hitler supported both Antonescu's suppression of the Iron Guard and his establishment of a military dictatorship in Romania. Owing his position to Hitler's support, Antonescu proceeded to move Romania even closer to **Nazi Germany**. This new arrangement between the two countries resulted in Romania becoming "Hitler's favorite ally."

Despite its fall from power in January 1941, the Iron Guard continued to exert its influence on Romania's policy toward the Jews. In March 1941, Antonescu succumbed to pressure from the Iron Guard and enacted a series of laws that practically removed Jews from Romanian life. Ultimately, Romania's participation in the **Final Solution**, which resulted in the extermination of 420,000 of Romania's 770,000 Jews, can in part be explained by the radical anti-Semitism that the Iron Guard legitimized in Romania.

IRVING, DAVID (1938–). A specialist in the military history of World War II, Irving's books on **Nazi Germany** have proved highly controversial due to allegations against him of undue sympathy for the **Third Reich**, **anti-Semitism**, and his involvement in the **Holocaust denial** movement. Irving has been described as the most skillful preacher of Holocaust denial in the world. He is the author of 30 books, including *The Destruction of Dresden* (1963), *Hitler's War* (1977), and *Goebbels—Mastermind of the Third Reich* (1996). Irving's reputation as a historian was widely discredited after he brought an unsuccessful libel case against American historian Deborah Lipstadt and Penguin Books in 1996. During the trial, an English court found that Irving was an "active Holocaust denier," as well as an anti-Semite and racist, and that he "associates with right-wing extremists who promote **neo-Nazism**."

ISAAC AFFAIR. A term used by the **Nazis** for the **Kristallnacht pogrom**. "Isaac" was used pejoratively by the Nazis to describe the Jews in **Germany**.

"ISRAEL" AND "SARAH." In its efforts to isolate and identify **Germany**'s Jews, the **Nazi** government on 17 August 1938, ordered that all Jewish men were required to add "Israel" to their name, and all Jewish women, "Sarah."

ISRAEL, STATE OF. The State of Israel was founded on 14 May 1948, against the background of the **Holocaust**. Ultimately approximately 350,000 **survivors** of the **death camps** left Europe and immigrated to the Jewish state. One of the first decisions faced by Israel, in the aftermath of the Holocaust, was the emotional issue of its relationship with the West German Federal Republic. Under the leadership of Chancellor **Konrad Adenauer**, West Germany displayed a desire to compensate the Jews for the horrors of the **Nazi** epoch. Despite protests from Holocaust survivors and Israeli politicians such as Menachem Begin, the future prime minister, that compensation was "blood money " the decision was made to accept the reparations and seek a cordial relationship with West Germany. In 1952, the **World Jewish Congress**, led by Nahum Goldmann, negotiated a reparation agreement whereby West Germany made **restitution** of $845 million to Israel in the form of goods over a span of 12 to 14 years. The West German Parliament also passed a restitution law that compensated survivors for their suffering. Although a controversial and emotional issue, the reparations brought badly needed capital equipment, such as passenger and merchant vessels, tractors, heavy machinery, and concrete mixers, to the fledgling Jewish state. The reparation agreements with West Germany, for many Israelis, did not imply forgiveness for the suffering endured during the Holocaust. Rather, the action of West Germany was viewed as recognition of its responsibility to the victims of **Nazi Germany**.

An accounting of a different kind, however, occurred in May 1960 when the Israeli public learned that **Adolf Eichmann**, a major figure in the implementation of the **Final Solution**, had been kidnapped from Argentina by the Israeli secret service (Mossad) and brought to Israel to stand trial. Eichmann was the first Nazi to be tried in the Jewish state, an event that was televised in Israel as well as in the **United States**. Eichmann was found guilty and hanged on 31 May 1962. The Eichmann trial marked a turning point in Israel's understanding of the Holocaust. Native-born Israelis could not comprehend how their European brethren allowed themselves to be murdered by the Nazis with so little **resistance**. The Eichmann trial educated Israelis to understand how difficult it was to defy the Nazi objective of annihilating the Jews of Europe. As the trial brought home the anguish of the Holocaust, a new appreciation for the suffering and martyrdom of Europe's Jews took hold of the population. The interest in the Holocaust led to its memorialization with the establishment in 1962 of **Yad Vashem**, a museum for Holocaust remembrance, located in Jerusalem.

On 5 July 1950, the Israeli parliament (*Knesset*) enacted the Law of Return. The act guarantees the right of every Jew to enter Israel as an immigrant and to become a citizen immediately upon arrival. The passage of the law reflected not only the **Zionist** movement's objective to restore the Jews of the world to their ancient homeland but also the painful lessons of the Holocaust. Had there been a Jewish state at the time the Nazis came to power, would there have been a Holocaust? The Law of Return guarantees to Jews everywhere that the reenactment of restrictive immigration laws that prevented Jews from finding a refuge from persecution would no longer be a concern. Thus the Law of Return has become, for many Jews, an insurance policy against the day when Jews might once again be threatened with persecution, if not annihilation. In this respect, Israel has become the immediate haven that was denied to them on the eve of the Holocaust. *See also* PALESTINE; ZIONISM.

ITALY. Until the passage of the Italian racial laws in 1938, **anti-Semitism** was a marginal phenomenon in Italy. In fact, many Jews had supported **Benito Mussolini's** fascist movement until the mid-1930s. This changed in 1938 when Mussolini succumbed to **Adolf Hitler's** pressure and promulgated the "Declaration of Race," which was ostensibly modeled after the German **Nuremberg Laws** but had the effect of satisfying no one, least of all the **Nazis,** who criticized the many exceptions in the new racial laws. Yet the racial laws were enforced and took their toll on Italy's Jewish community.

There were approximately 57,000 Jews in Italy at the time of the passage of the racial laws in 1938. Jews constituted about 1 percent of the population, and about 10,000 were refugees from **Germany** and **Austria**. The Jewish community was predominantly middle class, and thoroughly assimilated into Italian life, characterized by a growing rate of intermarriage. Thus, the passage of the anti-Jewish laws in November 1938 came as a shock to Italian Jewry. Jews were excluded from the civil service and the army, and prohibited from owning enterprises that employed large numbers of Italians. In June 1939, the government barred Jewish professionals from serving non-Jewish clients, and limitations were placed on land ownership as well as on property in general. Consequently, what had once been a prosperous community was reduced to penury.

Jews, however, could take solace that, despite their economic, political, and social privation, the government resisted German demands to deport them. Although Mussolini was increasingly dependent on his German ally, the protection of Jews, both within the country and in Italian-occupied territories in **France**, **Yugoslavia**, and **Greece**, was a way in which Italy asserted its independence from its **Axis** partner. Combined with humanitarian concerns, Italian-occupied territories became havens of refuge for Jews. This protection, however, ended when Germany occupied Italy in September 1943. Between September and January 1944, at least 3,110 Jews were deported from Italy to **Auschwitz**, and an additional 4,056 arrived at the **death camp** a few months later as the Germans systematically deported Jews from northern and central Italy.

Because of the assistance of ordinary Italians, however, about four fifths of Italian Jewry was saved. But it is also true that the Germans were aided by Italian **collaborators** in the roundup and **deportation** of Jews to Auschwitz. Thousands of Jews were arrested by the Italian police, and others were betrayed in exchange for monetary rewards that the Germans offered for the denunciation of Jews. Approximately 8,000 Italian Jews perished in the **Holocaust**.

– J –

JAGERSTAB (HUNTER STAFF). The German central planning board whose responsibility was to provide conscripted labor for the armaments industry and other war-related industries. The *Jagerstab* seized workers from transports arriving from German-occupied territory, requisitioned **forced labor** from the **concentration camps**, and entered into contracts with the **Schutzstaffel** (SS) for concentration camp inmates. This activity resulted in the presence of an increasing number of emaciated and starving Jews in factories and labor camps.

JAPAN. Although allied with **Nazi Germany** during World War II, the Japanese did not share their **Axis** partner's solution to the **Jewish question**. The government, however, was influenced by **Nazi** propaganda and "specialists" on Jewish affairs, who wrote and translated

anti-Semitic works into Japanese. Nevertheless, prior to the outbreak of World War II in September 1939, 15,000 stateless Russian Jews were recognized as an autonomous community in Japanese-occupied Manchuria and northern China. The Japanese also provided a sanctuary in occupied **Shanghai** in 1938 to approximately 17,000 Jewish refugees from **Germany, Austria**, and **Poland**.

The ambivalent attitude of the Japanese toward the Jews may be explained by the absence of a tradition of anti-Semitism. Their ambiguous reaction manifested itself in the so-called **Fugu Plan**, whereby Japan adopted its pro-Jewish policy. The Japanese calculated that by providing a safe haven for Jewish **refugees**, "world Jewry," as an expression of its gratitude, would bring pressure on the **United States** government to accept Japan's "New Order" in Asia. Although many of Japan's Jewish "experts" accepted the negative imagery of Jews depicted in the **Protocols of the Elders of Zion**, they also believed that Jewish wealth and political influence could be turned to Japan's advantage. Ironically, the same anti-Semitism that resulted in Jews being sent to **gas chambers** in German-occupied Europe served to inspire Japan's pro-Jewish policy. This policy was further evident between December 1940 and November 1941, when approximately 3,500 to 5,000 Jews from Poland and **Lithuania** found sanctuary in Kobe, Japan. The fortunate Jewish refugees were the recipients of the travel visas issued by **Sempo Sugihara**, the Japanese vice-consul in Kaunas (Kovno).

Although 40 Jewish families already lived in Kobe, they did not have the resources to care for the large number of refugees. The necessary help came, however, from an unexpected source, the Japanese citizens of Kobe. They provided ration cards so that the Jews could purchase food, and in general showed many kindnesses to the newly arrived refugees. For example, they presented gifts to the synagogue on the Jewish holidays and helped the Talmudic students of the *Mir Yeshiva* (Hebrew house of study) to reconstitute their academy.

Toward the end of January 1942, however, the Germans placed pressure on the Japanese to change their policy toward the Jews. To please its Axis partner, the Japanese government established a **ghetto** for all Jews in February 1943. But because of Japan's sensitive relationship with the **Soviet Union**, approximately 3,500 stateless Russian Jews were exempted from residing in the ghetto. While

Jews endured many hardships in the ghetto, it did not compare with its European equivalent. Thus, the Jewish refugees of Japan lived in relative safety throughout the rest of the war.

JEHOVAH'S WITNESSES. Among the religious beliefs of Jehovah's Witnesses was their refusal to swear allegiance to any secular government or to bear arms for any nation. After the **Nazis** came to power in 1933, attacks against Jehovah's Witnesses commenced because of their beliefs and particularly their refusal to pay obeisance to the Nazi state. Between 1935 and 1939, the persecution of Jehovah's Witnesses took the form of placing many of their followers in "**protective custody**," and then moving them from prison to **concentration camps**, wherever they totaled a substantial percentage of camp prisoners. In May 1938, for example, 12 percent of all prisoners at **Buchenwald** and 18 percent at the women's camp at Lichtenburg were Jehovah's Witnesses. At **Dachau**, as well as in other concentration camps, the Jehovah's Witnesses were isolated and assigned to **forced labor**. At **Flossenbürg**, they were assigned to work in the **crematoria** and required to work on Sunday in violation of their religious beliefs.

After 1938, the Jehovah's Witnesses were offered the opportunity to be released from concentration camps if they renounced their faith and membership in the International Jehovah's Witness Association. Few did and their refusal resulted in the execution of more than 40 Witnesses in **Sachsenhausen** and brutal treatment in Buchenwald. In the camps, Jehovah's Witnesses were marked by an inverted purple **triangle** sewn on their prison jackets and trousers. About 2,500 of the 10,000 imprisoned Jehovah's Witnesses perished in the concentration camps. Once at war following **Nazi Germany**'s invasion of **Poland** in 1939, the Nazi military tribunals issued death sentences and executed more than 250 Jehovah's Witnesses for refusing to serve in the German military.

JEW HOUSE. Although **ghettos** were not set up for Jews inside **Germany** during the course of the **Third Reich**, between 1940 and 1942 Jews were evicted from their homes and moved into "Jew houses," where they were forced to live under increasingly overcrowded conditions. Based on a **Nazi** law promulgated in April 1939, landlords were allowed to evict Jewish tenants if alternative accommodations were available. Increasingly, municipalities began to concentrate the Jewish populations in unused barracks and similar types of buildings. In Mungersdorf, near Cologne, for example, 2,000 Jews were put into a dilapidated fort, 20 to a room. Some 38 such "residence camps" were created after the outbreak of the war.

JEWISH AGENCY. Under the mandate for **Palestine** that was assigned to **Great Britain** by the League of Nations in 1921, a provision was included for the establishment of a Jewish Agency that would serve as the executive and political policy-making body for the Jewish settlement (**Yishuv**) in Palestine.

Following the start of World War II, the Jewish Agency sided with Great Britain against **Nazi Germany**. Despite the restrictions of the British **White Paper of 1939**, the position of the Jewish Agency was, to paraphrase David Ben-Gurion, the agency's head, that it would fight the war as if there were no white paper, and fight the white paper as if there were no war. The contribution of Palestine Jewry to the war effort manifested itself in the participation of more than 30,000 men and women who served in the British army. In September 1944, the British granted permission for the Jewish Brigade group, which saw action in **Italy** under its own flag.

Under pressure from the British, the Jewish Agency authorized the deployment of volunteers from the kibbutzim (collectives) to parachute into Europe for the objective of locating and aiding **partisan** bands in **Hungary**, **Romania**, and **Yugoslavia**. The most famous of these Jewish volunteers was **Hannah Szenes**, who, at the age of 23, was captured and executed by Hungarian fascists. Her poem, *Blessed Is the Match That Is Consumed in Kindling Flame*, is among Israel's most famous poems.

The Jewish Agency also employed agents in Turkey to assist refugees who had escaped from **Nazi**-occupied Europe. Through the "illegal" immigration organization operating in Istanbul, Jewish Agency operatives were able to transport 3,500 to 5,000 Jewish refugees by sea, and 1,500 by the overland route to Palestine. The Jewish Agency, in the summer of 1944, also added its voice to those who called for the **Allies** to bomb **Auschwitz** and the railway lines leading to the camp, but to no avail, as these requests were rejected.

Inasmuch as its resources were limited in its efforts to rescue the millions of Jews targeted for extermination, the Jewish Agency focused on saving as many Jews as possible, with an eye to strengthening the Jewish community in Palestine, so that at the end of the war, it would be prepared to absorb what remained of European Jewry. *See also* ALIYA BET; TRANSFER AGREEMENT.

JEWISH ANTI-FASCIST COMMITTEE (JAC). In the spring of 1942, **Joseph Stalin** approved the creation of the Jewish Anti-Fascist Committee. One of the primary reasons for the creation of the organization was to appeal to world Jewry, but in particular to American Jews, for funds for the Red Army. The organization was founded at the time when the Red Army was staggering from the German offensive, and Stalin saw the need to create a committee of recognizable Jewish figures who could enlist the support of Jews the world over in support of the **Soviet Union** in their struggle against **Nazi Germany**. The initial members of the JAC included actor **Solomon Mikhoels**, who became its chairman; writer Ilya Ehrenburg; Yiddish poets such as Itsik Feffer, David Bergelson, and Lev Kvitko; and other Soviet Jews drawn from the fields of science and the military.

One JAC project was the publication of *The Black Book*, a collection of firsthand testimony of **Nazi** atrocities written by both Jews and non-Jews under the direction of Ilya Ehrenburg. The writer Vasily Grossman, for example, visited **Majdanek** soon after its **liberation** and was among the first to describe the horrors of the camp. Other contributors described atrocities that were committed by the **Einsatzgruppen** on Soviet territory. Stalin after the war, however, did not allow the book to be published and it did not appear in print until 1980.

The committee was allowed to publish a Yiddish newspaper, *Einikkeyt* (Unity), and Stalin allowed Mikhoels and Itsik Feffer to travel to the **United States** and **Great Britain** in order to win support for the Soviet Union from the Jewish communities in both countries. With the defeat of Nazi Germany and the dawning of the Cold War, Stalin no longer had use for the JAC, which had important contacts with Western countries. Stalin feared that the organization might call attention to the existence of ongoing **anti-Semitism** in the Soviet Union, and so the JAC was disbanded in November 1948. Many of its activists were arrested and tried for treason, espionage, and bourgeois nationalism. On 12 August 1952, 13 of the defendants were executed. As for Mikhoels, Stalin had already personally ordered his murder in February 1948.

JEWISH COMBAT ORGANIZATION (ZOB). The ZOB, first under the command of **Mordecai Anielewicz** and then **Marek Edelman,** was the force that fought the **Nazis** during the **Warsaw ghetto uprising**. The ŻOB confronted German troops under the command of **Schutzstaffel** (SS) General Jurgen Stroop, who sought to seal off the **Warsaw ghetto** for the purpose of deporting the some 60,000 remaining Jews to the **Treblinka death camp** on the eve of Passover in April 1943.

"JEWS NOT WANTED HERE." This phrase was displayed on signs that appeared throughout **Germany** after the **Nazi** seizure of power in 1933. The signs were temporarily removed prior to the Olympic Games in 1936.

JEWISH POLICE (JUDISCHER ORDNUNGSDIENST). *See* JUDENRÄTE.

JEWISH QUESTION. The "Jewish question" refers to the hostile response of European nationalists in the post-Emancipation era to the presence of Jews as a people in the midst of the newly created nation-states of the 19th century. The term became associated with the increased **anti-Semitism** in the later part of the century and into the 20th century.

In **Nazi Germany**, the term "Jewish Question" (*Judenfrage*) referred to the anti-Semitic racial theories and policies of the **Third Reich**. Initially the Jewish question was to be solved by resettling Jews in **Madagascar**, and following the **Nazi** invasion of the **Soviet Union** in 1941, the plan was to resettle the Jews in the vast lands of Siberia. After initial setbacks in the war, the decision was made by mid-December 1941 at the latest, to implement a so-called **Final Solution** to the Jewish question, the systematic annihilation of European Jewry.

JUDENBEGUNSTIGUNG. Often at great risk, some Gentiles in **Germany** disobeyed the law and helped Jews. The Germans pejoratively referred to this as *Judenbegunstigung*, or favoring or supporting Jews.

JUDENFREI **(FREE OF JEWS)**. Phrase used by **Nazis** to indicate that a given area under their control was empty of Jews as a result of **deportation** and extermination operations. *See also* EUPHE-MISMS.

JUDENJAGD **(JEW HUNT)**. The term was used by Germans in **Poland** to describe search-and-destroy missions against Jews.

JUDENRÄTE (sing. JUDENRAT) (JEWISH COUNCILS). Once the decision was made in 1941 to implement the **Final Solution**, the Germans were determined to involve the Jews in their own demise. Toward this end, the Germans established *Judenräte*, or Jewish Councils, in each of the **ghettos** in **Poland**. In November 1939, **Hans Frank**, the chief administrator of the **General-Gouvernement** in Poland, issued a decree that established the structure of the *Judenräte*. Communities of up to 10,000 Jews were to have a 12-member council, and ghettos in excess of that number had a 24-member council. The councils were to be elected by the community but subject to German approval. The reality was that the Germans appointed the membership of the Jewish Councils, and those who refused to serve were beaten or shot. The prototype for these councils was the *Reichsvereingung der Juden in Deutschland*, the Jewish Council in **Germany**, that the government established in February 1939. Members of the *Judenräte* were discouraged from displaying any independence but were expected to implement instructions received from the Germans.

The responsibilities of the Jewish Councils included maintaining law and order, allocating the meager food rations, providing a postal system, selecting people for **forced labor**, preparing a census of the Jewish ghetto population, collecting fines, providing shelter for the ghetto inhabitants, and rounding up Jews to fill the daily quotas for **deportation** to the **death camps**. The latter responsibility entailed the use of the ghetto police, whose task was to uncover those Jews who went into hiding in order to escape deportation. The ghetto police consisted primarily of Jews or converts who found themselves consigned to the ghetto.

In structure, the *Judenräte* varied from one part of German-occupied Europe to another. In the Eastern European countries, the councils operated in the local ghettos organized by the Germans. In **Romania**, however, the ghetto, and, therefore, the *Judenräte*, was national in jurisdiction, as was the case in **France**, the **Netherlands**, and Germany. In **Hungary**, the Jewish Council in Budapest was both national and local, and was the primary link between the **Nazis** and the Jews in the countryside.

Regardless of organizational structure, the *Judenräte* faced enormous difficulties. The most pressing may have been the shortage of food, which invariably led to near-starvation conditions. In a number of ghettos, the *Judenräte* leadership sought to purchase food from the "**Aryan**" side or obtain food by bartering products produced in the ghetto. Despite these efforts, there was never enough food, and starvation among the ghetto population remained a chronic problem. Although food often was smuggled into the ghetto from the outside, the Jewish Council was expected to arrest those involved in the practice.

Overcrowding and the lack of sanitary facilities, in turn, led to the spread of contagious diseases, which were endemic throughout the ghettos. The Germans welcomed the attrition rate caused by disease, although they held the *Judenräte* accountable for preventing its spread to the "Aryan" side. The Jewish Councils attempted to counter the spread of disease by organizing clinics and hospitals as well as providing aid for the suffering.

The moral dimension of the *Judenräte*'s responsibilities was tested in 1940 when the Germans demanded that the councils select Jews for the forced labor camps in Poland and in the rest of German-occupied Europe. This required the *Judenräte* to draw up lists of the Jews who would be torn away from their families and homes and sent to distant locations where they would endure severe brutality and suffering. At first, the Jewish Councils hesitated when the Germans demanded Jewish workers for the labor camps, but they eventually complied with the orders, fearing that if they failed to assume this responsibility, the Germans would undertake the task and inflict even greater brutality on the ghetto population.

The apparent "cooperation" of the Judenräte with the Germans often led to friction between the Jewish Councils and the community. As the Nazi pressure increased on the ghettos and the Jewish Councils implemented decrees from the Germans, their unpopularity grew proportionately among the Jewish population. The strain in the relationship between the Jewish leadership and the community was welcomed by the Germans. The Nazis calculated that the frustration and anger of the Jewish masses, trapped in a sea of despair, would be deflected onto the *Judenräte* rather than on themselves. The situation worsened when the Jewish Councils were instructed to round up Jews for deportation to the death camps. The initial batches of Jews who were gathered for deportation consisted of the sick and infirm. The *Judenräte*, in complying with German orders, may have felt that they were saving the majority of the Jews by weeding out the weak and the elderly. For many of the heads of the *Judenräte*, survival was linked with productive labor, and a great effort was made to keep the able-bodied off the lists for deportation.

The work of the Jewish Councils was assisted by the Nazi-created ghetto police or **Jewish police**. Unprecedented in Jewish communal life, the *Judischer Ordnungsdienst*, or Jewish police, ostensibly was responsible for protecting the Jewish community, but in fact its primary duty was to enforce German decrees. Those who joined the police did so for a myriad of motives, including the desire to serve the Jewish community. Others enrolled for their own personal gain, using their position to obtain food or an exemption from being seized for forced labor, or to protect their families from deportation. Requirements for police service were minimal, and the Germans insisted only that the recruits be able-bodied and, where possible, have had military training. Although the *Judenräte* sought police who would serve the interests of the Jewish community, they were not always successful. Some 70 percent of the police officers in the ghettos of the *General-Gouvernement* played no part in Jewish life, and many of them were strangers to the ghetto population.

The Germans were careful in approving candidates for police work inasmuch as they wanted only those who would blindly follow their orders. For this reason, they actively recruited apostates to Judaism as well as known **anti-Semites**. For example, the **Warsaw ghetto** police force included a large number of converts to Catholicism, who because of the German racial laws were designated as Jews. This reclassification to the status of a Jew made them bitter toward the Jewish population and, therefore, unsympathetic to its plight. Their bitterness translated into a zealous implementation of German directives.

Opposition to the leadership of the Jewish Councils appeared in some countries under German occupation. Generally the **Zionists** or Jews in the resistance movement challenged the authority of the Jewish Councils. This was true in Brussels, Budapest, and, at the end, the Warsaw ghetto. In the main, resistance to the authority of the *Judenräte* was not endemic throughout the ghettos of Europe, and where it did exist, it took on different levels of intensity. In fact, in some of the smaller ghettos in Poland, the Jewish Councils cooperated with the underground. Similarly, there is a mixed record in regard to the Jewish police. In the Warsaw ghetto, the Jewish police tried to uproot the underground, but in other ghettos the police ignored the existence of Jewish **resistance** movements. In the **Kovno ghetto**, the Jewish police actively helped the underground and participated in the resistance. Thus, although there was tension between the Jewish police and the underground, the response of one to the other varied from ghetto to ghetto.

JUDENREIN (CLEAR OF JEWS). Following the turn to the **Final Solution**, the Germans referred to the liquidation of a **ghetto** and the **deportation** of the Jews to the **death camps** as making an area "free" or "clear" of Jews. *See also* EUPHEMISMS.

JUDENTRANSPORT (JEWISH TRANSPORT). Inscription placed on segregated trolley cars and other modes of public transportation in **Nazi Germany**.

JUDENVERRAT (BETRAYAL OF THE JEWS). The most common invective directed against the **Judenrat** (Jewish Council) in the **Warsaw ghetto** was *Judenverrat* or "Betrayal of the Jews."

JÜDENZÄHLUNG (JEWISH CENSUS). In 1916, the German High Command conducted a *Jüdenzählung* (Jewish census) that disproved allegations of a lack of patriotism among German Jews, but the survey was not made public despite the fact that most German Jews viewed the war as an opportunity to prove their commitment to the fatherland. **Adolf Hitler**, in particular, accused the Jews of betraying the German war effort and Jewish soldiers of lacking ability and courage in battle. The reality, however, was far different. Despite charges made by **anti-Semitic** groups that they evaded military service, Jews flocked to the front and contributed 100,000 soldiers or nearly 18 percent of the 1 percent German Jewish population. Four fifths of these volunteers served on the front lines, 35,000 were decorated, and 12,000, or 12 percent, were killed in battle. The participation of the Jews in the war entitled them to believe that through the crucible of battle, they had proved their loyalty beyond question to **Germany**.

JUDISCHER ORDNUNGSDIENST (JEWISH POLICE). *See* JUDENRÄTE.

– K –

KALTENBRUNNER, ERNST (1903–1946). Kaltenbrunner, a radical **anti-Semite** and brutal **Nazi**, was **Reinhard Heydrich**'s successor as head of the **Reich Security Main Office** (RSHA) and the **Sicherheitsdienst** (SD) of the **Schutzstaffel** (SS) from 1943 to 1945. The nearly seven-foot Kaltenbrunner was responsible for the growth of the **Gestapo** in his native **Austria** as well as the organization of the **concentration camp** at **Mauthausen**.

Kaltenbrunner's antipathy toward the Jews manifested itself in his personal interest in the means by which Jews were killed in the **gas chambers**. During his tenure as head of the RSHA, Kaltenbrunner was responsible for the extermination of several million Jews. He was sentenced to death by the **Nuremberg** tribunal for crimes against humanity.

KANADA. *See* CANADA.

KANTOR, ALFRED (1923–2003). Alfred Kantor's watercolors and sketches recreating daily life in **Auschwitz**, **Theresienstadt**, and Schwarzheide constitute one of the few visual records of existence in a Nazi **concentration camp**. At the **Nazi** war crimes trials in **Nuremberg**, the **Allies** showed horrific films of the conditions discovered when they **liberated** the camps. But very few pictures exist that depict the workaday life of prisoners. Kantor sketched and painted surreptitiously, mainly at night.

Kantor's 127 paintings and sketches of concentration camp life were published in 1971 by McGraw-Hill as *The Book of Alfred Kantor*, which included his account of his experiences. In the introduction to his book, Kantor wrote, "My commitment to drawing came out of a deep instinct of self-preservation and undoubtedly helped me to deny the unimaginable horrors of that time." While some of the book's paintings were made inside the three camps and smuggled out, Kantor—who had destroyed most of his work, fearing that the Nazis would find it and kill him—re-created many pictures from memory at the end of the war.

At Theresienstadt, Kantor sketched daily scenes in the "model **ghetto**," including the new shops and fresh food that suddenly appeared in the town when an **International Red Cross** delegation visited. Theresienstadt, however, for most Jews was only a stopping place on the way to the **death camps**. Kantor was eventually herded into a cattle truck and transported to Auschwitz, where he sketched all the horrors of that camp: naked women being sorted into those who would live and those who would die; prisoners loading corpses from the **gas chambers** into trucks; the desperate search for food; the red glow of flames from the **crematorium** chimneys at night; brutal guards; and the infamous chief physician, **Josef Mengele**, in Nazi uniform. (An attached note said that "a motion with his stick" was sufficient to send a prisoner to his death.)

In 1944, Kantor was sent with other prisoners to help rebuild a German synthetic fuel plant at Schwarzheide, near Dresden. There he continued drawing, despite grueling 12-hour work shifts. When the war ended the next year, he was one of only 175 prisoners out of 1,000 who survived a **death march** back to Theresienstadt. The last picture, "Happy End," shows a liberated concentration camp inmate, still in his prison stripes, talking with friends on a Prague street on 10 May 1945, two days after V-E Day. *See also* ART AND THE HOLOCAUST.

KAPO. The term refers to a Jewish or Gentile inmate supervisor of laborers in the **concentration camps**, or a prisoner who was given an assignment and collaborated with the **Nazis**. The Kapos often exercised their authority over the concentration camp prisoners with great brutality.

KARAITES. A Jewish sect that originated in the eighth century in Babylonia and then spread throughout the Middle East. From the 13th century on, the Karaites made their way into Europe, where many of them settled in the Crimea. The Karaites also migrated to **Lithuania** and Russia, where they attained full civil rights in the 19th century.

The Karaites were granted their rights in **anti-Semitic** Czarist Russia because they claimed they were not Jews. This became an issue for the **Nazis** in 1935 when they enacted the **Nuremberg Laws**. The small Karaite community in **Germany** petitioned for an exemption from the anti-Jewish laws on the grounds that they were not of Jewish origin. In January 1939, the Germans concluded that the Karaites were not Jews and exempted them from the hostile measures that were directed toward the Jewish community in Germany and elsewhere in German-occupied Europe.

KARSKI, JAN (1914–2000). Karski, a member of the Polish underground and a courier of the Polish government-in-exile, was sent on a mission in 1942 to evaluate the conditions in occupied **Poland** as the situation of the Jewish population deteriorated. Twice Karski slipped into the **Warsaw ghetto** and met with Jewish leaders who briefed him on the terrible conditions faced by Polish Jewry. In November 1942, Karski arrived in London and reported on his mission to Prime Minister **Winston Churchill** as well to other prominent members of the British government. Based on his report, the Polish government-in-exile called on the **Allies** to take measures to prevent the murder of European Jewry. Karski subsequently went to the **United States**, where he met with President **Franklin D. Roosevelt** and disclosed the terrible plight of Polish Jewry. Assured by the president that something would be done, Karski spent his remaining time in the United States arousing public opinion about the **Nazi** atrocities against the Jews. In 1944, he published *Story of a Secret State*, an account of his witness to the unfolding tragedy of Polish Jewry. *See also* RIGHTEOUS GENTILES.

KASZTNER, RUDOLF (1906–1957). *See* KASZTNER TRAIN.

KASZTNER TRAIN. In his mistaken belief that the Germans had permitted the ransoming of **Slovakia**'s Jews for large sums of money, Rudolf Kasztner, a member of the Relief and Rescue Committee of Budapest, attempted a similar negotiation with the Germans as the **deportations** of Jews to the **death camps** began in 1944. After meeting with **Adolf Eichmann** and agreeing to pay a fee of $1,000 per person, a train with 1,684 Jews left **Hungary** in the summer of 1944, supposedly bound for **Spain** or **Switzerland**.

Instead, the train went to **Bergen-Belsen**, where the passengers were detained. The passengers included members of Kasztner's family as well as some of Budapest's more prominent Jews. Kasztner believed that this would be the first of many trains that would rescue the Jews of Hungary from the death camps. But subsequent trains filled with Jews did not follow, and Kasztner was accused of giving preference to his family and friends. Subsequently, he would also be accused of creating the illusion of rescue by promoting the idea that the trains would take the Jews to safety, instead of warning them of the deportations to **Auschwitz**. In a subsequent trial in Israel, Kasztner stood accused of making the roundup of the Jews of Hungary that much easier for Eichmann.

In July 1944, **Heinrich Himmler** gave permission for the **Schutzstaffel** (SS) to further negotiate with Kasztner, and subsequently Sally Mayer, a representative of the **American Joint Distribution Committee,** a Jewish relief organization, met with the SS at a location near the Swiss border. The meeting resulted in a halt to the deportations of the Jews of Budapest in August 1944, and the release of 318 Jews from the Kasztner train, who were subsequently allowed to enter Switzerland. In December, the balance of the "Kasztner train" Jews detained at Bergen-Belsen were set free and also allowed to enter the Swiss state. Shortly thereafter, the negotiations came to a halt and the deportations from Budapest continued. The Kasztner episode was a momentary interruption in a process that had the highest priority among the planners of the **Final Solution.**

KATYN. Following the Soviets occupation of the eastern part of **Poland** on 17 September 1939, the Red Army interned 200,000 Polish prisoners of war, many of whom were subsequently released or transferred to **forced labor** camps in southeastern Poland. The Polish officers, however, were **deported** to camps in the **Soviet Union**, where they were soon joined by Polish police, prison guards, and military police, but during April and May 1940 some 4,443 were taken by the Soviet NKVD to the Katyn Forest near Smolensk, where they were individually shot in the back of the head and buried in mass graves. An additional 20,000 Polish prisoners were killed, including reserve officers, doctors, professionals, landowners, civil servants, and others. Initially, the Soviet Union charged that the killings were committed by the Germans, but eventually it was proved that the murders were perpetrated by the Soviets. The extermination of the Polish prisoners of war was part of a much larger objective by the Soviets to eradicate the Polish national culture.

KAUFMAN, THEODORE N. The eccentric American Theodore Kaufman, in 1941 self-published *Germany Must Perish*, a 104-page pamphlet that called for the **sterilization** of all German men and dividing **Germany**'s territory among its European neighbors The book was used by **Nazi Germany** as propaganda to allege that "the Jews" were plotting against the country. In fact, **Joseph Goebbels**, months before Pearl Harbor, used the pamphlet to supposedly portray Kaufman as an advisor to President **Franklin D. Roosevelt**, thus revealing the true intentions of the president's administration toward Germany.

KENNKARTE. In July 1938, the **Third Reich** introduced a mandatory identification card for all people living in **Germany** that they were required to produce when confronted by a government official. The color of the Kennkarte was based on ethnicity with both Jews and **Gypsies** issued yellow ones. Grey Kennkartes were introduced in German-occupied **Poland (General-Gouvernement)** between 1941 and 1943.

KLARSFELD, SERGE (1935–) and BEATE (1939–). The Klarsfelds, best known to the public as "**Nazi** hunters," have for more than 30 years located and confronted Nazis who remained untried for their participation in the **Holocaust**. In 1968 Beate, the Christian daughter of a father who was a soldier in the **Wehrmacht**, publicly slapped Kurt Kiesenger, the German chancellor, in an attempt to expose his Nazi past. The controversy that ensued led three months later to Kiesenger's defeat at the polls by Willy Brandt, a leading anti-Nazi politician. Subsequently, the Klarsfelds located and exposed many Nazis who had managed to escape trial as war criminals. The list of names includes **Klaus Barbie**, Rene Bousquet, Kurt Lischka, **Maurice Papon**, and Paul Touvier.

Serge Klarsfeld published the *Memorial of the Deportation of Jews of France* (1978), which consists of a listing of more than 80,000 names of Jews deported to the East or killed in **France**. Each entry includes names, birth date, and birthplace of each deportee. In 1996, Serge Klarsfeld published a similar memorial entitled *French Children of the Holocaust*, a collection of photos and personal data on more than 11,000 Jewish children who were **deported** from their homes in France and put to death in the German extermination camps. The Klarsfelds head the Committee of Children of Deportees, a French organization whose objective is to bring French **collaborationists** to justice.

KOMMANDO. *Kommando* is a generic term for prisoners in **concentration camps** who were divided into different labor gangs—for example, building gangs, cleanup gangs, road-building gangs, and bodies gangs. In the **death camps**, the **Sonderkommandos** moved the dead from the **gas chambers** to the **crematoria**. Gangs extracted the gold-fillings from the dead, others were responsible for sorting the clothes of the victims, and gangs were assigned to shear the hair from the departed. In some *Kommandos*, which were considered more important by the **Nazis** due to the steady turnover of workers due to the high death rate, they received extra rations of bread and sausage, sometime margarine and jam.

KOMMANDOSTAB REICHSFUHRER SS. Heinrich Himmler organized this special unit of **Waffen-Schutzstaffel** (SS) and **Ordnungspolizei** (ORPO), or Order Police, following the German invasion of the **Soviet Union** in June 1941. The purpose of this force of 25,000 men was to engage in killing actions behind the front lines against **partisans**, Jews, communist officials, **Gypsies**, and the mentally ill.

KOVNO GHETTO. The **ghetto** was located in the **Lithuanian** city of Kovno (Kaunas). On the eve of World War II, there were approximately 40,000 Jews in a city of 160,000. During the period of Soviet rule from 1940 until the German invasion of the **Soviet Union** in June 1941, the rich Jewish cultural life of Kovno was destroyed and hundreds of Jewish families were rounded up by the Soviets and exiled to Siberia.

On 24 June 1941, the Germans occupied Kovno, but not before bands of Lithuanians set upon Jews in a killing spree. Between June and July 1941, more than 10,000 Jews were killed by Lithuanians and the Germans. The Germans followed the action against the Jews by establishing two ghettos in Slobodka, a suburb of Kovno, with a **Judenrat** (Jewish Council) appointed to implement German decrees. Thus the **Nazis** spared from immediate death the lives of approximately 30,000 Jews for the purpose of using them as **slave labor**. However, the reprieve did not last, inasmuch as the Germans resumed the killing of Jews. In the following two and a half months, more than 12,000 Jews were killed by the Germans.

Following the German *Aktion*, the Jews were given a period of respite from the killings, which lasted until March 1944. During this period, however, the Kovno ghetto was converted into a central **concentration camp** under orders issued by **Heinrich Himmler**. Jews were now moved to work camps where they endured the most excruciating hardships. In March 1944, the Germans resumed the killings when 1,800 persons, including infants, children, women, and the elderly, were dragged from their homes and murdered.

As Soviet troops approached Kovno in July 1944, the Germans decided to transfer the Jews to concentration camps in **Germany**. About 4,000 Jews were taken to Germany, where they were joined by a number of Kovno Jews who had been held in camps in **Estonia**. Many Jews, however, refused to be **deported** to Germany, and as a consequence went into hiding in underground bunkers. The Germans used bloodhounds, smoke grenades, and fire bombs to drive them from their shelters. The result was that approximately 2,000 Jews died as a result of the explosions. Only 90 Jews survived the German attack, and in August 1944 the Red Army liberated Kovno.

When the German concentration camps were liberated, nearly 2,000 Jews from Kovno survived. Together with those who went into hiding, the number of Kovno Jews who survived was 8 percent of the original Jewish population of the city.

KRISTALLNACHT (NIGHT OF BROKEN GLASS). The events of 9–10 November 1938 marked a turning point for the Jews of **Germany**. For the first time the government sanctioned the use of violence against its Jewish population, ostensibly in retaliation for the assassination of a German official in the French embassy by Herschel Grynspan, a 17-year-old Jewish refugee living in Paris. Grynspan's action resulted from information he received about his parents, who—like so many **Polish** Jews living in Germany—had been deported to an area on the Polish–German border. Feeling helpless to aid them, he vented his rage on Ernst vom Rath, the third secretary in the German embassy, although his intention had been to assassinate the German ambassador. The German government, upon learning of the shooting, immediately retaliated against the German Jewish community.

Joseph Goebbels organized a nationwide **pogrom** against the Jews. Led by **Sturmabteilung** (SA) groups, an orgy of violence spread through the country, with the police having been told to not interfere. Starting in Munich, about 500 synagogues were burned throughout Germany. Windows of hundreds of Jewish shops were shattered, and looters were encouraged to haul away jewelry, furs, and other items that they could carry. Jewish establishments were forcibly entered and trashed. Before it was over, 90 Jews were killed and about 30,000 Jewish men were placed under **"protective custody"** in **concentration camps** or **Gestapo** prisons. In Berlin, despite the prohibition on racial mixing, a number of Jewish women were raped by the Germans.

On 12 November 1938, **Hermann Goering** announced a series of measures that were designed to punish the Jewish community and reduce it to poverty. Jews were prohibited from owning retail stores as well as working as independent craftsmen. Jews were banned from attending concerts, the cinema, or other forms of public entertainment. They were even prohibited from driving automobiles.

The most devastating blow, however, was the announcement that German insurance companies were released from their obligation to cover the full damage done to Jewish property. Instead, Goering decreed that the Jews themselves would be fined for the cleanup. The total bill charged to the Jewish community was one billion reichsmarks, or $400 million, approximately 3,000 marks for every Jewish man, woman, and child living in Germany. In the aftermath of *Kristallnacht*, between 100,000 and 150,000 Jews **emigrated** from Germany. The pogrom also marked a change in German policy regarding the Jews. Prior to 9–10 November, **Nazi** strategy toward the Jews was to make their lives so miserable that they would leave voluntarily. After Kristallnacht, the German government embarked on a new policy of forced emigration, signaled by the roundup of Jews and their internment in concentration camps until they agreed to leave Germany.

The term *Kristallnacht* is not used in present-day Germany. Rather, the Germans use the word *Reichspogromnacht* to describe the events of 9–10 November 1938. The first use of the term *Kristallnacht* is attributed to Hermann Goering. It struck him as humorous to describe the shattered glass from the windows of Jewish stores and the broken glass from the synagogues that glistened on the wet cobblestones as Jewish "crystals" or "diamonds."

K-Z. German abbreviation for *Konzentrationlager* or **concentration camp**.

– L –

LABOR UTILIZATION (*ARBEITSEINSATZ*). The **euphemism** was used by **Reinhard Heydrich** at the **Wannsee Conference** in January 1942. At the meeting, Heydrich brought together representatives of the German bureaucracy whose participation was deemed necessary for the coordination of the **Final Solution**. The euphemism refers to Heydrich's decision to ship Jews from all over German-occupied Europe to the east, where they would be separated by sex. Those Jews capable of labor would be used to build roads, but he also anticipated that a great many would die because of the severity of the labor conditions or, as Heydrich put it, they would fall away through natural reduction. Those who survived "labor utilization" would have proved to be the toughest elements of Jewry, and consequently would have to be dealt with "appropriately," Heydrich's euphemism for the murder of Jews.

LANGE SONDERKOMMANDO. Named after its leader Herbert Lange, the special **Sonderkommando** unit was assigned to a euthanasia project, which gassed patients from asylums in East and West Prussia. Having accomplished its task by using **gassing trucks** to kill the targets of the **Euthanasia Program**, Lange and his squad were sent to **Chelmno**, where they introduced the method of piping in deadly **carbon monoxide** gas in the back of vans crowded with Jews from the **Lodz ghetto**.

LARGE SPACES. In the fall of 1939, Einsatzkommandos, under orders from the **Reich Security Main Office** (RSHA), accompanied the German army into **Poland** and carried out executions that were similar to the mass executions subsequently enacted in the **Soviet Union**. It was in **Poland** that numerous **Schutzstaffel** (SS) leaders who were later complicit in the **Holocaust** learned to think in "large spaces," a **euphemism** for mass murder. In violating civilized norms of behavior, according to historian Michael Wildt, the mass murder in Poland marked "the actual founding act of the Reich Security Main Office." *See also* COMMISSAR ORDER; EINSATZGRUPPEN.

LATVIA. When the German army entered Latvia in June 1941, many Latvians who had suffered under Soviet rule greeted them as liberators. The commanders of **Einsatzgruppe** A, therefore, had little difficulty in enlisting Latvians, who identified Jews with **Bolshevism**, to kill Jews. The major Latvian militia, the Arajs Commando, which numbered 400 men, engaged in killing operations in Riga and in the provinces. It is estimated that as many as 30,000 Jews were murdered by the Arajs Commando. About 2,000 Latvians also served in the German **Sicherheitsdienst** (SD) or Security Service. It is impossible to accurately estimate the number of Latvians who participated in the overall killing of Jews, although it is clear that the native population made it easier to implement the **Final Solution**. It is estimated that of the 70,000 Jews in Latvia, not more than 3,000 survived the massacres. In addition, the Germans **deported** about 20,000 Jews from the Greater **Reich** to Latvia, and about 1,000 survived the war.

LAW AGAINST THE OVERCROWDING OF GERMAN SCHOOLS AND UNIVERSITIES. Following the passage of the **Law for the Restoration of the Professional Civil Services** on 7 April 1933, the new **Nazi** government continued its anti-Jewish policies with the promulgation of this law on 25 April 1933, which restricted the percentage of newly admitted Jewish pupils and students to 1.5 percent and the overall percentage of Jews at any educational institutions to no more than 5 percent.

LAW FOR THE RESTORATION OF THE PROFESSIONAL CIVIL SERVICES. On 7 April 1933, the German government promulgated a law that barred anyone not of **Aryan** descent from public employment and established the principle of racial differences between Jews and Germans. The law marked the start of the **Nazi** policy to drive Jewish professionals, such as academics and attorneys, from public employment. German Jews who served in World War I were exempt from the law.

LAWS AGAINST HOLOCAUST DENIAL. **Holocaust denial** is illegal in a number of European nations. Many countries also have broader laws that criminalize **genocide** denial. In addition, the European Union has issued a directive to combat racism and xenophobia, which makes provision for member states criminalizing **Holocaust** denial, with a maximum prison sentence of between one and three years. In addition, the Council of Europe's 2003 *Additional Protocol to the Convention on Cyber Crime*, which concerns the prosecution of acts of a racist and xenophobic nature committed through computer systems, includes an article entitled "Denial, Gross Minimization, Approval or Justification of Genocide or Crimes against Humanity," although this does not have the status of law. Of the countries that ban Holocaust denial, a number (**Austria**, **Germany**, and **Romania**) were among the perpetrators of the Holocaust, and many of these also ban other elements associated with Nazism. The following is the status of Holocaust denial country by country where such laws are applicable:

- **Belgium**: Holocaust denial was made illegal in 1995.
- **Czech** Republic: In addition to Holocaust denial, the negation of purported communist atrocities was made illegal in 2001.

- European Union: While the European Union has not prohibited Holocaust denial outright, a maximum term of three years in jail is optionally available to all member nations for "denying or grossly trivializing crimes of genocide, crimes against humanity and war crimes."
- **France**: The Gayssot Act, voted for on 13 July 1990, makes it illegal to question the existence of the category of crimes against humanity as defined in the London Charter of 1945, on the basis of which **Nazi** leaders were convicted by the International Military Tribunal at **Nuremberg** in 1945–1946. When the act was challenged by Holocaust denier **Robert Faurisson**, the Human Rights Committee upheld it as a necessary means to counter possible **anti-Semitism**.
- Germany: *Volksverhetzung* (incitement of the people) is a concept in German criminal law that bans the incitement of hatred against a segment of the population. It often applies in (although is not limited to) trials relating to Holocaust denial in Germany. In addition, laws outlaw various symbols such as the **swastika** and **Schutzstaffel** (SS) runes.
- **Israel**: A law to criminalize Holocaust denial was passed by the Knesset on 8 July 1986.
- Liechtenstein: Although not specifically outlining **National Socialist** crimes, Item 5 of Section 283 of the criminal code prohibits the denial of genocide.
- **Luxembourg**: Article 457–3 of the Criminal Code, Act of 19 July 1997 outlaws Holocaust denial and denial of other genocides. The punishment is imprisonment for between eight days and six months and/or a fine.
- The **Netherlands**: While Holocaust denial is not explicitly illegal, the courts consider it a form of spreading hatred and therefore an offense. According to the Dutch public prosecution office, offensive remarks are only punishable by Dutch law if they equate to discrimination against a particular group. Article 137 of Dutch law stipulates "He who in public, orally, in writing or image, deliberately offends a group of people because of their race, their religion or beliefs, or their hetero- or **homosexual** orientation, shall be punished with imprisonment not exceeding one year or a third category fine."

- **Poland**: In addition to Holocaust denial, the denial of communist crimes is punishable by law.
- **Portugal**: Although denial of the Holocaust is not expressly illegal in Portugal, Portuguese law prohibits genocide denial.
- **Romania**: Emergency Ordinance No. 31 of 13 March 2002 prohibits Holocaust denial. It was ratified on 6 May 2006. The law also prohibits racist, fascist, and xenophobic symbols, uniforms, and gestures, proliferation of which is punishable with imprisonment from between six months to five years.
- **Russian Federation**: Russia does not have laws pertaining to Holocaust denial but its penal code provides for the investigation and prosecution of crimes motivated by racial, ethnic, or religious bias.
- **Spain**: Genocide denial was illegal until the Constitutional Court of Spain ruled that the words "deny or" were unconstitutional in its judgment of 7 November 2007. As a result, Holocaust denial is legal, although justifying the Holocaust or any other genocide is an offense punishable by imprisonment in accordance with the constitution.
- **Switzerland**: Holocaust denial is not expressly illegal, but the denial of genocide and other crimes against humanity is a punishable offence.
- **United States** and **Great Britain**: Holocaust denial is not criminalized in the United States because of the First Amendment of the U.S. Constitution. It is also not an offence in the United Kingdom, although laws against libel or inciting racial hatred may apply.

LAZARETT **(INFIRMARY).** The term was used to describe the sick bay at **Treblinka** where those who were deemed too weak or ill to work were sent. The camouflaged area, with a Red Cross flag flying over it, hid a large ditch where **Schutzstaffel** (SS) men and **Ukrainian** guards killed the Jews on the spot.

LEBENSBORN **(FOUNTAIN OF LIFE). Heinrich Himmler** believed that in the distant past, when the German empire stretched as far as Livonia, the Nordic German ruling class intermarried with the Slavic population, thus creating a population of mixed "blood." He was convinced that the Nordic traits of the Slavs made them dangerous to **Germany**. Thus, Germany had the choice of incorporating this remnant of mixed Nordic and Slavic blood into the nation or exterminating it. Himmler ordered the **Schutzstaffel (SS)** in **Poland** to search for this valued stock and bring the offspring to Germany, where they would be placed in special kindergartens or children's homes. The *Lebensborn* organization placed kidnapped Polish and other Slavic children who had Nordic or **Aryan** physical traits in the *Lebensborn* facilities, where it was anticipated that they would be adopted by SS families.

LEBENSRAUM (LIVING SPACE). A primary objective of **Germany** during World War II was the acquisition of living space for the purpose of extending the ethnic boundaries of "Germandom" eastward, in order to reclaim land that had once been part of German territory. Much of the territory was to be annexed at the expense of **Poland** and included Danzig, West Prussia, Pozaan, and eastern Silesia. **Heinrich Himmler**, however, believed that the German empire of the Middle Ages stretched as far east as Livonia, now part of the territory of **Latvia** and **Estonia**. *Lebensraum* was also a product of **Nazi** racial **ideology**, which held that the Slavic peoples of the east were inferior to the **Aryan** race. Ultimately, the millions of ethnic Germans living in the east would be resettled on the conquered territory, and the former inhabitants would serve as a source of cheap labor for the **Reich**.

LEMKIN, RAPHAEL (1901–1959). *See* GENOCIDE.

LEVELS DECREE. As part of the **Reich Security Main Office**'s (RSHA) continuing war on enemies of the Reich, **Reinhard Heydrich** issued on 1 January 1941 the so-called Levels Decree (Schadstoffwerteverordnung), which stipulated that "prisoners in **protective custody** who were less incriminated and absolutely capable of improvement were to be sent to the **concentration camps** in **Dachau** and **Sachsenhausen** and to the main camp in **Auschwitz**. Prisoners in protective custody, who were seriously incriminated but still capable of education and improvement, were to be sent to **Buchenwald**, **Flossenbürg**, and **Neuengamme**. . . . Those prisoners in protective custody who were seriously incriminated and had also been convicted of previous offenses and were 'asocial' were to be sent to the **Mauthausen**, where conditions were particularly severe."

LIBERATION. The **Allied** liberation of the **concentration camps** in late 1944 and 1945 resulted in an incidental and unexpected encounter with the victims of **Nazi Germany**. Units of both the American and British armies were therefore totally unprepared for what they found: piles of dead bodies, emaciated human beings, inmates near death because of **typhus**, and the most vile living conditions ever encountered by the Allied soldiers. Generals **Dwight Eisenhower**, George S. Patton, and Omar Bradley, the three most senior commanders, visited the Ohrdruf camp, and Patton became physically ill from the experience. Eisenhower insisted that the local Germans view the camps where the genocidal actions of the **Nazis** had been committed. The practice of exposing the local townsfolk to the horrors of the concentration camps was duplicated in almost all of the liberated camps.

The films and photographs taken by the Allied liberators have become part of the evidence of the Nazi **genocide**. The following is a list of the camps that were liberated by the Allies.

- **Great Britain**: **Bergen-Belsen** was liberated by the 63rd Anti-Tank Regiment of the Royal Artillery, accompanied by the British 2nd Army, with Canadian units, on 15 April 1945.
- **Soviet Union**: **Auschwitz** was liberated by the Red Army on 27 January 1945.
- **United States**: Ohrdruf was liberated by the U.S. 4th Armored Division on 4 April 1945; **Buchenwald** by the 9th Infantry Division on 11 April 1945; Nordhausen by the 104th Infantry and 3rd Armored Divisions also on 11 April; **Dachau** by the 42nd and 45th Infantry Division on 29 April; Woeblin by the 82nd Airborne Division on 2 May; Gunskirchen by the 71st Infantry Division on 4 May; and **Mauthausen** and Ebensee by the 11th Armored Division on 5 and 6 May 1945.

"LIFE UNWORTHY OF LIFE." *See* EUTHANASIA PROGRAM; T-4.

LINDBERGH, CHARLES (1902–1974). On 20–21 May 1927, Lindbergh, then a 25-year-old U.S. Air Mail pilot, emerged from virtual obscurity to almost instantaneous world fame as the result of his Orteig Prize–winning solo nonstop flight from Roosevelt Field on Long Island to Le Bourget Field in Paris in the single-seat, single-engine airplane, the *Spirit of St. Louis*. Lindbergh, an army reserve officer, was also awarded the nation's highest military decoration, the Medal of Honor, for his historic exploit. Before the **United States** entered World War II in December 1941, the iconic Lindbergh had been an outspoken advocate of keeping the United States out of Europe's conflict and he became a leader of the antiwar and isolationist America First Committee. In the aftermath of his visit to **Germany** in 1936, Lindbergh praised German accomplishments in aviation, and in 1938 he received a medal, the Service Cross of the German Eagle, from the German government. In the months prior to Pearl Harbor, however, Lindbergh gave a speech under the auspices of the American First Committee in Des Moines, Iowa, on 11 September 1941, where he criticized America's involvement by way of its support of **Great Britain** and singled out the British, the Roosevelt administration, and the Jews as the "major agitators for war." Although he understood the Jews' desire for "the overthrow of **Nazi Germany**," Lindbergh expressed concern over "their large ownership and influence in our motion pictures, our press, our radio, and our government."

The speech severely damaged Lindbergh's reputation inasmuch as he had repeated the same types of stereotypes that one associated with **anti-Semites**. Rabbi Irving F. Reichart of Temple Emanu-El of San Francisco retorted, "**Hitler** himself could not have delivered a more diabolical speech." Lindbergh claimed he was not anti-Semitic but simply responding to facts. He never apologized for his remarks because he believed that what he had said was true. President **Franklin D. Roosevelt** disliked Lindbergh's outspoken opposition to intervention and his policies such as the Lend-Lease Act. Roosevelt said to Treasury Secretary **Henry Morgenthau** in May 1940, "If I should die tomorrow, I want you to know this, I am absolutely convinced Lindbergh is a **Nazi**." Nonetheless, Lindbergh supported the war effort after Pearl Harbor and flew many combat missions in the Pacific theater of World War II as a civilian consultant, even though President Roosevelt had refused to reinstate his Army Air Corps colonel's commission that he had resigned earlier in 1939.

LITERATURE AND THE HOLOCAUST. The literature of the **Holocaust** consists of all the literary responses to the destruction of European Jewry, including **survivor** testimony, diaries of victims, memoirs of survivors, and documents collected by the Jewish community in the form of archives and memorial books, but it also includes novels and poetry written about the **Shoah**. Historian James Young has noted that memoirists like **Elie Wiesel** and Primo Levi have lamented the sheer impossibility of describing the **concentration camp** experience in what to them seemed to be an indescribable task. Nevertheless, since the end of World War II, there has appeared a growing body of literature about the Holocaust, especially in the form of memoirs, novels, and poems, that seeks to capture the suffering of the victims of the **Nazi genocide**.

Examples of the more significant memoirs, novels, and poems of the Holocaust would include *Night* by Elie Wiesel, who lost most of his family in **Auschwitz**. Until his father's death in **Buchenwald**, Wiesel and his father were together throughout their internment, the experiences of which he recounts in his autobiographical memoir, *Night*. After honoring his vow of silence for years, Elie Wiesel first published a Yiddish version of his Holocaust story in 1956. An English translation of the shortened French version of *Night* appeared in 1960. It was not the first book to detail the experiences of a Holocaust survivor, but *Night* has become one of the most widely read, if not *the* most read, book on the Holocaust.

Primo Levi and Elie Wiesel are among the better-known Holocaust memoirists. Levi's memoir, which recounts the year he spent as a prisoner in Auschwitz, *If This Is a Man* (1947), published in the **United States** as *Survival in Auschwitz* (1958), has been described by a number of critics as one of the most important works of the 20th century. A chemist by training, Levi was also a prolific writer. His work include a second memoir, *The Truce* (U.S. title, *The Reawakening*, 1963), two novels, short stories, poems, and essays, many of which deal with his experiences in Auschwitz. Levi died on 11 April 1987. Elie Wiesel said at the time that "Primo Levi died at Auschwitz forty years earlier." The coroner interpreted Levi's death as suicide, since in his later life Levi indicated he was suffering from depression.

One of the more controversial Holocaust novels is *Treblinka* by Jean-Francois Steiner. Written in 1967, his book remains unsettling because Steiner, a French Jew whose father died in a concentration camp, argues that many Jews perished in the Holocaust because they were too cowardly to fight back. His novel describes the prisoners' revolt in **Treblinka** in 1943 when the Jewish **Sonderkommando** (the laborers detailed to wrench gold teeth from corpses and bury the dead), with smuggled arms, killed 20 of their captors. Some 300 prisoners escaped from the camp, but all but 40 of them were eventually hunted down and executed. This, stated Steiner, was the honorable way for Jews to respond to their Nazi captors. Instead, in an interview he lamented, "I felt ashamed to be the son of this people of 6,000,000 victims who permitted themselves to be pushed into **gas chambers**. In the camps the victims themselves, the Jews, made themselves the accomplices of their extermination."

Steiner's rendering of the revolt in Treblinka is one of a number of novels that re-create actual events during the Holocaust. Novels such John Hersey's *The Wall* (1950) and Leon Uris's *Mila 18* (1961) depict the **Warsaw ghetto uprising**, and Leslie Epstein's *King of the Jews* (1979) satirically re-creates Chaim Rumkowski's leadership of the **Judenrat** in the **Lodz ghetto**. Epstein's novel was one of the first fictional treatments of the Holocaust to use humor and absurd situations. A novel told in a different vein is Giorgio Bassani's *The Garden of the Finzi-Continis* (1962), a work of autobiographical fiction. The story is set in the years 1938–1943 when an aristocratic Italian Jewish family became subject to **Benito Mussolini**'s racial laws. Like similar events in **Nazi Germany**, the 1938 racial laws clamped down on the rights of **Italy**'s Italian Jewish community. The author conveys the steady deterioration of the Continis as their precarious situation worsens during the war and **deportation** to the camps appears imminent. The novel was turned into a film and *The Garden of the Finzi-Continis* won the Oscar for Best Foreign Language Film in 1971. Robert St. John's 1962 novel, *The Man Who Played God*, tells the story of **Rudolf Kasztner**, who bartered with the Nazis to save Jews in Nazi-occupied **Hungary**, only to be assassinated in 1957 after an **Israeli** court accused him of having **collaborated** with the Nazis.

Babi Yar, where 33,771 Jews were massacred by the Nazis in a ravine outside Kiev on 29–30 September 1941, is the subject of Anatoly Kuznetsov's novel *Babi Yar* (1966). Published in the **Soviet Union**, the uncensored novel was carefully researched and included previously unknown materials about the killings. The same atrocity is the subject of poet Yegeny Yevtushenko's most famous poem, *Babi Yar* (1961). In his poem, Yevtushenko denounced the Soviet distortion of historical fact regarding the Nazi massacre of the Jewish population of Kiev, as well as the **anti-Semitism** then still widespread in the Soviet Union. The usual Soviet policy in relation to the Holocaust was to describe it as atrocities against Soviet citizens, and to avoid mentioning that it was a genocide specifically of the Jews. Therefore, Yevtushenko's work *Babi Yar* was quite controversial as it spoke not only of Nazi brutality but also of the Soviet government's own persecution of its Jewish population.

Different approaches to the Holocaust can be found in the fiction of Ahron Appelfeld, who is recognized worldwide as among the most profound literary novelists of the Holocaust and has met with international critical and popular acclaim. His books are written in Hebrew but many have been translated into English, such as *Badenheim 1939* (1980). Tadeusz Borowski's *This Way for the Gas Chamber, Ladies and Gentleman* (1967) is a classic of the Holocaust genre. Borowski was part of the **resistance** against the Nazis in Warsaw and was incarcerated at the Auschwitz **death camp**. In searing, satiric prose, Borowski details what life and death were like in the Nazi concentration camps.

The traumatic effects of the Holocaust on survivors have influenced the writing of novels on the subject. Two notable works of fiction that confront the trauma of survivors are American novelist Edward Lewis Wallant's *The Pawnbroker* (1961) and William Styron's *Sophie's Choice* (1979). Wallant's novel centers on Sol Nazerman, a Jewish pawnbroker who survived imprisonment in a Nazi concentration camp, even though his wife and family did not. The devastating experience and unrelenting memories inhibit Sol from emotional involvement with life. He has no faith in religion and less in mankind. Though he carries on an affair with a woman who was also a victim of the Nazi camps, it is without emotion and Sol grows increasingly bitter and callous, withdrawing still further from the world around him. *Sophie's Choice* is one of the few works of fiction dealing with the Holocaust that centers on a non-Jewish survivor (Polish Catholic) of the Nazi concentration camps. The novel was an instant best-seller and the basis of a successful film, and considered by some critics as both Styron's best work and a major novel of the 20th century. The plot revolves around Sophie's darkest secret: On the night that she arrived at Auschwitz, a sadistic doctor makes her choose which of her two children would die immediately by gassing and which would continue to live, albeit in the camp. Of her two children, Sophie chose to sacrifice her seven-year-old daughter in a heart-rending decision that leaves her with a guilt that she cannot overcome. Sophie's difficult "choice" has become an idiom of the English language. A "Sophie's choice" is a tragic choice between two unbearable options.

The following are significant works of fiction that continue to inform our understanding of the Holocaust: Saul Bellow's *Mr. Sammler's Planet* (1970), Cynthia Ozick's short story *The Shawl* (1999), Jakov Lind's *Landscape in Concrete* (1963), and Philip Roth's *The Ghost Writer* (1979), a satiric novel that illustrates how much **Anne Frank** has entered into the landscape of American culture and become an icon of the imagination. Also noted for their particular power in providing a sense of the terror of the Holocaust are *Jakob the Liar* by Jurek Bicker (1975), D. M. Thomas's *The White House* (1981), and *The Sunflower* (1976) by **Simon Wiesenthal**, a novel that raises moral questions when a Holocaust survivor is asked for forgiveness by a wounded Nazi soldier.

Popular novels whose themes focus on the Holocaust would include, among others, Herman Wouk's *Winds of War* (1971), which became a widely viewed television miniseries (1983) and *War and Remembrance* (1978), which also was made into a television miniseries (1988). Both of Wouk's novels were best-sellers. Two works of fiction that became best-sellers in the early 1960s were Katherine Anne Porter's *Ship of Fools* (1962), a novel that traces the rise of Nazism and **anti-Semitism** on the eve of the Holocaust, and *The Last of the Just* by Andre Schwartz-Bart (1961), a novel that chronicles the colossal horror of Christian Europe's thousand-year history of violence against its Jews, culminating in the Nazi Holocaust.

Theodor Adorno stated that not only is poetry after Auschwitz barbaric, but it is immoral to derive the slightest bit of aesthetic pleasure from the suffering of Holocaust victims. Adorno would later retract this dictum after reading, perhaps, the most famous poem relating to the Holocaust, poet Paul Celan's 1944 masterpiece *Todesfuge* (Death Fugue). Celan was only one of a number of poets who, through their poetry and figurative language, have allowed us to gain insight into the Holocaust. In addition to Celan, the verses of poets such as Nelly Sachs (*O the Chimneys*), Jakov Glatstein (*Dead Men Don't Praise God*), and Itzhak Katzenelson (*Song of the Murdered Jewish People*), among others, lament that there is no redemption, no consoling beauty to be found in the ashes of the *Shoah*. Many of these poets wrote their poems in Yiddish in the camps and the **ghettos**, and had Adorno been aware of their work, he might never have issued his condemnation of writing poetry after Auschwitz. *See also* ART AND THE HOLOCAUST; FILM AND THE HOLOCAUST; THEATER AND THE HOLOCAUST.

LITHUANIA. Following the pact between **Nazi Germany** and the **Soviet Union** in August 1939, Lithuania fell into the German sphere of influence. This arrangement was altered in September 1939 when Lithuania refused to join **Germany** in the war against **Poland**. In response, Germany exchanged its interest in Lithuania for territory in central Poland and Lithuania became part of the Soviet sphere of influence in the Baltic region. Following the invasion of the Soviet Union in June 1941, Nazi Germany occupied Lithuania, whose people, at first, welcomed them as liberators from **Bolshevik** tyranny. Among the Lithuanian population there was a sizable German-speaking population who sought a union with Germany.

Since the early 1930s, a nascent **Nazi** movement had operated in Lithuania that grew to about 15,000 people on the eve of World War II. The Lithuanian "**storm troopers**" modeled themselves after the **Schutzstaffel** (SS) and received their training in Germany. Following the German occupation of Lithuania, most of the country's Jews were killed by the *Einsatzgruppe*, who were aided by pro-Nazi Lithuanian supporters. On 25 June 1941, in one *shtetl*, for example, hundreds of Lithuanian Jews were killed, synagogues destroyed, and an entire residential district burned down. An additional thousand Jews were murdered the following night, many brutally beaten to death with clubs and iron rods. All of this was witnessed by the **Wehrmacht**, who did not interfere. Members of the surviving Jewish population were herded into **ghettos** in Vilnius, Kaunas, and Siauliai, where they were used for **forced labor** and gradually worked to death.

Perhaps the most brutal of the German massacres of Jews took place at Ponary located about six miles from Vilnius (Vilna) in July 1941. Tens of thousands of Jews from Vilna, as well as Soviet prisoners of war, were brought to the wooded area of Ponary and were shot to death in pits by the Einsatzgruppe and their Lithuanian **collaborators**. Estimates of the number of persons murdered at Ponary range from 70,000 to 100,000; the great majority of the victims were Jews.

The bulk of Lithuania's Jews were killed between mid-July and December 1941. The strategy employed by the *Einsatzgruppen* with regard to the Jews demonstrated to the outside world that the local population issued measures on its own as a natural reaction to decades-long repression of the Jews and to the terror of the communists during the previous occupation.

Beginning in the fall of 1942, tens of thousands of Jews were **deported** to Lithuania from other parts of Europe to be used as slave labor. They were used to mine oil shale for the production of synthetic fuel, and when they became too ill to work, many of them were killed, and others died of disease or hunger. With the approach of the Red Army in the fall of 1944, the remaining Jews from the camps were sent to the **Stutthof** forced labor and **death camp**. The number of Jews killed, including those deported to Lithuania from other parts of Europe, is estimated at between 200,000 and 500,000. About 20,000 Jews were able to escape to the Soviet Union, and another few thousand were rescued by Lithuanians.

LITZMANNSTADT. Following the **Nazi** conquest of **Poland** in September 1939, German officials began the process of replacing the name of Polish towns and cities with German ones. The Nazis, for example, renamed the city of **Lodz** to Litzmannstadt in an attempt to obliterate all aspects of its Polish identity. Other sites that were renamed include Kulmhof for **Chelmno**, and **Auschwitz** for Oswiecim.

LODZ GHETTO. After Warsaw, Lodz was the second-largest city in **Poland** and included the country's second-largest Jewish population.

Like Warsaw, Lodz was an important center of Jewish culture and commerce, and more than 50 percent of the city's Jewish population engaged in industry. The Germans occupied Lodz on 8 September 1939 and renamed the city **Litzmannstadt** in honor of the German World War I general Karl Litzmann. German documents concerning the Lodz **ghetto** refer to it as the "Litzmannstadt ghetto."

The brutal treatment of Jews began immediately after the German occupation of the city. The Germans next promulgated a series of decrees on 18 September 1939 that crippled its economic life. Jewish business establishments were confiscated, and Jews were forbidden from using public transportation. Bank accounts were blocked, and the amount of cash holdings was restricted. From 15–17 November, the Germans destroyed all of the city's synagogues, and Jews were ordered to wear a yellow armband.

As was the case in other occupied Polish cities, the Germans established a **Judenrat** (Jewish Council) in Lodz in October 1939, which was followed in December with the establishment of the Lodz ghetto. Between 1941 and 1942, some 38,500 Jews from outside Lodz, including Jews from **Germany**, **Austria**, and **Czechoslovakia**, were crowded into the ghetto, which by the beginning of 1941 numbered about 205,000 Jews. Although the Lodz ghetto was the last to be liquidated by the Germans, the living conditions were, at all times, deplorable. As in the **Warsaw ghetto**, the Jews endured insufferable hunger and were victims of illness because of the overcrowded conditions. Approximately 43,500 Jews, or 21 percent of the population, died from starvation and disease.

The Germans began the process of moving Jews from the ghetto to **forced labor** camps between December 1940 and June 1942, when 7,200 Jews were sent to a labor camp in the Poznan area. But in the beginning of January 1942, 55,000 Jews from the Lodz ghetto were deported to the **Chelmno death camp**, where they were gassed. This first **deportation** of Jews was followed by a second during the summer of 1942. About 20,000 of the children, and those deemed too sick to work, were **"resettled"** in Chelmno. The final series of *Aktions* against the Jews occurred between September 1942 and May 1944, and differed from the earlier deportations insofar as most Jews were not sent to Chelmno. Rather, the Germans turned the ghetto into a forced labor camp, with 90 percent of the Jews employed in factories. By August 1944, however, German plans for the ghetto changed, and the 77,000 remaining Jews were sent to **Auschwitz** to be gassed.

LONDON CHARTER OF 8 AUGUST 1945. The trials of major **Nazi** war criminals proceeded in accordance with the procedures outlined in the London Charter: the reading of the indictment; the accused entering pleas of guilty or not guilty; presentation of the evidence by the prosecution and defense; interrogation of witnesses and defendants; addresses of the defense and prosecution; final statement by the defendants; and judgment and punishment. *See also* NUREMBERG TRIALS.

LUBLIN GHETTO. Located in eastern **Poland**, the district of Lublin had a population of 40,000 Jews out of a total of 120,000 on the eve of World War II. Jews participated in the **resistance** to the German invasion forces, but as soon as the city was seized by the **Wehrmacht** (German army), Jews were taken and placed in **forced labor** gangs. The Germans also looted Jewish possessions, including the confiscation of their apartments. By the end of November 1939, Jews were ordered to wear the **yellow Star of David badge**, and their movements were restricted. Lublin was also linked to the ill-fated Lublin Plan, which would have moved Jews under German occupation to the region that bordered on the **Soviet Union**. Before the plan was dropped, however, approximately 63 Jews from other parts of the **General-Gouvernement** were deported to the area. The Lublin district was also the headquarters of the **Aktion Reinhard** chief, **Odilo Globocnik**, who was responsible for the operation of the **death camps** in the area, which included **Majdanek**, located in a Lublin suburb.

In the spring of 1941, the Germans established the Lublin **ghetto**, but not before deporting some 10,000 Jews to the surrounding areas, where they endured horrendous living conditions. The ghetto crowding peaked at 34,000 Jews and resulted in the periodic outbreak of **typhus**, which was caused by starvation, overcrowding, and the lack of adequate medical supplies. The **deportation** to the death camps began in March 1942, and by April 1942, more than 30,000 Jews had been exterminated in **Belzec**. An additional 4,000 Jews were consigned to a suburb of Lublin, which was called the "little ghetto," where the Germans engaged in frequent raids that resulted in the death of more than 2,000 Jews at Majdanek.

We know about the detailed conditions faced by the Jews of Lublin because a small number managed to escape and made their way to the **Warsaw ghetto**, where they told about the brutal treatment of the Jews. The unfortunate Jews who remained in the ghetto were eventually killed by early 1944. Following Lublin's **liberation** in July 1944, the city became a gathering place for **survivors** of the city and its vicinity as well as for Jews who had fought as **partisans** against the Germans and for those Jews who had taken refuge in the **Soviet Union**.

LUBLIN RESERVATION. *See* NISKO PLAN.

LUXEMBOURG. At the time of the German occupation of Luxembourg in May 1940, there were about 3,500 Jews, who constituted 1 percent of the population. Until September 1940, some Jewish property was confiscated but no **anti-Semitic** legislation was passed. All of this changed in September, when the Germans applied the **Nuremberg Laws** to Luxembourg, and subsequently forced the Jews into a **ghetto**. Jews were now required to wear the **yellow Star of David badge** and were assigned to **forced labor** brigades. Between August 1940 and October 1941, approximately 1,500 Jews managed to escape to **Vichy France** and **Portugal**. This was the last opportunity for the Jews to leave Luxembourg, as the Germans commenced the roundups that culminated in approximately 2,000 Jews being **deported** to **Auschwitz** and **Theresienstadt** between October 1941 and April 1943. It is estimated that about 1,950 Jews were exterminated, with about a third killed in the **death camps**. The rest either were killed in Luxembourg or became victims of the deportations in the countries that they fled to for sanctuary.

– M –

MACDONALD WHITE PAPER. *See* WHITE PAPER OF 1939.

MADAGASCAR PLAN. Following the German occupation of **Poland** in September 1939, the **Nazis** made plans to remove the Jews from the annexed areas of Poland and resettle them in the Lublin district, where they would reside in the transit camp at **Nisko**. When this scheme failed, the Germans focused on the French colony of Madagascar as an area of Jewish resettlement. The defeat of the French in 1940 made the Madagascar Plan feasible, but its implementation required the defeat of **Great Britain**, which controlled the seaway to the colony. The inability to defeat the British, however, forced **Germany** to abort the plan. Had the Madagascar Plan been realized, it would have resulted in the **deportation** of tens of thousands of Jews to an area ill-suited to absorb such a large number of people. Because the colony could not have provided infrastructure to sustain life, it is not unreasonable to conclude that the plan was a prescription for **genocide**.

MAJDANEK. Located in a suburb of Lublin, **Poland**, Majdanek was initially constructed in the winter of 1940–1941 as both a labor and an extermination camp for Jews, Poles, and Soviet prisoners of war. In 1942, the first Jews arrived in the camp from **Slovakia** and the **Protectorate of Bohemia and Moravia**. Subsequently, Jews from **Belgium, France, Greece**, the **Netherlands**, and Poland were sent to Majdanek. By the end of 1943, more than 125,000 of the 130,000 Jews in the camp were killed. In all, nearly 500,000 persons from 28 countries passed through the camp, with approximately 360,000 killed as a result of starvation, disease, and beatings, with about 40 percent exterminated in the **gas chambers** or through other forms of execution. Although Jews made up a minority of those killed in the camp, they made up a majority of the gassing victims. In addition, sadism among the guards was rampant toward the inmates, with reported cases of infants and children being killed before their mothers' eyes. The most notorious act of murder at Majdanek was the mass shooting of 17,000 Jews on 3 November 1943. *See also* DEATH CAMPS.

MASTER RACE (*MEISTERRASSE*). The fundamental belief of the **Nazis** held that in nature there is a hierarchy among human beings. The Nazis contended that the **Aryan** race was superior to all other races, and this earned it the right to rule over inferior peoples, such as the Slavs. The mission of **National Socialism**, therefore, was to weed out those who had corrupted German blood through intermarriage, such as the Jews, and breed future generations of blond, blue-eyed Germans who would restore the pure blood of Aryan superiority. *See also* IDEOLOGY; *LEBENSBORN*.

MAUTHAUSEN. The Mauthausen **concentration camp** was located near Linz, **Austria**. It was constructed in 1938, soon after the **Anschluss**, and consisted of two main camps as well as 49 subcamps. Mauthausen was both a **forced labor** camp and a **death camp**, inasmuch as it also included a **gas chamber** and a **crematorium**. The camp also used the gassing facilities in the nearby **Schloss Hartheim** to supplement its own killing process. The camp was the hub of the **Schutzstaffel** (SS) industrial empire in Austria. Those engaged in forced labor consisted of both Jews and non-Jews who were employed in the construction of subterranean tunnels to house factories for rocket assemblies and the production of plane parts. Approximately 120,000 prisoners were murdered or worked to death at Mauthausen. This included approximately 38,000 Jews. The camp was **liberated** by American forces on 5 May 1945.

MAX HERLIGER ACCOUNT. Fictitious **Schutzstaffel** (SS) bank account set up in **Swiss banks** by **Heinrich Himmler** in September 1940 for the purpose of depositing all of the valuables confiscated from the Jews. This included precious jewelry, gold and silver items, and the gold teeth extracted from the Jewish victims in the camps. "Saintly Max," as Himmler referred to the alleged account holder, did not exist.

MEDICAL EXPERIMENTS. During the course of World War II, the Germans conducted more than 70 medical research projects in the **concentration camps**. Using camp inmates as "guinea pigs," the experiments received the support of the entire medical complex of the **Third Reich**. Approximately 200 German medical doctors were assigned to the camps, where they carried out projects designated to them by German and **Austrian** research institutions. Camp inmates at **Dachau** were exposed to experiments involving high-altitude testing, whereby the victims were placed in pressure chambers with low pressure and little oxygen in order to duplicate the conditions prevailing at an altitude of 13 miles. The purpose of the experiment was to determine the necessary type of equipment required to save the crew of a damaged aircraft at 13 miles' altitude. The experiments took place with the full knowledge that human beings cannot properly function at an altitude of 3.7 miles or above without an adequate supply of oxygen.

Freezing experiments were also carried out at Dachau, whereby efforts were made to determine the most effective way of treating persons who were in a state of shock following a prolonged stay in freezing water or exposed to dry cold. Camp inmates were put into tanks with ice water and remained there for 70 to 90 minutes, or as long as it took for them to lose consciousness. Once removed from the tanks, the victims were denied painkillers to relieve their suffering.

The most notorious of the medical experiments, however, were those associated with **Dr. Josef Mengele**, the chief medical doctor at **Auschwitz** from 1943 to 1945. Because of his research interests, Mengele monitored the *Selektionen* in Auschwitz in hopes of identifying suitable victims for his experiments. Jews and **Gypsies** served as guinea pigs for his experiments on infants, dwarfs, giants, hunchbacks, and other malformed prisoners who piqued his interest. The most infamous of his experiments, however, were those performed on twins in hopes of finding a method that would produce a race of blue-eyed **Aryans**, thus realizing a prime objective of **Nazi** racial science. In Auschwitz's notorious **Block 10**, Mengele, along with other physicians, organized **sterilization** stations, which included the intensive use of **X-rays** on their victims. Mengele was also involved in the special dissection wards in Auschwitz, where autopsies were performed on murdered camp inmates and their body parts shipped back to German medical schools to be used for research purposes.

MEIN KAMPF **(MY STRUGGLE).** The part autobiography and part political testament was written by **Adolf Hitler** in 1924 while he was incarcerated in Landsberg prison following his conviction for attempting to overthrow the government of Bavaria. *Mein Kampf* is filled with animus toward Jews and his radical solutions for resolving **Germany**'s "**Jewish question.**" A comparison of the book with Hitler's speeches and writings about Jews on the eve of World War II reveals his consistent radical **anti-Semitism** as well as his extreme remedies in regard to the future of the Jews in Germany. The book, however, was not taken seriously by German Jews, even when he established a dictatorship in Germany. Many Jews believed that Hitler would moderate his anti-Semitic views lest he become a pariah in the world community.

Those who argue that the Holocaust was already in Hitler's mind when the **Nazis** seized power in 1933 (intentionalists) point to the autobiography as proof that he was obsessed with his hatred of Jews from the start of his political career, and that a straight road leads from Hitler's autobiography to the ovens of **Auschwitz**. This view supports the argument that the seeds of the **Holocaust** were already planted in *Mein Kampf.*

MENGELE, JOSEF (1911–1979). *See* ANGEL OF DEATH; MEDICAL EXPERIMENTS.

MEXICO. The term refers to Section B3 in **Auschwitz**-Birkenau where the seemingly colorful clothes of the **Hungarian** Jews were stored.

MIKHOELS, SOLOMON (1890–1948). *See* JEWISH ANTI-FASCIST COMMITTEE; STALIN, JOSEPH VISSARIONOVICH.

MILA 18. The bunker headquarters of the **Jewish Combat Organization** (ZOB), commanded by **Mordecai Anielewicz**, that fought the German troops during the **Warsaw ghetto uprising** in April 1943 was located at Mila 18. *See also* LITERATURE AND THE HOLOCAUST.

MILGRAM, STANLEY (1933–1984). In 1974, Milgram published *Obedience to Authority*, the results of a series of experiments in social psychology, in what has come to be known as the "Milgram experiment." After the disclosure of the horrors of World War II, many wondered, and not for the first time, how human beings could be motivated to commit acts of such brutality toward each other—not just those in the armed forces, but ordinary people who were coerced into carrying out the most cruel and gruesome acts. Stanley Milgram was one of those asking these questions and his subsequent experiments were inspired by the 1961 trial of **Adolf Eichmann** in **Israel**, from which he sought to comprehend the psychological dynamic that turned ordinary people like Eichmann into perpetrators of mass murder.

But Milgram did not investigate the extreme situation of war; he wanted to see how people would react under relatively "ordinary" conditions in the laboratory. How would people behave when told to give an electrical shock to another person? To what extent would people obey the dictates of the situation and ignore their own misgivings about what they were doing? Milgram, who taught at Yale University, conducted a series of social psychology experiments that measured the willingness of his participants in the study to obey an authority figure who instructed them to perform acts that conflicted with their personal conscience. The experiments began in July 1961, three months after the start of the Eichmann trial in Jerusalem, when Milgram devised his psychological study to answer the question: "Was it that Eichmann and his accomplices in the **Holocaust** had mutual intent, in at least with regard to the goals of the Holocaust?" In other words, "Was there a mutual sense of morality among those involved?"

Milgram's testing revealed that it could have been that the millions of accomplices were merely following orders, despite violating their deepest moral beliefs. This conclusion was based on the experiments where 37 out of 40 participants administered the full range of shocks up to 450 volts, the highest obedience rate Milgram found in his whole series. In this variation, the actual subject did not pull the shock lever; instead, he only conveyed information to the peer (a confederate) who pulled the lever. Thus, according to Milgram, the subject shifts responsibility to another person and does not blame himself for what happens. This resembles real-life incidents in which people see themselves as merely cogs in a wheel, just "doing their job," allowing them to avoid responsibility for the consequences of their actions. *See also* ARENDT, HANNAH.

MISCHLINGE. The **Nuremberg Laws** of 1935 established the definition of who was a Jew. Those persons having one or two Jewish grandparents were designated as part Jews, or *Mischlinges*.

MIT BRENNENDER SORGE. *See* "WITH BURNING CONCERN."

MORGENTHAU, HENRY, JR. (1891–1967). As secretary of the Treasury, Morgenthau was the highest-ranking Jew in the administration of **Franklin D. Roosevelt**. During his tenure as Treasury secretary, Morgenthau had considerable influence with the president and, as the conditions of the Jews in Europe deteriorated under the **Nazis,** Morgenthau used his position to initiate rescue efforts on their behalf. The creation of the **War Refugee Board** (WRB) in January 1944 was Morgenthau's most important achievement in his effort to save the remaining Jews of Europe. As the Nazi onslaught against the Jews intensified in 1942, Morgenthau concluded that the State Department was to blame in thwarting the efforts of those Jews who were legally entitled to enter the country under the immigration laws. By 1943, Morgenthau was deeply concerned about the impending fate of European Jewry as the massacres of Jews and the news of **gas chambers** reached the shores of America.

In January 1944, Morgenthau's assistant, Josiah DuBois Jr., a non-Jew, handed him his "**Report to the Secretary on the Acquiescence of This Government in the Murder of the Jews,**" which documented the State Department's "willful failure to act." Morgenthau tempered the title of the report and it was changed to "A Personal Report to the President" before delivering it to Roosevelt on 16 January 1944. Along with two other Jewish advisors to the president, Benjamin V. Cohen and Samuel Rosenman, Morgenthau met with President Roosevelt. In the aftermath of the meeting, the president established the War Refugee Board. The creation of WRB came too late to save the lives of millions of Jews, but it did manage to rescue approximately 200,000 Jews from **deportation** to the **death camps**. In 1945, Morgenthau promoted the so-called Morgenthau Plan, which called for the "pastoralization" of the former **Third Reich**, because he feared the rebirth of an industrialized **Germany** could bring about World War III. Roosevelt's successor, President **Harry S. Truman**, dismissed the plan as impractical.

MOSCOW DECLARATION. On 1 November 1943, Prime Minister **Winston Churchill**, President **Franklin D. Roosevelt**, and General Secretary of the Communist Party **Joseph Stalin** issued the Moscow Declaration, which condemned **Nazi** atrocities in Europe and promised to prosecute Nazi perpetrators after the war.

MUSELMANN. The term refers to **concentration camp** inmates who were on the verge of death from starvation and exhaustion. They were characterized by aimless wandering and their lack of response to any stimuli, whether it be a conversation or a savage beating from a guard. The origin of the term remains obscure, although camp inmates compared the condition of the *Muselmann* to that of a Muslim prostrating himself in prayer.

MUSSOLINI, BENITO (1883–1945). Mussolini, the Italian fascist leader, became prime minister of **Italy** in 1922 and subsequently became the country's dictator. Although viewed by historians as a pragmatic politician who did not consider **anti-Semitism** politically effective in Italy, Mussolini regarded anti-Semitism as morally repugnant and alien to the Italian people. Historian Meir Michaelis quotes Mussolini as stating that "**Hitler**'s anti-Semitism has brought him more enemies than necessary." Elsewhere, it is recorded that Mussolini considered **Nazi** racism and anti-Semitism as barbaric. In fact, Italian Jews, who consisted of 0.1 of the country's population, played a disproportionately important role in supporting Mussolini and the growth of Italy's fascist movement. By 1936, however, Mussolini moved closer to becoming an ally of Adolf Hitler as **Nazi Germany** supported Italy's invasion of Ethiopia. Thus from being critical of Hitler's early policies, Mussolini became an admirer of the Nazi leader, and emulated the Nazi **Nuremberg Laws** when he promulgated the Italian Racial Laws of 1938. These laws were partially imitative and partly written by Mussolini himself and were not due to pressure exerted on him by Adolf Hitler.

A number of historians attribute these anti-Semitic measures to a trend by the fascist government toward racism, but recent revelations from the diaries of Mussolini's mistress, Clara Petacci, present a different picture of Mussolini's true feeling about Jews. She records him as saying, "These disgusting Jews, I must destroy them all," and elsewhere Mussolini boasts to Petacci, "I've been a racist since 21." He even boasts in words that foreshadow the coming **Final Solution**, "I shall carry out a massacre like the Turks did," an illusion to the Armenian genocide in 1915. Historian Paul Corner of the University of Siena, Italy, commenting on these revelations released after more than 50 years in the Italian state archives, states, "People have always assumed the racial laws were a political instrument, not part of a policy in which he sincerely believed. This would suggest quite the opposite."

– N –

NANSEN PASSPORTS. The Nansen Passport was named after Fridtjof Nansen (1861–1930), the League of Nations administrator for refugee problems from 1919 to 1921. The passport was the work of the League of Nations, which authorized their use to help stateless refugees. League diplomats, such as James G. McDonald, unsuccessfully tried to issue Nansen Passports to Jewish refugees escaping **Nazi** persecution, but many countries, like the **United States**, refused to accept the passport as a legally binding document. *See also* EVIAN CONFERENCE; REFUGEE CRISIS.

NATIONAL COMMITTEE FOR THE RESCUE FROM NAZI TERROR. The British organization was founded in March 1943 for the purpose of devising strategies to rescue Europe's Jews from the **Nazi genocide**. The chief organizers of the group were Eleanor Rathbone, a Unitarian and one of the first women in Parliament, and Victor Gollancz, a publisher and the author of an influential pamphlet, *Let My People Go*. The organization's supporters included the Archbishops of Canterbury and York, the Moderators of the Church of Scotland and the Free Church of Scotland, Harold Nicolson, and other influential leaders of both the Jewish and non-Jewish communities.

NATIONAL SOCIALISM. *See* NAZI.

NATIONAL SOCIALIST GERMAN WORKERS' PARTY (NSDAP). *See* NAZI PARTY.

NATIONAL SOCIALIST PARTY. *See* NAZI PARTY.

NAZI(S). Nazi is an acronym formed from the syllables of the words National and Socialist. Depending on the context, the term is used to describe the German government under **Adolf Hitler** as well as its policies and **ideology**. The word is also used to characterize those who belonged to the **Nazi Party**.

NAZI GERMANY. **Nazi** Germany refers to the totalitarian rule of **Adolf Hitler** and the **National Socialist Party** between 1933 and 1945. Appointed chancellor in April 1933, Hitler established his dictatorship over **Germany** following the death of President Paul von Hindenburg on 2 August 1934, when he took the title of **Führer** or "leader." Hitler immediately imposed his will over the German people by creating a police state and a network of **concentration camps** that served to incarcerate his political enemies as well as elements in German society that he sought to eliminate.

Hitler sought to establish a racial state in Nazi Germany that distinguished between those of **Aryan** "blood" and non-Aryans. To that end he sought to remove Jews from German life and subsequently through the **Reich** Citizenship Law of 1935, defined citizenship as applying only to Germans or people of "related blood." Through this law, the Jews were effectively removed as nationals of Germany.

Nazi Germany was constructed on certain beliefs that emanated from Hitler. In addition to its racial policies, the **Third Reich** instituted a **Euthanasia Program** in 1939, which was grounded in the Führer's understanding of Darwinism, whereby he sought to "weed" out the *Volk*'s most unfit people. Racial hygiene became the policy whereby the handicapped, the mentally retarded, the chronically ill, and other categories of the population that were deemed **"life unworthy of life"** were murdered through the organization of so-called health courts, which were administered by physicians. This was not all. Anticipating the coming of war in the east, Hitler believed that one cause for Germany's loss in World War I was the severe food shortages that had led to the demoralization of the population, and he was determined not to allow this to happen in the future. Unproductive members of society, therefore, were targeted for elimination because they ingested the nation's food resources. The Euthanasia Program was also about reproduction. In war, the best of the *Volk* die in battle and the least fit survive, thus the nation is genetically weakened, and Nazi policy was to strengthen the nation's gene pool by eliminating the unfit.

The above policies, among others, were grounded in the Nazi held belief in the organic community. This concept implied that the Führer was like the human brain, giving unquestioned direction to the body or nation. Early in the history of the Third Reich, the concept of the *Fuhrerprinzip* was implemented wherein all authority derived from the unquestioned directives of the leader. In Nazi Germany, Hitler provided direction and his subordinates were expected to unhesitatingly implement his orders. The extermination of the Jews, for example, did not require a written order from Hitler because a verbal order, even a nod, had the same authority as a document.

The human body corresponding to the population of the Third Reich was defined in the expression *Volksgemeinschaft* or "people's community." The term implied the establishment in Nazi Germany of a national community based on the Aryan race. The expectation was that all institutions of German life were to be synchronized (*Gleichschaltung*) to conform (like the human body) to the policies of Hitler. Those who refused to adapt were targeted for concentration camps or worse.

Following Nazi Germany's invasion of **Poland** in September 1939, a primary objective was to acquire "living space" (*Lebensraum*) in the east for the purpose of extending the ethnic boundaries of Germany with the purpose of uniting ethnic Germans into the Reich. The policy of *Lebensraum* was also the product of Nazi racial **ideology**, which held that the Slavic peoples of the east were inferior to the Aryan race. The objective was to resettle the Slavic population on the conquered territories, which stretched as far as **Latvia** and **Estonia**, and the inhabitants were to serve as a source of cheap labor for the Reich.

Hitler was also obsessed with conquering the **Soviet Union** and destroying the base for the spread of **Bolshevism**, which he believed was a Jewish creation. In accordance with his theories of race, the invasions of both Poland and the Soviet Union were designed as a *Volkstumkampf*, or racial war, a term used by Adolf Hitler and the hierarchy of the **Schutzstaffel** (SS) to describe Nazi Germany's war against the Jews, Poles, and the Slavic peoples of Eastern Europe in general. The war in the east was not an ordinary war but an ethnic struggle that combined Nazi Germany's ideological racial goals with Germany's military and political objectives of *Lebensraum*, or the establishment of a German empire in Eastern Europe.

The late historian Lucy Dawidowicz titled her classic history of the **Holocaust** *The War against the Jews* (1975). What she inferred was that World War II was both a conventional war fought by competing nations and also a racial war in which Nazi Germany's objective was to murder every last Jewish man, woman, and child. It was no coincidence that with the invasion of the Soviet Union, which Hitler associated with Jewish Bolshevism, the decision was made to implement the **Final Solution** to the **Jewish question**. The deliberate **genocide** of the Jews was the unique crime of Nazi Germany and what separates it from previous wars in German history.

NAZI PARTY (NATIONALSOZIALISTCHE DEUTSCHE ARBEITERPARTEI) (NSDAP). In 1918, Anton Drexler and Karl Harrar, both railroad workers, founded the German Workers' Party with the financial help of the **Thule Society**. In 1919, **Adolf Hitler** was sent by his army regiment commander to spy on the activities of the party. However, he quickly became impressed with the party's program and soon became its chairman of propaganda. It was Hitler who added the term "National Socialist" to German Workers' Party as well as making **anti-Semitism** central to the party platform. In July 1921, Hitler became chairman of the NSDAP, and later that year he was designated as party **Führer**, or leader.

Included in the 25-point program that the fledgling Nazi Party approved in February 1920 was its demand that all Jews who had arrived in **Germany** prior to 1914 be forced to leave. In anticipation of the **Nuremberg Laws** of 1935, Article 4 of the party program declared that only Germans of pure blood could be countryman, "hence no Jew can be a countryman." Article 24 called for a struggle against "the Jewish materialist spirit within and without."

Following Hitler's failure to overthrow the Bavarian government in the so-called **beer hall putsch** in November 1923, for which he was imprisoned, Hitler moved the NSDAP away from attempting to overthrow the **Weimar Republic** through violence and focused on political means to attain power. The reorganization of the Nazi Party in 1925 focused not only on anti-Semitism but also on an economic program that stressed protectionism, autarkic development, tax relief, and the mandatory application of impartible inheritance. Between 1925 and 1932, the **Nazis** attracted voters as much because of their anti-Jewish agitation as they did because of their economic program.

In 1932, more than 14 million Germans (37.3 percent of the electorate) voted for the Nazis, who became the largest single party in Germany, although they did not attract a majority of the German population. The political crisis of 1932, which led to Hitler's appointment as chancellor of Germany, also marked the ascent of the Nazi Party as the real center of power in the Nazi dictatorship. Major decisions that affected the Jewish population of Germany, such as the Nuremberg Laws, were approved by the Nazi Party.

NEBE, ARTHUR (1894–1945). Nebe was the chief of the criminal police (Kripo) in the **Reich Security Main Office** (RSHA). Following the German invasion of the **Soviet Union**, he commanded **Einsatzgruppe** B between June and November 1941. During this period, Nebe was responsible for the execution of approximately 46,000 Jews in White Russia and in areas near the Moscow front. Nebe, however, was repelled by the mass murders conducted under his command and returned to his former position in the criminal police. His alleged repulsion to the massacres, however, did not prevent him from recommending in June 1944 the use of so-called half-breed "asocials" from **Auschwitz** for **medical experiments**, such as forcing the prisoners to drink seawater. A month later, Nebe was implicated in the 20 July 1944 plot against **Adolf Hitler**, and he was executed by the **Nazis** in March 1945.

NEO-NAZISM. The term "neo-Nazism" refers to any post–World War II social or political movement seeking to revive Nazism or some variant that echoes core aspects of Nazism. The West German government passed strict laws prohibiting **Nazis** from publicly expressing their beliefs as well as barring them from the political process. Displaying the **swastika**, for example, was an offense punishable by up to one year's imprisonment. There was little overt neo-Nazi activity in Europe until the 1960s. However, some former Nazis retained their political beliefs and passed them down to the next generation. After German reunification in the 1990s, neo-Nazi groups gained more followers, mostly among disaffected teenagers in the former East **Germany**. Many were groups that arose amidst the economic collapse and high unemployment in the former communist state.

Neo-Nazis have confronted people from Slavic countries (especially **Poland**) and people of other ethnic backgrounds who moved from the former West Germany into the former German Democratic Republic after Germany was reunited. German neo-Nazis have attacked migrant workers from Turkey and were involved in the murders of three Turkish girls in a 23 November 1992 arson attack in Mölln, in which nine other people were injured. Other neo-Nazi acts of violence include a 1993 arson attack by far-right **skinheads** on the house of a Turkish family in Solingen, which resulted in the deaths of two women and three girls, as well as in severe injuries for seven other people. These and similar incidents preceded demonstrations in many German cities involving hundreds of thousands of people protesting against far-right violence. The protests precipitated massive neo-Nazi counterdemonstrations and violent clashes between neo-Nazis and their anti-Nazi opponents. Statistics show that in 1991, there were 849 hate crimes, and in 1992 there were 1,485.

In four decades of the former East Germany, 17 people have been murdered by far-right groups. Beginning in the late 1990s and early 2000s, neo-Nazis started holding demonstrations on the anniversary of the bombing of Dresden in World War II, and in one such rally in 2009, 6,000 neo-Nazis were confronted by tens of thousands of anti-Nazis and several thousand police. German law forbids the production of pro-Nazi materials, so when such items are procured they are smuggled into the country mostly from the **United States**, Scandinavia, the **Czech** Republic, **Hungary**, and **Italy**. Neo-Nazi rock bands such as Landser have been outlawed in Germany, yet bootleg copies of their albums printed in the United States and other countries are still sold in the country. Neo-Nazis, however, are not found only in Germany. The influence of Neo-Nazi ideas and political parties also resonate in countries such as **Austria**, **Belgium**, **Croatia**, **Estonia**, **France**, **Great Britain**, **Greece**, **Russia**, and the United States.

NETHERLANDS. At the time of the German occupation of the Netherlands in May 1940, there were 140,000 Jews who represented about 1.6 percent of the population. The Jews of the Netherlands, many of whom were working class, were among the poorest of western

European Jewry. In addition to the native-born Dutch Jews, there were approximately 15,000 refugees from **Germany**, **Austria**, and the **Protectorate of Bohemia and Moravia**. Prior to the German occupation, Jews enjoyed full civic equality, and many of their religious and welfare institutions were beneficiaries of government subsidies. The 75,000 Jews of Amsterdam constituted the largest concentration of Jews in any city in Holland. During the **refugee crisis** of the 1930s, the Netherlands Jewish community created a Committee for Special Jewish Affairs (COJE), which assumed responsibility for the care of refugees who had migrated to Holland from Germany. In 1939, the government opened a special camp in the village of Westerbork for the purpose of detaining illegal immigrants. The COJE shouldered both the cost and the responsibility for running the camp.

Following the German occupation of the Netherlands, the Germans, at first, acted with restraint in regard to the Jews. This, however, changed in August 1940, when the first anti-Jewish measures were enacted. The Jewish ritual practice of *shehita*, which enabled meat and poultry to become kosher, was prohibited. This was quickly followed by decrees that required the registration of Jewish businesses as well as the posting of financial assets as a first step toward the **Aryanization** of Jewish property. When Jewish professors at the universities of Leiden and Delft were dismissed, however, the students protested the measures, thus forcing the Germans to close both institutions. In January 1941, Jews were ordered to register or face a five-year prison term and immediate confiscation of their property. This was followed by the requirement that all civil servants take an **Aryan** oath, which effectively led to the dismissal of Jews from the civil service, the schools, and the universities. The registration decree was particularly useful for the Germans because it provided them with a detailed profile of the Jewish population by city, street, age, gender, and the number of those who had intermarried.

The Dutch population responded to these measures mostly with indifference, thus confirming the German conviction that most of the Dutch shared their ideological disposition toward the Jews. The measures were followed by acts of violence between Jews and Dutch **Nazis**, which led the occupation authority to establish a *Joodse Raud*, or Jewish Council, for the purpose of preserving order among the Jewish population and implementing the Nazi decrees. The Jewish

Council, however, was unable to prevent a subsequent act of violence in February 1941 that involved a Jewish cafe owner and the police in Amsterdam. In response, the Germans blockaded the Jewish quarter of the city and seized 389 young Jewish men and deported them to **Buchenwald** and later to **Mauthausen**. The arrests, the brutal treatment of the Jews, and their **deportation** to the **concentration camp** angered the Amsterdam municipal workers, who called for a general strike in protest against the Germans. The strike was joined by all segments of the population, and it took the Germans three days to suppress the strikers.

Both sides drew conclusions in the aftermath of the strike. The Dutch realized that the Germans would not moderate their treatment of the Jews, and the Germans concluded that **anti-Semitism** was not as widespread among the population as they had believed. Nevertheless, in the weeks that followed, the Germans intensified their anti-Jewish measures. Starting in March 1941, they began the process resulting in the Aryanization of Jewish property, and in May a decree ordered the confiscation of all Jewish valuables, except for personal items such as wedding rings and gold-capped teeth. At the same time, the **Reich Security Main Office** (RSHA) opened the **Central Bureau for Jewish Emigration**, which replicated the offices in Berlin and Vienna.

Toward its objective of removing the Jews from the Netherlands, the Germans placed all Jewish organizations under the authority of the Joodse Raud and proceeded to issue additional decrees that resulted in the segregation of the Jews from the rest of their countrymen. For example, Jews were dismissed from work in the arts and the stock exchange, and were even barred from public parks. When in August 1941 the Germans prohibited Jewish children from attending public and vocational schools, it fell to the Jewish Council to fill the educational vacuum by opening its own schools. Once the total segregation of the Jews was completed, the Germans turned to the confiscation of Jewish property and then to deportations.

The confiscation of Jewish property in the Netherlands was placed under the jurisdiction of two bureaucracies. The first was that of the **Rosenberg Special Operations Staff** (Einsatzstab Rosenberg), which was responsible for the confiscation of Jewish property for redistribution among the resettled Germans in the eastern territories.

Rosenberg's agency moved more than 16,941,249 cubic feet of furniture from apartments owned by Jews to the east in 1941 alone.

The Aryanization of Jewish property was under the aegis of **Arthur Seyss-Inquart**, chief civilian administrator of the occupied Netherlands. Under his direction, a series of decrees was issued beginning in March 1942 that led to the liquidation of Jewish enterprises and the transfer of Jewish establishments into Aryan hands. Only in the diamond trade did the Germans allow Jews to continue their work, and this was due to their belief that Jewish expertise in diamond cutting was irreplaceable.

In early 1942, the Germans opened **forced labor** camps and made the Jewish Council responsible for supplying the manpower. Similarly, the Germans also ordered the Jewish Council to round up Jews to meet the timetable for deportation to the east. The deportation of Jews to the **death camps** began with their concentration in Amsterdam, and then moving them to the Westerbork transit camp. To facilitate the roundups, the Jews were required to wear the **yellow Star of David badge**. Many among the Dutch population were outraged by this decree, and some began to wear the yellow badge as an act of solidarity with the Jews. When the deportations began in July 1942, segments of the Dutch population as well as the churches protested the German action. Eventually the Dutch Reformed Church agreed to halt its protest when the Germans agreed to exempt Jewish converts from the deportations. When the Catholic archbishop, Johannes de Jong, insisted that his protest against the deportation be read in church, the Germans retaliated by arresting 201 converts to Catholicism, including monks and nuns, and deporting them to **Auschwitz**. Although the Vatican was silent in regard to the deportation of the Jews, the Roman Catholic Church in the Netherlands proved to be the most outspoken Catholic church in Europe protesting the movement of the Jews to the death camps.

The public protest against the deportations from the Netherlands failed to sway the Germans. Orchestrated from **Adolf Eichmann**'s office in Berlin, the Germans continued to move Jews to Westerbork, and from there to Auschwitz and **Sobibor**. Although most of Holland's population appeared to be in opposition to the deportation of the Jews, it is also true that a segment of the Dutch population **collaborated** with the Germans. This took the form of volunteers who joined Dutch Nazi paramilitary and military organizations. Dutch Jews were also betrayed by some of their fellow citizens, as was the case for **Anne Frank** and her family. The participation of Dutch officials in the deportation process, however, may have resulted not from their inbred anti-Semitism but from their respect for the law, even the law of the occupier. The political culture of Holland stressed deference for the law. For many bureaucrats and citizens, it was unimaginable to disobey the law, even if the law resulted in the death of their neighbors. It has been estimated that between 120,000 and 150,000 persons, or one out of every 70 Dutchmen, were charged with collaboration after the war.

Despite the long tradition of religious tolerance and the sympathy of a majority of the Dutch population, a much higher percentage of Dutch Jews were killed in the **Holocaust** than in **Belgium**, **France**, and any other country in Western Europe under German occupation. All told, approximately 110,000 Jews were deported to Auschwitz and Sobibor, and about 5,000 survived. The result was the destruction of 75 percent of Dutch Jewry.

NEUENGAMME. Situated in the outskirts of Hamburg, **Germany**, Neuengamme was an annex of the **Sachsenhausen concentration camp**. The first group of prisoners was brought to the camp in 1938 for the purpose of reactivating a brick factory that the **Schutzstaffel** (SS) wanted to use for the huge public structures planned for the city of Hamburg. In 1942, the Walther weapons factory set up various branches of its armament industry. By 1945, the total number of satellite camps at Neuengamme reached 70. In 1944, the main camp had a prison population of 12,000 prisoners and twice that number were in the satellites whose prisoners were used as **forced labor** for various aspects of the German armaments industry. The camp served the needs of the German war machine and also carried out **exterminations through labor**. The inmates were spread over the main camp and approximately 80 subcamps across the north German area. Many prisoners succumbed to the subhuman conditions in the camp from hard manual work with insufficient nutrition, very unhygienic conditions, and violence from the guards.

In 1944, a large transport of Jewish prisoners from **Hungary** and **Poland** was brought to the camp. All told, some 13,000 Jewish prisoners passed through the camp between 1944 and 1945. It has been estimated that more than 106,000 prisoners were sent to Neuengamme through the life of the camp, and an excess of 50,000 prisoners perished. Among those who died in the camp was Fritz Pfeffer, one of the occupants of **Anne Frank**'s secret annex. The main camp was evacuated in mid-April 1945.

NIEMOLLER, MARTIN (1892–1984). Niemoller was a leader of the German Evangelical Church (Confessing Church), which opposed the German attempt to Nazify the churches in **Germany**. In particular, it protested the **Aryan Paragraph**, which was used to purge converted Jews from positions in the churches. A World War I hero who served as a U-boat commander, Niemoller was ordained as a pastor in 1924. At first, he welcomed **Adolf Hitler**'s ascension to power, but he quickly became an opponent of the regime. In 1934, Niemoller formed the Pastor's Emergency League, and in 1937 he assumed leadership of the Confessing Church (**Bekennende Kirche**). Subsequently, he was arrested on Hitler's orders for his refusal to capitulate to **Nazi** intimidation, and incarcerated first at **Sachsenhausen** and then **Dachau**, where he was imprisoned for seven years.

As was the case among many of the leaders in the Confessing Church, Niemoller's anti-*Judentum* was grounded in traditional Christian religious prejudice against the Jews. Many Christian clergy in Germany were indifferent to the growing persecution of the Jews. They believed that the Jews, in first rejecting Jesus as the Christ and then crucifying him, had brought their punishment upon themselves. Niemoller and his colleagues opposed the Nazi persecution of Jewish converts to **Christianity** on the basis that the racial definition was antithetical to Christianity and negated the salvational effects of baptism. Consequently, most of those affiliated with the Confessing Church were reticent in challenging Nazi **anti-Semitism** but protested the treatment of Jewish converts to Christianity.

Niemoller was released from Dachau by the **Allies** in 1945. Subsequently, he joined other leading German churchmen in issuing the Stuttgart Confession of Guilt (1945), a statement of repentance for their failure to confront the evils of Nazism. A few years later, before an audience of college students in the **United States**, Niemoller expressed his famous cautionary words:

"First they came for the Jews. I was silent. I was not a Jew. Then they came for the Communists. I was silent. I was not a Communist. Then they came for the trade unionists. I was silent. I was not a trade unionist. Then they came for me. There was no one left to speak for me."

The quotation adorns the wall of the **United States Holocaust Memorial Museum** in Washington, D.C.

NIGHT AND FOG (*NACHT AND NEBEL*). Adolf Hitler's secret order issued on 7 December 1941 regarding the method to be used in combating resistance in **Nazi**-occupied Europe. The immediate cause of the **Führer**'s order was to quell the growing **resistance** movement in **France**. Those arrested under the Hitler directive were to be subjected to torture, and then disappear into the "fog of the night." Hitler's order prescribed that their deaths not be divulged. In February 1942, special courts were convened to conduct the Night and Fog trials. By April 1944, the courts had sentenced 1,793 defendants to death.

Night and Fog is also the name of an influential documentary film directed by Alain Resnais in 1956. The film scans the ruins of **Auschwitz** in all of its graphic detail. Resnais, however, does not mention Jews in the film's narration but refers to the dead as "deportees." Perhaps, because of his leftist politics (Resnais was a socialist), he eschewed singling out the Jews in exchange for a universal condemnation of the Nazi **genocide**. *See also* FILM AND THE HOLOCAUST.

NISKO PLAN. Following the German occupation of **Poland** in September 1939, the Germans commenced the process of expelling Poles and Jews from territories intended for Germanization. In September 1939, **Germany** and the **Soviet Union** agreed on the area along the Bug and Vistula rivers as the demarcation line between both countries. The Lublin region, which fell on the German side of the line, was set aside as a "reservation" for the Jews who found themselves in German-occupied territory. The establishment of the Nisko transit camp, located in the Lublin region, marked the initial step in the German objective of **deporting** all of the Jews from **Reich**-held territories.

The Nisko Plan was aborted by **Heinrich Himmler** for logistical reasons when plans to move ethnic Germans from the **Baltic states** to the newly acquired territories in western Poland became difficult because of the lack of jobs and housing in the area. The failure to implement the Nisko Plan, however, was not the end of Germany's objective of removing the Jews from Reich territory. Subsequently, the Germans turned to the **Madagascar Plan** as a means of solving their Jewish problem through a territorial solution.

NOONTIDE PRESS. Willis Carto was a leading figure in the postwar **Holocaust denial** movement. In 1969, he founded Noontide Press, which published *The Myth of the Six Million* by David Hoggan, the first major book declaring that the **Holocaust** was a lie promoted by a Jewish-led conspiracy. Noontide Press soon became the major publisher of **anti-Semitic**, Holocaust denial, and racist literature in the **United States**.

NORWAY. At the time of the German occupation of Norway in April 1940, there were approximately 2,100 Jews in the country, with about 200 from central Europe. Most Jews lived in Oslo, where they were integrated into all aspects of the city's life. Despite the presence of the **anti-Semitic** National Unity or NS Party, which modeled itself after the **Nazis**, there was little anti-Jewish feeling in Norway. After the Germans' occupation of the country, they installed Vidkun Quisling, the founder of the NS Party, as prime minister of Norway, but real authority rested with the occupying force. Following the German invasion of the **Soviet Union** in June 1941, a number of Norway's Jews were arrested and sent to **forced labor** camps or prisons. Subsequently, the Germans promulgated anti-Jewish decrees, accompanied by a campaign of violence by Quisling's **storm troopers**. In the spring of 1942, all business establishments were ordered to submit lists of their employees by religion. This was followed by the demand for an inventory of all Jewish real estate, and by the end of June, Jewish businesses were placed under German control. These decrees were accompanied by measures that insisted that the word "Jew" be marked on all passports and identity cards held by Jews.

The roundup of Norway's Jews began in October 1942 in the city of Trondheim, where all male Jews over the age of 14 were arrested. This was followed by the arrest and **deportation** of approximately 700 men, women, the elderly, the mentally retarded, the sick, and children to **Auschwitz**. The deportations were organized by Quisling's bureaucracy in cooperation with the Germans, and were accompanied by the confiscation of Jewish property.

The deportation of Norway's Jews was not supported by the population. In November 1942, the bishop of Norway, together with other Protestant congregations, wrote to Quisling in protest over the deportations. The letter sent to the prime minister was supported by the people of Norway, who stood behind the clergy in its confrontation with Quisling and the German occupation force. Despite the protest, however, the deportations continued. Yet, due to the assistance of the Norwegian underground, most of Norway's Jews managed to escape the German roundups and make their way to **Sweden**. Ironically, between those who were sent to the **death camps** and the others who fled to Sweden, Norway had, in fact, become *Judenrein* (free of Jews). In June 1998, the government of Norway proposed the payment of $60 million to Norwegian Jews and international Jewish organizations as compensation for property seized during World War II.

NUREMBERG LAWS. The death of President Paul von Hindenburg in August 1934 removed the last restraint on **Adolf Hitler**'s efforts to remove the Jews from German life. While Hindenburg was alive, he insisted that Jewish war veterans be exempted from the increasing civil disabilities that affected Jewish life in **Germany**. Following Hindenburg's death, Hitler assumed a new role as both chancellor and president of Germany as a result of the 1934 plebiscite that gave him 88 percent of the vote. Hitler now offered the Jews one of two choices: either leave Germany or, for those who remained, accept the loss of their citizenship and a segregated place in the **Third Reich**. The problem arising from these objectives was to determine who was a Jew and what constituted membership in the Jewish community. On 15 September 1935, the Nuremberg Laws were decreed at a special session of the Reichstag summoned to Nuremberg during the annual **Nazi Party** rally in that city.

The special session produced two laws that became the basis for the exclusion of Jews from German life. The **Reich** Citizenship Law declared that only Germans or people "of related blood" could be citizens of Germany. As a result of the law, Jews lost their political rights and were relegated to being subjects of the state. The Law for the Protection of German Blood and Honor prohibited marriage and extramarital intercourse between Jews and Germans. Jews were also prohibited from employing German maids under the age of 45. Although the provision was haphazardly enforced until 1938, Jews were also forbidden to raise the German flag.

A Jew was defined as someone who descended from at least three Jewish grandparents or from two Jewish parents and belonged to the Jewish religious community on 15 September 1935 or joined the community on a subsequent date or was married to a Jewish person on 15 September 1935 or was the offspring of a marriage contracted with a three-quarter or a full Jew after the Law for the Protection of German Blood and Honor had been implemented or was "the offspring of an extramarital relationship with a three-quarter or full Jew and was born out of wedlock after 31 July 1936." Not defined as a Jew but counted as *Mischlinge*, or of mixed Jewish blood, was "any person who [was] descended from two Jewish grandparents but who did not adhere to the Jewish religion on 15 September 1935, and who did not join it at any subsequent time and was not married to a Jewish person on the 15 September date, and who did not marry such a person at any subsequent time." Such persons were designated as *Mischlinges* of the first degree. Any person descended from one Jewish grandparent was designated as a *Mischlinge* of the second degree.

The Nuremberg Laws had the effect of dividing non-**Aryans** into categories, Jews and *Mischlinges*, with the latter excluded from the civil service and the Nazi Party, and restricted to the rank of common soldier. *Mischlinges* were also prohibited from marrying Germans without official permission. *See also* IDEOLOGY.

NUREMBERG TRIALS. The trials of the 22 major **Nazi** war criminals were held from October 1945 to October 1946 in the German city of Nuremberg. The court's legal designation was the International Military Tribunal (IMT). The court, consisting of judges and prosecutors from **France, Great Britain**, the **Soviet Union**, and the **United States**, brought charges against the 22 defendants who were major officials in the hierarchy of the **Nazi Party**. They were accused of war crimes against humanity and peace, by planning, executing, and organizing crimes as well as ordering others to do so during World War II.

The Nuremberg Trials were unprecedented in history and established the principle that wars of aggression in any form are forbidden. The Nazi leaders tried at Nuremberg were found guilty of crimes against humanity and having engaged in a criminal conspiracy by virtue of their membership in a criminal organization, the Nazi Party. Of the 22 defendants, 12 were sentenced to death: Martin Bormann, head of the Chancellery and **Adolf Hitler**'s secretary; **Hans Frank**, governor-general of the General-Gouvernement; Wilhelm Frick, minister of the interior; **Hermann Goering**, Reich marshal and commander-in-chief of the Luftwaffe; **Ernst Kaltenbrunner**, head of the **Reich Security Main Office**; Wilhelm Keitel, chief of the armed forces; Alfred Jodl, Hitler's chief adviser on military operations; Joachim von Ribbentrop, **Reich** foreign minister; **Alfred Rosenberg**, Reich minister for the eastern occupied territories; Fritz Sauckel, plenipotentiary general for manpower; **Arthur Seyss-Inquart**, Reich commissioner for the occupied **Netherlands**; and **Julius Streicher**, founder of *Der Stürmer*. Sentenced to life imprisonment were Walther Funk, president of the Reichsbank; Rudolf Hess, deputy führer; and Erich Raeder, commander of the navy. Lesser sentences were meted out to Karl Donitz, the head of the navy (10 years); Baldur von Shirach, leader of the Hitler Youth and *Gauleiter* of Vienna (20 years); Konstantin von Neurath, Reich protector of Bohemia and Moravia (15 years); and Albert Speer, minister for armaments and war production (20 years). Only Hans Fritzsche (head of the Radio Division, Propaganda Ministry), Franz von Papen (the ambassador to Turkey), and Hjalmar Schacht (president of the Reichsbank until 1939) were acquitted.

Subsequent Nuremberg proceedings against lower-echelon Nazis were enacted in a series of trials that continued from 1946 through 1948. Among the more sensational of the trials that disclosed the full horror of the Nazi regime were the prosecution of physicians who performed **medical experiments** in the **concentration camps** (1946), the trial of I. G. Farben (1947), the Krupp case (1947), and the trial of the **Einsatzgruppen** (1947).

The revelation that the Nazi regime was responsible for the murder of millions of innocent people made it imperative to conduct additional trials in order to bring to justice the Nazi perpetrators and their accomplices in mass murder. Despite the overwhelming nature of the task, the trials of the Nazis and their **collaborators** continued in **Great Britain** in the 1950s, and in the following decades in **Poland, Israel,** and more recently **France,** with the trial of **Maurice Papon** (1998). The trials of the Nazis and their collaborators for complicity in the murder of millions of Jews and others have become an ongoing legacy of the **Holocaust.**

Because many of the Nazis tried by the Nuremberg Tribunals were among the second tier of those who implemented criminal acts, questions arose in regard to personal responsibility. Were those involved in mass murder acting under orders from their superiors, thus exculpating them from charges of participating in genocide? The judgment at Nuremberg was an emphatic no! The trials at Nuremberg established the principle that under international law an individual is responsible for disobeying an order that entails committing a war crime.

– O –

OFFICE OF SPECIAL INVESTIGATION (OSI). The Office of Special Investigations was founded in 1979 as a unit within the Criminal Division of the U.S. Department of Justice as a direct legacy of **Simon Wiesenthal.** The OSI has focused on the prosecution of **Nazi** war criminals who lived in the **United States.** Many war criminals, mostly from Eastern Europe who participated in the murder of Jews and **Gypsies,** entered the United States after World War II, often by lying on affidavits about their Nazi past. Since its founding, the OSI has investigated more than 1,500 persons, and more than 100 have been prosecuted for violating U.S. immigration and naturalization laws in obtaining their American citizenship. Those convicted of participating in Nazi war crimes were subsequently denaturalized and **deported** to their native countries. Many, such as Adam Friedrich, lived in the United States for decades and led obscure lives. Friedrich, for example, had lived in the United States since 1955 and had been a citizen since 1962 before the OSI found out that he had been a member of the **Waffen-Schutzstaffel** (SS), assigned as a prison guard at the Gross-Rosen **concentration camp**. He was denaturalized in 2004 but died in 2006 before he could be deported.

The most recent case of war crimes prosecuted by the OSI was that of John Demjanjuk, a **Ukrainian**-American who was stripped of his U.S. citizenship and recently deported to **Germany** by the Office of Special Investigations for concealing his involvement in war crimes at the **Sobibor death camp** in order to immigrate to the United States. On 13 July 2009, Demjanjuk was formally charged in Germany with 27,900 counts of acting as an accessory to murder, one for each person who died at Sobibor during the time he is accused of serving as a guard at the Nazi death camp. Demjanjuk's trial commenced in Berlin in December 2009.

OHLENDORF, OTTO (1907–1951). A high official in the **Reich Security Main Office** (RSHA), Ohlendorf was the commander of **Einsatzgruppe** D in southern **Ukraine** in 1941–1942. Although born to a peasant family, Ohlendorf went on to study at the University of Leipzig and Gottingen, where he graduated in 1933. In 1925, while still a student, he joined the **Nazi Party**, then the **Schutzstaffel** (SS) in 1926. Although a specialist in the theories of **National Socialism** and Italian fascism, he was also a lecturer on economics and had addressed institutions such as the Institute of World Economy at the University of Kiel.

Ohlendorf joined the **Sicherheitsdienst** (SD) in 1936 and became chief of the SD Inland Section of the RSHA in 1939. In June 1941, **Heinrich Himmler** appointed the intellectually minded Ohlendorf to head Einsatzgruppe D, which subsequently swept through the Crimea and the Ciscaucasia, killing more than 90,000 men, women, and children, who were mostly Jews. Fearing that the mass killings might have damaging psychological consequences on his men, Ohlendorf insisted that his men shoot their victims at the same time, thus avoiding personal responsibility for their actions. At the **Nuremberg Trials** where he was tried as a war criminal, Ohlendorf defended the mass shooting of Jews as a necessary consequence of the policy of *Lebensraum*. When asked whether children also had to be murdered, he replied that it was unavoidable "because the children were people who would grow up, and surely, being the children of parents who had been killed, they would constitute a danger no smaller that than of their parents."

Ohlendorf was tried by the Nuremberg Military Tribunal and sentenced to death in 1948. He was hanged along with other Einsatzgruppen commanders in Landsberg prison on 8 June 1951.

"ON THE JEWS AND THEIR LIES." Written by Martin Luther in 1543, "On the Jews and Their Lies" attacked Jews as the sworn enemy of **Christianity**. In this vituperative essay, Luther states that "With their accursed usury they hold us and our property captive. . . . Worse than that, they mock and deride us because we work an d let them play the role of lazy squires at our expense and in our land. Thus they are our masters and we are their servants, with our property, our sweat, and our labor." Elsewhere in the essay, Luther's **final solution** to the **Jewish question** is "to set fire to their synagogues or schools and to bury and cover with dirt whatever will not burn, so that no man will ever again see a stone or cinder of them. . . . I advise that their houses also be razed and destroyed" and that the Jews themselves "be lodged under a roof or in a barn, like the **gypsies**. . . . I advise that all their prayer books and Talmudic writings, in which such idolatry, lies cursing, and blasphemy are taught be taken from them. . . . I advise that their rabbis be forbidden to teach henceforth on pain of loss of life and limb." It is not surprising that a number of scholars who studied the roots of the **Holocaust** would find a direct line from Luther to **Adolf Hitler**. *See also* KRISTALLNACHT.

"ONE PEOPLE, ONE REICH, ONE LEADER." The slogan *"Eine Volk, Eine Reich, Ein Führer"* was used by **Nazi** ideologues to return to the **Third Reich** those ethnic Germans who lived across Eastern Europe. *See also* ETHNIC CLEANSING.

ONEG SHABBAT. Compiled by the Jewish historian **Emanuel Ringelblum**, the Oneg Shabbat Archive documented the **Nazi** treatment of the Jews in the **Warsaw ghetto** and enlisted the testimony of Jews who arrived from German-occupied Europe to the **ghetto**. Ringelblum was aware of the unprecedented nature of the Nazi persecution of the Jews and was determined to leave behind a record of the events that were destroying the Jewish community. During the final weeks of the ghetto's existence, Ringelblum and his colleagues collected every available piece of evidence that related to the **deportation** of the Jews and passed them on to the Polish underground. It was due to Ringelblum's work that the **Allies** first learned about the **Chelmno death camp** and the deportation of 300,000 Jews from the Warsaw ghetto. The Oneg Shabbat or Ringelblum Archive is the most extensive documented source on the Jews during the Nazi occupation of **Poland**.

OPERATION BERNHARD. The **Reich Security Main Office** in 1942 introduced a plan to flood **Great Britain** with counterfeit sterling pound notes with the objective of undermining the British currency. This **Nazi** "economic weapon" was directed by **Schutzstaffel** (SS)-SBF Bernhard Krüger, an engineer appointed director of banknote production. In July 1942, orders were sent out from the central office for the economic administration of the **concentration camps** (K-Z) to the commandants of **Auschwitz**, **Buchenwald**, Ravensbruck, and **Sachsenhausen** with the orders that Jewish prisoners in these camps who were qualified as printers, paper experts, and related skills were to be selected for the project. Between 1942 and 1945 as part of the Nazi war effort, there were 142 Jewish prisoners, faced with incessant death threats, who were forced to forge British and later American bank notes worth billions, as well as bonds, stamps, and other documents. The forgery workshop was based in Sachsenhausen. The story of Operation Bernhard was the basis for the 2007 award-winning **film** *The Counterfeiters*.

OPERATION ERNTEFEST (OPERATION HARVEST FESTIVAL). On 3–4 November 1943, the Germans shot 43,000 Jews residing in **Schutzstaffel** (SS) work camps located in the **General-Gouvernement**. The operation was the largest single shooting massacre of Jews in the war and had as its objective the total elimination of the Polish Jews still remaining in the Lublin region. Jews were shot and hurled into mass graves. As part of the operation, the 18,000 Jews remaining in **Majdanek** were ordered to dig their own graves before they were executed. *See also* TRAWNIKI LABOR CAMP.

OPERATION HARVEST FESTIVAL. *See* OPERATION ERNTEFEST.

OPERATION ILTIS. Approximately 1,000 Jews in Brussels and Antwerp, **Belgium**, were rounded up by the Security Police and **Sicherheitsdienst** (SD) on 3 September 1943 and brought to the Malines detention camp in order to be transported to **Auschwitz**.

OPERATION INTELLIGENTSIA. In October 1939, **Reinhard Heydrich** directed office heads of the **Reich Security Main Office** (RSHA) to carry out the liquidation of the Polish leadership by the beginning of November. Members of the Ethnic German Self-Defense, under the leadership of the **Einsatzgruppen**, were primarily responsible for the executions that followed. According to historian Bogdan Musial, more than 45,000 Poles, including 7,000 Jews, had been killed in Operation Intelligentsia by the end of 1939. *See also* POLAND.

OPERATION MUSY. In February 1945, 1,200 prisoners in **Theresienstadt** were allowed to enter **Switzerland** as free people. The rescue of the Jews was the result of negotiations between the Vaad Ha-Hatsala (Rescue Committee of **United States** Orthodox Rabbis), Jean M. Musy, a Swiss politician, and **Heinrich Himmler**. The negotiations, which began in January 1945, initially called for the release of 1,200 Jews at two-week intervals. Fearing his own fate with regard to **Germany**'s imminent defeat in the war, Himmler, in exchange for releasing the Jews, demanded an end to anti-**Nazi** propaganda and that he be portrayed as a humanitarian.

OPERATION REINHARD. *See* AKTION REINHARD.

OPERATION TANNENBERG. The code name for the deployment of the **Sicherheitsdienst** (SD) in **Poland** following **Germany**'s invasion of the country on 1 September 1939.

OPERATION TODT. Its founder, Dr. Fritz Todt (1891–1942), in 1938 organized large-scale construction work in the military and armaments industries. Todt became minister for armaments and munitions in March 1940, and during the war, the Todt organization was active in occupied countries using foreign workers as well as Jews as slave laborers. Todt was killed in an accident in February 1942 and was succeeded by Albert Speer (1943–1945) as head of the Todt organization. In 1944, the number of Organization Todt employees numbered 1,360,000, including about a million foreign workers, prisoners of war, and about 20,000 **concentration camp** prisoners.

Organization Todt's best-known endeavor was the construction of a cavernous underground factory, cut out of solid rock. Prisoners from the Dora-Mittelbau concentration camp, located near Nordhausen, were put to work excavating tunnels that were to serve as the site for the building of the V-2 rockets. The conditions were deplorable, with more than 10,000 prisoners being forced to live in the tunnels under unbearable conditions. The Jews who were brought to Dora-Mittelbau were treated with great brutality, and their mortality rate was higher than that of the non-Jewish workers.

OPERATION ZEPPELIN. Following the German army's defeat near Moscow, the **Nazi** high command realized that the war would take longer than anticipated. Seeking to foster unrest in the **Soviet Union**, the **Reich Security Main Office** (RSHA) at the end of 1941 and the beginning of 1942 deployed behind Soviet lines members of Russian national minorities, supporters of Czarist Russia, and even communist anti-Stalinist groups, for the purpose of gaining intelligence, engaging in sabotage, and using brigades to implement revolt against the Stalinist regime. The Zeppelin units were ordered to fight against both **Bolshevism** and the Jews. Many of those in the Zeppelin units were recruited from among prisoners of war in **concentration camps**, using the criteria that the agents selected for the operation were both anticommunist and **anti-Semitic**, rather than being chosen for their racial purity.

ORDNUNGSPOLIZEI (ORPO) (ORDER POLICE). This body arose out of a reorganization that occurred in **Germany** in 1936, when the conventional police and the gendarmerie were merged into a single police force on **Heinrich Himmler's** orders. Subsequently, the Order Police and its auxiliaries played an important role in the **Final Solution**. Because the **Schutzstaffel** (SS) did not have enough personnel to guard the trains that took Jews to the **death camps**, they enlisted the Order Police or police battalions for this responsibility. Composed of "ordinary Germans," these policemen had already participated with the **Einsatzgruppen** in the invasion of the **Soviet Union**, and had participated in the mass shootings of Jews. Following the decision to implement the Final Solution, the Order Police, under the command of Kurt Daluege (1897–1946), became the intermediaries between the **deported** Jews and the death camps as they came to regard the guarding of the "**special trains**" as part of their duties. Although, in the occupied countries, these units were supposed to perform police duties, their primary role was to fight against **partisans**, and on occasion they were enlisted to support combat units. The number of men serving in ORPO in 1944 is estimated at 3,500,000.

OSTARA. A popular pulp magazine edited by Jorge Lanz von Liebenfels. **Adolf Hitler** was greatly influenced by the magazine during his Vienna years between 1909 and 1914. The story line depicted the conflict between heroic blond men and dwarfish apelike creatures. The struggle to protect blond blue-eyed women from the apelike men resonated in the **anti-Semitic** imagination as the struggle between the **Aryan** race and the Jews. "The Blood Protection and Marriage Law" (1935), which forbade Jews from engaging in sexual relations with non-Jews, was an example of how the **Nazi** ideological fantasy became a reality. *See also* IDEOLOGY; NUREMBERG LAWS; *RASSENSCHANDE*; *VOLKISCH*.

OSTJUDEN. The term used to denote Jews from Eastern Europe. The *Ostjuden* evoked images of ultra-Orthodox Jews, their long sideburns, and the caftans they wore that marked them off from the rest of the population. Both among the Germans and German Jews, the word *Ostjuden* had a pejorative connotation, and they were considered as primitive as the rest of the peoples of Eastern Europe. *See also MEIN KAMPF.*

OSWEGO. One of the accomplishments of the **War Refugee Board** (WRB) was the organization of a haven for **refugees** in an unused army camp in Oswego, New York. The WRB evacuated 982 Jewish refugees from **Italy** and moved them to the camp in the **United States** in August 1944. The president, ever sensitive to **anti-Semitic** demagoguery of those who accused his administration of favoring the Jews, insisted that non-Jews be added to the mix of refugees.

Although the WRB hoped that the Oswego haven would be the first of many to follow, President **Franklin D. Roosevelt** agreed only to the Oswego project.

– P –

PALESTINE. On 2 November 1917, the British government issued the **Balfour Declaration**, which permitted the Jews, after almost 1,900 years of exile, to return to their home in Palestine. Seeking to replace the Turks as the protector of the Suez lifeline to India, there were those in Prime Minister Lloyd George's cabinet who believed that the Jews would be a more dependable ally than the Arabs in protecting **Great Britain**'s imperial interests in the Middle East. Not everyone in Lloyd George's government agreed with the decision. The Arabists in the British Foreign Office opposed the decision, as did Sir Edwin Montagu, a Jew, who was a member of the cabinet. The support for a Jewish national home in Palestine also marked the culmination of years of intense persuasion by **Chaim Weizmann**, the leader of British **Zionism**, among the leaders of the British establishment.

In 1922, the League of Nations incorporated the Balfour Declaration into the document that assigned Great Britain the mandate over Palestine, and gave its final approval on 29 September 1923. Almost from the beginning of the mandate, it became clear that the Arabs resented the presence of Jews in large numbers in Palestine.

Fearing that the Jews would attempt to create a state in Palestine rather than to live as a "guest" in their homeland, the Arabs agitated against Jewish immigration into Palestine and discouraged Jews from purchasing land from the Arab landowners. Following the arrival of approximately 35,000 Jews from **Poland** in 1925 because of **anti-Semitism** and a severe economic crisis, the Arabs of Palestine, under their leader **Hajj Mohammad Amin al-Husseini**, the grand mufti of Jerusalem, intensified their attacks against Jewish settlements. The growing violence between the Arabs and the Jews led the British to investigate ways of resolving the conflict.

Against the background of intensified violence, the British government established a series of commissions to make recommendations regarding the deteriorating conditions in Palestine. The first of these commissions, chaired by Sir Walter Shaw, took place in 1930, and criticized the Zionist leadership for encouraging immigration and for actively pursuing land purchases. The report became the basis for the British government's white paper issued in late 1930, when Lord Passfield (the former Sidney Webb) was secretary of state for the colonies. The white paper was the first direct sign that many in the British government regretted the decision to support a Zionist home in Palestine. The white paper threatened to prohibit land purchases and recommended a cessation of Jewish immigration into Palestine.

Under pressure from pro-Zionist elements in the government, Prime Minister Ramsay MacDonald backed down from the implications of the white paper. The issue of immigration into Palestine, however, became an urgent matter once **Adolf Hitler** attained power in January 1933. As the persecution against the Jews in **Germany** intensified, Zionist leaders in Palestine entered into the so-called **Transfer Agreement** with **Nazi** authorities. The agreement facilitated Jewish immigration to Palestine by allowing the transfer of their capital in the form of German goods. In 1935, 69,000 Jews from Poland and Germany arrived in Palestine, the largest number to arrive since the start of the British mandate. The Arab response was to form the Arab Higher Committee in April 1936, which demanded that the British halt immigration into Palestine and prohibit land sales to Jews. The Arab demands were followed by a six-month strike that was accompanied by an armed uprising. In October 1936, the British promised to investigate the Arab demands, and the strike was called off. Arab agitation resumed in the summer of 1937 when the British government endorsed the recommendation of the Peel Commission, which called for the partition of Palestine into a Jewish and Palestinian state. The **Jewish Agency** accepted the plan but the Arabs rejected it, and a revolt against Great Britain followed that continued throughout 1937–1938.

In the same year as the Arab revolt, the Haganah, Palestine Jewry's defense force, organized a committee for illegal immigration to rescue the Jews of Europe and bring them into Palestine (**Aliya Bet**). As violence between Jews and Arabs intensified, Great Britain wavered in its support for a Jewish home in Palestine. In May 1939, the British government issued a white paper (**White Paper of 1939**) that called for an independent Palestinian state within 10 years and a limit on

Jewish immigration to Palestine to 75,000 over a five-year period, and limited the sale of land to Jews. The British government's repudiation of the Balfour Declaration was made because of the certainty of war and its awareness that Jews would be on their side regardless of what happened.

On the day when Germany invaded Poland in September 1939, a ship carrying illegal Jewish immigrants from Europe was intercepted by the British navy off the coast of Palestine, and the passengers were interned in Mauritius. The efforts of the Haganah to circumvent the white paper through illegal immigration would continue throughout the war. As news reached the Jewish Agency concerning the **Final Solution**, an Extraordinary Zionist Conference was convened in the Biltmore Hotel in New York City in May 1942. The assembled delegates voted to support the creation of a Jewish commonwealth in Palestine as expeditiously as possible, inasmuch as it was obvious that Palestinian Jewry could no longer rely on Great Britain to carry out its mandatory responsibilities.

Although Great Britain's unwavering enforcement of the white paper was calculated on keeping the Arabs from siding with **Nazi Germany**, it wasn't the only reason. As the violence in Palestine escalated between Arabs and Jews, the pro-Arab officials in the British colonial office found support from members of the British government. Oliver Harvey, Foreign Minister Anthony Eden's private secretary, noted in his diary that "Eden was immovable on the subject of Palestine inasmuch as he loved the Arabs and hated the Jews." British anti-Semitism intensified as the British came under attack from dissident Jewish underground groups such as the Irgun Zvai Leumi (National Military Organization) and the Stern gang. Bombings, the kidnapping of British soldiers, and the assassination of Lord Moyne, the British deputy minister of state for the Middle East and a close friend of Prime Minister **Winston Churchill**, by the Stern gang in Cairo in 1944 all contributed to a growing estrangement between the **Yishuv** and the British. In January 1944, the conflict intensified as the Irgun organized an armed revolt against British authorities in protest over Great Britain's enforcement of the white paper. The Jewish Agency condemned the Irgun because their attack against the British would impair their ability to defeat Nazi Germany. Following the end of the war, the British continued to rigidly enforce the provisions of the white paper, although during the war approximately 20,000 of the allotted 75,000 certificates available for immigration went unfilled. The Jewish Agency responded by intensifying its illegal immigration operation. Between November 1945 and April 1948, 54 ships brought more than 67,000 survivors of the **Holocaust** to Palestine. The conflict over the white paper came to a head when Ernest Bevin became foreign secretary in November 1945. Bevin denied that Great Britain ever intended to support a Jewish state in Palestine. He urged that Jewish refugees seeking to leave Europe should not try and get ahead of the queue but wait their turn.

If Great Britain's pro-Arab policy during the war was grounded on keeping them out of the enemy camp, its policy after the war was based on the importance of oil, and that it was in the country's national interest to curry favor with the Arabs. The anti-Jewish policy of the Bevin government, in turn, gave rise to further violence between the British and the Yishuv. Ultimately, it was the United Nations that stepped in to resolve the clash. Between April 1946 and May 1947, several commissions were appointed to study and make recommendations regarding the future of the area. At the same time, the British announced that all illegal Jewish refugees attempting to enter the country would be sent to Cyprus. The most sensational of Great Britain's efforts to enforce its policy occurred in July 1947, when the British ordered the return of 4,550 Jews from **displaced persons** (DP) camps on board the ship *Exodus 1947* to be returned to their point of origin.

On 14 February 1947, Bevin announced that Great Britain had decided to turn the entire question of Palestine over to the United Nations. The cost of supporting 100,000 British soldiers in Palestine, as well as being on the receiving end of negative world opinion, took its toll. In April 1947, the General Assembly of the United Nations appointed the United Nations Special Commission on Palestine (UNSCOP) to study the issue of Palestine. On 31 August 1947, UNSCOP recommended the termination of the British mandate and proposed the partition of Palestine into separate and sovereign Arab and Jewish states. On 29 November 1947, the General Assembly voted in favor of partition by a vote of 33 to 14. The Arab Higher Committee rejected the partition, and subsequently violence broke out between the Jews and Arabs of Palestine. Although ostensibly a neutral, Great Britain increasingly sided with the Arabs in the conflict. Bevin, in fact, was determined not to cooperate with the implementation of partition and insisted that as long as the mandate remained in effect, it would not permit any interference by the United Nations in any part of Palestine. Convinced that a Jewish state could not survive the attack of an army composed of military from the combined Arab states, Bevin appears to have been determined to facilitate an Arab victory by leaving Palestine in chaos.

The British mandate came to an end on 14 May 1948, and on the same day, David Ben-Gurion, the head of the Jewish Agency, proclaimed the new State of Israel. Within two days, the Jewish state was recognized by the **Soviet Union** and the **United States**. The proclamation that established the State of Israel was followed by the invasion of the Arab states in a war that continued until the United Nations negotiated an armistice between both sides in July 1949. *See* ISRAEL, STATE OF.

PAPON, MAURICE (1911–2007). Papon served as secretary general of the Gironde Prefecture in Bordeaux, **France**, between May 1942 and August 1944. During this time, he signed orders to the French police to round up thousands of foreign-born Jews, who were sent to French **concentration camps** at **Drancy** in preparation for **deportation** to **Auschwitz**. But it was not until over a half a century later that he was tried by the French government, in October 1997, for these acts.

In April 1998, Papon was found guilty by the French court of complicity in **Nazi** crimes against humanity. Papon, however, was absolved by the court of knowingly furthering Nazi plans for the extermination of the Jews.

Because Papon after the war went on to become an official in the government of Charles de Gaulle, his conviction forced the French to reevaluate their role during the German occupation and the **collaborationist Vichy** government. Papon's conviction raises questions as to whether there was a clean break between Vichy and the postwar French governments, and about the belief that the **Gestapo** and not the French police was responsible for the roundup of the Jews for deportation to the **death camps**.

PARTISANS. *See* RESISTANCE.

Warsaw Ghetto: Children in Rags.
Pictorial History of the Holocaust, p. 121. Permission: Yad Vashem

The Deportation of Slovakian Jews to Auschwitz.
Pictorial History of the Holocaust, p. 231. Permission: Yad Vashem

Arrival at Auschwitz.
Pictorial History of the Holocaust, p. 270. Permission: Yad Vashem

U.S. Soldiers Uncover Bodies at the Woeblin Camp, 1945.
Jessel Hollingsworth Collection

U.S. Soldiers Uncover Bodies at the Woeblin Camp, 1945.
Jessel Hollingsworth Collection

U.S. Soldiers Uncover Bodies at the Woeblin Camp, 1945.
Jessel Hollingsworth Collection

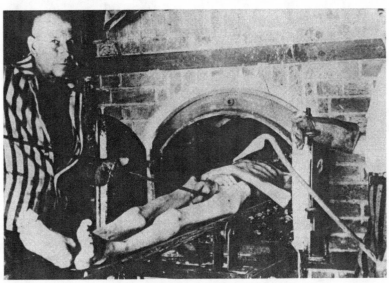

Taken from a German POW at Nordhausen, 1945.
Jessel Hollingsworth Collection

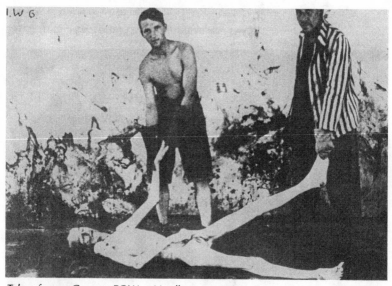

Taken from a German POW at Nordhausen, 1945.
Jessel Hollingsworth Collection

PASSING THROUGH. Nazi euphemism for the process of exterminating Jews.

PIUS XI (1857–1939). Achille Ratti was elected pope in 1922. A strong advocate of the separation of electoral politics and cultural activities, Pius XI was a believer in the binding force of written documents, best exemplified by the 18 **concordat** signed during his papacy, which included those agreed to with fascist **Italy** in 1929 and **Nazi Germany** in 1933.

When the German government violated the provision of the concordat that promised that they would respect the integrity of Catholic schools in **Germany**, Pius XI issued the encyclical "**With Burning Concern**" (*Mit Brennender Sorge*), which attacked **Adolf Hitler**'s nonobservance of the concordat. The logic of the pope's attack on the Hitler dictatorship soon led him to address the issue of the **Nazi** persecution of the Jews. The Nazis responded by spreading the falsehood that Ratti himself was half-Jewish. Instead of denying the accusation, the pope, speaking before a group of Belgian pilgrims in 1938, stated that "we are the spiritual offspring of Abraham. . . . We are spiritually Semites." Before his death in 1939, Pius XI had authorized the draft of "The Unity of the Human Race" (*Humani Generis Unitas*), an encyclical that would have attacked Nazi racism and **anti-Semitism**. The encyclical was never completed and was buried in the **Vatican** archives until its discovery in 1972 and its publication in 1997. *See also* CHRISTIANITY.

PIUS XII (1876–1958). Monsignor Eugenio Pacelli became pope following the death of **Pius XI** in 1939. As papal nuncio in **Germany**, he had negotiated the **concordat** with **Nazi Germany** in 1933. Skilled in diplomacy, the future Pius XII was a vehement anticommunist who viewed Nazi Germany sympathetically because of its strong stand against **Bolshevism**. With the outbreak of World War II, Pius XII adopted a policy of strict "impartiality" that resulted in his refusal to condemn **Nazi** atrocities, lest it compromise the **Vatican**'s ability to bring about a diplomatic solution to the conflict.

Despite being among the first to learn of the **Final Solution**, Pius XII refrained from condemning Nazi Germany. He justified his silence with the argument that a public denunciation of Germany would have made matters worse for both Jews and German Catholics. Yet, despite his refusal to use the full force of his moral authority to condemn the Nazi extermination campaign against the Jews, Pius XII has been credited with saving the lives of hundreds of thousands of Jews and to have permitted Catholic clergy to open their monasteries and convents to hide Jews. In addition, he intervened in both **Hungary** and **Slovakia** and pleaded with their leaders to halt the **deportation** of Jews to **Auschwitz**. Pius XII's ambiguous record in regard to the **Holocaust** continued after the war when in 1948 he requested mercy for all Nazi war criminals but was refused by General Lucius D. Clay. *See also* CHRISTIANITY; PIUS XI.

POGROM. The term is usually associated with the government promoted violence against Jews in Czarist Russia. In **Nazi Germany**, however, a pogrom, mockingly referred to by **Hermann Goering** as **Kristallnacht**, was initiated by the government on 9–10 November 1938. Jews were arrested and sent to **concentration camps**, their business establishments looted, the synagogues set afire, and a number of Jews beaten to death.

POGROMS IN POLAND. Allegations of the medieval "**blood libel**" led to violence against the Jewish community of Kielce in **Poland** on 4 July 1946. The **pogrom** was instigated by the police and resulted in 42 Polish Jews being murdered and 40 being injured out of some 200 **Holocaust survivors** who had returned to Kielce after the war following their **liberation** from **Nazi concentration camps**. The Kielce pogrom was preceded by a pogrom based on the blood libel in the Polish town of Rzeszow when a rabbi and other Jewish leaders were arrested by police and accused of ritual murder of a nine-year-old girl. They were eventually released but not before a riot against Jews resulted in beatings and robberies. This pogrom was followed by one in Krakow, where the blood libel ignited a riot wherein a mob stormed and plundered a synagogue, killed several Jews, and seriously injured dozens more. The pogroms shocked the surviving remnant of Polish Jewry as well as the international community, as it indicated that following the disclosure of the near **genocide** of the Jewish people, virulent **anti-Semitism** continued to be present in Polish life.

POHL, OSWALD (1892–1951). Pohl was the head of the Wirtschafts Verwaltungshauptamt (WVHA) (Economy and Administration Main Office), and the WVHA was responsible for the **forced labor** projects in the **concentration camps**. The WVHA was also responsible for collecting the valuables taken from gassed Jewish prisoners.

Pohl joined the **Nazi Party** in 1922 and subsequently joined the **Schutzstaffel** (SS), where he caught **Heinrich Himmler**'s eye because of his organizational ability. Throughout the decade of the 1930s, Pohl was given many important posts in government. By 1940, he was in charge of SS interests in the concentration camps and the labor camps, where he set up a chain of SS enterprises.

Under Pohl, the **death camps** proved lucrative for **Germany**, as the personal possessions of murdered Jews, including hair, clothing, gold teeth fillings, wedding rings, and jewelry, were sent back to the **Reich**, where they were turned into cash or used commercially. The gold loot was melted down in the form of bars and sent to **Switzerland** in exchange for needed currency, or placed in a special SS account in the Reichsbank. By the end of 1942, Pohl had become the most important functionary in the German concentration camp system, presiding over 700,000 slave laborers and committed to Himmler's order to annihilate camp inmates through hard work.

Pohl was sentenced to death by an American military tribunal on 3 November 1947, and after spending three and a half years in the Landsberg prison, he was hanged on 8 June 1951. *See also* OPERATION TODT; SWISS BANKS.

POISONOUS MUSHROOM. *See STÜRMER, DER.*

POLAND. Following the end of World War I in November 1918, the Versailles Treaty created the Second Polish Republic. The new state, however, was obliged by the League of Nations to sign a treaty that protected the ethnic and religious rights of minorities. Poland's independence had followed a bitter war from 1918 to 1920 against the **Soviet Union** that was accompanied by anti-Jewish riots. Although Poland promised to abide by the treaty provision that prevented it from discriminating against minorities, **anti-Semitism** was an ever-present factor in daily life in Poland. Polish anti-Semitism stemmed from the large number of Jews in the country's population. Jews constituted 10 percent of the population, 30 percent in the cities. Poles claimed that Jews played an inordinately large role in Polish economic life at a time when there was a drive on the part of Polish politicians for the "Polonization" of the nation's economic life. Jews were subsequently barred from the civil service and restricted in the professions and certain sectors of the economy. In May 1926, Jozef Pilsudski staged a military coup and established an authoritarian regime that lasted until 1935. Pilsudski's regime showed little interest in encouraging anti-Semitism, but upon his death in 1935, life for the Jews of Poland was radically altered. Against the background of a severe economic depression, the government encouraged anti-Jewish attitudes as a means of strengthening Poland's internal cohesion. Jewish economic concerns became targets of boycotts, and the government actively encouraged the **emigration** of the Jews as a means of reducing the country's Jewish population.

On the eve of the German invasion in September 1939, a large number of the Polish population supported the move to deprive the country's 3.5 million Jews of the right to live in Poland. Polish Jews, however, had few places open to them, inasmuch as restrictive immigration laws throughout much of the world prevented them from finding a viable refuge. Following the German occupation of Poland in September 1939, Polish government institutions dissolved but were reestablished as an underground organization by the Polish government-in-exile, which was based in **Great Britain**.

The attitude of the Polish underground toward the Jews was one of ambivalence, with prewar anti-Semitic attitudes often governing the response of the Polish underground to Jewish pleas for assistance, as in the case of the **Warsaw ghetto uprising**. Notable exceptions were the **Zegota** underground organization and the efforts of individual Poles who risked their lives to save Jews. The Germans organized Poland into separate districts with specific objectives in mind. Western Poland was set up as the **Warthegau**, and the Germans expected to "Germanize" the area by resettling ethnic Germans (*Volksdeutsche*) on land vacated by Poles and Jews. By the end of 1939, about 90,000 Jews and Poles were expelled from the annexed area into the **General-Gouvernement**. Ultimately, a total of about 900,000 persons, not counting the Jews who were deported for extermination, were replaced by 600,000 Germans from other parts of

Poland and other countries of Eastern Europe. In addition, approximately 400,000 from **Germany**'s annexed territories were resettled in the area. Under the treaty between Germany and the Soviet Union that was signed in August 1939, the eastern part of Poland fell under Soviet occupation.

The unannexed area of central Poland, the General-Gouvernement, was used to place Jews in **ghettos** prior to their **deportation** to the **death camps**. Of the 3.5 million Jews who lived in Poland in September 1939, about 310,000 survived: 30,000 in **concentration camps**, 30,000 in Poland, and approximately 250,000 fled to the Soviet Union. It is estimated that about 15,000 out of 3.2 million Jews, or less than half of 1 percent, were saved by the Poles. At the end of the war, the German occupation of Poland was followed by the Soviet Union. Although the Poles had suffered more than 3,000,000 killed at the hands of the Germans, anti-Semitism continued to inform a large percentage of the Polish population. Some Poles identified Jews with the Soviet occupation. Others continued to view Jews with the traditional anti-Jewish bias that was associated with church teachings. Polish animosity toward the Jews came to a head in the town of Kielce, where a **pogrom** was directed toward some 150–250 Jewish **Holocaust survivors** who had returned to their homes. On 4 July 1946, the riot, which took the lives of 42 Jews, broke out after a Polish woman charged that the Jews were killing **Christian** children and drinking their blood. This event convinced Polish Jews that life was unsafe for Jews in Poland and many of them left the country. More recently, tensions between Poles and Jews surfaced when in 1984 Carmelite nuns sought to establish a convent in a vacant building that bordered the **Auschwitz** death camp.

The controversy mirrored the unresolved issues between Polish Jews and non-Jews regarding the **Holocaust**. For Jews, the Auschwitz death camp has become a symbol of the approximately six million Jews who died in the Holocaust. But the death camp also has meaning for Poles inasmuch as the camp was initially created to eliminate the Polish intelligentsia. More than 270,000 of the Polish political and cultural elite were killed in Auschwitz. The conflict was temporarily resolved in 1987 when an agreement was reached to remove the convent and to create, instead, a center for information, education, meeting, and prayer. But then a series of inflammatory events occurred that threatened the settlement. This included the repudiation of the 1987 agreement by Polish Primate Cardinal Glemp and the attempt by a group of American Jews, led by Rabbi Avi Weiss, to enter the convent by force. Finally Pope John Paul II intervened and agreed that the convent must be moved, and supported the construction of a new center. The resolution of the conflict was achieved but not before it dealt a blow to Polish–Jewish relations. The controversy revealed that despite the absence of Jews in Poland, anti-Semitism continues to resonate among segments of the population and informs, for many, their understanding of the Holocaust.

POLITICAL HOUSECLEANING. Reinhard Heydrich's **euphemism** for the orders given to the **Einsatzkommandos** to eliminate the clergy, the aristocracy, the intelligentsia, and the Jews, following the German invasion of **Poland** in September 1939.

PORAJMOS. The word translated literally means the "Great Devouring" as a description for the **Gypsy Holocaust.**

PORTUGAL. During the **refugee crisis** of the 1930s, thousands of Jews sought to reach Portugal via **Spain** in order to escape from Europe by ship. In May 1940, the officially neutral but pro-German Portuguese government prohibited the passage of refugees through its territory. The Portuguese government instructed its consular agents in **France** not to issue visas to persons who had no final destination or who were seeking asylum in Portugal.

Specifically, visas were not to be issued to Jews. This action left thousands of Jews stranded in the south of France. It was under these circumstances that the Portuguese consul in Bordeaux, **Aristides de Sousa Mendes**, issued almost 10,000 entry visas to Jews and 20,000 to other refugees, including American actor Robert Montgomery. Because Sousa Mendes disobeyed his government's orders, he was dismissed from the Foreign Service. The visas, which saved thousands of lives, read, "The Portuguese government requests of the Spanish government the courtesy of allowing the bearer to pass freely through Spain. He is a refugee from the European conflict." *See* RIGHTEOUS GENTILES.

POSEN. Following **Nazi Germany**'s occupation of Poland, the Germanization of the incorporated territories under **Heinrich Himmler**'s direction commenced with the arrest of 88,000 Poles and Jews in Posen in December 1939. Located in the **Warthegau**, the Poles and Jews of Posen were taken by train and **resettled** in the **General-Gouvernement**, dumped there upon arrival. Posen was also where inmates from psychiatric hospitals in the Warthegau were sent and crammed into a sealed room in the local headquarters of the **Gestapo**. Here they were forced to inhale **carbon monoxide** gas released from canisters. This was the first time in history that a **gas chamber** had been used for mass killing.

POSITIVE CHRISTIANITY. During the early years of the **Third Reich**, the **Nazis** attempted to purge the German churches of Jewish converts to **Christianity**. Toward this end, the government introduced the concept of Positive Christianity—that is, a German church devoid of any Jewish influences. *See* NIEMOLLER, MARTIN.

PROTECTIVE CUSTODY. *See* EUPHEMISMS.

PROTECTORATE OF BOHEMIA AND MORAVIA. *See* CZECHO-SLOVAKIA.

PROTOCOLS OF THE ELDERS OF ZION. A forgery that purported to be an eyewitness account of a meeting in a cemetery, where rabbis and other Jewish elders unfolded their plan to rule the world. The *Protocols* was first published in Czarist Russia in 1905, where Tsar Nicholas II financed its distribution. The *Protocols* was brought to **Germany** by Baltic German émigrés who managed to escape the **Bolshevik** victory in the Russian Revolution. **Alfred Rosenberg** is generally credited with calling **Adolf Hitler**'s attention to the *Protocols*. For Hitler, the *Protocols* was a revelation, inasmuch as it explained, to his satisfaction, how it was possible for the Jews to dominate international finance and at the same time undertake the leadership of communist movements throughout Europe. For Hitler, the Jewish conspiracy to rule the world meant that regardless of the victor in the conflict between capital and the proletariat, the Jews would still triumph because they had assumed the leadership of both sides.

PRUSSIC ACID CONGRESS. The congress was held in Frankfurt-am-Main on 27–28 January 1944. The purpose of the meeting, which was initiated by the **Schutzstaffel** (SS) leadership, was to inform companies that produced and distributed prussic acid to the **death camps** of plans for the further use of **Zyklon B** gas. Among the many firms represented at the congress were Degesch, Tesch and Stabenow, Heerdt-Lingler, the Dessau Works, and I. G. Farben.

– Q –

QBVII. Queen's Bench VII is the courtroom in London where a libel trial was held against American novelist Leon Uris in 1964. The libel action was brought by a Polish physician, Dr. Wladislaw Alexander Dering, a prisoner in **Auschwitz**, who was accused by Uris of performing 17,000 **medical experiments** in surgery without anesthetics on prisoners in the **death camp** in Uris's 1958 best-selling novel *Exodus*, where he referred to the physician as Dr. Dehring and substituted the fictional Jadwiga **concentration camp** in place of Auschwitz.

During the trial, survivors of Auschwitz who had undergone the ordeal of irradiation and mutilation of their sexual organs by surgery were brought forth to provide testimony. Although the evidence pointed to Dering's guilt, he won the case because the defense could not prove that he had performed the large number of surgeries Uris had accused him of. The award, however, brought no solace to Dering inasmuch as he was compensated with the smallest coin of the realm, one halfpenny. The trial was one of the earliest of its kind to expose the intolerable medical abuses performed on the mostly Jewish victims in Auschwitz. Uris published his version of the trial in his novel *QBVII* (1970).

QUARANTINE. The inmates chosen for hard labor at **Auschwitz** were sent to an area of the camp called the "quarantine," where their clothes were taken and exchanged for prison-striped garb. In addition, both men and women inmates had their hair shorn; subsequently the hair was sent to **Germany**, where it was processed as mattress filling. Life in the quarantine was characterized by extreme privation, and if a prisoner was not selected for **forced labor**, the victim's life expectancy was only a few months. Many of those in the quarantine were so weak and emaciated from hunger that they were referred to as *Muselmann*, camp jargon for someone who could not react to his environment. Once selected for forced labor, inmates were removed from the quarantine area and sent to different sections of the camp, where they were worked until they could not continue, whereupon they were gassed.

– R –

RACIAL SIFTING (*RASSENSIEBEND*). In May 1940, **Heinrich Himmler** completed the memo, "Reflections on the Treatment of Peoples of Alien Races in the East," which he presented to **Adolf Hitler**, who approved it. In this memorandum, Himmler recommended that "people of alien races in the East be cultivated into as many ethnic groups as possible," which would be the basis for carrying out the policy of racial sifting. Himmler's objective was to select racially valuable people and bring them to **Germany** where they would be assimilated into the **Third Reich**. Himmler acknowledged that this operation might be "cruel and tragic," but it "is still the mildest and best one" for those who "reject as un-German . . . the physical extermination of a people."

***RASSENSCHANDE* (RACIAL POLLUTION).** In 1935, the German government enacted the Blood Protection and Marriage Law, which proscribed sexual intercourse between Jews and **Aryans**. Shortly thereafter the concept prohibited any form of touching or caressing. Jewish men accused of violating the law were found guilty of assaulting German blood, and their punishments ranged from imprisonment to sentences of death. Jewish women were not tried under the law because women were held to be passive in sexual encounters and, therefore, could not be found guilty of sexual transgressions. By the 1940s, all German Jews were being rounded up and **deported** to the **death camps**. Thus trials for *Rassenschande* were no longer necessary, as Jewish men accused of violating the law were immediately sent to **concentration camps**. *See also* IDEOLOGY; NUREMBERG LAWS; *OSTARA*.

RATHENAU, WALTHER (1867–1922). German industrialist, politician, writer, and statesman who served as the foreign minister of **Germany** during the **Weimar Republic**. Walther Rathenau was assassinated by an **anti-Semitic** ultranationalist, but prior to his murder, he anonymously published an article where he advised German Jews to avoid doing anything that might arouse scorn or ridicule on the part of their non-Jewish countrymen. "They should be careful," he wrote, "not to make themselves a laughing stock by a slouching and indolent way of walking amid a race which has been raised and bred in a strictly military fashion. . . . In the meantime they should not try to look like 'lean Anglo-Saxons.' . . . They simply could not alter nature by wearing a sailor's costume on the beach." It was obvious to Rathenau that "two thousand years of misery have left marks too deep to be washed away by eau de cologne." Years later, the **Nazis** used Rathenau's article as evidence that even Jews admitted that differences between **Aryans** and non-Aryans were ineradicable.

RATLINES. A number of leading **Nazis** involved in the mass murder of Jews, such as **Walter Rauff** and **Adolf Eichmann**, were able to escape from **Germany** at the close of World War II through the so-called ratlines. This was an escape route that led them to safe havens in South America, particularly Argentina, Paraguay, Brazil, and Chile. Other destinations included the **United States**, Canada, and the Middle East. There were two primary routes: the first went from Germany to **Spain**, and then Argentina; the second from Germany to Rome, Genoa, and then South America. One ratline, made famous by the Frederick Forsyth novel *The Odessa File*, was run by the ODESSA ("Organization of Former SS Members") network organized by Otto Skorzeny, an SS *Obersturmbannführer* (lieutenant-colonel) in the German **Waffen-SS**. Another ratline was organized by a number of **Vatican** priests sympathetic to the **Nazi** cause.

RAUFF, WALTER (1906–1984). He was a **Schutzstaffel** (SS) officer in **Nazi Germany**, attaining the grade of colonel (*Standartenführer*) in June 1944. In January 1938, he was an aide to **Reinhard Heydrich**, first in the **Sicherheitsdienst** (SD), and then in 1939 where he served in the **Reich Security Main Office** (RSHA). In 1941–1942, Rauff was involved in the development of **gas trucks** or mobile **gas chambers** used to fatally poison Jews, persons with disabilities, communists, and so forth who were considered by the SS to be enemies of the German state. Rauff is thought to be responsible for nearly 100,000 deaths during World War II. In the late 1970s and early 1980s, he was arguably the most wanted of the **Nazi** fugitives still alive.

RAUS. German word for "out." This was the "greeting" that Jews and others received as they disembarked from the railcars upon arriving at **Auschwitz**.

RED HOUSE AND WHITE HOUSE. The term refers to the two **gas chambers** at **Auschwitz**-Birkenau located in Bunkers I and II, or the "red house" and the "white house."

REFUGEE CRISIS. Between 1933 and 1938, most refugees **emigrating** from **Germany** sought entry into **France**, the **Netherlands**, **Switzerland**, **Czechoslovakia**, and **Austria**. Not all of these countries were willing to absorb large numbers of Jews. For example, Switzerland allowed some 21,000 Jews to enter the country, but approximately 30,000 others were refused entry at the borders. In many instances, when Jews were allowed entry, it was on a temporary basis. A number of Jews went to **Palestine**, the **United States**, and **Great Britain**. In the aftermath of the **Anschluss** on 13 March 1938, approximately 96,000 Jews from Germany and Austria migrated, with the majority going to Palestine and the United States.

Between 1939 and October 1941, approximately 121,500 escaped from Germany. Once the war broke out, the refugee crisis became more acute and centered on approximately 100,000 Jews who were spread throughout Europe. In some countries, such as France, the Netherlands, and **Belgium**, Jews were interned. Jewish refugees who fled the **Nazis** in **Poland** and the **Baltic states** migrated to the **Soviet Union**, where many of them were placed in Soviet Gulags in Siberia. *See also* EVIAN CONFERENCE; *ST. LOUIS.*

RE-GERMANIZATION. The term refers to **Reinhard Heydrich**'s plan to clear territory in German-occupied western **Poland** for the purpose of resettling ethnic Germans in the eastern provinces. The objective necessitated the expulsion of Jews and Poles from their homes as well as the seizure of farmsteads for **Schutzstaffel** (SS) men or army veterans. *See also* GENERAL-GOUVERNEMENT; *LEBENSRAUM*; WARTHEGAU.

REGULATION FOR THE BAN ON JEWISH EMIGRATION FROM THE GENERAL-GOUVERNEMENT OF POLAND. The ban on Jewish **emigration** from **Poland** was issued by the **Reich Security Main Office** (RSHA) on 23 November 1940, shortly after the creation of the **Warsaw ghetto**. The ban heralded a change in **Nazi** policy toward the Jews, from officially encouraging their emigration to forbidding it. The regulation anticipated the conditions necessary for **genocide** that began with the German invasion of the **Soviet Union** in June 1941. By October 1941, Jewish emigration was prohibited throughout German-occupied territory.

REICH. Reich refers to three former German states: The First Reich, the Holy Roman Empire (962–1806); the Second Reich, which followed the unification of Germany (1871–1918); and the **Third Reich**, the **Nazi** regime (1933–1945), which saw itself as the successor to the first two Reich's. *See also* THOUSAND-YEAR REICH.

REICH SECURITY MAIN OFFICE BUREAU (REICHSSICHER-HEITSHAUPTAMT) (RSHA). The RSHA was the German agency responsible for the **resettlement** of the Jews in the aborted **Nisko Plan** and **Madagascar Plan**. **Reinhard Heydrich**, who headed the RSHA, would subsequently assume responsibility for the **Final Solution**. The RSHA was organized in September 1939 when the **Nazi Party** merged its intelligence apparatus, the security services of the **Schutzstaffel** (SS), the **Sicherheitsdienst** (SD), the **Sicherheitspolizei** (SIPO), and the state security and the criminal police (**Gestapo** and Kripo) into the RSHA under the command of Heydrich, who reported directly to **Heinrich Himmler**, the head of the SS. The RSHA consisted of seven bureaus, of which Section B of the fourth bureau was responsible for the **Jewish question**, with **Adolf Eichmann** in charge of the Jewish section.

REICHSBAHN (RAILWAY ADMINISTRATION). The **death camps** ran efficiently because the German railway system cooperated in the **Final Solution**. German trains, under the jurisdiction of the German Ministry of Transportation, carried Jews from every part of Europe to the **death camps**. The German railroad system stretched from Bordeaux to Dnepropetrovsk, and although the railway system was the prime vehicle for moving soldiers, military cargo, and industrial products for the war effort, officials were also assigned to schedule **special trains** to move Jews to the extermination centers. Administrators designed the train schedules so that there would be an uninterrupted movement of Jews to the camps. Once the allocation of freight cars and locomotives was arranged, Jews were herded like cattle into the sealed cars and dispatched to the extermination camps. The trains were generally overcrowded, with the norm in Western Europe or **Germany** being 1,000 persons per train. The crowding was greater in the east but subsequently, to save on engines and the frequency of the trips, the number of Jews herded into the cattle cars was doubled. The crowded freight cars were filled with men, women, and children who traveled in unheated conditions in the winter and terribly hot temperatures in the summer. There was little air, food, or water, and the **Ordnungspolizei** (ORPO), who were responsible for escorting the trains, shot anyone attempting to escape from the freight cars. Rarely did a transport arrive without 1 or 2 percent of the deportees having died en route.

The movement of trains to the death camps was a high priority, and large numbers of transports of Jews were scheduled even as the **Wehrmacht** (German army) launched its final offensive in the Moscow area in order to avoid the Russian winter. Raul Hilberg put it best when he wrote, "Apparently, military considerations also were not to be considered in the 'Final Solution' of the Jewish problem." Moving millions of Jews to the death camps was an expensive proposition. The use of trains, the use of the ORPO to guard the victims, and the salaries of railway personnel all created a financial burden. To help make the books balance, the Railway Administration charged the Jews for the cost of transportation to the extermination camps. Train tickets were "sold" to Jews at the third-class rate, children aged four to 10 were charged at half-fare, and those under the age of four traveled free of charge. Half-fare group rates were also charged for more than 400 "passengers." The fare was billed to the **Gestapo**, which, in turn, passed on the cost to authorities in foreign areas where Jewish property had already been confiscated, or charged the Jewish communities themselves. In Germany, the Gestapo billed the **Reichsvereinigung** (Jewish Association) for defraying the cost of moving the deportees to the east. The German Railway Administration was indispensable to the running of the extermination camps, inasmuch as camp officials depended on the trains to bring them victims on a regular basis. There is no evidence that a single Jewish life was spared because of the lack of transportation. At the conclusion of the war, however, only one official of the Railway Administration was tried for participating in the Final Solution.

REICHSFLUCHSTEUER. The **"emigration** tax" that the German government forced Jews to pay before leaving **Germany** during the 1930s. *See also* CENTRAL BUREAU FOR JEWISH EMIGRATION.

REICHSSICHERHEITSHAUPTAMT. *See* REICHS SECURITY MAIN OFFICE.

REICHSVEREINIGUNG DER JUDEN IN DEUTSCHLAND. *See* REICHSVERTRETUNG DER DEUTSCHEN JUDEN.

REICHSVERTRETUNG DER DEUTSCHEN JUDEN (REICH REPRESENTATION OF GERMAN JEWS). The body refers to the organized Jewish community from 1933 to 1939, which the **Nazis** recognized as the official spokesmen for German Jewry. In 1939, the Germans renamed the organization the Reichsvereinigung der Juden in Deutschland. The Reichsvertretung became the model for the subsequent **Judenräte** (Jewish Councils), which the Germans established in the **ghettos** of **Poland** and the rest of German-occupied Europe.

The Reichsvertretung's responsibilities included retraining a large number of Jews who had lost their positions as a result of Nazi measures and providing vocational training for those who sought to **emigrate**. When the German government "racially cleansed" all public elementary schools in September 1935, it fell to the Reichsvertretung to expand its support of Jewish schools.

REPORT NUMBER 51. During the course of the **Einsatzgruppen's** murderous action in the **Soviet Union, Adolf Hitler** was frequently informed, and approved, the killing operations. In a meeting between Hitler and **Heinrich Himmler** on 18 December 1941, according to the latter's notes, the extermination of Soviet Jews was to be continued under the pretext that they were **partisans**. This policy is described in "Report number 51," dated 29 December 1942, sent by Himmler to Hitler, in which the **Schutzstaffel** (SS) leader notes that among those assisting bandits or those suspected of banditry, the number of Jews executed in southern Russia, the **Ukraine**, and the **Bialystok** district in the months from August to November 1942 was no less than 363,211. A marginal note written by Hitler's adjutant confirms that the **Führer** had seen and read the report. *See also* COMMISSAR ORDER.

REPORT TO THE SECRETARY ON THE ACQUIESCENCE OF THIS GOVERNMENT IN THE MURDER OF THE JEWS. *See* WAR REFUGEE BOARD.

RESETTLEMENT. *See* EUPHEMISMS.

RESISTANCE. When the opportunity presented itself, Jews resisted the Germans. The many acts of defiance, however, did not prevent the annihilation of the bulk of European Jewry. Yet there is a record of thousands of Jews who in different situations managed to confront their **Nazi** tormentors.

Ghettos. The most famous act of Jewish resistance was the **Warsaw ghetto uprising** in April 1943. The courageous defiance of the Germans by the relatively few Jews in the ghetto inspired other acts of revolt in the remaining ghettos of **Poland**. In the ghetto of Lvov, the Germans faced Jewish opposition in the form of grenades and Molotov cocktails when they attempted to liquidate the ghetto. German and Ukrainian casualties totaled nine dead and 20 wounded. The

Germans crushed the resistance but not before blowing up houses where Jews were concealed in order to force them to surrender. In the **Bialystok ghetto**, members of the Jewish Socialist Bund, the communists, and the **Zionists** put their differences aside and formed an organization to oppose the Germans. The revolt in the ghetto lasted five days but was no match for the armored cars and tanks, as well as manpower, that the Germans brought to battle. Facing defeat, the leaders of the revolt committed suicide.

Partisans and Resisters. In the **Baltic states, Belarussia**, and western **Ukraine**, it is estimated that 20,000 to 30,000 Jews were in partisan units that fought the Germans. Among the better known of these Jewish partisan fighters was Alexander Bielski, who along with his brothers formed the **Bielski Otriad**, which consisted of more than 300 fighters who fought a guerrilla war against the Germans in Belarussia. They engaged in different acts of sabotage, including the derailment of troop trains and blowing up of bridges and electric stations. In Ukraine, Diadia Misha (Uncle Misha) fought the Germans in forests and villages. Jews also assumed leadership positions in over 200 partisan bands but fought under assumed Ukrainian or Russian names, lest they call attention to their Jewish ancestry.

Between 1942 and 1944, there were 27 Jewish partisan units fighting against the Germans in Poland, and about 1,000 who participated in the Warsaw uprising in the summer of 1944. In general, Jewish partisans fought under the authority of the national groups that fought the Germans, since they lacked support from a country or government-in-exile.

The record indicates that Jewish partisan groups fought with the resistance in **Yugoslavia, Bulgaria**, and **Greece**, where they were accepted as equals. In Western Europe, Jews fought in the resistance movements in German-occupied countries. Jews participated in the French underground, fought in the Belgian resistance movement, and were active in the resistance to **Adolf Hitler** in **Germany**. Active opposition to the government in Germany, however, was limited to distributing leaflets and publishing illegal literature. The most important group in this regard was the Herbert **Baum** band, which operated in Germany from 1937 to 1942. Its most noteworthy act of defiance occurred in May 1942, when it set fire to the anti-Soviet exhibit that had been organized by **Joseph Goebbels**. Baum and the rest of his group were arrested, tortured, and executed.

Death Camps. Despite the difficulties, there was also resistance in many of the death camps as well as in the **concentration camps**. In **Auschwitz**, the Auschwitz Fighting Group engaged in acts of sabotage, organized escapes, and was able to find food and medicine for ill comrades. In October 1944 in Auschwitz-Birkenau, a revolt occurred at the moment when the mass extermination of **Hungarian** Jews was coming to an end. The Jewish **Sonderkommandos**, realizing that their days were numbered, pleaded with the Auschwitz Fighting Group, which consisted of many nationalities, to revolt against its captors. The underground force, however, rejected their plea, whereby the Sonderkommandos launched the revolt by themselves. Limited in weapons, they nevertheless were able to obtain explosives and proceeded to blow up **Crematorium** 3, destroying the facility. The revolt was immediately crushed by the **Schutzstaffel** (SS), and all of the participants were rounded up and executed.

On 14 October 1943, Jewish prisoners at the **Sobibor** death camp rose up in revolt. The plan was to kill the SS guards, seize weapons from the armory, cut the barbed wire, clear the mines outside the camp, and escape to the nearby forest. About 300 prisoners were able to escape, but many of the Jews who participated in the revolt were shot by the Germans or blown up by the mines. Many of those who escaped were tracked by the Nazis and shot. Some made it to the forest and joined up with partisan groups, and others were killed by **anti-Semitic** Polish partisan units. In the aftermath of the uprising, the Germans liquidated the Sobibor camp after executing the remaining Jews.

The Jews at **Treblinka** rose in revolt in August 1943. The uprising was led by a Jewish underground that had been organized in the camp. The plan was similar to the one at Sobibor, and once the revolt commenced, the prisoners seized weapons and called on the rest of the inmates to join in. But once the Germans recovered from the surprise, they quickly turned the tide against the resistance and apprehended many of those who had managed to escape. Of the approximately 750 prisoners who succeeded in escaping, 70 managed to survive the war. After the Germans crushed the revolt, they demolished Treblinka. Jewish underground resistance groups were also organized at **Majdanek** and **Buchenwald**.

Aside from the fact that the Jews were small in number and therefore ill equipped to defend themselves against the Germans and their helpers, Jews relied on the willingness of their fellow partisans to support the cause of Jewish survival. Given the endemic anti-Semitism that characterized much of Europe, it is not surprising that the number of Jewish lives saved as a result of aid from the rest of the population was small.

RESTITUTION FOR HOLOCAUST SURVIVORS. In **Nazi**-occupied Europe, Jewish property and assets, including life insurance policies, bank accounts, and works of art, were seized by the Nazi government. In addition, Jews deposited millions of dollars of assets in banks outside the **Third Reich**, such as in **Switzerland**, from fear that the Nazis would seize their insurance policies and other liquid capital. Millions of these Jews, however, perished in the **Holocaust** and after the war **survivors** and children of those who perished demanded that financial institutions, such as the **Swiss banks**, make payments on the matured assets. However, without documentation, such as death certificates, many European banks, including the Swiss institutions, refused to honor the requests from the families of the victims. To address the issue of compensation, Jewish organizations were formed to enter into negotiations, if not legal action, to provide restitution for the Holocaust survivors and their families. The primary organizations that represented the claimants included the Conference on Jewish Material Claims against Germany, or **Claims Conference**, which represents world Jewry in negotiating for compensation and restitution for victims of **Nazi** persecution and their heirs.

The Claims Conference, which was founded in 1951, administers compensation funds, recovers unclaimed Jewish property, and allocates funds to institutions that provide social welfare services to Holocaust survivors. These services include hunger relief, home care, medical assistance, and emergency cash grants. Nahum Goldmann, then president of the **World Jewish Congress** (JWC), was a co-founder of the Claims Conference, and JWC designates two members to its board of directors. The Claims Conference negotiated with the newly united German government in 1990 to enable original Jewish owners and heirs to file claims for properties in the former East **Germany**. In order that unclaimed properties should not revert to the state or to beneficiaries of Nazi policies, the Claims Conference also negotiated to recover unclaimed formerly Jewish properties in the former East Germany. The Claims Conference uses a small portion of the proceeds from the East German properties to support programs engaging in Holocaust education, documentation, and research.

The International Commission on Holocaust Era Insurance Claims (ICHEIC) was established in August 1998 to identify, settle, and pay individual Holocaust-era insurance claims at no cost to claimants. The ICHEIC entered into negotiations with representatives of international Jewish and survivor organizations, the **State of Israel**, European insurance companies, and U.S. insurance regulators. The result of the negotiations, a Memorandum of Understanding (MOU), was signed on 25 August 1998 by several European insurance companies.

RIEGNER CABLE. In mid-summer 1942, Gerhart Riegner, the **World Jewish Congress** (WJC) representative in Geneva, Switzerland, was informed by **Eduard Schulte**, a German businessman, of the planned extermination of the European Jews by means of poison gas and other methods. On August 8, Riegner forwarded the information in a cable to Rabbi **Stephen S. Wise**, the president of the WJC and a close friend of President **Franklin D. Roosevelt**, and to Sidney Silverman, a member of the British Parliament.

The Riegner cable was intercepted by the State Department, and Wise did not actually receive the cable until 28 August 1942 from Silverman. Wise passed the information on to Undersecretary of State Sumner Welles, who asked that the content of the cable not be made public until the information was confirmed. The information was subsequently made public on 24 November 1942 by Wise, but only after the government was convinced that the information in the Riegner cable was indeed true. Wise would later be criticized for withholding the information for three crucial months, at a time when Jews were being murdered on a daily basis.

RIGHTEOUS GENTILES (aka RIGHTEOUS AMONG THE NATIONS). The Avenue of the Righteous, located outside **Israel's Yad**

Vashem Holocaust memorial museum in Jerusalem, honors those Gentiles who saved Jewish lives during the Holocaust, despite the fact that if caught it would entail severe punishment or execution. It is estimated that between 10,000 and 20,000 Gentiles risked their lives by hiding Jews from **deportation** to the **death camps**. Many of the names of these heroic people are unknown, but Israel has honored more than 8,000 persons who have been designated "Righteous Gentiles" because of their efforts on behalf of Jews.

The manner in which the Righteous Gentiles saved Jews took many forms, such as hiding Jews in one's own home, as was the case of Countess Maria von Maltzen, who hid Jewish writer Hans Herschel, along with other Jews, in her small Berlin apartment. **Oskar Schindler** provided Jews with work in his factory as a means of protecting them from being deported to the death camps. Rescuers were always aware that they might be the subject of searches conducted by the **Nazis** to uncover those in hiding but, nevertheless, they were willing to share their scarce supply of food with the Jews and risk denunciation by **collaborators**.

In southern **France**, the small Protestant village of Le Chambon-sur-Lignon, led by its minister, Andre Trocmé, concealed Jews in full view of **Vichy** officials and a nearby division of the **Schutzstaffel** (SS). In the Dutch village of Nieuwlande, each villager agreed to hide one Jewish family or individual Jew. The collective effort of the Danish people to save 7,000 Jews by ferrying them in small boats to Sweden is well known. The record of the **American Friends Service Committee** (AFSC) in aiding Jews in Paris, Marseilles, Lisbon, and Madrid, and its role in feeding and rescuing Jewish children in France, provides an outstanding example of what other Christian denominations might have accomplished had they had the same interest as the Quakers in helping Jews to survive. Active participation in protecting Jews from deportation often placed the lives and careers of individuals in danger. **Jan Karski**, a courier for the Polish underground, twice slipped into the **Warsaw ghetto** in 1942 and subsequently made his way to London and later the **United States** to report on the deplorable conditions that he witnessed. **Raoul Wallenberg**, a Swedish diplomat, confronted the **Nazis** in **Hungary** by issuing protective passports, which saved the lives of tens of thousands of Jews on the eve of the German **deportations**. **Sempo Sugihara**, the Japanese consul general in Kaunas (Kovno), **Lithuania**, lost his position when he defied his government by issuing thousands of entry visas to Jews escaping the Nazis. Similarly, **Aristide de Sousa Mendes**, a Portuguese diplomat, was dismissed from the Foreign Service for issuing approximately 10,000 transit visas to Jewish **refugees**.

RINGELBLUM, EMANUEL (1900–1944). *See* ONEG SHABBAT ARCHIVE.

ROAD TO HEAVEN. The **euphemism** was used by guards at **Treblinka** to describe the tube or path leading to the **gas chambers**.

ROCKWELL, GEORGE LINCOLN (1918–1967). Rockwell was a major figure in the **neo-Nazi** movement in the postwar **United States**, and his beliefs and writings have continued to be influential among white nationalists and neo-**Nazis**. More than any other neo-Nazi personality, Rockwell was able to develop a strategy that bridged the transition from **National Socialism** to a form of Nazi **ideology** that was more politically viable in the United States. Rockwell redefined "white" to mean anyone not born black or a Jew, thus opening his movement to a wider pool of potential recruits. It was Rockwell who, in countering the Black Power movement, coined the slogan "White Power." In 1959, he founded the American Nazi Party (ANP), which, despite early notoriety, never gained a national following. Rockwell was murdered in Arlington, Virginia, on 25 August 1967 by John Patler, a member of the ANP and captain of his "**storm troopers**."

ROMANIA. On the eve of World War II, there were approximately 770,000 Jews living on Romanian soil. The situation of the Jews, however, was a precarious one because of the vehement **anti-Semitism** of the Romanian fascist **Iron Guard** and the pressure exerted on the Romanian government by the Germans, once World War II commenced. Prior to the outbreak of war, King Carol II attempted to maintain a policy of neutrality between **Germany**, and **Great Britain** and **France**. Once the war began, Romania tilted toward the Axis, and after the **Soviet Union** invaded the country in June 1940, it was forced to cede the territories of northern Bukovina and all of Bessarabia. The Germans also pressured Romania to cede the northernmost part of Transylvania to **Hungary**. Accompanying the departure of Romanian troops from the ceded territories was a campaign of terror against the Jews living in the area.

Romania's national humiliation as a result of its loss of territory was partially assuaged by the enactment of a law in August 1940 that canceled citizenship for most Romanian Jews and prohibited mixed marriages. The law was a popular one because the Romanian government accused the Jews of aiding the communists and serving the interests of the Soviet Union.

The situation of Romania's Jewish population further deteriorated when King Carol II, hurt by a loss of popularity as a result of the loss of the territories, was forced to install the National Legionary State in September 1940, with Ion Antonescu as prime minister and members of the Iron Guard placed in key government positions. King Carol II himself was deposed in a bloodless coup as the Iron Guard became the country's only legal party. Two months after its accession to power, the Iron Guard celebrated its political triumph with a rampage, slaughtering scores of its political opponents and massacring Jews. As the power of the Iron Guard grew in the Legionary State, the situation of the Jews continued to deteriorate. The government legally confiscated Jewish enterprises and removed Jews from the economy. These acts were accompanied by a further campaign of terror, and when Antonescu insisted on the maintenance of law and order, he was opposed by the Iron Guard. On 21–23 January 1941, the Iron Guard staged a coup against the Antonescu government that was accompanied by anti-Jewish riots. In Bucharest, 123 Jews were killed as the Iron Guard invaded the city's Jewish section. Synagogues were burned, property destroyed, and the apartments of Jews thoroughly trashed. The coup failed, however, as **Adolf Hitler** allowed Antonescu to suppress the Iron Guard.

Hitler, preparing for the invasion of the Soviet Union, required a stable Romania and viewed the indiscriminate violent behavior of the Iron Guard with displeasure. Units of the **Wehrmacht** were placed at Antonescu's disposal, and with this support he overcame the Iron Guard and replaced the National Legionary State with his own military dictatorship. In turn, Antonescu and the **Third Reich** forged a new relationship that made Romania "Hitler's favorite ally."

The failed coup, however, did not result in the alleviation of anti-Jewish measures. The German government sent a special adviser to Romania to advise Antonescu on legislation against the Jews that was similar to the types of laws enacted in Germany. The result was the enactment of the Law for the Protection of the State, which was passed on 5 February 1941. Under the law, Jews would receive double the punishment as Christians for the same offense. In a subsequent law, Jewish-owned dwellings were legally confiscated, and many Jews already dismissed from employment were now also evicted from their homes and made destitute. Additional laws were passed that sought as their objective the "Romanianization" of the country, with the final goal of removing the Jewish population from Romanian life.

In June 1941, Romania joined Germany in the invasion of the Soviet Union. Antonescu was in personal command of the Romanian army, which committed 15 divisions to the **Nazi** cause. Following the invasion, the Antonescu regime expelled Jews from various areas of Romania. Forty thousand Jews were driven from villages and towns, and their property confiscated. Romanian troops cooperated with **Einsatzgruppe** D in the killing of Jews in the Soviet Union. As a reward for its alliance with Germany, Romania was able to reoccupy Bukovina and Bessarabia as well as receive territory in **Ukraine**. Along with the territory, Romania also acquired a large number of Jews.

Subsequently, thousands of Jews were rounded up by Romanian soldiers and sent off, without bread or water, in freight cars that had no apparent destination. Those who did not die as a result of suffocation or hunger were shot. The remaining Jews from Bessarabia and Bukovina were interned in transit camps and **ghettos**, from where they were deported to Transnistria in August 1941. The 200,000 Jews of Bessarabia deported to Transnistria, which was located between the Dniester and Bug rivers, were part of Antonescu's solution to Romania's **Jewish question**, whereby thousands of Jews would die of starvation or disease.

Antonescu's Jewish policy, however, made a distinction between the Jewish populations of Bessarabia and Bukovina, and of Jews in Romania living in the pre–World War I borders, as well as those in southern Transylvania. Antonescu consented to the **Final Solution** of the Jews in Bessarabia and Bukovina, which was dutifully carried out by German and Romanian army units, and assisted by Einsatzgruppe D. In September 1941, the surviving 150,000 Jews in both areas were expelled to the Transnistria "reservation." Between 1941 and 1944, when the area was under Romanian control, some 90,000 Jews died as a result of terrible conditions. By early 1942, however, Antonescu doubted that Germany would win the war or that Hungary would be forced to return northern Transylvania, with its millions of Romanians, to the mother country. Adding to Antonescu's doubts were the reports of heavy Romanian losses on the Russian front. Together, they forced him to reconsider his cooperation with Germany. In the summer of 1942, **Adolf Eichmann** sent one of his operatives to Bucharest to coordinate with the government the **deportation** of the city's Jews. Intervention, however, by the Romanian clergy and the papal nuncio, together with the appeal of the Jewish community, led Antonescu to cancel his agreement with Germany to deport the country's 292,000 Jews to the **Belzec death camp**. The large number of Jews given this reprieve from deportation reflected the Romanian racial laws passed during Antonescu's regime. The racial definition of a Jew also included converts and their offspring.

In a diplomatic visit to Adolf Hitler in March 1943, Antonescu refused to bow to pressure and reverse his decision. By the end of the year, Antonescu concluded that the solution to Romania's "Jewish problem" was to allow them to **emigrate** in return for a considerable payment. Although Eichmann was determined to abort Antonescu's plan, the Nazis ultimately failed to execute their extermination plan in Romania. Nevertheless, large numbers of Jews were murdered by Romanian troops and deported by the Germans. In Transnistria, only 50,000 out of 300,000 Bessarabian and Bukovinian Jews survived. Most of the others were killed by Einsatzgruppe D and their auxiliaries, including Romanian troops. Out of an estimated total of 770,000 Jews in all of Romania, 420,000 were killed.

ROOSEVELT, FRANKLIN DELANO (1882–1945). During the war against the **Third Reich**, the policy of the Roosevelt administration toward the ongoing annihilation of European Jews was one of inaction. Prior to America's entry into the war, a number of members of Congress justified restricted immigration from German-occupied territory by announcing their fears that Jews who **emigrated** from **Germany** would have their families held hostage by the **Nazis**, thus blackmailing them to do their bidding once they arrived in the **United States**. Others argued that among **refugees** entering the country, the Nazis would introduce a "fifth column," that is, planting spies among the new arrivals. The Roosevelt administration did not counter these arguments. Once the country went to war in December 1941, and the president received evidence of the Nazi **death camps**, he told American Jewish leaders that the quickest way to save Jewish lives was to win the war.

President Roosevelt remains a figure of controversy among historians, notably in the scholarly works of David Wyman, in regard to his criticism that President Roosevelt did not do enough to prevent the murder of millions of Jews. Wyman cites Roosevelt's hesitancy to urge the liberalization of American immigration laws so as to allow refuge to European Jews, escaping Nazi persecution, and the refusal of the **Allies** to bomb **Auschwitz** when the president had full knowledge of the **Final Solution**. Roosevelt's defenders, however, cite the political limitations facing the president that prevented him from a more activist role in the rescue of European Jewry. They point to the growing **anti-Semitism** in the **United States**, exemplified by Father **Charles Coughlin**, **Charles Lindbergh**, and reinforced by Nazi propaganda, which fostered the belief among segments of the country's population that Jews exerted undue influence in politics and were manipulating the Roosevelt administration to wage war on Germany in behalf of their persecuted European brethren. The consequence of these political realities led the president, once Germany declared war on the United States, to conclude that the support of a massive rescue operation to save European Jews would be construed by his opponents that the war was being fought in behalf of the Jews. Lastly, prior to our entry into the war, the president understood that many Americans feared that the massive influx of refugees would only compound the chronic problem of high unemployment.

It was only when members of his own administration, primarily in the Treasury Department, threatened to reveal the obstructionist and anti-Semitic inaction of the State Department that prevented the limited efforts to rescue Jews, that the president created the **War Refugee Board** (WRB). At the time the WRB was created in 1944, millions of Jews had already perished at the hands of the Nazis. Nevertheless, the WRB has been credited with saving the lives of some 200,000 Jews.

ROSENBERG, ALFRED (1893–1946). Born in **Estonia**, Rosenberg was an early mentor of **Adolf Hitler** and became the foremost racial philosopher of the **Third Reich** as well as the head of the **Nazi Party**'s Foreign Affairs Department. The son of an Estonian mother and a **Lithuanian** father, both with Baltic German roots, Rosenberg studied architecture at the University of Moscow but fled to the West following the Russian Revolution in 1917. In Munich he was involved in White Russian émigré circles as well as being a member of the **anti-Semitic Thule Society**. Rosenberg was obsessed with conspiracy theories that accused Jews, Freemasons, and the **Bolsheviks** as the cause of the world's disorder. According to Rosenberg, Freemasons were responsible for World War I, while "international Jews" were responsible for the Russian Revolution. In line with his belief in conspiracy theory, Rosenberg was a primary disseminator of the **Protocols of the Elders of Zion** in **Germany**. He joined the Nazi Party in 1919, and Hitler appointed him editor of the *Volkischer Beobachter* in 1923.

Rosenberg impressed Hitler with his "erudite" learning, and Hitler came to depend on him during the formative years of the Nazi Party in the 1920s. Like Hitler, Rosenberg was driven by a fanatical nationalism, a virulent anticommunism, and anti-Semitism. His works include *The Track of the Jew through the Ages* (1919), *Immorality in the Talmud* (1919), and *The Crime of Free Masonry* (1921). Soon after being elected to the Reichstag in 1930, Rosenberg published *The Myth of the Twentieth Century*, which, together with *Mein Kampf*, became the bible of the Nazi movement, although Rosenberg's book was ridiculed in some Nazi circles. The book was influenced by the racial theories of Comte de Gobineau and **Houston Stewart Chamberlain**'s *The Foundations of the Nineteenth Century*.

After the Nazi seizure of power in 1933, Rosenberg served as Hitler's deputy for monitoring the spiritual and **ideological** education of Nazi Party members. During the war, Hitler appointed him **Reich** minister for the occupied eastern territories. But Rosenberg's role in the inner circle of Hitler's advisers was eclipsed by his more powerful rivals, such as **Joseph Goebbels, Hermann Goering, Heinrich Himmler**, and Hitler's secretary, Martin Bormann. Toward the end of the war, he became a pathetic figure who was not taken seriously by the party hierarchy, including Hitler. At **Nuremberg** he was found guilty of war crimes and hanged. *See also* ROSENBERG SPECIAL OPERATIONS STAFF.

ROSENBERG SPECIAL OPERATIONS STAFF (EINSATZSTAB ROSENBERG). The first German agency in the **Netherlands** to engage in the confiscation of Jewish property. **Adolf Hitler** authorized the agency to confiscate any item that it believed was vital to **Germany**. The operation was headed by **Alfred Rosenberg, Reich** minister for the eastern territories. Property, such as furniture, was confiscated from deported Dutch Jews and redistributed to the resettled Germans in the occupied eastern territories. In 1941 alone, the Germans shipped from the Netherlands to the east the contents of 17,235 apartments, totaling 16,941,249 cubic feet of furniture. Rosenberg's "enterprise," however, was independent of the **Aryanization** process, which reached its peak of confiscated Jewish property in 1942.

ROSENSTRASSE PROTEST. In February 1943 in Berlin, hundreds of Gentile women who were married to Jews protested the **deportation** of their husbands to the **death camps**. The wives and children of those targeted for deportation protested for six days and demanded that the government "Give us back our husbands!" Subsequently, **Joseph Goebbels** ordered that the men be set free. Twenty-five of those who had already been sent to **Auschwitz** were returned and sent to a **concentration camp** in Thuringia. The Rosenstrasse episode is the only known mass protest against the deportations in **Nazi Germany**.

RUMKOWSKI, MORDECHAI CHAIM (1877–1944). As head of the Lodz **Judenrat**, Rumkowski devised a strategy to save as many Jews as possible by acquiescing to **Nazi** demands for the **deportation** of the Jewish population to the **Chelmno** death facility, as well as complying with their demand for labor, reasoning that they would become indispensable to **Germany**'s war effort. Rumkowski staked all on "forestalling" the dissolution of the **ghetto** through deportations, which included children, in the hope that the end of the war was near and, for this reason, opposed armed **resistance** because he feared that in defying Nazi decrees, such an act would have brought the ghetto to a swift and bloody end. Rumkowski himself was deported to **Auschwitz** when the **Lodz ghetto** was liquidated in 1944.

RUSSIA. *See* SOVIET UNION.

RUSSIAN EAST. *See* EUPHEMISMS.

– S –

SACHSENHAUSEN. The **concentration camp** located near Berlin on the outskirts of Oranienburg was built in 1936. In November 1938, following **Kristallnacht**, 1,800 Jews were sent to the camp, where some 450 Jews were murdered after their arrival. During its early history, the executions at Sachsenhausen were done in a trench, either by shooting or by hanging the victims. By 1941, the **Schutzstaffel** (SS) set up installations for mass executions by shooting and the primary victims were Soviet prisoners of war. By the fall of 1941, 13,000–18,000 Soviet prisoners had been murdered. In 1942, large numbers of Jewish inmates were relocated to **Auschwitz**. In 1943, the construction of a **gas chamber** and **crematoria** provided for large numbers of prisoners to be killed. The gas chamber murdered prisoners with liquid **Zyklon B**, which was placed in small glass bottles into the ventilation system next to the door. The bottle was broken with a spike and the gas mixed with the air and was forced into the chamber.

On the front entrance gates to Sachsenhausen was the infamous slogan *Arbeit Macht Frei* (Work Liberates). About 200,000 people passed through Sachsenhausen between 1936 and 1945. Some 30,000 inmates died there from exhaustion, disease, malnutrition, or pneumonia from the freezing winter cold. Many were executed or died as the result of brutal **medical experimentation**.

Sachsenhausen was also the site of **Operation Bernhard**, the largest counterfeiting operation ever. The Nazis forced prisoners, mostly

Jewish artisans, to produce forged British and U.S. currency as part of a plan to undermine the British and **United States'** economies. Over £1 billion in counterfeited banknotes were recovered.

With the advance of the Red Army in the spring of 1945, Sachsenhausen was prepared for evacuation. On 20–21 April, the camp's SS staff ordered 33,000 inmates on a forced march northeast. Most of the prisoners were physically exhausted and thousands did not survive this **death march**; those who collapsed en route were shot by the SS. On 22 April 1945, the camp's remaining 3,000 inmates, including 1,400 women were **liberated** by the Red Army and the Polish 2nd Infantry Division .*See also* NEUENGAMME.

ST. LOUIS. In May 1939, more than 900 **German** Jewish **refugees** boarded at the port of Hamburg on the passenger ship SS *St. Louis*, in the hope of finding refuge abroad. However, on arriving at the port of Havana, they were refused entry into Cuba. Fearing the rising **anti-Semitic** sentiment sweeping his country, Cuban president Laredo Bru declared the permits held by the refugees invalid. Jewish-American organizations appealed to President **Franklin D. Roosevelt** and other American officials to allow them haven in the **United States**. Over 700 of the passengers were on the American immigration waiting list, and they pleaded that they be permitted to wait their turn in America, but to no avail. The passengers were returned to Europe, where they were admitted to **Great Britain**, **Belgium**, the **Netherlands**, and **France**. Many of the refugees would eventually be sent to **concentration camps** as a result of the German occupation of most of Europe. *See also* EVIAN CONFERENCE.

SALONIKA. See GREECE.

SAN RIVER. The San River is located in southeastern **Poland** and western **Ukraine**. Following the **Nazi** defeat of Poland in September 1939, the **Wehrmacht** expelled thousands of Polish Jews into Russian-occupied territory. The San River was the demarcation line between German- and Soviet-occupied Poland. On 12 September 1939, the Wehrmacht deported Jews from East Upper Silesia over the San River into Soviet territory. Subsequently, the German 14th Army gave the **Einsatzkommandos** the responsibility for "cleansing" operations and **deporting** Jews over the river. The Einsatzkommando was also given the responsibility of securing the demarcation line bordering on the Soviet part of Poland and forcibly preventing refugees who had fled to the east during the first days of the war from returning home by crossing the San River. *See also* SOVIET UNION.

SARAH. *See* "ISRAEL" AND "SARAH."

SCHINDLER, OSKAR (1908–1974). Although not a diplomat, Oskar Schindler contributed to the rescue of Jews at great personal risk. The subject of Steven Spielberg's epic film, *Schindler's List*, he was one of several German businessmen, including Julius Madritsch and Raimund Titsch, who aided Jews interned in the Plaszow labor camp by providing them with ample food rations and protection from the brutal whims of Amon Goeth, the camp commandant.

Because of his connections with German officials, Schindler was able to acquire two firms that had previously been owned by Jews. The firms, which produced enamel kitchenware products, came under the jurisdiction of the German occupation administration in Krakow. Schindler employed mainly Jewish workers in his factories, thereby protecting them from **deportation** to **Auschwitz**. When the Krakow **ghetto** was liquidated in early 1943, many of its Jews were sent to the Plaszow labor camp, administered by Goeth. Schindler was able to arrange with Goeth for the transfer of about 900 Jewish workers from the camp to his factory. Some of the workers in Schindler's factory were totally unfit for the tasks assigned to them; had this been discovered by the Germans, they would have been worked to death at the labor camp or deported to Auschwitz.

For reasons that remain unclear, Schindler was determined to protect "his Jews." When the Soviets approached Krakow in 1944, the Germans allowed him to reorganize his firm as an armaments production company in Brunulitz, located in the Sudetenland, and he was permitted to take his workers with him. Because the company produced shells for rocket casings, the Germans considered Schindler's firm vital to the war effort. Schindler, therefore, was given permission to transfer about 1,100 Jewish men from the Gross Rosen camp and 300 Jewish women from Auschwitz. In Brunulitz, the 1,100 Jews were provided with food and medical care, and allowed to practice their religion. Schindler also rescued 100 Jews from the Goleszow camp, who were left stranded and nearly frozen to death in a railway car, and brought them to the Brunulitz factory, where he nourished them back to health. After the war, Schindler was impoverished and lived on the sufferance of the "Schindler-Juden (Jews)," as those he saved came to be known. In 1962, he was honored by **Yad Vashem** when a tree bearing his name was planted in the Garden of the Righteous. *See also* FORCED LABOR; RIGHTEOUS GENTILES.

SCHLAUCH **(TUBE).** The method of killing at the **Belzec death camp** required the victims to hand over their personal possessions and undress, before being ushered through a tube-like corridor leading to the **gas chambers**.

SCHLOSS HARTHEIM. Located near **Mauthausen**, Schloss Hartheim had at one time served as a sanitarium for the chronically ill, but with the introduction of the **Euthanasia Program**, it became an institution for extermination.

SCHULTE, EDUARD (1891–1966). Schulte was a German industrialist and businessman who informed Gerhard Riegner, the **World Jewish Congress** (WJC) representative in Geneva, **Switzerland**, in July 1942 that the **Nazi** regime had decided to murder the Jews of Europe. This became the basis for the **Riegner cable**, which alerted both the **United States** and **Great Britain** of Nazi intentions toward the Jews. Schulte also provided information to **Allied** and Jewish organizations on other topics, as well as being instrumental in helping individual Jews escape from the Nazis. He escaped to Switzerland in 1943 and remained there for the rest of his life.

SCHUTZSTAFFEL (SS) (PROTECTIVE SQUADS). The organization was founded in 1923 to serve as **Adolf Hitler**'s personal bodyguard. The SS replaced the **Sturmabteilungen** (SA), following its purge in 1934, as the instrument of terror in the **Third Reich**. Under the leadership of **Heinrich Himmler**, who was appointed **Reich** leader of the SS in 1929, the organization broadened its responsibilities to include the operation of the **concentration camps**, as well as responsibility for implementing the **Final Solution** through the organization of the **Einsatzgruppen** units and the supervision of the **death camps**. Additional responsibilities of the SS included the organization of the *Wirtschafts und Verwaltungshauptamt* (WVHA) (Economy and Administration Main Office), which provided **forced labor** in the camps for German corporations such as I. G. Farben and Krupp. The war also witnessed the organization of the **Waffen-SS** units, which served as Hitler's personal multinational brigade. By 1945, the Waffen-SS numbered some 800,000 men who fought alongside the **Wehrmacht** (German army) in the war, but under the army's operational control.

Racial pedigree and **ideology** were institutionalized in the SS. **Aryan** racial characteristics were primary criteria for admission to the elite organization. Membership in the SS required that recruits and their wives prove that their "racial purity" extended back as far as the year 1700.

SECOND JEWISH LAW OF HUNGARY. The law recognized the conversion of those Jews who had converted to **Christianity** before 1919 and whose family had resided in **Hungary** since 1848. There were about 90,000 converts in Hungary in 1941. About 60,000 Jews who had converted after 1919 were deported in 1944 along with the other Jews of the Hungarian countryside and towns. Converts who resided in Budapest, however, were exempt from the **deportations**, as were priests, nuns, and lay church officials. About 53,000 converts survived the **Holocaust** in Hungary.

SELEKTION. Upon arrival at the **death camps**, able-bodied Jews were selected for **forced labor**. Those who appeared too ill or young or physically impaired, and thus incapable of work, were immediately sent to their death. At **Auschwitz**, **Josef Mengele** conducted the *Selektion* for the purpose of identifying suitable victims for his **medical experiments**. The term also refers to the selection of Jews in the **ghettos** who were marked for **deportation** to the death camps.

SELF-CLEANSING EFFORTS. In **Lithuania**, following the **Nazi** invasion of the **Soviet Union**, **Reinhard Heydrich** ordered his **Einsatzgruppen** leaders to instigate "self-cleansing efforts" among the local population. This **euphemism** called for inciting anti-Jewish

pogroms, disguised as the spontaneous actions of patriotic **Lithuanians**, against the **Bolshevik** and Jewish enemy.

SENDLER, IRENA (1910–2008). Sendler was a Polish Catholic social worker in German-occupied **Poland**. A member of the Polish Council for Aid to the Jews (**Zegota**), she helped alleviate the suffering of numerous Jews. Because she worked for the Social Welfare Department of the Warsaw municipality, Sendler had access to the **Warsaw ghetto**, where she provided Jews with money, medicine, and clothing. Identifying with the plight of the suffering Jews she encountered, Sendler wore the **yellow Star of David** armband as a symbol of solidarity with the Jewish people when she walked the streets of the **ghetto**. Her most dangerous activity in behalf of the Jews, however, was in smuggling Jewish children out of the ghetto and placing them with non-Jewish families. In the course of her commitment to save Jewish children, she at one time oversaw eight apartments where Jews were in hiding under her care. In 1943, when the Germans became suspicious of her activity, she was arrested by the **Gestapo** and jailed in the Pawiak prison, where she was brutally tortured. She survived her ordeal and, on her release from prison, Sendler continued her work with Zegota until the end of the German occupation. In 1965, she was recognized by **Yad Vashem** as one of the "**Righteous amongst the Nations.**"

SERBIA. The number of Jews living in Serbia at the start of World War II was approximately 12,000 with 8,000 residing in Belgrade. Following the German occupation of **Yugoslavia** in April 1941, Serbia was placed under a military administration. Between the end of April and mid-June 1941, the Germans issued numerous directives in regard to the Jews. For example, Jews were required to register and wear the **yellow Star of David badge**. In early May, Jews were forced into labor brigades, and by the end of the month, they were removed from the country's economic life. The **Aryanization** of Jewish property began in July. The economic measures against the Jews were accompanied by violence on the part of the German troops. In August 1941, the Germans set up three internment camps for male Jews. Since the **death camps** were not as yet operational, the Germans resorted to shooting Jews on a daily basis. By mid-November

1941, 5,000 male Jews had been murdered by German troops. In December, Jewish women and children were interned and shot by the Germans. By mid-1942, Serbia was *Judenfrei* (free of Jews). In all, Jewish losses in Serbia are estimated at 30,000.

SEYSS-INQUART, ARTHUR (1892–1946). A lawyer by training, Seyss-Inquart was appointed by Austrian chancellor Kurt von Schuschnigg as a mediator between himself and the Austrian **Nazis**. In February 1938, **Adolf Hitler** pressured Schuschnigg to appoint Seyss-Inquart as **Austria**'s minister of the interior with total control of the police and public safety. Following Schuschnigg's resignation in March 1938, Seyss-Inquart became the new chancellor and immediately invited the Germans to enter Austria, allegedly to maintain law and order. Following the **Anschluss** on 13 March 1938, Seyss-Inquart was appointed **Reich** commissioner of Ostmark (Austria).

In the aftermath of **Germany**'s occupation of **Poland**, Seyss-Inquart in October 1939 was appointed deputy governor-general in the **General-Gouvernement** under **Hans Frank**. Following the German occupation of Holland, he was appointed Reich commissioner of the occupied **Netherlands**. It was in this position that Seyss-Inquart initiated anti-Jewish legislation as well as sanctioning the pillage of Jewish property. He was also instrumental in the **deportation** of the Dutch Jews to the **death camps**. In regard to this responsibility, Seyss-Inquart engaged in a successful political struggle with **Adolf Eichmann** and **Heinrich Himmler** over the jurisdictional responsibility for dealing with the **Final Solution** in the Netherlands. During his tenure as Reich commissioner, Seyss-Inquart was answerable for the deportation and extermination of more than 110,000 Dutch Jews, or 75 percent of the Dutch Jewish population. Seyss-Inquart was sentenced to death at the **Nuremberg Trials** that commenced on 18 October 1945.

SHANGHAI. In 1937, the Japanese conquered China and imposed their rule over Shanghai. At the time, the port city consisted of four million inhabitants, which by 1939 included approximately 25,000 Jews, many of whom arrived in Shanghai after **Kristallnacht**. Jewish **refugees** from **Germany**, **Austria**, and **Hungary** made their way to the Asian city because refugees were not required to produce a visa, passport, or official papers of any kind. In Shanghai, the refugees were able to replicate much of Jewish life as it had existed in Germany and Austria prior to the advent of the **Nazi Party**. The refugee community organized religious services, ranging from Reform to Orthodox, and fostered a **Zionist** movement, a German-language press, and many different forms of cultural and educational institutions such as a theater and adult education centers.

As was the case for Jewish refugees in **Japan**, the Japanese government, under pressure from its German partner, established a **ghetto** on 18 February 1943. Because help from Jewish relief organizations, such as the **American Joint Distribution Committee**, was cut off as a result of the war, the Jewish Shanghai community was reduced to penury. In December 1943, the situation improved as a result of both the **United States** State and Treasury Departments granting permission for the transfer of funds to Europe and China. Life in the ghetto was not, however, subject to the cruelty and privations that characterized its counterparts in **Nazi**-occupied Europe.

At war's end, most of the Jews in Shanghai were either unwilling or unable to leave. The creation of **Israel** in 1948, however, led to an exodus to the Jewish state. Others, fearful that the Chinese communists would occupy the city, were able to resettle in the Western hemisphere. When the Maoist communist regime occupied the city in 1949, most of the Jews had already departed, and the small numbers that remained were allowed to leave by the mid-1950s.

SHOAH. The Hebrew word for the **Holocaust** that denotes the destruction of the Jews of Europe. An early use of the term can be found in a booklet published in Jerusalem in 1940 entitled "*Shoat Yehudi Polin*" (Devastation of Polish Jewry). The word attained wider currency in **Palestine**, when the **Jewish Agency** in 1942 began to use the term to describe the Jews being murdered in Europe. Historian Zev Garber points out that the Jewish poet Shaul Tschernichovsky (1875–1943) used the term before a group of colleagues when he referred to "the horrible Shoah that is coming upon us."

SHTETL. The Yiddish word refers to the small Jewish villages or towns in Eastern Europe before World War II. During the war, thousands of *shtetls*, located in Eastern Europe, **Poland, Lithuania, Belarussia**, and the Western **Ukraine**, were destroyed by the **Nazis** and their Jewish population either murdered or moved into **ghettos**.

SICHERHEITSDIENST (SD) (SECURITY SERVICES). The organization was founded by **Reinhard Heydrich** in 1931 and merged into the **Reich Security Main Office** in 1939. Its primary function was to gather information on opponents of the **Nazis** as well as on the **Sturmabteilung** (SA).

SICHERHEITSPOLIZEI (SIPO) (Security Police). The agency consisted of the **Gestapo**, the criminal police, and the border police. SIPO was merged with the **Sicherheitsdienst** (SD) when **Reinhard Heydrich** became head of the **Reich Security Main Office** (RSHA).

SILBERBAUER, KARL (1911–1972). The Austrian-born **Gestapo** officer who on 4 August 1944 led the raid on the secret annex at 263 Prinsengracht, where **Anne Frank**, her family, and four other Jews had been in hiding for two years and one month. After the war, Silberbauer returned to **Austria**, where he was jailed for 14 months on charges of having roughed up some communists in 1938. He was later hired by the Vienna police force, where in 1963 **Simon Wiesenthal** tracked him down from a 1943 telephone directory that listed the names of all the Gestapo officials who had served in occupied Holland. Commenting on Silberbauer, Wiesenthal in his memoirs stated that in comparison with other names in his files, "He was a nobody, a zero. But the figure before the zero was Anne Frank."

SILBERTANNE. A unit of largely Dutch **Schutzstaffel** (SS) volunteers who were given the task of killing their countrymen for attacks on **Nazi collaborators**.

SKINHEADS. This is a white supremacist and **anti-Semitic** youth subculture, many of whom are affiliated with white nationalist organizations. The original skinhead subculture started in **Great Britain** in the late 1960s and was neither based on white power nor **neo-Nazism**, but some skinheads had engaged in "gay-bashing," "hippy-bashing," and random violence against Pakistanis and other South

Asian immigrants. The original skinhead movement had mostly died out by 1972, but a revival in the late 1970s came partly as a backlash against the commercialization of punk rock. The skinhead revival in Britain included a sizeable white nationalist faction, involving organizations such as the National Front, British Movement, Rock against Communism, and later Blood and Honour. Because of this, the mainstream media began to label the whole skinhead identity as neo-Nazi. The racist subculture eventually spread to North America, Europe, and other areas of the world. In the **United States**, for example, the Hammerskin Nation was formed in Dallas, Texas, in the late 1980s. Subsequently, racist skinheads gained acceptance among other organized hate groups such as Church of the Creator, White Aryan Resistance, and the Ku Klux Klan. In 1988, there were approximately 2,000 neo-Nazi skinheads in the United States.

According to a 2007 report by the Anti-Defamation League, groups such as White Power skinheads, neo-Nazis, and the Ku Klux Klan, have been growing more active in the United States in recent years, with a particular focus on opposing nonwhite immigration, specifically from Mexico, and attacks against Jews. White Power skinheads are known for wearing Dr. Martens or combat-style boots, flight jackets, jeans, and suspenders (also known as braces). White Power skinheads generally have tattoos that often feature explicitly racist content, such as the **swastika**. Some wear badges, chains, or rings featuring **Nazi** or White Power emblems. Together with other neo-Nazi groups, the White Power skinheads celebrate **Adolf Hitler**'s birthday on 20 April.

SKOKIE. In 1977 and 1978, Illinois **neo-Nazis** of the **National Socialist Party** of America (NSPA) attempted to march in Skokie, a suburb of Chicago. The **Nazis** made this decision after their original site for their political rally in Marquette Park, on the south side of Chicago, was denied because the city government required the NSPA to post an onerous public safety–insurance bond, then proceeded to ban *all* political demonstrations in Marquette Park. Seeking another free-speech political venue, the NSPA chose to march on Skokie. Given the many **Holocaust** survivors living in Skokie, the village's government thought the Nazi march would be politically provocative and socially disruptive, and refused the NSPA its permission. At this point, the American Civil Liberties Union (ACLU) interceded in behalf of the NSPA, in the case of the *National Socialist Party of America* v. *Village of Skokie*, wherein an Illinois appeals court denied the injunction issued by a Cook County Circuit Court judge, ruling that the presence of the **swastika** would constitute deliberate provocation of the people of Skokie. However, the court also ruled that Skokie's attorneys had failed to prove that either the Nazi uniform or their printed materials, which it was alleged that the Nazis intended to distribute, would incite violence. Subsequently, Chicago's city government lifted its Marquette Park political demonstration ban, and the NSPA held its rally in Chicago. In 1981, the attempted Illinois Nazi march on Skokie was dramatized in the television movie *Skokie*.

SLAVE LABOR. *See* FORCED LABOR.

SLOVAKIA. Following the dismemberment of **Czechoslovakia** in 1939, the Germans created Slovakia as an independent state. The Germans allowed Father Josef Tiso, a Catholic priest, to become its president, and the nationalist and **anti-Semitic Hlinka Guard** became the only legal political entity allowed in Slovakia. As a satellite state of **Nazi Germany**, Slovakia cooperated in the **Final Solution** by allowing the **deportation** of its Jews to the **death camps**. In 1939, the Jews of Slovakia numbered about 90,000, which constituted 3 percent of the population. In April 1940, Slovakia initiated anti-Jewish legislation that was based on religion rather than racial criteria. The religious definition resulted from the intercession of the Catholic Church, which eschewed the racial laws in order to protect those Jews who had converted to **Christianity**. However, under the prodding of the **Nazis**, a new definition was promulgated in September 1941, which was more in accordance with **Germany**'s racial laws. Together with the new racial definition came the requirement that all Jews were to wear the **yellow Star of David badge**, thus making them identifiable and available for work in the three **forced labor** camps that Slovakia established in the fall of 1941.

In August 1940, **Adolf Eichmann** sent his representative, **Dieter Wisliceny**, to Slovakia to advise the government on Jewish affairs. Under Wisliceny's direction, the Hlinka Guard and Slovak volunteers were reorganized along the lines of the **Schutzstaffel** (SS) and ordered to carry out anti-Jewish measures. The deportation of

Slovakia's Jews began in March 1942, and by October, more than 75 percent had been "**resettled**," most of them having been sent to **Auschwitz**. Although the racial laws were operative in Slovakia, a number of Jews sought protection from the Catholic Church by converting to Catholicism. The number of conversions is uncertain, but the estimate is that several thousand Jews became Christians in order to save their lives. In turn, the Catholic Church responded by exerting pressure on the Slovak parliament to protect the converts. On 15 May 1942, the parliament again changed the law, which now defined a Jew as someone who belonged to the Jewish religion or who had been converted after 14 March 1939. Exemptions extended to the families of Jews converted to Christianity prior to that date. The parliament's decision, which displeased the German government, was as much a result of the pressure emanating from the church as it was, perhaps, from its displeasure with the deportations. The Germans, after all, charged Slovakia 500 marks for each Jew who was deported from the country. Thus the Slovakian government saved 500 marks for each Jew exempted under the new definition.

At the time of the deportations, Rabbi **Michael Dov Weissmandel** (1903–1956), a leader of Slovakia's Jewish community and a member of the Working Group, a Jewish underground organization, embarked on a plan to save not only the Jews of Slovakia but also the Jews of German-occupied Europe. The **Europa Plan**, as it came to be known, sought to prevent the deportation of Slovakian Jewry through the payment of a ransom to the Germans. Wisliceny was given somewhere between $40,000 and $50,000 to freeze the deportations, and when they were subsequently halted, Weissmandel and his colleagues assumed it was because of the cash payment. There is, however, no evidence to suggest that Wisliceny was responsible for the cessation of the transports. Weissmandel, nevertheless, moved on the assumption that the ransom strategy was successful and proceeded to make plans to ransom the Jews of **Poland**. The Working Group, consisting of prominent Slovakian Jews, attempted to raise between $2 million and $3 million from Jews in the free world.

The Europa Plan failed because the **Allied** nations would not allow the transfer of large sums of money into the hands of the Germans. When Wisliceny commenced deportations in the fall of 1944, Weissmandel and his group blamed the failure of the plan on Jewish organizations for not raising the necessary $200,000 down payment, thus allowing European Jewry to face an uncertain future at the hands of the Germans.

In mid-1944, communists, disaffected Slovak nationalists, and other political groups who were determined to free Slovakia from its dependence on Germany rose in revolt. About 2,000 Jews participated in the Slovak national uprising, including four parachutists from **Palestine**. When the uprising failed, deportations resumed and approximately 13,500 Jews were deported to **Auschwitz, Sachsenhausen**, and **Theresienstadt**. An additional 5,000 Jews joined the **partisans** in the mountains or in the towns of Slovakia until the end of the war. After the gas installations were dismantled in Auschwitz, a few thousand Slovakian Jews were sent to **Bergen-Belsen** and some to Theresienstadt. Approximately 10,000 Jews who were deported after the uprising survived and eventually returned to Slovakia.

SOAP. During World War II and for many years thereafter, the story persisted that the Germans made soap from the fat of their Jewish victims. The soap-from-Jewish-fat rumor, in fact, was used by **Schutzstaffel** (SS) personnel at **Auschwitz** to taunt Jewish prisoners. **Holocaust** historians, such as Yehuda Bauer and Raul Hilberg, indicate that there is little evidence to support this charge. It is true, however, that Germans made soap from human bodies at the Danzig Anatomic Institute in 1944. Although the Germans sought to further experiment with the process, there was no industrial production, and the pieces of soap that Jewish victims were told were made of human fat turned out to be nonorganic fats. Yehuda Bauer has written that this is "one of those things that we know today didn't happen." Thus we are left with the probability that had subsequent experiments proved successful, Germany would have manufactured soap from human fat. Germany's defeat in World War II prevented this **Nazi** atrocity from occurring. *See also* MEDICAL EXPERIMENTS.

SOBIBOR. The **Aktion Reinhard death camp** was located near the village and railway station of Sobibor in the eastern section of the Lublin district in **Poland**. The camp was constructed in March 1942 after the extermination operations had already begun in **Belzec**. Under camp commandant Franz Stangl, the gassing of Jews by **carbon monoxide** commenced in May 1942. Stangl, like many of the operatives in the Belzec camp, came to Sobibor experienced in killing with gas because of his participation in **Germany's Euthanasia Program**. Unlike Belzec, there was no barracks for the arrivals once they disembarked from the trains. Rather, the undressing took place in the railway square under the watchful eyes of the Ukrainian guards. In order to avoid panic, the victims were told upon arrival that following their baths, they would have their possessions returned to them and be sent to **Ukraine**, where they would be able to live and work. The sick and the infirm were told that they would be taken to the infirmary, but instead were taken to open ditches and shot. At the "Cash Office," Jews were required to "deposit" their money and valuables, and were warned that they would be shot should they attempt to hide anything.

The entire process, from their arrival at the camp to entry into the **gas chamber**, was often accompanied by beatings administered by German and Ukrainian guards. Jews were humiliated even more by a dog called **Barry**, which **Schutzstaffel** (SS) men had trained to bite, especially when the victims were naked. The humiliation was, however, calculated. The beatings, the dog's bites, and the screaming guards had the effect of forcing the Jews to escape these indignities by running through a tube that led to the "baths" where they were gassed. Fewer convoys of Jews arrived at Sobibor than at Belzec, and their size rarely exceeded 20 freight cars with a total of 2,000 to 2,500 people. By September 1942, there was additional construction at the camp that resulted in a new building containing six gas chambers, which increased the extermination capacity to 1,200 to 1,300 people a day. In July 1943, **Heinrich Himmler** ordered that Sobibor be converted to a **concentration camp** in order to store and process captured munitions. Before the conversion took place, however, a revolt of Jewish prisoners broke out in the camp on 17 October 1943. Despite the odds against a successful revolt, a number of prisoners managed to escape, and their accounts remain the most detailed sources that we have about Sobibor. The number of Jews exterminated in Sobibor range from a low estimate of 225,000 to a high of 250,000. *See also* RESISTANCE.

SOCIAL DARWINISM. The application of the biological theories of Charles Darwin to society. Although the social interpretation of Darwin varied from country to country, for **Adolf Hitler** it became the core of his political philosophy. Hitler and the **Nazi Party** believed that the "struggle for existence" was at the core of human behavior, or what Hitler called the "granite foundation" of existence. In adopting the "survival of the fittest" as a component of his politics, Hitler professed his belief in brutal struggle, cruelty, destruction, and the right of the strong to rule over the weak. The **ideology** of **National Socialism** mirrored Hitler's interpretation of Social Darwinism.

SONDERBEHANDLUNG **(SPECIAL HANDLING).** *See* EUPHE-MISMS.

SONDERKOMMANDO (SPECIAL COMMANDO). The term has three different applications. The first applies to the special units of the **Schutzstaffel** (SS) who were reserved for special assignments in the **Final Solution**. There were 10 Sonderkommandos operating in tandem with the **Einsatzgruppen** in the invasion of the **Soviet Union** in June 1941. The Lange **Sonderkommando**, subsequently known as *Sonderkommando* Bothmann, was in charge of the extermination operation at **Chelmno**.

The second use of the term refers to Jewish prisoners in the **death camps** who were assigned work in the **gas chambers** and **crematoria**. Their function was to carry out the bodies of the gassed victims from the inside of chambers, search the bodies for any valuables that they might have concealed, pull out gold fillings from their teeth, and then move the bodies to the crematoria to be incinerated or heave them into large burial pits. The Sonderkommandos were relieved every few months and sent to their deaths in the gas chambers.

The third application refers to the Jewish *Sonderkommando* in the **Lodz ghetto**. As part of the **ghetto's Jewish police**, they dealt with criminal offenses. *See also* BOTHMANN SECTION.

SOUSA MENDES, ARISTIDE DE (1885–1954). A Portuguese diplomat who risked his career to help Jews. He was the consul-general of **Portugal** in Bordeaux when he found himself besieged by refugees seeking visas to reach Portugal by way of **France**. Although specifically ordered not to extend visas to refugees, and under no circumstances to Jews, Sousa Mendes nevertheless issued transit visas to approximately 10,000 Jews. For his act of courage, he was dismissed from the Foreign Service and denied his pension. He died in 1954, an almost forgotten hero of the **Holocaust**. In 1966, he was posthumously honored as one of the **Righteous among the Nations** by **Yad Vashem**. Sousa Mendes was formally rehabilitated by the Portuguese government in 1988. In 1994, Bordeaux belatedly paid homage to Sousa Mendes by erecting a bust in his memory. *See also* REFUGEE CRISIS.

SOVIET UNION. From August 1939 to June 1941, the Soviet Union and **Nazi Germany** were linked by treaties that permitted a Soviet sphere of influence in eastern **Poland** and **Ukraine**, and the occupation of the **Baltic** states. On the eve of World War II in September 1939, the Jewish population of the Soviet Union ranged between 3,020,000 and 3,050,000. The Soviet annexation of eastern Poland, the Baltic states, and Bessarabia and Bukovina added an additional 1,900,000 Jews under Soviet rule. An additional 250,000 to 300,000 Jews were allowed to enter the Soviet Union as refugees from German-occupied Poland.

Soon after the German invasion of the Soviet Union in June 1941, the Soviets found their country partially occupied by the **Wehrmacht** (German army). The Jews found themselves until 1943 either under German occupation, which included the Baltic states and all of Poland, or under the protection of the Soviet government. In the territories captured from the Soviet Union, orders were given by **Heinrich Himmler** and **Reinhard Heydrich** for the extermination of the Jews. Within 12 to 18 months, the Germans exterminated the total population of Jews living on occupied Soviet soil.

The extermination of the Jews within the Soviet Union's pre-1939 borders was based on **Adolf Hitler**'s conviction that Jews were the main supporters of the Soviet government. Hitler's **Commissar Order** implied the complete extermination of the Jewish population, inasmuch as the murder of the Jews was viewed as a strategic component of **Nazi** objectives in the Soviet Union. The special units known as the **Einsatzgruppen** accompanied the Wehrmacht into Russian territory and were primarily responsible for the killing operations against Jews.

The roundup and murder of the Jews in German-occupied Soviet territory took several forms. Where possible, the Germans sought help from the local population. The Einsatzgruppen would move from town to town and gather local support for the roundup of Jews, who were then brought to ditches or ravines and shot. In other parts of the Soviet Union, the Germans concentrated Jews in **ghetto**-like conditions. Jews were required to wear either a white armband or a **yellow Star of David badge** on their clothing. The Germans placed the young and the skilled in **forced labor** units, but this lasted only a short time. Subsequently, all of the Jews living in the ghettos were shot to death by the Germans.

Although there was no organized **resistance** by the Jews in the Soviet Union, individual Jews withstood the Germans in many different ways. The main form of resistance for those Jews who opposed German rule was to flee to the forests and join the partisans. A few of these partisan groups were composed mostly of Jewish fighters, but in the aggregate they were Russian. Despite acts of sabotage against the Germans, the record of the partisan movement, as a whole, was a poor one when it came to saving Jewish lives. As additional numbers of Russians fled the Nazis and joined partisan groups, they also brought with them their **anti-Semitism**. Jews in the partisan movement were objects of ridicule, and their willingness to fight was always questioned.

During the course of the war, most Jewish men were either drafted or volunteered for the Red Army. The percentage of Jews in the military was, in fact, higher than their percentage in the population. Some 500,000 Soviet Jews fought in the Red Army, and approximately 200,000 lost their lives in battle. Close to 161,000 medals were awarded to Jews for their heroism in battle. In the Soviet Union proper, Jews suffered hardships during the war like their non-Jewish Soviet citizens. But this did not prevent the intense anti-Semitism, which was exacerbated by returning indoctrinated disabled war veterans who spread anti-Jewish Nazi propaganda. The Soviet government did little to counter anti-Semitism with its own propaganda. What **Joseph Stalin**'s government did do was to create the **Jewish Anti-Fascist Committee** (1943), which became the temporary representative body of Soviet Jewry. The appearance of the committee also helped to defuse the criticism that the government was indifferent to anti-Semitism.

Starting in 1944, when the Soviet Union went on the offensive against Germany, the Jews who had sought refuge in Russia commenced their return home to the former German-occupied territory. What they witnessed upon their arrival was not only the full extent of the Nazi **genocide** but also the complicity of their neighbors in the murder of Jews and the seizure of their property. Jews found that their former apartments were occupied by those who took advantage of their absence, and they were not permitted to work in some of the occupations that they had held before the war. From Poland to the Baltic states, Nazi propaganda had succeeded in intensifying an already existing anti-Semitism.

SPAIN. Although it was officially neutral during World War II, Spain's sympathies were with **Germany**. After the fall of **France** in 1940, tens of thousands of **refugees**, mostly Jews, attempted to enter Spain so as to reach seaports where they hoped to find a ship that would sail them to a safe haven. Spain's policy was to allow refugees to enter if they possessed entry visas to **Portugal** or some other country. Despite this restriction, tens of thousands of refugees entered the country in 1940–1941. When it was demanded, however, the Spanish security police handed over refugees to the Germans. Nevertheless, the regular **emigration** of Jews to Spain continued until October 1941, when it was halted by the Germans.

The Spanish government on the whole was concerned about the influx of thousands of refugees into Spain, and in formulating a policy to meet the crisis, it did not discriminate against Jews, nor did it share the racial **anti-Semitism** of **Nazi Germany**. In fact, the government countered Germany's threat to Spanish Jews living in other European countries by issuing a document that protected more than 4,000 Spanish Jews living in various European countries. The Spanish government authorized the use of "protective documents" and issued a special passport that allowed for a person to obtain Spanish citizenship without residing in the country. When the Germans in January 1943 demanded that Spanish Jews living in Western European countries leave by March 31, the Spanish government was positioned to save the lives of thousands of Spanish Jews living in **Nazi**-occupied countries.

The Spanish authorities, however, did limit the number of refugees seeking asylum to enter Spain. They demanded that refugees claiming Spanish citizenship produce complete documentation of their Spanish origins. This requirement resulted in many of the refugees being denied entry into Spain. The government also insisted that refugees who entered Spain depart shortly after their arrival. Toward the implementation of this policy, the Spanish government stipulated that only after one group of refugees left the country would the next group be allowed residence in Spain. As a result of these restrictions, it has been estimated that a total of only 800 Spanish Jews were allowed to enter Spain from 1943 to the end of the war.

Similarly, between 1942 and 1943, when refugees fled from France in order to escape **deportation**, they sought sanctuary in Spain. The Spanish government, at this point, was ready to turn over the Jewish refugees to the Germans, but threats from British prime minister **Winston Churchill** led it to rescind this decision. In April 1943, the Spanish government announced that the refugees could stay, provided that they were cared for and that they would, as in the case of the Spanish Jews who were expelled by the Germans, leave the country for another destination as soon as possible.

Under these circumstances, the number of Jewish refugees who found refuge in Spain between mid-1942 and the fall of 1944 was approximately 7,500. Despite pressure from the Germans, the Jewish refugees in Spain were not singled out for persecution nor were they discriminated against. The Spanish authorities treated Jewish and non-Jewish refugees alike. They permitted Jews to live in towns and in the cities of Madrid and Barcelona, where Jewish relief agencies covered the cost of their upkeep.

SPECIAL RESPONSIBILITIES ON ORDERS OF THE FÜHRER. Following Nazi Germany's invasion of the **Soviet Union** in June 1941, the **Einsatzgruppen** units of the **Reich Security Main Office** (RSHA) were ordered to liquidate "Jewish **Bolsheviks**," which meant the murder of Soviet party and state functionaries as well as the intelligentsia. The Führer's order issued to **Heinrich Himmler** in March 1941 served as the basis for the Einsatzgruppen to act independently of the **Wehrmacht** and subsequently to decide who was considered part of the "Jewish-Bolshevik intelligentsia, rather than the military." *See also* COMMISSAR ORDER.

SPECIAL TRAINS. The term used by the Germans to describe the trains that carried the Jews to the **death camps**. *See also* EUPHE-MISMS; REICHSBAHN.

STAB IN THE BACK. In the early 1920s, **Adolf Hitler**, the leader of the **Nazi Party**, accused the Jews of **Germany** of inflicting a "stab in the back" upon the nation that resulted in Germany's defeat in World War I and the country's subsequent economic and political ills. The use of the phrase "stab in the back" was, at one time, erroneously associated with Friedrich Ebert, the first president of the **Weimar Republic**. In extending greetings to troops returning from the war, Ebert told the assembled soldiers that they had never been defeated in the field. The phrase "stab in the back" was added by others to his remarks, although he never included the phrase to the troops. The term was used, however, by General Paul von Hindenburg when he was summoned by the Reichstag to explain the causes of Germany's defeat in the war, although he did not associate the phrase with the Jews. Hitler employed the phrase for political propaganda purposes, and he used it exclusively in association with the Jews.

STALIN, JOSEPH VISSARIONOVICH (1879–1953). After consolidating his dictatorship over the **Soviet Union** in 1929, Stalin introduced the first of his Five-Year Plans to turn the country from an agrarian into an industrialized state. Toward this objective, he introduced a policy of forced collectivization to finance his policy of industrialization, and nowhere was this transition more brutal than in **Ukraine**. Although Stalin would later be a party to the **Moscow Declaration** in November 1943, which condemned **Nazi** atrocities, he was no stranger to mass murder.

It was also in 1929 that Stalin directed the OGPU to eliminate perceived enemies to his increasingly paranoid and arbitrary political leadership. In 1936, Stalin unleashed the "Great Purge," whereby suspect Soviet citizens were arrested and executed by the NKVD, which had replaced OGPU. Many of those imprisoned were Jews, including many prominent "Old Bolsheviks," such as Gregory Zino-viev, Lev Kamenev, as well as an earlier exile of Stalin's main politi-cal rival, Leon Trotsky. As a group, they were accused of conspiracy and treason and, with the exception of Trotsky whom Stalin had murdered in Mexico in 1940, were executed after public show trials. Subsequently Stalin purged the top leadership of the Red Army. The result of the purges and mass killings led to the emergence of a new generation, largely of peasant origin, who became the new political leadership of the Soviet Union. They brought with them not only total loyalty to Stalin but also their **anti-Semitism**.

Most historians agree that Stalin was anti-Semitic, but this facet of his personality was not openly evident until after World War II, al-though he did enter into a treaty with **Nazi Germany** in August 1939. Following **Germany**'s invasion of the Soviet Union in June 1941, Stalin rallied the Russian people to fight the war in defense of the homeland. But the Nazi attack also marked the decision to implement the **Final Solution**. As it became apparent that the Germans were specifically targeting Jewish men, women, and children for extermi-nation, Stalin announced in April 1942 the formation of the **Jewish Anti-Fascist Committee**, the only such organization he allowed to speak on behalf of a national group. The committee's stated purpose was to disseminate antifascist propaganda among world Jewry, but its primary objective was to raise funds for the Red Army from the Jews of the **United States** and **Great Britain** in support of the war against Nazi Germany Throughout the war Stalin not only acknowl-edged the Nazi bloodletting of the Jews but specifically alerted the West to the Nazi massacre at **Babi Yar**, where the **Einsatzgruppen** murdered 33,000 people. Stalin's policy toward the Jews changed during the Cold War. Stalin, speaking of the "Great Patriotic war," re-fused to distinguish between Jew and non-Jew in the conflict against Nazi Germany, which was fought predominately on Soviet soil and resulted in the loss of approximately 26.6 million lives. He ignored the revelations of the **Holocaust** and refused to acknowledge Jews as having a separate fate at the hands of the Nazi invaders from that of the rest of the Soviet population. Between 1948 and 1953, Stalin waged an anti-Semitic campaign against the Jews, which included the disbanding of the Jewish Anti-Fascist Committee and the murder of its chairman, **Solomon (Shlomo) Mikhoels**, killed on Stalin's orders in February 1948.

STANGL, FRANZ (1908–1971). *See* SOBIBOR; TREBLINKA.

STERILIZATION. The road that led the **Nazis** to the **Euthanasia Program** and then to the **death camps** began with the passage of the Law to Prevent Hereditarily Sick Offspring (the "Sterilization Law") in 1933. The law allowed for medical practitioners to sterilize an entire group of people with hereditary diseases. Carriers of the following hereditary "defects" were subject to sterilization: hereditary feeble-mindedness, schizophrenia, manic depression, epilepsy, Huntington's chorea, deafness, physical malformations, and chronic alcoholism. The law also contained a provision that allowed physicians to castrate homosexuals. The Nazis established a bureaucracy that included racial hygiene courts that decided one's hereditary status. The 1933 law also created institutes and clinics for hereditary and racial care. Provisions in the law allowed for the maintenance of files on criminals and the study of hereditary diseases among the non-Aryan races. Between 1933 and 1945, approximately 1 percent of the German population was sterilized. The support and participation of the medical profession in the implementation of the 1933 law was based on their belief that sterilization was a necessary moral action in order to preserve the nation's racial purity.

STOKERS. The **Nazi euthanasia** process entailed among other methods of killing those deemed as **"life unworthy of life,"** the murder of patients in **gas chambers.** Following their deaths, orderlies known as "stokers" (*Heiser*) came in, disentangled the bodies, and dragged them out to the "death room," where selected corpses were dissected and their organs removed for the purpose of sending them to research centers for study. The bodies of the dead were burned in the **crematorium** and their ashes shoveled in urns by the stokers. Subsequently ashes, not necessarily those of the deceased, were sent in urns to the grieving families.

STORM TROOPERS. *See* STURMABTEILUNG.

STREICHER, JULIUS (1885–1946). *See STÜRMER, DER*; NUREM-
BERG TRIALS.

STRUMA **AFFAIR.** In December 1941, a cattle boat was purchased by
Zionists for the purpose of smuggling Jews into **Palestine**. Approximately 769 immigrants from **Romania** set sail with the hope that
they would successfully challenge the British ban on immigration
into the region. The British intercepted the ship before it left port and
announced that they would not allow the passengers to reach their
destination. Nevertheless, the *Struma* set sail but broke down and
barely reached the port of Istanbul. The British pressured the Turkish
government not to allow the passengers to leave the ship or to supply it with fuel, food, and other necessities. Subsequently, the ship
was hastily repaired and dragged out into the Black Sea. The ship's
engines again broke down, and a day later on 23 February 1942 the
Struma exploded, leading to the drowning of 768 Jews with only one
survivor.

Theories abound in regard to the responsibility for the explosion.
One view holds that the *Struma* was hit by a torpedo sent by a Soviet
or German submarine. Another theory argues that the ship was hit by
a naval mine. The fate of the *Struma* also marked the termination of
illegal immigration into Palestine until the end of the war. *See also*
WHITE PAPER OF 1939; YISHUV.

STURMABTEILUNG (SA). Sometimes referred to as the "Brown
Shirts," the paramilitary organization was founded in 1923 and
served as the militia for the **Nazi Party**. The plebeian street fighters were also the "storm troopers" of the early **Nazi** movement. The
SA's virulent **anti-Semitism** often resulted in violence against Jews
as well as against its political opponents. Its reputation for brawling
gave the SA an image of an undisciplined and dangerous element
within the Nazi movement. Under the leadership of Ernst Rohm
(1887–1934), the SA enlisted close to 3,000,000 members by 1934
and was viewed by the Reichswehr (German army) as a potential
threat to its military leadership. Possibly fearing that Rohm might attempt to replace him as the leader of the Nazi movement, and at the
same time determined to placate the Reichswehr high command, **Adolf Hitler** ordered a purge against the SA in 1934 that resulted in the

murder of Rohm and many of his top officers. The Nazis took advantage of the bloodletting and shot many of their political enemies in a massacre that historians refer to as the "Night of the Long Knives." The SA never recovered from the purge and faded from importance in the Nazi movement.

***STÜRMER, DER* (THE STORMER).** The **anti-Semitic Nazi** propaganda weekly published by Julius Streicher that sought to inflame public opinion in **Germany** against the Jews. The journal included stories about ritual murder, Jewish pornography, excerpts from the **Protocols of the Elders of Zion**, and repellent photographs of Jews. The Stürmer Publishing House also circulated the **Poisonous Mushroom**, a primer for schoolchildren. Included in this vile **anti-Semitic** "text" is this couplet: "from a Jew's appearance, Evil Satan speaks to us. The Devil, who in every land is known as a terrible plague." *Der Stürmer*, the most radical of the Nazi anti-Semitic publications, sought to guarantee that the next generation of Germans would recognize the Jew as the nation's archenemy. Streicher, a radical in regard to resolving Germany's "Jewish problem," was tried and hanged in the aftermath of the **Nuremberg Trials** in 1946.

STUTTHOF. This **concentration camp** was located east of Danzig (Gdansk), at the mouth of the Vistula River. Initially designated as a camp for civilian prisoners of war following the German invasion of **Poland** in September 1939, it became a concentration camp in January 1942 and remained in operation until May 1945. Initially the camp had few Jewish inmates and was used to incarcerate Soviet prisoners of war. In 1944, however, Stutthof was turned into a **death camp** when large transports of Jews consisting primarily of women were brought to the camp from the **Baltic states** and **Auschwitz**. As was the practice in the other extermination camps in Poland, the Jews were put through a *Selektion*, and many were sent to the **gas chambers**. Of the 50,000 Jews who were sent to Stutthof, nearly all were killed.

SUGIHARA, SEMPO (1900–1986). Sugihara was the Japanese consul-general in Kaunas (Kovno), **Lithuania**, who with the Dutch consul Jan Zwartendijk issued entry visas from their respective countries that allowed thousands of Jews to pass through the **Soviet Union** and **Japan** toward their destination to colonies in the Dutch East Indies. The Soviets had made the visas a condition for allowing refugees who fled the German army to travel by train across Siberia to Vladivostok. The Japanese government, however, refused to allow the issuance of the visas, and after repeatedly being denied his request for the passports, Sugihara issued them himself. Sugihara was punished for his action and was forced to resign from the Japanese Foreign Service in disgrace.

Most of the Jews who used the Sugihara visas ended up in Japan for a short time but spent much of the war in Shanghai, although none made it to the Dutch colony of Curacao, which was their original destination. Included among those saved by the efforts of both Zwartendijk and Sugihara were the 400 Talmudic scholars of the *Mirrer Yeshiva* (house of study). The Talmudic academy was the only one from Eastern Europe to survive the war intact. *See also* RIGHTEOUS GENTILES.

SUITABLE TREATMENT. The term is a **euphemism** for the killing process directed toward the Jews following the **Nazi** decision to implement the **Final Solution** in mid-1941. **Reinhard Heydrich** stated that Jews capable of work would be moved into the anticipated conquered areas of the **Soviet Union** to build roads and provide other forms of **forced labor**. Heydrich envisioned that a large number of Jews would die as a result of the work conditions, but that a small remnant would survive. Because these Jews would represent the most physically resistant, they would ultimately be targeted for "suitable treatment, lest they become the germ-cell of a new Jewish revival." *See also* EXTERMINATION THROUGH LABOR.

SURVIVORS OF THE HOLOCAUST. The estimates of living **Holocaust** survivors range from 834,000 to 960,000, with between 360,000 and 380,000 in **Israel**, followed by 184,000–220,000 in the former **Soviet Union**, 140,000–160,000 in the **United States**, 80,000–100,000 in Western Europe, 50,000–80,000 in Eastern Europe, and about 20,000 in other countries. The definition of a Holocaust survivor refers to any Jew who lived under the **Nazi** regime or German occupation, or in a state that collaborated with the

Germans or was its ally, and those who fled from any of the above. The category of survivors also includes those who survived the **death camps**, fought as **partisans** against the Germans, or were hidden and protected by Gentiles from the Germans.

SWASTIKA. An ancient Indo-European symbol of Hindu origin in the form of a twisted cross or sunwheel that was adopted by the **Nazi Party** as its logo in the 1920s. The swastika was an important symbol in the heathen religion of the pre-Christian Germanic people. The arms of the sunwheel in antiquity turned toward the left and represented the spiritual realm. The **Nazi** swastika turned to the right, symbolizing the material world. The logo was also used by the **Thule Society**, which helped to finance the Nazis in their early years.

SWEDEN. Although Sweden was officially neutral during World War II, its neutrality was tempered by the German occupation of **Norway** and **Denmark**. Surrounded by the Germans and subjected to the British blockade, Sweden was forced to rely on **Germany** for many of its raw materials as well as chemical products. In turn, Sweden provided Germany with iron ore, which was indispensable for its war effort. Early in the war, therefore, Sweden allowed Germany to use its railways and coastal waters to ship its troops to Norway and later to **Finland** during its war against the **Soviet Union**. With the invasion of the Soviet Union in June 1941, Germany gained even more influence over Sweden as it made demands regarding the shipment of soldiers and war materials to its Finnish ally.

After the German defeat at Stalingrad during the winter of 1942–1943, Swedish neutrality tilted toward the **Allies** as the German reversals in the Soviet Union and North Africa reduced the ability of the **Reich** to place pressure on the Swedes. By 1944, Swedish policy had become pro-Allied without interrupting its trade with Germany. Sweden's bittersweet relationship with Germany mirrored its response to the issue of the Jews.

Sweden's response to the plight of the Jews may best be described as a cautious one. In January 1938, Sweden limited the number of Jewish **refugees** allowed to enter the country. Following both the **Anschluss** and **Kristallnacht**, Sweden did not alter its immigration law except to allow the entry of 500 Jewish children from Germany, but without their parents. In order to prevent additional Jewish refugees from entering the country, Sweden required that the letter "J" be stamped on German passports for all Jews. In the fall of 1938, the Germans introduced this requirement for Jewish émigrés, and those German Jews who arrived in Sweden without the proper stamped visa were forced to return to the Reich. However difficult the Swedes made it for Jewish refugees to find a haven in their country, it is also true that between 1939 and 1944 approximately 12,000 Jewish refugees found asylum in Sweden.

On the eve of World War II, there were approximately 7,000 native-born Jews in Sweden, most of whom lived in Stockholm. The Swedish-Jewish community in the late 1930s was active in lobbying the government to bend the immigration laws but found their petitions rejected. Sweden, however, maintained the tradition of cooperation with its Scandinavian neighbors, and for this reason its doors were open to Jews escaping **deportation** from Norway, Denmark, and Finland. In the fall of 1943, the Swedish government requested the German government to place Denmark's Jews in camps in Sweden. When the Germans failed to respond to the request, the Swedish government announced its willingness to provide a haven for all of Denmark's Jews. Sweden's action resulted in the rescue of Danish Jewry from deportation to the **death camps**.

As Sweden's policy become more pro-Allied, it came to play an important role in helping Jews under German domination. In particular, the Swedish government cooperated with the **United States War Refugee Board** and sent **Raoul Wallenberg** to **Hungary** to help protect Jews from deportation to the **death camps** by issuing Swedish passports. The Swedish government also played an important role in the decision made by the **Hungarian** regent, Miklos Horthy, to halt the deportation of Hungarian Jewry to **Auschwitz** in July 1944.

SWISS BANKS. Following the **Nazi** "seizure of power" in **Germany** in January 1933, Jews who feared the worst from the new government attempted to protect their assets by placing funds in Swiss banks. This precaution against an uncertain future was encouraged by a Swiss law that protected the banks' clients from the scrutiny of the Nazis. During the war, the Swiss banks were recipients of gold from countries under Nazi occupation, as well as from the gold fillings extracted from the teeth of Jewish victims in the death camps. A **Schutzstaffel** (SS) officer, Captain Bruno Melmer, had the responsibility for collecting gold from the **death camps**, including **Auschwitz**, and subsequently a substantial portion of the victims' gold was sent to **Switzerland**. In exchange for the gold, the banks provided currency that enabled Germany to continue the war for at least two additional years.

There is little doubt that the Swiss banks knew, and had few scruples, about dealing in gold looted from banks in countries under German occupation. A report commissioned by the Swiss government in 1998 concluded that Swiss National Bank (SNB) officials were aware that some gold sent to Switzerland from German-occupied areas of Europe was looted and that some of this gold was stolen from **Holocaust** victims. The Swiss government and SNB officials, however, have since denied that the banks had knowledge at the time that they were accepting victims' gold. Swiss historians estimate that the amount of gold stolen from the murdered death camp victims and other casualties of **Nazi Germany** totaled some $146 million at 1945 prices. Recent revelations have disclosed that an estimated $2.8 million (or $2.5 billion at today's prices) flowed through the so-called Melmer Account. Furthermore, as it became evident that Germany would lose the war, the Swiss accepted the deposits of leading Nazi officials, who placed funds in the Swiss banks as seed money in anticipation of establishing the Fourth Reich.

In order to prevent a resurgence of Nazism, the United Nations' Monetary and Financial Committee met in July 1944 and adopted the "Safehaven" program, which called on the **Allies** to uncover and prevent the sale of German assets. One stipulation of the Safehaven program required that neutral nations prevent the Nazis from hiding funds and loot in their countries.

Uncovering the funds that the Nazis deposited in Swiss banks, however, was only one problem the Allies faced at the end of the war. There was also the matter of the deposits made by Jews who had since been murdered by the Nazis, and by **survivors of the Holocaust**, who came through their terrifying ordeal bereft of proper identification, let alone deposit books, that would enable them to claim the funds placed in the Swiss banks. The absence of death certificates for the victims of the Holocaust enabled the banks to deny that such deposits had ever existed.

Following the end of World War II, Switzerland, in May 1946, agreed in the Washington Accord to return $5.8 million of gold that Germany had stolen and deposited in Swiss banks. The Swiss also agreed to locate the assets of Jews who were killed in the Holocaust and honor the claims of their relatives. For the next two decades, however, very few Jewish accounts were identified by the Swiss banks. Furthermore, it appears that the Swiss banks claimed the dormant accounts of the Holocaust victims and used the funds as a means of compensating those Swiss whose property had been confiscated in communist countries. For example, in July 1950, the Swiss signed an agreement with the communist government in **Hungary** whereby the heirless assets of Hungarian Jews would be exchanged for compensation to those Swiss whose property had been confiscated. The Swiss, however, insisted that the Hungarians would have to provide evidence about the existence of heirless assets in Swiss banks. A similar agreement was reached by the Swiss government with **Poland**, which transferred the heirless assets of Polish Jews to the Polish government.

In the mid-1990s, however, Jewish organizations, led by the **World Jewish Congress**, (WJC) demanded a reckoning of the unclaimed deposits. The Swiss banks agreed to investigate the dormant accounts and subsequently announced in February 1995 that the unclaimed deposits totaled $32 million. In April of the same year, **United States** Senator Alfonse D'Arnato opened hearings in Washington, D.C., into the manner in which the Swiss banks handled the unclaimed accounts. Soon after the D'Amato hearings commenced, a class action against the Swiss banks was filed in New York. The claimants sought $20 billion in restitution from the dormant accounts of the Holocaust victims. The response of the outgoing president of Switzerland, Jean-Pascal Delamuraz, was to accuse the Jews of attempting to blackmail his country, a statement for which he later apologized. In early 1997, the chairman of one of Switzerland's largest banks, Credit Suisse, proposed the creation of a fund of $72 million for Holocaust survivors and their relatives. By the end of the year, however, the fund had increased to $600 million when a consortium of Swiss banks and businesses pooled their resources to provide up to $1,000 to each of the eligible Holocaust survivors. The response of Jewish organizations, led by the World Jewish Congress, was to reject this offer as too small a sum. Based on present value, they insisted the figure should be closer to $1.5 billion. By the end of July 1998, despite the mediation of Stuart E. Eizenstadt, the U.S. Undersecretary of State for Economic Development, negotiations between Switzerland's three major banks and representatives of Holocaust survivors collapsed.

The threat made by New York, New Jersey, and California to impose sanctions against Swiss banks on 1 September 1998, however, may have been a major factor in the subsequent agreement reached in mid-August 1998, between the Swiss banks and Jewish groups led by the WJC. Accordingly, an estimated $1.25 billion agreement on compensation for unreturned Holocaust-era assets was reached by both parties. The agreement stipulated that the money would be paid out to Holocaust survivors over a three-year period. *See also* MAX HERLIGER ACCOUNT; RESTITUTION FOR HOLOCAUST SURVIVORS.

SWITZERLAND. In the past two centuries, Switzerland has provided asylum to political **refugees**. Prior to the outbreak of World War II, the Swiss welcomed thousands of refugees, including Jews, seeking to escape the **Nazis**. Some Jews also placed money in **Swiss banks** in fear that the German government would confiscate their assets. Jews felt secure in placing their money in Swiss banks because of the 1934 Swiss banking secrecy laws that sought to protect their clients' deposits from Nazi scrutiny. After the **Anschluss** in March 1938, Switzerland changed its policy of providing political sanctuary when it closed its borders to some 30,000 Jewish refugees streaming toward them. The Swiss had already provided a haven for approximately 21,000 Jews when the new policy went into effect. In the fall of 1938, Heinrich Rothmund, Switzerland's chief of police, persuaded the German government to require that Jews of German or Austrian extraction have their passports stamped with the letter "J" (for *Jude* or Jew). The Swiss were now able to employ a means of identification to keep Jews out of Switzerland.

With the outbreak of war in September 1939, Switzerland maintained its policy of neutrality but was intimidated by the presence of foreign troops along the borders with **Germany** and **Austria**.

Furthermore, the Swiss depended on Germany for the importation of gold, iron, coal, and other products that were produced by **slave labor**. In turn, the **Swiss banks** laundered the gold ingots they received from Germany and exchanged them for hard currency, which enabled Germany to continue the war. But the Swiss never questioned the source of the gold. The Germans, in fact, had confiscated gold from the countries under their occupation, as well as extracting gold fillings from the teeth of the victims of the **death camps**.

Under these circumstances, Swiss "neutrality" was a benevolent one toward Germany, especially when it came to the Jews. The Swiss government, in curtailing the number of Jewish refugees allowed entry into Switzerland, defended its action with the argument that "a life raft can only absorb so many people." In short, the Swiss boat was full. In August 1938, the Swiss government officially closed its borders to Jewish refugees. There were, however, Swiss officials, such as Paul Gruninger (1891–1972), the chief of police of the Swiss canton of St. Gallen, who disobeyed the order closing the borders. He lost his position as a result of providing a haven in Switzerland for 2,000 Jewish refugees who crossed into Switzerland from Germany and Austria in 1938–1939.

During the war, tens of thousands of refugees entered Switzerland, and among them were Jews, some of whom came in special transports, such as the 1,684 Hungarian Jews who arrived from **Bergen-Belsen** in 1945. About 1,200 Jews arrived from **Theresienstadt** as a result of negotiations between **Heinrich Himmler** and representatives of the American **War Refugee Board** that took place toward the end of the war.

Recent disclosures, however, shed new light on the relationship between Switzerland and Germany during the war years. Documents uncovered in the mid-1990s unearthed evidence that gold looted by the Nazis was discreetly sold on the world markets by the Swiss National Bank, with the proceeds used to help the Germans finance their faltering war effort.

Additionally, the Swiss also traded freely with the Germans in stolen artworks and jewelry. The **United States** government concluded that not only did the Swiss help the Nazis prolong the war by at least two years, but they also shielded millions of dollars worth of German assets in the immediate postwar period.

The same documents also raised the question as to the fate of the bank accounts, insurance policies, and other wealth deposited in Switzerland by Jews who subsequently perished in the **Holocaust**. The record shows that the Swiss commercial banks did little to help **survivors of the Holocaust** gain access to assets deposited by relatives who died at the hands of the Germans. Rather, they used the dormant accounts of Holocaust victims to compensate Swiss businesses for expropriated assets in the former communist East European countries. *See also* DENTISTS; SWISS BANKS; WORLD JEWISH CONGRESS.

SZENES, HANNAH (1921–1944). A prime example of Jewish **resistance** during the **Holocaust**, Hannah Szenes was a poet who was a parachutist in the Jewish commando unit of the British army. Szenes was born in Budapest, **Hungary**, and moved to **Palestine** in 1939 where she joined a kibbutz. In 1943, she volunteered to join parachutists, along with 36 other Hungarian-Palestinian Jews, who planned to infiltrate occupied Hungary to help save Jews who were about to be **deported** to **Auschwitz**. After being parachuted into **Yugoslavia** and spending time with a partisan band, Szenes crossed over into Hungary where she was arrested at the border, imprisoned, and tortured, but she refused to reveal details of her mission and was eventually tried and executed by firing squad. She is regarded as a national heroine in **Israel**, where several streets and a kibbutz are named after her, and her poetry is widely read. Her best-known poem is "Blessed Be the Match," which was written while she was in the partisan camp in Yugoslavia and includes the memorable lines,

> Blessed is the match consumed in kindling flame.
> Blessed is the flame that burns in the secret fastness of the heart.
> Blessed is the heart with strength to stop its beating for honor's sake.
> Blessed is the match consumed in kindling flame.

– T –

T-4. Code name for the German **Euthanasia Program**, which killed more than 100,000 people who were defined as "**life unworthy of**

life" by the **Nazi** regime. The code name refers to the government department of the **Reich** chancellery responsible for the operation, which was located on Tiergarten Strasse 4 in Berlin.

TANNENBERG. The code name for the planned operations of the **Einsatzgruppen** following **Germany**'s invasion of the **Soviet Union** in June 1941. *See* COMMISSAR ORDER.

TATTOOING. The tattooing of prisoners was first used in **Auschwitz** in March 1942 for the purpose of keeping a record and identifying the bodies in the mortuary and the **crematorium**.

10-DEKO. In many parts of **Nazi**-occupied **Poland**, Jews were entitled to one slice of bread daily, called "10-deko" because it supposedly weighed 10 decagrams, or about three and a half ounces. It provided a few hundred calories at most. Made of rye flour, it was dark and moist and, for many, tasted like clay.

THEATER AND THE HOLOCAUST. The threat of Nazism was dealt with in a number of notable stage plays in the 1930s and 1940s. They include N. Behrman's *Rain from Heaven* (1934), Lillian Hellman's *Watch on the Rhine* (1941), and Elmer Rice's *Flight to the West* (1940) and *Judgment Day* (1934), about the Reichstag fire trial.

The earliest stage representation of the **Holocaust** was *The Diary of Anne Frank* in 1954. At the time, the full horror of the Nazi **genocide** was yet not fully comprehended by the public, and the producers of the play were unwilling to confront its horrors in the theater. The stage tended to portray the Holocaust in an oblique manner, with few references to the **ghettos** and none to the **concentration camps**.

The murder of the Jews, however, reached audiences with the adaptation of *Der Stellvertreter. Ein christliches Trauerspiel (The Deputy, a Christian Tragedy)* by Rolf Hoccuth. The play was first produced in Germany in 1963 and brought to Broadway in 1964. *The Deputy* was controversial because of its criticism of **Pope Pius XII**'s failure to speak out against the **Nazi** use of **gas chambers** in the killing of Jews. The play is based on the true story of Kurt Gerstein, a devout Protestant and later a member of the **Schutzstaffel** (SS), who witnessed the use of poison gas in the killing process. In the play Gerstein confronts the pope with his information, which the pope disregards. *The Deputy* sparked the ongoing controversy among historians over the "silence" of Pius XII during the Holocaust.

The first Broadway musical to seriously treat Nazism was the award-winning *Cabaret* (1966), based on John Van Druten's 1951 play *I Am a Camera*, which in turn was adapted from the novel *Good-bye to Berlin* by Christopher Isherwood. The musical is set in 1931 Berlin as the Nazis are rising to power, and focuses on nightlife at the seedy Kit Kat Klub, attended by **swastika**-wearing "Brown Shirts." The play includes an ill-fated romance between a German boardinghouse owner and her elderly suitor, a Jewish fruit vendor. Overseeing the action is the Master of Ceremonies at the Kit Kat Klub, who serves as a constant metaphor for the state of society in **Weimar Germany**.

American playwright Arthur Miller, over the course of his career, wrote three plays with themes relating to the Holocaust: *Incident at Vichy* (1964) portrays a roundup of Jews for **deportation** from wartime **France**; in *Playing for Time* (1980), a television play, a French cabaret singer's music keeps her alive in **Auschwitz**; and in *Broken Glass* (1994), an American woman is paralyzed by news reports of **Kristallnacht**. The Holocaust was also the theme of *The Man in the Glass Booth*. This Robert Shaw play was based on the **Adolph Eichmann** kidnapping and subsequent trial in Jerusalem in 1961. The play opened on Broadway in 1969 and was made into a film in 1975.

In the past few decades, however, a number of plays have appeared that do not deal directly with the Holocaust but with how people responded to those who were **survivors**, such as Barbara Lebow's *A Shayna Maidel* (1984), Donald Margulies' *The Model Apartment* (1990), and Jeffrey Sweet's *The Action against Sol Schumann* (2001). Still other plays have dealt with growing up as the child of survivors, including Leeny Sack's *The Survivor and the Translator* (1980), Adam Melnick and John Tarjan's *Camp Holocaust* (2000), and Deb Filler's *Punch Me in the Stomach* (1992). The shadow of the Holocaust even pervades plays focused on entirely other subjects, such as the end of Neil Simon's *Brighton Beach Memoirs* (1983), and imposes troubling dimensions in Jon Robin Baitz's *The Substance of Fire* (1991) and Donald Margulies's *Sight Unseen* (1992). *See also*

ART AND THE HOLOCAUST; FILM AND THE HOLOCAUST;
LITERATURE AND THE HOLOCAUST.

THERESIENSTADT. The **Nazi** plan to establish a **ghetto** in Theresienstadt, located in northwestern **Czechoslovakia**, is first mentioned
in a document dated 10 October 1941. The ghetto was opened on 24
November 1941, and following the **Wannsee Conference** in January
1942, **Reinhard Heydrich** ordered that all **Reich** Jews over the age
of 65 be interned in Theresienstadt and be allowed to die a natural
death. Subsequently, Jewish war veterans who were disabled or decorated with the Iron Cross First Class were added to the list. Heydrich
was also careful to add "prominent Jews" to the group, lest they be
missed and questions be raised about their whereabouts. Although
committed to the objective of the **Final Solution**, Heydrich did not
regard elderly Jews as a threat to **Germany**, and by sending them
to an "old age ghetto," he could perpetuate the hoax that Jews were
being **resettled**. The inclusion of Jewish war veterans appeased the
leadership of the German army, which took an interest in the fate of
Jewish war veterans, inasmuch as they had fought for Germany and
deserved some consideration. German Jews, however, were not alone
in being **deported** to Theresienstadt. The Germans also deported
Jews from Central and Western Europe to the ghetto.

By September 1942, there were 53,000 internees in Theresienstadt,
and by mid-1943, 90 percent of the Jews of Bohemia and Moravia
(75,500) and nearly all of the Jews left in Germany, some 42,000,
including their leader, Rabbi Leo Baeck, were deported to the ghetto.
Subsequently, the ghetto included 15,000 Jews from Austria, 5,000
Jews from the **Netherlands**, and 500 from **Denmark**. Beginning in
January 1942, Jews were deported from the ghetto to **Auschwitz**
and **Treblinka**. Under **Adolf Eichmann**'s direction, the ghetto was
allowed an inordinate variety of cultural and educational activities.
Primed to disguise its real purpose, the **Schutzstaffel** (SS) encouraged artists, writers, and scholars to contribute to a number of cultural
programs and events, which included several orchestras, an opera, a
theater group, and a cabaret. The ghetto also included a 60,000-vol-
ume library as well as weekly lectures and concerts.

At the end of 1943, when news of the **death camps** had reached
the outside world, the German government invited the **International**

Committee of the Red Cross to inspect conditions in the ghetto. In preparation for the visit, the Germans constructed temporary stores, cafes, banks, schools, and flower gardens, all for the purpose of disguising the reality of the ghetto. **Joseph Goebbels** even made a propaganda film to show how pleasant life in Theresienstadt was for the Jews. Shortly after the visit from the Red Cross, the participants in the film, including the children, were deported to Auschwitz. Throughout its life, approximately 144,000 Jews were deported to the ghetto. When the ghetto was **liberated** on 8 May 1945, there were 19,000 survivors; however, 33,000 had already died from the outbreak of epidemics, and 88,000 had been deported to the death camps. *See also* BRUNDIBAR.

THIRD REICH. The phrase "The Third Reich" was coined by the German writer Arthur Moeller von den Bruck, who in 1923 published a book entitled *Das Dritte Reich*, which eventually became a catch-phrase that survived the **Nazi** regime. *See also* REICH.

"THE THIRTEENTH." In the **Warsaw ghetto**, the Germans organized Jews from the criminal element for the purpose of informing and performing duties that the regular **Jewish police** refused to participate in. The largest of these groups was located in Warsaw under the name of the Control Office to Combat Black Marketing and Profiteering in the Jewish Residential District. Warsaw's Jews referred to the **Gestapo**-directed group as "the Thirteenth," because its headquarters was located at 13 Leszno Street. "The Thirteenth" served primarily as an intelligence agency for the Gestapo, and consisted of about 300 uniformed Jewish police. Similar groups existed in the **Lodz**, Kovno, and Lublin **ghettos**.

THOMALLA, RICHARD (1903–1945). *Obersturmführer* (Security Lieutenant) (**Schutzstaffel** (SS) Richard Thomalla, an architect by training, was responsible for the construction of the **Aktion Reinhard death camps**, Belzec, **Treblinka**, and **Sobibor**. He was executed by the Soviets in 1945.

THOUSAND-YEAR REICH. In Western culture, a thousand years is referred to as the millennium, which in some Christian denominations represents a "Golden Age" or Paradise on Earth in which "Christ will reign" prior to the final judgment. This belief is derived primarily from the book of Revelation 20:1–6. **Adolf Hitler** envisioned that the **Third Reich** would last a thousand years, but it lasted for 12 years (1933–1945).

THULE SOCIETY. This conspiratorial racial society was founded in 1918 by Rudolph von Sebbendorf (Rudolf Glauer), who was a prime financial contributor to the fledgling **Nazi Party**. The Thule Society was committed to German nationalism, the occult, and the promotion of **anti-Semitism**. Its members included **Alfred Rosenberg**, **Hans Frank**, and Rudolph Hess as well as **Dietrich Eckert**, who exerted a great deal of influence on **Adolf Hitler**'s political thought. *See also VOLKISCH.*

TOTENSLAGER. Burial pits in **Poland** and the **Soviet Union** where Jews were dumped after they were executed by German soldiers and **Einsatzgruppen**. *See also* BABI YAR.

TRANSFER AGREEMENT (HEBREW *HAAVARA*). From the time the Transfer Agreement was signed in August 1933, approximately 50,000 Jews were able to **emigrate** from **Germany** to **Palestine**. According to the accord made between the German government and the **Zionist** leadership in the **Yishuv**, Jews could migrate to Palestine and receive their capital in the form of German-produced goods. Germany benefited from this agreement because it could thereby rid the country of its Jews, gain access to their personal wealth, and at the same time export its manufactured goods. For the **Jewish Agency**, the agreement allowed for an orderly transfer of population from Germany to Palestine, thus achieving an objective of the Zionist movement. Despite a great deal of criticism from Jewish groups that were advocating a boycott of German goods, the World Zionist Congress continued to support the Transfer Agreement.

TRAWNIKI LABOR CAMP. The **Schutzstaffel** (SS) established the camp, located southeast of Lublin, **Poland**, in the fall of 1941 to hold Soviet prisoners and Polish Jews. The Trawniki camp was part of a network of camps under the supervision of **Odilo Globocnik**.

In the spring of 1942, Jews from the Greater **Reich** were brought to the camp, where many of them were brutalized; others were sent to the **Belzec death camp** or were shot in the forest near the camp. Following the liquidation of the **Warsaw ghetto** in 1943, the Fritz Schulz Works, which produced army uniforms and other necessities for the war effort, was moved to Trawniki along with its 10,000 workers. Included among the workers were **Emanuel Ringelblum** and 33 members of the **Jewish Combat Organization** (ZOB). Following the revolt at **Sobibor** in October 1943, **Heinrich Himmler** ordered the liquidation of all the camps in the Lublin district. Fearing similar uprisings in the camps, the Germans proceeded to murder some 43,000 Jews in the so-called **Operation Erntefest**. On 5 November 1943, the 10,000 Jewish prisoners of the Trawniki camp were brought to pits that had already been prepared, and killed. Led by the members of the Jewish Combat Organization, those Jews who belonged to the camp's underground attempted **resistance**, but all were killed in battle. During its existence, approximately 20,000 Jews passed through the Trawniki labor camp. *See also* LUBLIN GHETTO; ONEG SHABBAT.

TRAWNIKIS. Sometimes referred to as Hiwis. The term refers to Eastern Europeans, mainly **Ukrainians**, who worked as German auxiliaries in mass **death camps** such as in **Sobibor**. The Trawnikis would actually do the killing under German supervision.

TREBLINKA. Treblinka was the last of the **Aktion Reinhard** camps to be constructed. The **death camp** was located in the northeastern part of the **General-Gouvernement** near a railway station on the main Warsaw-Bialystok line. The site was in a wooded area and thus naturally concealed. Although construction of the camp began in late May or early June 1942, there already existed nearby a **forced labor** camp where Polish and Jewish prisoners were made to process raw materials from a gravel pit for border fortifications. The death camp was modeled after that of **Sobibor**. In fact, personnel who had been involved in the construction of Sobibor were transferred to Treblinka, including technical specialists from the **Euthanasia Program**. The **gas chambers** at Treblinka were located in a massive brick building, and the access paths, including the tube (which the guards at

Treblinka called the "**road to heaven**"), were modeled on the tubes in **Belzec** and Sobibor.

During its first stage, there were three gas chambers in operation at Treblinka. The walls of the chambers were covered with white tile, shower heads were installed, and water pipes ran across the ceiling, all constructed in order to give the appearance of "showers. " In reality the pipes conducted the carbon monoxide gas into the chambers. After the gassing operation, the bodies were thrown into huge ditches located east of the gas chambers.

The process that awaited the arrivals at Treblinka was not unlike that at Sobibor. The deportees were ushered out of the freight cars and led through a gate into the camp where men were moved to the right and women and children to the left. As was the case in Sobibor, the prisoners were ordered to undress and tie their clothes into a bundle, leave their valuables with a cashier, and then told that after they showered, they would get back their personal belongings and receive clean clothes. The men, women, and children were subsequently forced to run naked through the tube that led to the gas chambers. During the camp's first phase, more than 5,000 to 7,000 Jews arrived each day. Then the number of arrivals increased to about 12,000 a day, although thousands were already dead on arrival.

Germans with dogs stood along the path to the gas chambers. The dogs had been trained to bite the men's genitals and the women's breasts, ripping off pieces of flesh. The Jews were beaten with whips and iron bars so that they would press on to the "showers." To escape from the blows, the victims ran to the gas chambers as quickly as they could, the stronger ones pushing the weaker aside. The Germans assigned two **Ukrainian** guards at the doors of the gas chambers, and as soon as the chamber was full, the Ukrainians closed the doors and started the engine. Some 20 to 25 minutes later, an SS officer would check through the window to be sure that everyone had been asphyxiated. Jewish prisoners (**Sonderkommandos**) were then ordered to remove the corpses.

The system, however, did not always work properly. Sometimes the engines that produced the carbon monoxide gas failed, and the victims already inside the gas chamber would be left standing until the engines were repaired. On one occasion, the doors to the gas chambers were opened prematurely and the victims were still alive, so the doors were again closed and the engines restarted. In a five-week period between 23 July and 28 August 28 1942, approximately 268,000 Jews were annihilated. Because of frequent breakdowns in the gas chambers, Franz Stangl was transferred to Treblinka from Sobibor to deal with this "embarrassing" problem.

The second phase in the killing operations at Treblinka began with Stangl's appointment as the commandant of the extermination camp and the construction of new and more efficient gas chambers. Ten additional gas chambers were added to the existing three old ones. In addition, Stangl "invented" new methods of subterfuge. In one of the buildings containing the new gas chambers, a dark curtain from a synagogue hung at the entrance to the passage. Its inscription in Hebrew read, "This is the gate through which the righteous may enter." Above the entrance door was affixed a Star of David. The new gas chambers were able to hold 4,000 people at a time, the old ones only 600. Under Stangl, a more efficient way of burning corpses was undertaken. The incineration of corpses was carried out by placing train rails on blocks of concrete. The corpses were then piled upon these rails. Brushwood was placed under the rails, and the wood was drenched with gasoline. Not only were the most recently gassed corpses burned this way but also those exhumed from the ditches.

In early March 1943, after **Heinrich Himmler** visited the headquarters of Operation Aktion Reinhard, he ordered the dismantlement of Treblinka. Before the camp could be closed, however, the bodies of hundreds of thousands of victims had to be exhumed and incinerated in order to destroy all incriminating evidence. It was at this point, during the final phase of the camp's existence, that the Jewish prisoners revolted on 2 August 1943. The revolt failed, and the last group of 30 Jewish prisoners was shot in November 1943. The number of Jews who were exterminated in Treblinka is estimated from a low of 700,000 to a high of 900,000.

TRIANGLES. In the **concentration camps** the prisoners were categorized according to nationality and the causes for their incarceration. This took the form of identifying inmates by the color of the triangular patches that were required to be worn on their clothes. For example, **homosexuals** were required to wear a pink triangular patch, communists a red triangle, criminals wore green, **Jehovah's Witnesses** wore purple, "asocials" wore black, **Gypsies** were identified by brown triangles, and the Jews by a **yellow Star of David**. Foreigners had a letter printed on their triangles. For example, the Poles were marked with the letter P, the French an F, and so on.

TRUMAN HARRY S. (1884–1972). Although the **Nazi concentration camps** were being **liberated** when Harry Truman inherited the presidency in April 1945, the effects of the **Holocaust** lasted throughout his two terms in office. The problems he faced, including the prosecution of German war criminals at the **Nuremberg Trials**, the Jewish **refugee crisis** in Europe after the war, and the creation of the **State of Israel**, which Truman recognized immediately after its government's declaration of statehood, are all issues that grew out of the Holocaust. In August 1945, President Truman appointed Earl Harrison (1899–1955) as his special envoy to inquire into conditions of the Jewish **displaced persons** (DP) in the American zone in **Germany**. Harrison was appalled by what he saw, and his report was a devastating indictment of **Allied** military policy toward the surviving Jews. Based on the report's findings, President Truman strongly urged the British to grant 100,000 visas to Jewish refugees to enter **Palestine**. Guided by the provisions of the **White Paper of 1939**, the British were willing to grant only 6,000 visas.

In recent years, however, evidence has been disclosed that President Truman was not as sympathetic to Jews as had earlier been believed. Based on his diary entries and other research, it has been disclosed that the 33rd president of the **United States** expressed **anti-Semitic** sentiments such as in his 1947 diary entry that "the Jews have no sense of proportion," that "the Jews are very, very selfish," and that "neither **Hitler** nor **Stalin** has anything on them for cruelty or mistreatment to the underdog." Historian Michael Cohen documented additional examples in his book, *Truman and Israel* (1991), when he quotes Truman as privately describing New York City as "kike town," and referring to his friend Eddie Jacobson as his "Jew clerk." Elsewhere, Cohen cites Truman stating in a private letter about New York City: "This town has 8,000,000 people, 7,500,000 of 'em are of Israelitish [*sic*] extraction, 400,000 wops and the rest are white people." During one cabinet session in 1946, Truman had this to say about Jewish criticism of his Palestine policy: "If Jesus

Christ couldn't satisfy the Jews while on earth, how the hell am I supposed to?"

Rafael Medoff, director of the David S. Wyman Institute for Holocaust Studies, has noted that during the Holocaust, Truman displayed little interest in the plight of the refugees. When a constituent, a Missouri rabbi, wrote to then-senator Truman urging him to support action to rescue Jewish refugees, Truman replied: "I do not think it is the business of Senators who are not on the Foreign Relations Committee to dabble in matters which affect our relations with the Allies at this time. . . . [I]t is of vital importance that the Jewish Congregations be patient and support wholeheartedly the foreign policy of our government" (the policy of refraining from taking any meaningful steps to aid refugees from Hitler). Medoff also charges that after the war, Truman did urge the British to admit 100,000 Holocaust **survivors** to Palestine—but that he never took concrete steps to pressure London to do so. Truman did grant diplomatic recognition to the State of Israel just minutes after the state was created, concedes Medoff, but he refused to send Israel weapons to defend itself against five invading Arab armies.

Despite his critics, it is also true that Truman—a biblical literalist and a Christian **Zionist**—had long been a fierce believer in Jewish statehood for reasons both religious and moral because the Old Testament stated that the Jews belonged in the "Holy Land." There is also evidence that suggests that his feelings about the plight of the refugees in the DP camps preceded receiving the Harrison Report, because Truman was concerned about the scandalously poor treatment of postwar Jewish refugees in the displaced persons camps, and so he waged a long and often bitter campaign to help ensure that the Jews got a country of their own.

TYPHUS. Typhus, also known as spotted fever, is a feared epidemic disease caused by poor hygiene, filth, famine, and extreme cold. The louse (*pediculis corporis*) is the vector of typhus and breeds in times of disaster such as in wartime and in overcrowded conditions. The **Nazis** believed that typhus was innate to the Jews and that the disease was spread by the Jewish population. For this reason, the Germans forbade **Aryan** doctors to treat sick Jews because of the belief that they would directly or indirectly infect the Aryan population. Jews contracted typhus, stated German health officials, not because of the unsanitary living conditions in the crowded **ghettos**, but because Jewish blood and genes predisposed Jewish bodies to infection. In fact, typhus caused only 3 percent of the deaths in the ghettos. **Anne Frank** and her sister, Margot, however, both died of typhus in **Bergen-Belsen** in March 1945. Diseases associated with crowded and unsanitary conditions, such as typhus fever, dysentery, tuberculosis, and starvation, constituted the vast majority of Jewish deaths in the ghettos of **Poland**.

In the spring of 1943, an exhibit opened in Warsaw that had as its theme the association of Jews with typhus and lice. It is estimated that more than 50,000 people attended the exhibit, including children whose attendance was made compulsory. Literature was distributed that warned that Jews were to be feared because they were the primary carriers of typhus-infested lice and that Jewish flesh poisoned all those who touched it. One handout cautioned that coming anywhere near a Jew caused illness, fever, and possibly death.

– U –

U-BOOTE (U-BOATS). The expression refers to an estimated 6,800 Jews who lived an underground existence in **Germany** during the war. They were hunted down by the **Gestapo** with the aid of Jewish informers known as **catchers**. About 1,400 of Berlin's Jews survived the war thanks to the protection that they were given by Berliners who risked their own lives to hide Jews. *See also* RIGHTEOUS GENTILES.

UKRAINE. The Jewish population of Soviet Ukraine in September 1939 was approximately 2.4 million people. When the Germans invaded the **Soviet Union** in June 1941, they were joined by Ukrainian nationalist units that had a deep hatred for communism In addition, volunteer Ukrainian **Wehrmacht** (German army) units fought alongside the Germans on the eastern front in hopes of regaining their independence. By October, the Germans occupied most of Ukraine and were welcomed by the population as liberators from Soviet rule.

Accompanying the German army into Ukraine were **Einsatzgruppen** C and D. The *Einsatzgruppen* proceeded to wage a relentless campaign of terror against the Jews, which resulted in the murder of hundreds of thousands of Jews as well as thousands of Ukrainians suspected of being communists. In the eastern area of Ukraine, however, approximately 800,000 Jews were evacuated or escaped to the Soviet Union, and about 50,000 Jews from the western Ukraine and Bukovina similarly were able to escape the Germans.

Almost immediately after their occupation of Ukraine, the Germans replaced Soviet rule in Ukraine with their own. The larger area of the former Soviet republic was administered by the German civilian government, and the eastern part of Ukraine was placed under a military rule. It quickly became apparent that the Germans were no better than the Soviets inasmuch as the population was subjected to starvation and millions of Ukrainians were sent on **forced labor** into the **Reich**.

In the western Ukraine, where many in the population identified Jews with communism, a series of pogroms, assisted by Ukrainian auxiliary police, was waged against the Jews, which resulted in thousands of deaths. In Lvov, 5,000 Jews were killed in two such **pogroms**, and the *Einsatzgruppen* added to the total in other areas of western Ukraine. In eastern Ukraine, the *Einsatzgruppen* war of extermination against the Jews moved into high gear. The pattern commenced with the military command issuing a decree that required Jews to wear the **yellow Star of David badge**. This was followed with the requirement that Jews form committees, not unlike the **Judenräte**, and monitor the confinement of Jews to special streets. After a time, Jews were rounded up and taken to ravines and ditches where they were shot. It was also in the eastern Ukraine that the Germans and their Ukrainian police auxiliaries introduced eight gas vans that were used to increase the numbers targeted to be killed. On September 29–30, two weeks after the occupation of Kiev, the Germans marched the city's Jews to the ravine of **Babi Yar**, where 33,771 were murdered.

By the end of 1942 and mid-1943, the *Einsatzgruppen* and their Ukrainian helpers had achieved their objectives. Most of Ukraine had become *Judenrein* (free of Jews), and no Jews were left "officially" alive, even in the forced labor camps.

UMSCHLAGPLATZ. The staging area near the railway tracks in the **Warsaw ghetto** where Jews were forced to report before boarding the trains that **deported** them to the **death camps**. The ghettos of **Poland** all had embarking areas equivalent to the *Umschlagplatz.*

UNCONDITIONAL SURRENDER. At the Casablanca Conference in January 1943, the **Allies** agreed that negotiations with **Germany** would be based on its "unconditional surrender" as the prerequisite for concluding the war. This meant that the Allies would neither barter nor negotiate with the **Nazis** for Jewish lives, lest the Allies violate the policy of unconditional surrender.

UNION OF SOVIET SOCIALIST REPUBLICS (USSR). *See* SO-VIET UNION.

UNITED STATES. The U.S. response to the **Holocaust** can be divided into two phases. The first is the period between 1933 and 1938, when American immigration policy was governed by the provisions of both the National Origins Act of 1924, which limited the number of immigrants to 2 percent of the 1890 census, and the law's modification in 1929, which placed a ceiling of 150,000 immigrants, with 130,000 visas allocated to northern and western Europe. Unfilled quotas from western and northern Europe were not transferable to immigrants from other parts of the world, including eastern and southern Europe. Because of the rigid enforcement of the immigration laws by the State Department, the United States has been accused of taking in fewer **refugees** than it was capable of absorbing.

Historians have offered many reasons for the failure of the United States to become a sanctuary for European refugees fleeing political persecution. As the plight of Jewish refugees unfolded in the years from 1933 to 1938, the Roosevelt administration found itself caught between those who strongly advocated help for **Adolf Hitler**'s victims and those who warned against liberalizing the immigration laws, lest an influx of refugees jeopardize recovery from the economic depression. President **Franklin Roosevelt** was also aware of polls that showed that as late as 1938, 60 percent of the American people believed that the persecution of the Jews was entirely or partly their own fault. Pressure on the administration was also exerted by the strong current of **anti-Semitism** that was being fanned by such personalities as Father **Charles Coughlin**, Gerald Winrod, and Gerald L. K. Smith. In fact, anti-Semitism in the United States reached its peak in the years between the outbreak of the Great Depression and World War II.

Absorbing large numbers of refugees was also complicated by a law that required that immigrants not become a public charge and prove that they had an "adequate means of support." Most American Jews lacked the financial resources to sponsor their European brethren. Those Jews, therefore, who obtained visas were among the fortunate minority who had relatives able to provide the necessary financial support. This financial requirement limited the number of German Jews who were admitted into the United States, although less than a third of the German quota was filled.

The liberalization of the immigration laws was not helped by the attitude of the State Department, which was directly responsible for enforcing the immigration laws. Much has been written about the apparent anti-Semitism of Undersecretary of State Breckinridge Long, who was in charge of implementing immigration policy. Did Long's personal dislike of Jews influence the rigid manner in which he enforced the law? As for the president, although he made several speeches that showed concern about victims of **Nazi** persecution, he was also careful not to identify them as Jews. Roosevelt was mindful that any display of support for the Jews would be used by anti-Semites to support the argument that the Roosevelt administration was under the influence of the Jews. Prior to the outbreak of the war, President Roosevelt did convene the **Evian Conference** in July 1938, in an effort to deal with the intensifying refugee crisis following **Germany**'s annexation of **Austria**, but he made it clear that the United States did not contemplate any changes in its own immigration laws.

The second phase, from 1939 to 1945, was marked by news of the escalating German atrocities against the Jews. The government, at first, disregarded this information as exaggeration, ever mindful of the British propaganda campaign about German atrocities that permeated the American media during World War I. But even after the Roosevelt administration was convinced of the Nazi plan to implement the **Final Solution, Allied** policy militated against the rescue of the doomed Jews in German-occupied Europe. Rather, the Allies insisted that the best way to save European Jewry was to defeat **Nazi Germany**. The creation of the **War Refugee Board** (WRB) in 1944 was a grudging concession to this policy.

When **Henry Morgenthau Jr.**, secretary of the Treasury, threatened to release to the press a report that accused the Roosevelt administration of covertly acquiescing in the murder of European Jews, the president responded. The creation of the War Refugee Board was a case of too little and too late. Although the government agency was active in saving Jews in war-torn Europe, the reality was that millions of Jews had already been exterminated by the Nazis. Furthermore, the WRB suffered from a lack of cooperation from the State Department and the War Department.

The source of disagreement between the government agencies stemmed from both the State Department and the military's suspicion that the WRB would agitate for special bombing missions to destroy the installations and railway tracks leading to **Auschwitz**. Ever responsive to the currents of anti-Semitism, President Roosevelt was sensitive to the political risk of being accused of risking the lives of American soldiers to save Jews. Even when American pilots flew bombing missions only a few miles from Auschwitz, the policy to destroy specific military targets precluded any mission to bomb the railroad tracks leading to the death camp.

Similarly, the Allied war strategy of demanding an **"unconditional surrender"** from Germany militated against the United States entering into negotiations with the Nazis on behalf of the Jews. Thus, the response of the U.S. government to the Holocaust was to maintain that the best way to save the lives of the Jews was through victory over Nazi Germany. *See also* BERMUDA CONFERENCE; RIEGNER CABLE; WISE, STEPHEN S.

UNITED STATES HOLOCAUST MEMORIAL MUSEUM (USHMM). The **United States Holocaust** Memorial Museum was created by a unanimous act of the U.S. Congress in 1980. The museum was built on federal land adjacent to the National Mall in Washington, D.C., and is located on **Raoul Wallenberg** Place, named for the Swedish diplomat who saved tens of thousands of Jews in **Hungary** during World War II. The architect, James Ingo Freed, who designed the building, fled **Germany** as a child in 1939. Since its opening, the museum has welcomed more than 25 million visitors and reaches millions more through its outreach programs. The museum's mission, however, is education and through its extensive programs, it reaches students from junior high school to graduate researchers, educators, law enforcement officials, and the military,

Using text, photos, maps, films and artifacts, the museum's permanent exhibition tells the history of the Holocaust with particular emphasis on the murder of millions of Jews, although it also includes the history of other victims of **Nazi** persecution and murder.

Also included in the museum is a library of more than 72,000 items in 55 languages as well as an archive with more than 42 million pages of documents, 77,000 photographs, 9,000 oral histories, and 985 hours of historical footage. The museum's Center for Advanced Holocaust Studies is a venue for Holocaust scholarship and allows visiting scholars to share the fruits of their research with their colleagues. The museum's website (www.ushmm.org), reaches both a national and international audience, providing the most recent updates on Holocaust research.

UNTERMENSCH. The word was used by the **Nazis** to describe Jews and Slavs whom they considered to be inferior or subhuman. *See also* ARYAN; EUGENICS; IDEOLOGY.

USTASA. Loosely translated as "to stand up for the homeland," it was the name of the nationalist and **anti-Semitic** political organization that ruled **Croatia** from 1941 to 1945. During this period, Croatia served as a German satellite state. The Ustasa was responsible for the murder of thousands of **Serbs**, Jews, and **Gypsies**.

– V –

VATICAN. *See also* CHRISTIANITY; PIUS XI; PIUS XII.

VERNICHTUNGSLAGER. See DEATH CAMPS.

VICHY FRANCE. The southern part of **France**, which was not occupied by the Germans after France's defeat in 1940, and the headquarters of the government headed by Marshal Philippe Petain. Vichy France collaborated with the Germans and passed laws in tandem with **Germany**'s **anti-Semitic** laws. The Vichy regime especially cooperated in the **deportation** of French Jews to **Auschwitz**. The Germans eventually occupied Vichy in November 1942.

VITAMIN P. As conditions worsened in the **ghettos** of **Poland**, having connections became important in order to avoid heavy-duty **forced labor** and subsequent **deportation**. Knowing the right people or having influence with officials in authority was the most sought-after commodity for self-protection. Someone who found himself engaged in forced labor details would complain that he lacked protection or "Vitamin P."

VOLK **(ETHNIC PEOPLE OR NATION).** As in the German *Volk*. The word was used by racial nationalists to distinguish between those who racially belonged to the German nation and those considered as foreigners. The **Nazis** employed the word to exclude Jews, **Gypsies**, and other non-**Aryan** people from their rights as citizens of **Germany**. *See also* BLOOD AND SOIL; IDEOLOGY; *VOLKISCH*.

VOLKISCH. The German word pertains to the racial **anti-Semitic** movement of German nationalists that appeared in **Germany** at the end of the 19th century. Viewing the Jews as a racial threat to Germany, they preached solutions to the **Jewish question** that ranged from expelling them from Germany to their extermination. **Adolf Hitler** as well as **National Socialism** in general were influenced by the ideas espoused by the *Volkisch* movement. *See also* IDEOLOGY; *VOLK*.

VOLKISCHER BEOBACHTER **(ETHNIC/RACIAL OBSERVER).** The official newspaper of the **Nazi Party** that was printed from 1921 to 1945. At its peak in 1944, the paper's circulation reached 1,700,000. The paper was edited for much of its life by **Alfred Rosenberg**.

VOLKSDEUTSCHE **(ETHNIC GERMANS).** **Adolf Hitler** sought to resettle on the occupied territory in western **Poland** those ethnic

Germans who resided in countries outside the **Reich**. An important objective of the policy of *Lebensraum* was the removal of Poles and Jews from the annexed territory and the **resettlement** of millions of ethnic Germans in their place. Hitler also demanded that regardless of their political status in other countries, the primary allegiance of all Germans, both inside and outside the Reich, should be to **Germany**.

VOLKSGEMEINSCHAFT. *Volksgemeinschaft* is a term used by the **Nazi** leadership to describe the new political arrangement in **Germany** under **Adolf Hitler**'s dictatorship. The term means a "people's community," which translated into the establishment on **Reich** territory a national community based on the **Aryan** race. In the early years of the **Third Reich**, the Nazis distinguished between laws and legal protection for the *Volksgemeinschaft* (or Aryan racial community) and other categories of people, who were deprived of the protection of the law. This included Jews, asocial persons, the handicapped, **Gypsies**, and foreigners, who were not considered part of the *Volksgemeinschaft*. Deprived of the protection of the law, they were subject to the arbitrary decisions of the police and whatever means the police chose to apply against them.

VOLKSTUMKAMPF. *Volkstumkampf* or racial war is the term used by **Adolf Hitler** and the hierarchy of the **Schutzstaffel** (SS) to describe **Nazi Germany**'s war against the Jews, Poles, and the Slavic peoples of Eastern Europe in general. The war against **Poland** was not an ordinary war but a new kind of conflict, a *Volkstumskampf*, or ethnic struggle, that combined Nazi Germany's **ideological** racial goals with the traditional military and political objectives of *Lebensraum* (living space), or the creation of a German empire in Eastern Europe. The brutality of the German occupation of Poland served as a laboratory for the German invasion of the **Soviet Union** in 1941.

– W –

WAFFEN-SS (ARMED SS). The Waffen-SS was the military wing of the **Schutzstaffel** (SS) during the war. The SS combat unit was also

Adolf Hitler's personal multinational brigade, which fought on the front line under the command of the **Wehrmacht**. By April 1945, the Waffen-SS numbered approximately 800,000 men in 40 divisions. *See also* HIMMLER, HEINRICH.

WAGNER-ROGERS BILL. Legislation introduced into the **United States** Congress in 1939 by Senator Robert F. Wagner of New York and Congresswoman Edith Rogers of Massachusetts that proposed to bring 20,000 mostly Jewish European refugee children into the United States. The bill called for the arrival of 10,000 children in 1939 and 10,000 more in 1940. The legislation was similar to efforts made by the Dutch and British governments to rescue Jewish children from the **Nazis**. The legislation, however, was amended in committee whereby the 20,000 children would gain entry into the United States, but only if the quota that allowed Jewish **refugees** to be admitted was reduced by 20,000. The bill died in the House after the sponsors withdrew support for the bill in frustration. A bill that allowed in thousands of children from **Great Britain**, non-Jewish victims of the 1940 blitz, was enthusiastically endorsed by Congress.

WALLENBERG, RAOUL (1912–?). A **Swedish** diplomat who was responsible for saving the lives of tens of thousands of Jews in Budapest, **Hungary**, on the eve of the **Nazi deportations** in 1944. Recruited by the Swedish government upon the recommendation of the **War Refugee Board**, Wallenberg had a task to help protect the 200,000 Jews residing in Budapest from deportation to the **death camps**. The strategy devised by the Swedish embassy was to issue provisional Swedish "protective passports" to Hungarian Jews. As the Swedish legation attaché, Wallenberg over a period of three months issued thousands of these passports to Jews that the Hungarian and German officials reluctantly honored. He also exhibited courage in his response to the **death marches**, whereby thousands of Jews were being force-marched to the **Austrian** border. Wallenberg followed the convoy and was able to secure the release of those Jews with protective passports.

Wallenberg was also instrumental in setting up special hostels that came under the protection of the foreign embassies in Budapest. Some 15,000 Jews found their way into the 31 protected houses, which formed an "international ghetto." Wallenberg also established a number of centers for children under the protection of the **International Committee of the Red Cross**, thereby saving the lives of about 8,000 Jewish children. Following the Soviet **liberation** of Hungary in January 1945, Wallenberg was arrested and accused of being an American agent, and was never heard from again. *See also* RIGHTEOUS GENTILES.

WANNSEE CONFERENCE. Following **Hermann Goering's** letter to **Reinhard Heydrich** on 31 July 1941, that authorized the **Final Solution**, plans were initiated that would lead to the murder of almost six million Jews. Heydrich, on 20 January 1942, invited officials of relevant German government departments to attend a meeting for the purpose of coordinating the Final Solution. Located in Wannsee, a suburb of Berlin, the meeting itself lasted little more than an hour, but in this abbreviated period of time, the officials were told by Heydrich that **Adolf Hitler** had decided on solving the so-called Jewish problem.

Heydrich outlined the new policy that called for using Jews, at first, for **forced labor**. Those who survived the rigors of labor would be "treated accordingly," a **euphemism** for their murder. Heydrich, in effect, stated that the 11 million Jews living in continental Europe and in the British Isles were now targets for extermination. The most heated aspect of the meeting, however, did not deal with the moral questions surrounding the decision to murder an entire people but focused on the fate of "mixed Jews," or **Mischlinges**. Heydrich's preference was to have half-Jews killed but to consider quarter-Jews as Germans provided that their appearance and behavior did not betray Jewish characteristics. Dr. Wilhelm Stuckart of the Interior Ministry argued that half-Jews be **sterilized** rather than be murdered. Ultimately the issue was deferred to later meetings.

From Heydrich's perspective, the meeting was a huge success. As **Adolf Eichmann**, who was Heydrich's second-in-command, later remembered, "During the conversation they minced no words. . . . They spoke about methods of killing, about liquidation, about extermination." Given the intense rivalries that characterized the bureaucracy of the **Third Reich**, Heydrich had every reason to expect difficulty in acquiring the support of the assembled government and party officials for coordinating the Final Solution. To his surprise, he found the assembled officials enthusiastic about the "project" and committed to doing their part in the extermination of European Jewry.

WAR REFUGEE BOARD (WRB). The board was created by an executive order from President **Franklin D. Roosevelt** in January 1944 for the purpose of rescuing Jews from German-occupied Europe. The circumstances under which the president established the board emanated from a threat, made by officials in the **United States** Treasury Department, to release to the press a statement that accused the administration of "acquiescing" to the German extermination program. Officials in the Treasury were incensed by their discovery that the Department of State was reluctant to carry out a July 1943 presidential directive to plan the rescue of thousands of **Romanian** Jews. The report was written by the assistant of Treasury Secretary **Henry Morgenthau Jr.**, Josiah Dubois Jr., and was titled "**Report to the Secretary on the Acquiescence of This Government in the Murder of the Jews.**" Prepared for the secretary of the Treasury, the report accused the State Department of a "willful failure" to pass on information or use its authority to offer aid to the victims of the **Nazi** extermination program. After Morgenthau changed the document's title to "A Personal Report to the President," he presented it to Roosevelt. Reacting to the politically explosive charges detailed in the report, the president, by executive order, created the War Refugee Board.

The War Refugee Board was the only **Allied** agency specifically established during the war to save the lives of the Jews still remaining in German-occupied Europe. The success of WRB rescue operations in Europe remains a subject of controversy among historians, but the best estimates regarding the number of Jews saved by the government agency range from 20,000 (William D. Rubenstein) to 200,000 (David Wyman). *See also* HUNGARY; WALLENBERG, RAOUL.

WARSAW GHETTO. On the eve of **Germany**'s invasion of **Poland** in September 1939, Warsaw had about 375,000 Jews, who constituted about 30 percent of the city's total population. Warsaw was the capital of Polish Jewry where both a religious and Jewish secular culture thrived. Poland's defeat at the hands of the Germans put an end to the creative life that characterized the Jews of Poland.

At first Jews had no reason to believe that the German occupation of Poland would be as severe as it later turned out to be. Rather, the memories of tolerance shown by German troops to the Jews during World War I led many to believe the German occupation would be no different. It did not take long, however, for the Jews to discover that the German troops who occupied Warsaw in 1939 were unlike their World War I counterparts. Almost from the beginning of the occupation, Jews were discriminated against and subject to attacks by the Germans. Jews were driven away from food lines, and religious Jews were frequently stopped and their beards shaved by mocking German soldiers.

In November 1939, the first of the German anti-Jewish decrees was promulgated, which included the requirement that Jews wear a white armband with a blue **Star of David** on it. Jews were required to register their assets, with a detailed list of clothes, household goods, and other items found in the home. The Germans also forbade the operation of Jewish institutions such as schools and cultural organizations. What the Germans did demand, however, was the formation of a *Judenrat* (Jewish Council). The Germans controlled the *Judenrat* by appointing those who were to serve on the council.

In mid-November 1940, the Germans confined Warsaw's Jews to a ghetto surrounded by a high wall and sealed it off from the rest of the population. It was situated in the Jewish section of Warsaw and placed under the administration of the Jewish Council, which was also given the responsibility of supervising a 2,000-man **Jewish police** force (*Judischer Ordnungsdienst*). The ghetto area was crowded inasmuch as the Jews, who constituted about 30 percent of Warsaw's population, were squeezed into 2.4 percent of the city's area. The daily food ration allocated to the ghetto inhabitants was 181 calories, about 25 percent of the Polish ration and 8 percent of the nutritional value of the food that the Germans received for their ration coupons. Between November 1940 and July 1942, the time of the major **deportation** of Warsaw's Jews to **Treblinka**, the monthly death rate of Jews in the ghetto increased from a few hundred a month at the end of 1940 to as many as 5,560 in August 1942. Disease and starvation were the most common causes of death in the ghetto.

Despite the crowded conditions and the extreme hardships faced by the ghetto Jews, they were still able to educate their young, create productive enterprises, organize cultural activities, and in general replicate life in the ghetto as it had been before the German occupation when organized Jewish life came to a standstill.

The steps that led Warsaw's Jews to the **death camps** began in July 1942 when the Jewish Council, led by **Adam Czerniakow**, was ordered by the Germans to prepare lists of the "nonproductive elements" in the ghetto population for deportation. Those whose names were on the list were expected to report to the *Umschlagplatz* (the area where Jews reported for deportation to the extermination camps), which was located near the railway station where freight trains waited to take them for **resettlement** to Treblinka. The German deportation quota was 10,000 Jews per day, although the rail facility had room for only 5,000.

The first deportation numbered 60,000 Jews but exempted the able-bodied who were fit for work and their families. It was under the pressure of these circumstances that Adam Czerniakow, having learned that the trains were taking Jews to their deaths, committed suicide rather than remain a party to the selection process. The July deportation was subsequently followed by additional roundups of Jews, including Dr. Janusz Korczak (pen name of Henryk Goldszmit, 1878–1942), the director of the ghetto orphanage, who was deported with his 200 children to Treblinka in August 1942. By 5 September 1942, there were approximately 130,000 Jews left in the ghetto, and on that day the Germans ordered the remainder of the Jews to present themselves at the *Umschlagplatz* for a *Selektion*. The Germans deported 60,000 Jews, thus reducing the ghetto population from a high of 380,000 to 70,000.

It was at this point that the various underground organizations in the ghetto joined to form the **Jewish Combat Organization** (ZOB) (*Zydowska Organizacja Bojowa*) in an effort to resist the Germans. When in January 1943 the Germans ordered another roundup of Jews for deportation, Jews refused to comply. Although the Germans managed to gather about 1,000 Jews, it was at a cost. The ZOB confronted the Germans in hand-to-hand fighting, and soon it become difficult for the Germans to fill their quotas for Treblinka, although 5,000 to 6,000 additional Jews were sent to the death camp. The Jewish Council also saw its authority weakened as the remaining Jews now took their lead from the Jewish Combat Organization. This was the situation in April 1943 when the Germans attempted to liquidate the ghetto and found themselves faced by a revolt that commenced on April 19 and was eventually crushed on May 16 when Brigade-führer Jurgen Stroop reported that "the Jewish quarter of Warsaw no longer exists." *See also* ONEG SHABBAT; RESISTANCE; WARSAW GHETTO UPRISING.

WARSAW GHETTO UPRISING. From the moment that the **Warsaw ghetto** was established by the Germans in November 1940, an underground **resistance** movement emerged in the **ghetto**. After the **deportation** of July 1942, when 60,000 of the ghetto's "nonproductive elements" were deported to **Treblinka**, a meeting of Jewish leaders took place to discuss the possibility of resistance. At the time, the decision was made to reject armed confrontation against the Germans because it would result in even greater hardships for the ghetto population. The Jews did request the Polish Home Army to send an appeal to the **Allied** nations that the German people be threatened with reprisals for their crimes against the Jews. The appeal was transmitted to London but the BBC maintained complete silence.

The sequence of events that led to the Warsaw ghetto uprising began with the 5 September 1942 deportation of Jews to Treblinka, which reduced the ghetto from its high of 380,000 in November 1940 to a population of 70,000. By October 1942, a coordinating committee consisting of various ghetto political groups formed the **Jewish Combat Organization** (ZOB). When in January 1943 the **Nazis** decreed another wave of deportations, Jews refused to comply with the order. When the Germans attempted to round up Jews, they encountered resistance from the ZOB, which engaged them in hand-to-hand combat. By mid-January the Germans reassessed the situation in light of Jewish resistance, and the outcome was a temporary halt in the deportations. Inasmuch as the remaining Jews now followed the orders of the ZOB, the **Judenrat** (Jewish Council) lost its authority.

Heinrich Himmler, monitoring the events, now ordered the dissolution of the ghetto and dispatched Brigade-führer Jurgen Stroop to raze the ghetto. The final liquidation of the Warsaw ghetto began on Monday, 19 April 1943, the eve of Passover. The Germans surrounded the ghetto, and subsequently the **Waffen-SS** entered the ghetto but was met with concentrated fire and incendiary bombs. At first, Jewish resistance forced the Germans to withdraw from the ghetto, inasmuch as they were unprepared for the armed response. Once they returned, however, the Germans engaged the Jews in street battles and adopted the tactic of systematically burning the ghetto, building by building. This strategy forced the resistance fighters to abandon their positions and use the sewers in order to escape from the fire. The Germans countered this by blowing up the manholes, and smoking candles were lowered into the sewer passages. As the Jews came up for air, the Germans shot them. On 8 May, **Mordecai Anielewicz**, the charismatic leader of the ZOB, was killed, and in subsequent attacks the German forces shot Jews in increasing numbers. Ultimately the revolt failed, and Stroop reported that 56,065 Jews were apprehended. Of this number, 13,929 were killed by the Germans, and the remainder deported to **death camps** such as Treblinka. In addition to the figure of 56,065 an estimated 5,000 to 6,000 Jews were killed in explosions or fires.

Stroop noted that German losses were 16 dead and 85 wounded. Stroop's figures may have underestimated German casualties, but the importance of the ghetto revolt was not found in the number of casualties. Rather, news of the revolt spread throughout the ghettos of occupied **Poland**. The Warsaw ghetto revolt became a legend even as the war and the deportations continued. The revolt gave hope not only to the Jews trapped in the ghettos of German-occupied Poland but to Jews throughout the world. The Warsaw ghetto uprising was perceived as marking the start of the Jewish resistance to the Nazi oppressors.

WARTHEGAU. Warthegau was the area of western **Poland** annexed by **Germany** after its defeat of Poland in September 1939. The **Nazi** objective was to resettle ethnic Germans in the incorporated territory, at the expense of Jews and Poles who were to be uprooted and **resettled** in the **General-Gouvernement**.

WAY TO HEAVEN. German guards referred to the passage leading to the **gas chambers** at Treblinka as the "way to heaven" (*Himmelstrasse*). The passage to the gas chamber was lined by **Schutzstaffel**

(SS) men with their dogs who, armed with whips and clubs, expedited the movement of the unsuspecting Jews to their deaths. *See also* BARRY; EUPHEMISMS.

WE REMEMBER: A REFLECTION ON THE SHOAH. In March 1998, the Catholic Church issued a long awaited document on the **Holocaust**. The Vatican document, 11 years in the making and issued by the Holy See's Commission for Religious Relations with Jews, acknowledged that centuries of **Christian** prejudice aimed at the Jews rendered many Christians less sensitive to the **Nazis'** anti-Jewish atrocities, but insisted that Nazism represented a pagan movement. It also acknowledged that individual Catholics did things that were wrong or even sinful in their support of **anti-Semitism** and the Nazi persecution of the Jews. However, to the dismay of many Jewish leaders, the document fell short of expectations inasmuch as it absolved the church as such from complicity in the **Holocaust** and gave credit to **Pope Pius XII** for saving the lives of several hundred thousand Jews, but skirted the issue of his silence in the face of his knowledge of the **Final Solution**.

WEHRMACHT. The word refers to the combined German armed forces. In 1935, the name *Wehrmacht* replaced *Reichswehr* as the designation for the army.

WEIMAR REPUBLIC. German Jews made important contributions in the short-lived Weimar Republic (1918–1933). Following **Germany**'s defeat in World War I, the victorious **Allies** abolished the monarchy and "imposed" a democratic form of government on the German people. The draft of the liberal constitution was written by Hugo Preuss, who was a Jew, one of many who were active in the wide spectrum of Weimar political parties and ideologies. Under the constitution, the Jews of Germany received full equality in the democratic republic.

It was not in politics alone, however, that Jews made their mark in the Weimar Republic. Although only about 1 percent of the population, Jews were visible in the arts, professions, commerce, and overall culture that made Weimar synonymous with modernism. It was also the visibility of the Jews in public life that made them easy targets for the **anti-Semitic** nationalist political parties that flourished in Germany during the period of the Weimar Republic.

Politics: A survey of some of the more prominent Jews involved in the politics of the Weimar Republic would include, in addition to Hugo Preuss, **Walter Rathenau**, a German-Jewish nationalist, who served as foreign minister in 1922 and was subsequently murdered by right-wing terrorists. Despite Rathenau's impeccable conservative credentials and his total alienation from the German Jewish community, he was despised by the right who manifested their hatred of him in a popular couplet: "Shoot down that Walter Rathenau / That cursed, goddamned Jewish sow."

The fear of a communist revolution in Germany was linked to Jews because some of the leaders associated with **Bolshevism** in both the **Soviet Union** and Germany were Jews. In particular, Rosa Luxemburg, a nominal Jew, was a leader of the Sparticist League, which called for a Soviet-style revolution in Germany. In Bavaria, Kurt Eisner, the minister-president, was a Jew with perceived "leftish" tendencies. He was assassinated by Count Arco-Valley, a member of the **Thule Society**, because one of the requirements of this **neo-Nazi** organization was to perform an act that would prove one worthy of membership. The assassin believed that Eisner and his Independent Socialists were responsible for all of Germany's troubles. **Adolf Hitler** was successful in attracting followers to the **Nazi Party** because of the willingness of large numbers of people to believe that the Jews sought to turn Germany into a Bolshevik state.

Commerce: Jews were prominent as bankers in Weimar Germany. Almost half of all private banks were owned by Jewish banking families such as the Mendelssohns, Bleichroders, and Schlesingers. Jews, however, were not owners of the important banks, although some of the largest of these types of banks employed Jewish managers. Arthur Salomonsohn, for example, directed the *Disconto-Gesellschaft* and was instrumental in forging the merger with the *Deutsche* Bank before his death in 1930, thus creating the main DD bank. Jews were also identified with the leading department stores such as Wertheim, Tietz, and Kaufhaus **Israel**. In 1932, Jews accounted for 79 percent of all such business enterprises.

Professional life: Jews were represented in all aspects of publishing. Ullstein and Mosse, for example, was one of the leading publishing houses in Weimar Germany. In medicine, Jews constituted approximately 11 percent of all physicians in Germany in 1933. Jews accounted for more than 16 percent of all lawyers and notaries public. In Berlin, where Jews numbered about 5 percent of the city's population, more Jews than non-Jews practiced law.

Cultural and intellectual life: A quarter of all Nobel Prizes that had been awarded to Germans by 1933 were won by Jews. In the **arts**, music, science, **literature**, **theater**, and **film**, Jews made important contributions to Weimar culture. A list of Jews whose names were familiar to the public would include such artists and intellectuals as Martin Buber, Albert Einstein, Fritz Haber, Max Lieberman, Max Reinhardt, Bruno Walter, Kurt Weil, and Richard Willstatter. If we add **Austrian** Jews, such as Sigmund Freud, the list becomes even more impressive.

WEISSMANDEL, MICHAEL DOV (1903–1956). Weissmandel was one of the leaders of the Working Group, a Jewish underground group in **Slovakia**. He strove tirelessly to find ways to rescue the Jews of Slovakia, as well as those in German-occupied Europe, from **deportation** to the **death camps**. Weissmandel was a proponent of the **Europa Plan**, which sought to ransom the Jews of Slovakia, and believed he had succeeded when deportations were halted in 1943 after **Dieter Wisliceny**, **Adolf Eichmann**'s deputy in charge of Jewish affairs in Slovakia, received a payment of between $40,000 and $50,000. Optimistic that he could raise money from Jews in the free world and thus ransom the rest of European Jewry, he proceeded to solicit the millions of dollars that were deemed necessary to save European Jewry. When deportations resumed in the fall of 1944, he blamed Jewish communities in the Allied countries for failing to raise the necessary $200,000 down payment toward the total sum of $2 million to $3 million demanded by Wisliceny.

When two Jews from Slovakia, Rudolf Vrba and Alfred Wetzler, managed to escape from **Auschwitz** in April 1944, they reported to the Working Group on the operation of the death camps. Weissmandel subsequently, along with Gisi Fleischmann, a member of the Working Group, initiated an information campaign about the horrors of the death camp and called on the **Allies** to bomb Auschwitz, the camp, and the railway lines, bridges, and tunnels leading to the death camp. Following the resumption of deportations in the fall of 1944, Weissmandel and his family were sent to Auschwitz, but he managed to escape and eventually made his way to the **United States**, where he established a Talmudic academy.

WEIZMANN, CHAIM (1874–1952). Weizmann was instrumental in procuring the **Balfour Declaration** in November 1917 from the British, which promised the support of **Great Britain** for a Jewish home in **Palestine**. The Russian-born Weizmann went on to become one of the most influential **Zionist** voices in international affairs. As president of the **World Zionist Organization** during the 1930s, Weizmann attempted to use his position to combat the racial persecution of Jews in **Germany** and elsewhere in Europe. On the eve of World War II, Weizmann pledged to British prime minister Neville Chamberlain his organization's full support against **Nazi Germany**. Apologists for Nazi Germany have seized on Weizmann's words to prove that the Jews had declared war on Germany once hostilities commenced in September 1939. The argument was made, therefore, that Germany's treatment of the Jews was justified because they were part of the Allied coalition against the **Third Reich**.

Despite his diplomatic skills and faith in the goodwill of Great Britain, Weizmann failed to gain support for the suspension of the British **White Paper of 1939**, the Brand mission, and the bombing of the **death camps**. After the war, he was removed from the presidency of the World Zionist Organization by his Zionist opponents, who included David Ben-Gurion and Abba Hillel Silver. Nevertheless, when the **State of Israel** was established in 1948, he became its first president. *See also* JEWISH AGENCY; YISHUV.

WHITE PAPER OF 1939. In the decades following **Great Britain**'s issuance of the **Balfour Declaration** and its legitimation by the League of Nations, violence between Jews and Arabs in **Palestine** grew in intensity, with the British mandatory government unable to find a formula for peace that would satisfy both sides. On the eve of World War II, British policy wavered in its support for a Jewish home in Palestine. Fearing that in a coming war with **Germany** the Arabs would side with their enemy, the British placated the Arabs by limiting Jewish immigration into Palestine in the hope of maintaining their support, if not neutrality. The British government further believed that given **Nazi Germany**'s **anti-Semitic** policies, it could take Jewish support for granted.

Beginning in 1937, the number of Jewish **refugees** issued visas to Palestine fell from a yearly average of between 6,800 and 8,400 to 3,286. The British White Paper of 1939 (also known as the MacDonald White Paper, after the British colonial secretary, Malcolm MacDonald) further curtailed Jewish immigration by limiting the number of Jews allowed to enter Palestine to 75,000 over a five-year period. In addition, the white paper called for the creation of an Arab state by 1949, a clear violation of the British mandate over Palestine. Thus, at a time when the issue of Jewish refugees from the Greater **Reich** had become a matter of international concern, the one haven available as an area of refuge for the unwanted Jews of Germany and **Austria** was subject to a quota of 5,000 Jews a year. *See also* ALIYA BET; JEWISH AGENCY; YISHUV.

WIESEL, ELIE (1928–). Born in Sighet, Transylvania, Wiesel is a survivor of the **Holocaust** who, through his novels and personal memoir, *Night* (1969), dedicated his life to keeping alive the memory of the **Shoah**. His outspoken condemnation of **genocide** has earned him unqualified prominence as a person of great moral stature. It was his worldwide prestige that earned him an audience when, on the occasion of his award of the Congressional Medal from President Ronald Reagan in 1985, he chastised the president for his visit to the cemetery in **Bitburg, Germany**, where 47 members of the **Waffen-Schutzstaffel** (SS) were buried. In 1986, Wiesel was awarded the Nobel Peace Prize. Wiesel has also played a major role in the planning of the **United States Holocaust Memorial Museum**, for which he served as chairman between 1980 and 1986. A professor of humanities at Boston University, Wiesel, through his lectures and writings, has kept the memory of the Holocaust in the forefront of the American conscience. *See also* LITERATURE AND THE HOLOCAUST.

WIESENTHAL, SIMON (1908–2006). The famed **Nazi** hunter was born in Galicia and resided in Lvov, **Poland**, at the outbreak of World War II in September 1939. A survivor of five **concentration camps**,

Wiesenthal was liberated from **Mauthausen** by the Americans on 5 May 1945. An architect by training, Wiesenthal based himself after the war in Vienna, where he subsequently founded the Jewish Documentation Center in 1961 in the wake of the trial of **Adolf Eichmann** in **Israel**. Through his center, Wiesenthal gathered information regarding Nazi criminals. Wiesenthal has been credited with discovering the whereabouts of over 1,000 Nazis, including Franz Stangl, the commandant of **Sobibor** and **Treblinka**.

In recent years, however, Wiesenthal has been accused of exaggerating his role in the pursuit of **Josef Mengele**, Martin Bormann, and Eichmann. The **World Jewish Congress** was also critical of Wiesenthal's defense of Kurt Waldheim, the former president of **Austria** who was accused of participating and covering up his role in Nazi war crimes in the former **Yugoslavia**.

Wiesenthal was also the author of many books on aspects of the Holocaust. Among his better known works are *The Murderers amongst Us* (1967), *The Sunflower* (1970), *Max and Helen* (1981), and *Justice Not Vengeance* (1989). In 1977, the Los Angeles Wiesenthal Center was established in his honor. *See also* ART AND THE HOLOCAUST.

WILD CAMPS. The term refers to the makeshift **concentration camps** the **Nazis** organized immediately after they came to power in 1933. The Nazis arrested political opponents, communists, Jews, and others they considered enemies of the **Nazi Party**. They were generally housed in abandoned warehouses, barracks, and an assortment of other temporary facilities, where those incarcerated were brutalized and denied any legal protection. The "wild" camps were subsequently replaced with the opening of **Dachau** in March 1933.

WIRTH, CHRISTIAN (1885–1944). Wirth was one of the first technicians of the **Nazi Euthanasia Program**. Because of the experience he gained using gas in the euthanasia killing process, he was assigned to Lublin, where he organized the first euthanasia center outside of **Germany**. Wirth was then given the responsibility of exterminating Jews at **Chelmno**. Working in tandem with **Odilo Globocnik**, Wirth was responsible for supervising the gassing of about 1,700,000 Jews in the **Aktion Reinhard** camps.

A brutal and often sadistic person, Wirth perfected the system by which the victims were led to the **gas chambers**. For example, Wirth introduced the method of disguising the gas chambers as shower stalls in order to lure his unsuspecting victims to their death. Wirth also took credit for the use of Jewish **Sonderkommandos** (prisoners), who were assigned to the gas chambers and **crematoria**, for the purpose of "burying" the dead. His primary contribution to the extermination of the Jews, however, was his development of new gassing techniques at **Belzec**, which were viewed by his superiors as an improvement over the methods used at Chelmno. Wirth's "expertise" in the use of **carbon monoxide** gas as a killing agent was subsequently applied to the **Sobibor** and **Treblinka death camps**. The enormous number of Jews who were killed by Wirth's techniques solidified his reputation as the most notorious of the Nazi war criminals.

WISE, STEPHEN S. (1884–1949). Wise was a Reform rabbi and one of the founders of the **World Jewish Congress** in 1936. Following the **Nazi** seizure of power in 1933, Rabbi Wise took a leadership role in organizing the boycott of German goods. Rabbi Wise was a friend of President **Franklin Delano Roosevelt** and as a consequence of this relationship, he sought to avoid criticism of the president in regard to the president's response to the **refugee crisis** of the 1930s and to the murder of European Jewry during the early 1940s. By 1943, Wise's leadership was seriously compromised when he adhered to the request of the State Department that he withhold information he had received in regard to the Nazi extermination policy against the Jews. His belief that the contents of the **Riegner cable** (August 1942) be verified before the information was made public was based on Wise's fear that if the information concerning the **Final Solution** proved unfounded, Jews would be accused of atrocity-mongering. Wise's eventual disillusionment with the president followed Wise's presentation of a booklet entitled "Blue Print for Extermination" (8 December 1942) that detailed the Nazi extermination campaign. The president subsequently issued a statement that condemned Nazi atrocities but refused to support Wise's request for a rescue plan that would include opening the doors to **Palestine** for Jews who could be **liberated** from the Nazis.

WISLICENY, DIETER (1911–1948). As a member of **Adolf Eichmann**'s staff, Wisliceny was responsible for the mass **deportation** of Jews from **Slovakia, Greece**, and **Hungary**. In 1931, he joined the **Nazi Party** and in 1934 joined both the **Schutzstaffel** (SS) and the **Sicherheitsdienst** (SD). In 1940, he acted as the advisor on Jewish affairs to the Slovak government, but because of his opportunism and concern for money, he soon acquired a reputation for accepting bribes. During the summer of 1942, Wisliceny was bribed by the Bratislava-based Jewish Relief Committee to delay the deportation of Slovakian Jews. He also negotiated the ill-fated **Europa Plan**, initiated by Rabbi **Michael Dov Weissmandel**, to save the remnants of European Jewry for a ransom of $2 million to $3 million, to be paid for by Jewish organizations abroad. Wisliceny accepted a bribe of $50,000 as a first installment, although he had no intention of halting the deportations.

In 1943 and 1944, Wisliceny was assigned to Salonika, where he introduced the definition of a Jew in accordance with the **Nuremberg Laws**. He ordered Jews to wear the **yellow Star of David badge**, and subsequently ordered Jewish physicians and lawyers to mount Jewish stars in their offices. Wisliceny also required the stars to be placed by Jewish tenants on their apartment doors for the purpose of identification. These directives were ordered in preparation for an efficient roundup and deportation of Greece's Jews to **Auschwitz**. Wisliceny's mission to Salonika was ultimately successful inasmuch as he was instrumental in the subsequent annihilation of Greek Jewry. His last assignment was in March 1944, when he joined Eichmann in **Hungary** to organize the deportation of the country's Jewish population to Auschwitz. In Hungary, Wisliceny served as the liaison in the failed **blood-for-goods** negotiations, in which Eichmann offered to save the lives of one million Jews in exchange for goods, including 10,000 trucks.

After the war, Wisliceny served as a witness at the **Nuremberg Trials** and presented a vivid description of the implementation of the **Final Solution**. He is the source of the alleged comment attributed to Eichmann that "he would leap into his grave laughing," because the feeling that he had the death of five million Jews on his conscience was to him "a source of extraordinary satisfaction." Soon after the trial, Wisliceny was extradited to **Czechoslovakia**, and while awaiting trial wrote several affidavits attesting to his role in the destruction of European Jewry, including his role in the Europa Plan, the bargaining over Jewish lives in Hungary, and Eichmann's central role in the implementation of the Final Solution. The latter affidavit was used at the Eichmann trial in Jerusalem in 1961. Wisliceny was found guilty by a Czech court for complicity in mass murder and was executed in February 1948.

"WITH BURNING CONCERN" (*MIT BRENNENDER SORGE*). Published on 21 March 1937, **Pope Pius XI**'s encyclical condemned racism and nationalism but pointedly said nothing about the persecution of the Jews in **Germany**.

WOLF'S LAIR. Convinced of a Soviet defeat at the hands of the German invading army, **Adolf Hitler** moved from Berlin to his new field headquarters in Rastenburg, East Prussia, in June 1941. The **Führer** called the new headquarters the "Wolf's Lair," a reference to his nickname in the 1920s.

WORLD JEWISH CONGRESS (WJC). The organization was founded in 1932 for the purpose of defending Jews against Nazism and **anti-Semitism**. Together with its affiliate, the American Jewish Congress, the organization in 1933 labored to mobilize public opinion in support of a boycott of German goods as a punishment for the **Nazi**'s brutal treatment of the Jews in **Germany**. The subsequent one-day boycott of Jewish business concerns in **Nazi Germany** on 1 April 1933 was the government's retaliation against the activities of the WJC and other Jewish organizations. Under the leadership of **Stephen S. Wise** and Nahum Goldmann, the WJC lobbied the **United States** government to alleviate the deteriorating situation of European Jewry. When the WJC representative in **Switzerland**, Gerhart Riegner, cabled Wise regarding the German implementation of the **Final Solution**, the organization, after a delay of a few months, staged mass rallies and in general took the lead in urging the Roosevelt administration to take more forceful action on behalf of European Jewry. Once the **Riegner cable** was verified by the **Allied** governments, President **Franklin D. Roosevelt**, under pressure from his secretary of the Treasury, **Henry Morgenthau Jr.**, established the **War Refugee Board**.

With the election of Edgar Bronfman as president of the WJC in 1981, the organization continued to monitor issues that affected the world's Jewish community. In the mid-1990s, the World Jewish Congress accused Kurt Waldheim, the former secretary-general of the United Nations, of concealing his wartime record as a German intelligence officer in the Balkans, where he was involved in the deportation of Jews and **Yugoslav partisans** to **concentration camps**. When Waldheim was denied entry to the United States under the Holtzman Amendment of the Immigration and Naturalization Acts, he accused the World Jewish Congress of organizing a conspiracy against him.

Under Bronfman's leadership, the World Jewish Congress accused **Swiss banks** of profiting from the **Holocaust**. The WJC called for an accounting of the whereabouts of millions of dollars that was entrusted to Swiss banks by terrified Jews seeking to escape Nazi persecution. The WJC confrontation against the Swiss banks was joined by U.S. Senator Alphonse D'Amato, who convened hearings in Congress to investigate the failure of the financial institutions to honor the claims made by survivors and relatives of the victims. President William Clinton endorsed the work of the WJC and appointed Stuart Eizenstadt, Undersecretary of State for Economic Affairs and the government's special envoy for property **restitution** in Central and Eastern Europe, to conduct an interagency investigation of the archival evidence against Switzerland.

Although a consortium of Swiss banks in 1998 offered close to $600 million for a "rough justice fund" for **survivors of the Holocaust**, the WJC dismissed the offer as insulting and insisted the restitution be calculated in today's values. The WJC calculated the sum owed the survivors and relatives of Holocaust victims to be approximately $1.5 billion. The Swiss banks as well as the president of Switzerland, Flavio Cotti, rejected the position of the WJC, and by the end of July 1998, negotiations had collapsed.

The threat made by New York, New Jersey, and California to impose sanctions against Swiss banks on 1 September 1998, however, may have been a major factor in the subsequent agreement reached in mid-August 1998, between the Swiss banks and Jewish groups led by the WJC. Accordingly, an estimated $1.25 billion agreement on compensation for unreturned Holocaust-era assets was reached by both parties. The agreement stipulated that the money would be paid out to Holocaust survivors over a three-year period.

– X –

X-RAYS. The **Nazi** used X-rays for the purpose of **sterilizing** designated victims in the **euthanasia** centers. In **Auschwitz**, the prolonged exposure to X-rays was used on women, without any protection, for the purpose of **medical experiments** by Dr. Josef Mengele.

– Y –

YAD VASHEM. The **Holocaust** Martyrs' and Heroes' Remembrance Authority, Israel's national institution of Holocaust commemoration, is located in Jerusalem. Yad Vashem was established by an act of the Knesset (parliament) on 18 May 1953. Yad Vashem was inspired by a verse in Isaiah that reads: "Ever unto them will I give within my house and within my walls a monument and a memorial . . . I will give them an everlasting memorial, which will never be cut off." The museum is the center for Holocaust archives and since 1957 has published *Yad Vashem Studies*, an annual in Hebrew and English that devotes each issue to the most recent research in Holocaust studies.

Yad Vashem also includes a Garden of Remembrance that honors over 13,660 **Righteous Gentiles** who aided Jews during the Holocaust. For the past several decades, Yad Vashem has also become a major shrine where more than a million people come each year to honor the memory of the six million Jews murdered by the **Nazis**. A visit to Yad Vashem has also become part of the itinerary for official guests of the **State of Israel**.

YELLOW STAR OF DAVID BADGE. The yellow badge, and less often the blue badge, was first introduced by the Germans in Lublin in November 1939 in order to readily identify Jews and to create a gulf between them and the rest of the population. The wearing of the Jewish badge, at first, was not uniform among the Jewish population in **Poland**. In Lublin, Jews were required to wear the yellow Star of David on the left side of their breast with the word *Jude* (Jew) inscribed on the patch. In **Bialystok**, the **Judenrat** (Jewish Council) called for Jews aged 14 and over to wear an armband with a blue Star of David. **Hans Frank**, attempting to bring uniformity to the wearing of the Jewish badge, ordered in November 1939 that a band with a blue Star of David be worn by all Jews. Following the German invasion of the **Soviet Union** in June 1941, guidelines were issued that contained the provision that at all times Jews must wear an identifiable yellow six-pointed star on the left side of their breast and on the back of their clothes.

The requirement to wear a distinctive badge also applied in the **ghettos**, where Jews were made responsible for fashioning the badges and circulating them throughout the ghetto. Jews who failed to wear the badges were subject to fines and prison sentences. An announcement of the Bialystok Judenrat of 26 July 1941, stated that "The authorities have warned that severe punishment up to and including death by shooting is in store for Jews who do not wear the yellow badge, on back and front."

The yellow badge was adopted by German satellite states such as **Slovakia**, **Hungary**, and **Romania**. The badge was also required by Jews in German-occupied countries where it was often resisted. In **Denmark**, for example, the Germans failed to force the yellow badge on Danish Jewry, although the legend continues to persist that King Christian X threatened to wear the badge should the Germans attempt to introduce it. Although the king opposed German anti-Jewish measures, he in fact never made such a declaration, nor did he appear in public wearing the yellow badge. Realizing that the Danes were resistant to the introduction any sort of anti-Jewish measures, the Germans did not attempt to force the yellow badge on the Jews of Denmark. In Western Europe, many Jews defied the orders to wear the yellow badge, and in the **Netherlands**, the Dutch underground newspapers printed 300,000 stars bearing the inscription "Jews and non-Jews are one and the same."

In the **Nazi concentration camps**, the Jews were required to wear a yellow Star of David patch.

YISHUV. The Hebrew word for the Jewish community in **Palestine** prior to the founding of **Israel** in 1948. At the outbreak of World War

II in September 1939, there were approximately 470,000 Jews in the Yishuv. In light of the **refugee crisis** in Europe that followed both the German annexation of **Austria** (March 1938) and **Kristallnacht** (9–10 November 1938), the efforts of the Yishuv to absorb Jewish refugees fleeing the **Nazis** were stymied by the British **White Paper of 1939**, which limited immigration into Palestine to 75,000 people for the following five years.

The Yishuv's response to the British restrictions was to organize an illegal immigration operation to smuggle Jewish refugees into Palestine (**Aliya Bet**). **Great Britain** responded by boarding ships carrying illegal immigrants and interning them in refugee camps.

It was at the beginning of 1942, however, that the Yishuv learned that the objective of the Nazis was to murder the Jews of Europe. The Yishuv also found itself threatened by German forces in North Africa. Furthermore, Great Britain made it clear that should Alexandria fall to the Germans, it would abandon Palestine. The Yishuv's leadership understood that a British retreat from Palestine would also lead to the destruction of the Jewish community in Palestine. It was only after the German defeat at El Alamein in November 1942 that the Yishuv felt secure enough to turn to the fate of European Jewry.

Given the lack of financial, political, and military resources, there was little the Yishuv could do to effect rescue. In fact, as the news of the **Holocaust** unfolded, the Yishuv, like most of the **Allied** countries, had difficulty comprehending the enormity of the Nazi **genocide**. Inasmuch as its resources and its ability to effect the course of the **Final Solution** were limited, it was not possible for the Yishuv to make a dramatic difference in the rescue of the victims of the Nazi extermination campaign. Consequently, the record of the Yishuv, given its limitations, was reduced to a few dramatic gestures, such as organizing periods of public mourning and demonstrations. Yet its leadership focused on saving thousands of Jews through illegal immigration with an eye to strengthening the Jewish community in Palestine, so that at war's end, it would be prepared to absorb the remaining Jews of Europe.

YIZKOR (MEMORIAL) BOOKS. The yizkor or memorial books were written during the **Nazi** rule by Eastern European Jews who managed to survive the **Holocaust**. Many of these memorial books were written to record the vibrancy of Jewish *shtetl* (village) life before the Nazi occupation as well as the destructive process itself.

YUGOSLAVIA. Founded on 1 December 1918, as the Kingdom of the Serbs, Croats, and Slovenes, Yugoslavia united the bulk of the South Slav population following the collapse of the Hapsburg Empire. On the eve of World War II, the population of Yugoslavia was about 15,500,000, consisting of 43 percent Serbs, 34 percent Croats, 7 percent Slovenes, and 7 percent Macedonians. The 1931 census, the last taken before the German occupation, tallied approximately 73,000 Jews. By 1941, the number increased to 80,000 as a result of the influx of Jewish **refugees** from **Germany** and **Austria**. Most of Yugoslavia's Jews lived in Belgrade, where **anti-Semitism** was a marginal phenomenon. Although Yugoslavia was neutral when World War II erupted in September 1939, the Germans exerted pressure on Yugoslavia that resulted in the passage of anti-Semitic measures. In October 1940, in the hopes of appeasing Germany, the government enacted a quota system for Jews in secondary schools and universities. This was followed by restrictions on Jews trading in certain sectors of the economy.

Between 1933 and 1941, about 50,000 Jews passed through Yugoslavia as they fled the **Nazis**. Yugoslav Jewry rallied to the support of the refugees with financial help as well as helping in the "illegal" immigration into **Palestine**. Following the German occupation of Yugoslavia in April 1941, the country was divided into separate states along religious and ethnic lines. The extermination of Yugoslavia's Jewish population followed, but the pace of the steps leading to the **deportations** varied in each of these areas. *See also* CROATIA; SERBIA.

– Z –

ZEGOTA. The code name of the *Rada Pomocy Zydom* (Council for Aid to the Jews). The Polish underground organization functioned from December 1942 until the **liberation** of **Poland** in January 1945. The *Zegota* consisted of five Polish and two Jewish political groups, and engaged in many operations against the Germans in behalf of the Jews. Included among its activities was to provide "**Aryan**" documents for Jews under its protection and the forging of false baptismal, marriage, and death certificates. It also provided identity employment cards for Jews.

Although hiding Jews was punishable by death, the *Zegota* was constantly finding shelter for Jews. It also sheltered Jewish children by placing them with foster families and public orphanages as well as convents. In Warsaw, more than 2,500 children were saved through the efforts of the underground organization. The *Zegota* was the only anti-German organization in Poland that was led by Jews and non-Jews. Politically, it petitioned the Polish government in-exile to urge the Polish population to help persecuted Jews and published leaflets that detailed the fate of the Jews under the Germans.

The *Zegota* also protested the activities of **anti-Semitic** elements within the Polish underground. At the height of its operations in the summer of 1944, it was providing financial and other assistance to about 4,000 Jews, mostly around Warsaw. *See also* SENDLER, IRENA.

ZIONISM. Although the idea of Zionism, or the return of the Jews to their ancestral homeland in **Palestine**, had been proposed by such diverse 19th-century personalities as Moses Hess, Rabbi Hirsch Zvi Kalischer, and the leaders of Russian Zionism, it was Theodor Herzl, an assimilated Hungarian Jew, who became the effective founder of the Zionist movement. It was Herzl who founded the **World Zionist Congress** in Basel, **Switzerland**, in August 1897. As a journalist based in Vienna, Herzl was sent to **France** to cover the trial of Alfred Dreyfus, a Jewish officer in the French army who was falsely accused of passing on military secrets to **Germany**. The atmosphere surrounding the trial shocked Herzl, who encountered a virulent form of **anti-Semitism** on the part of the anti-Dreyfusards. Herzl had already experienced the appeal of Jew-baiting in Vienna, where Karl Lueger had been elected mayor on an openly anti-Semitic platform, and he was also aware of the anti-Jewish policies of the czarist government in **Russia**. He did not, however, expect to find in democratic France the mobs that chanted "death to the Jews" because of their belief in Dreyfus's guilt.

It is not known exactly when Herzl took up the idea of a Jewish return to the ancestral homeland, but this solution to the endemic anti-Semitism that characterized much of Europe was promoted in a thin volume he titled *The Jewish State* (*Der Judenstaat*), a book he published in 1896. Herzl concluded that if in republican France anti-Semitism could continue to attract large segments of the population, then the future of the Jews in Europe was indeed a bleak one. Only in their own homeland could Jews realize the security and equality that the anti-Semites were attempting to deny them in Europe.

Although Herzl did not live to witness the fulfillment of his dream, one of his successors, **Chaim Weizmann**, was instrumental in convincing **Great Britain** to issue the **Balfour Declaration** in November 1917, which supported the creation of a Jewish homeland in Palestine. Despite the achievement, most Jews did not identify with Zionism. The bulk of Europe's Jews tended to describe themselves as a religious fellowship and not a nation. In **Germany**, for example, Jews viewed themselves as Germans of the Mosaic religious persuasion. In fact, many Jews felt threatened by Zionism and the implication that Jews were a nation within a nation, thus making them susceptible to charges of dual loyalty.

The **Nazi** seizure of power in 1933 and the subsequent persecution of the Jews in Germany reached its climax in the **Holocaust**. Tragically, the murder of six million Jews vindicated the Zionist assessment of the precarious nature of Jewish existence in Europe. As Jews throughout the world became aware of the **Final Solution**, many turned to the **Yishuv** as a refuge for the victims of Nazi persecution. The British **White Paper of 1939**, which restricted Jewish immigration into Palestine as the Germans systematically pursued their objective of annihilating the Jews of Europe, convinced many Jews to reevaluate Zionism. Jews the world over concluded that had there been a Jewish homeland, six million of their brethren would still be alive. On the eve of the establishment of the **State of Israel** in May 1948, most Jews embraced the Zionist idea and supported the creation of the Jewish state.

ZYGIELBOJM, SAMUEL ARTHUR (1895–1943). Samuel Arthur Zygielbojm, a Jewish Bundist (socialist) labor leader and a member of the Polish parliament-in-exile in London, committed suicide on 12 May 1943, when word of the liquidation of Warsaw's Jews reached him. Among those slain in the **Warsaw ghetto uprising** were his wife, Manya, and his 16-year-old son, Tuvia. In the letter he wrote before he took his life, Zygielbojm condemned the world's indifference to the mass murder of Polish Jewry and the lack of assistance to the **Warsaw ghetto** fighters.

ZYKLON B (PRUSSIC ACID). Experiments with Zyklon B pellets were initiated at **Auschwitz** in the fall of 1941. The gas, which was in general use as a pesticide, was distributed to the camp by the **Deutsche Gesellschaft fur Schadlingsbekampfung**, or German Vermin-Combating Corporation.

Bibliography

CONTENTS

INTRODUCTION

The imposing number of books and articles that have been published in recent years about the Holocaust has made it necessary to prioritize the literature in regard to significance. As a consequence, a bibliography of the Holocaust must by necessity be the product of choices made by the compiler. The books, articles, films, websites, and other information included in the bibliography have been selected for the purpose of providing the user the widest and most recent resources available for the purpose of research and general information. Included are a number of books that are indispensable as an introduction to the subject, as well as monographs that are reliable and likely to withstand the test of time. Additional titles have been included because they are the only available source on a particular topic or because of their controversial arguments. The choices, therefore, reflect the author's considered judgment as to which works continue to inform our understanding of the Holocaust.

Given the thousands of excellent titles on the subject, it may be presumptuous to single out the most important volumes on the subject. Nevertheless, a number of works continue to retain their significance in the literature of the Nazi genocide and remain essential for an understanding of the Holocaust. Take the section "General Holocaust Histories," for example. In this section a number of indispensable volumes on the Holocaust are listed. Readers will find Raul Hilberg's *The Destruction of the European Jews*, which details the Holocaust from Nazi records and describes how they organized the machinery of state to murder millions of people. The same section also includes Lucy Dawidowicz's *The War against the Jews, 1933-1945*, which is a comprehensive overview of the Holocaust and a book that makes the argument that the Final Solution was inherent in Nazi ideology. She goes on to argue that the war provided the opportunity to realize its objective of a *Judenrein* Europe. Dawidowicz also includes a valuable appendix that lists, country by country, the fate of European Jewry. Leni Yahil's *The Holocaust* is an exhaustive study of the subject that details the Holocaust from the perspective of the victims. Unlike Hilberg's work, Yahil accentuates the role of Jewish resistance in the Holocaust as well as the more sensitive issue of Jewish collaboration. Martin Gilbert's *The Holocaust* is a general history of the Holocaust told primarily from the perspective of the eyewitnesses. The volume is very readable and an excellent introduction to the subject.

Although a pioneering study, Hilberg's *The Destruction of the European Jews* did spark controversy. The dispute focused on the assertion that the Judenräte (Jewish Councils) contributed to the annihilation of European Jewry by their obedient implementation of Nazi orders in the ghetto. This argument was joined by Hannah Arendt, whose *Eichmann in Jerusalem*, listed under "Resistance," argues that had the Jewish Councils refused to carry out orders for the roundup of the Jews, it would have made it more difficult for the Nazis to conduct the deportations. The response to both Hilberg and Arendt can be found in *Judenrat* by Isaiah Trunk (same section). In the definitive work on the Jewish Councils in Eastern Europe, the author makes a compelling case that the Jewish Councils, given their enormous responsibilities, handled the situation circumstances as best they could under the most adverse conditions.

Although there is little doubt that Nazi Germany was committed to exterminating the Jews of Europe, there is a body of literature that contends that the Final Solution was the product of an impromptu decision-making process that responded to the exigency of war. A number of books take this approach, but few are better than the works of Christopher Browning. The so-called functionalist approach to the Holocaust can be found in his *Path to Genocide: Fateful Months, Ordinary Men* and *The Origins of the Final Solution* (see "The Final Solution"). This argument is countered by the intentionalist school, which contends that the destruction of European Jewry was part of Adolf Hitler's plans from the beginning of the Nazi movement. In addition to Lucy Dawidowicz's *The War against the Jews*, an important work that argues that Hitler was obsessed with annihilating the Jews is Gerald Fleming's *Hitler and the Final Solution* (see "Adolf Hitler"). A book that takes the intentionalist argument even further is Daniel Jonah Goldhagen's *Hitler's Willing Executioners* (see "Interpretative Works on the Holocaust"). Although his argument has been attacked by Holocaust historians, the book has received worldwide attention and has become, arguably, the most recognized title in Holocaust historiography.

Goldhagen argues that the Holocaust was not uniquely the creation of the Schutzstaffel (SS) or the Nazi Party. Rather, the Final Solution won the overwhelming support of the German people because they were motivated by a virulent anti-Semitism that led them to believe that the Jews were the demonic enemy. This "eliminationist" anti-Semitism made the annihilation of the Jews a German national project, and when Adolf Hitler turned to the mass extermination of the Jews, he was able to enlist vast numbers of Germans to support the Final Solution. This argument has been dismissed by leading Holocaust historians, such as Christopher Browning, Raul Hilberg, and Yehuda Bauer, as simplistic, and Goldhagen is accused of being selective in his use of evidence. But the book became a best-seller in both the United States and Germany, where Goldhagen received a sympathetic audience. The publicity attended to Goldhagen's book suggests that it is probable that if one book were read on the Holocaust, Goldhagen's tome would be the volume, and the reader's understanding of the Final Solution would be shaped by his arguments.

There appears to be a continuing interest in Anne Frank, whose diary is the most widely read book on the Holocaust in primary and secondary schools. Scholars, students, and interested readers will find a section in the bibliography on Anne Frank, which includes a number of the more important books on the subject, including *Anne Frank: The Book, the Life, the Afterlife* by Francine Prose.

The reader will find included in the bibliography a sufficient number of books that offer alternative explanations for the causes of the Holocaust. In addition to these monographs and interpretive works, a number of reference works are listed and should be consulted or purchased by libraries (see "Bibliographies and Encyclopedias"). The most indispensable of these books is the *Encyclopedia of the Holocaust*, edited by Israel Gutman. Also listed in this section and recommended are the *Bibliography of Holocaust Literature* by Abraham and Hershel Edelheit; *The Holocaust Encyclopedia*, edited by Walter Laqueur; and *The Columbia Guide to the Holocaust*, by Donald Niewyk and Francis Nicosia.

The indispensability of books on the Holocaust cannot be overestimated. However, additional sources of information on the Holocaust have also enriched our understanding of the destruction of European Jewry. Specifically, the Internet (see "Internet Resources") and film (see "Books on Holocaust Film" and "Selected Holocaust Films") have become sources by which the general public, as opposed to community of scholars, have learned about the Nazi genocide. Holocaust Internet websites continue to provide useful information in regard to the Holocaust and a number of the most important are listed in the bibliography, including *Yad Vashem* (www.Yadvashem.org), located in Israel, which includes probably the world's largest collection of information on the Holocaust. *March of the Living* (www.motl.org), a website for young people, is dedicated to teaching the lessons of the Holocaust. The *H-net* site brings together scholars and those interested in the Shoah to exchange issues relating to the Holocaust (h-net.org/~holoweb/), and the United States Holocaust Memorial Museum (www.ushmm.org) reconstructs the history of the Holocaust through multiple media (see "Internet Resources").

Holocaust awareness and its continued interest among the general public owes as much to work of scholars as it does to film. Film, especially the ever-growing numbers of documentaries, have become important teaching tools in our educational institutions, often supplementing texts on the subject of the Holocaust. It would be difficult to ignore the impact of commercial films and documentaries, such as *The Diary of Anne Frank*, *Judgment at Nuremberg*, *Schindler's List*, and the documentary *Shoah*, to name just a few, in calling the public's attention to the Holocaust in the decades following World War II. Similarly, made-for-television films (see "Television Films") such as *Holocaust* not only reached millions of viewers in the United States but also in West Germany, where it reached massive audiences and struck a nerve among the postwar generation. In fact, the film representation has spurred an increasing number of films and documentaries (see "Documentaries") in both the United States and throughout Europe. The importance of this medium is recognized by its place in the bibliography, which includes a select number of commercial films and documentaries, both foreign and domestic, that have been released in theaters and on television and are considered exemplary representatives of the genre. The films listed in this section are available on DVD. To supplement the section on film, the bibliography also includes scholarly books on the Holocaust.

The bibliography is divided into topical sections, each of which reflects a particular aspect of the Holocaust. The primary and secondary works listed under each section represent the most significant works on the subject. The choices also reflect a decision to make the bibliography "user friendly." Since much of the important foreign literature on the Holocaust has already been translated into English, the author has resisted the temptation to overload the reader with sources in other languages. Nevertheless, many important books and articles that have not, as yet, been translated into English are included in the bibliography.

The organization of the bibliography by subject necessitated combining secondary works with published articles, thus allowing the reader to find relevant citations in one place. Inasmuch as monographs and articles often become dated as a result of new research, the author has attempted to include the most recent scholarship in the bibliography as well as those scholarly works that remain important to our understanding of the Holocaust.

Whenever possible, consideration was given to the availability of books and periodicals still in print, as well as their accessibility in most university and public libraries.

REFERENCE WORKS

1. Atlases

Freeman, Michael. *Atlas of Nazi Germany*. London: Croom Helm, 1987.
Gilbert, Martin. *Atlas of the Holocaust*. New York: Pergamon Press, 1988.

2. Bibliographies and Encyclopedias

Bloomberg, Marty, and Buckley Barry Barrett. *The Jewish Holocaust: An Annotated Guide to Books in English*. San Bernardino, Calif.: Borgo Press, 1995.
Edelheit, Abraham J., and Hershel Edelheit. *Bibliography of Holocaust Literature*. Boulder, Colo.: Westview Press, 1986.
Gutman, Israel, ed. *Encyclopedia of the Holocaust*. 4 vols. New York: Macmillan, 1990.
———. *Encyclopedia of the Holocaust*. New York: Macmillan Library Reference, 1995. Reprint, 4 vols. into 2.
Laqueur, Walter. *The Holocaust Encyclopedia*. New Haven, Conn.: Yale University Press, 2001.
Levy, Richard S., ed. *Antisemitism: A Historical Encyclopedia of Prejudice and Persecution*. 2 vols. Santa Barbara, Calif.: ABC-Clio, 2005.
Megargee, Geoffrey, ed. *Encyclopedia of Camps and Ghettos: 1933–1945. Early Camps, Youth Camps, and Concentration Camps and Subcamps under the SS-Business Administration Main Office (WVHA)*. Bloomington: Indiana University Press and the U.S. Holocaust Memorial Museum, 2009. 2 vols., Part A and B.
Niewyk, Donald, and Francis Nicosia. *The Columbia Guide to the Holocaust*. New York: Columbia University Press, 2000.
Szonyi, David M. *The Holocaust: An Annotated Bibliography and Resource Guide*. New York: Ktav, 1985.

Wistrich, Robert. *Who's Who in Nazi Germany*. New York: Bonanza Books, 1982.

3. Dictionaries

Edelheit, Abraham J., and Hershel Edelheit. *History of the Holocaust: A Handbook and Dictionary*. Boulder, Colo.: Westview, 1994.
Epstein, Eric Joseph, and Phillip Rosen. *Dictionary of the Holocaust*. Westport, Conn.: Greenwood Press, 1997.

PRIMARY WORKS

4. Documents

Arad, Yitzhak, Yisrael Gutman, and Abraham Margaliot. *Documents of the Holocaust: Selected Sources on the Destruction of the Jews of Germany and Austria, Poland and the Soviet Union*. Jerusalem: Yad Vashem and Pergamon Press, 1981.
Dobroszycki, Lucjan, ed. *The Chronicles of the Lodz Ghetto, 1941–1944*. New Haven, Conn.: Yale University Press, 1984.
Eizanstadt, Stuart. *Report on Nazi Theft of Jewish Assets*. Washington, D.C.: U.S. Government Printing Office, 1997.
Friedlander, Henry, and Sybil Milton, eds. *Archives of the Holocaust*. 23 vols. Westport, Conn.: Garland Press, 1989.
Hilberg, Raul, ed. *Documents of Destruction: Germany and Jewry, 1933–1945*. Chicago: Quadrangle Books, 1971.
Kugelmass, Jack, and Jonathan Boyarin, trans. *From a Ruined Garden: The Memorial Books of Polish Jewry*. 2nd exp. ed. Bloomington: University of Indiana Press, 1998.
Mendelsohn, John, ed. *The Holocaust: Selected Documents*. New York: Garland, 1982.
Mendes-Flohr, Paul R., and Jehuda Reinharz, eds. *The Jew in the Modern World: A Documentary History*, 484–583. Oxford: Oxford University Press, 1980.
———. *Nazi Conspiracy and Aggression*. 8 vols. Washington, D.C.: U.S. Government Printing Office, 1946.
———. *The Trial of the Major War Criminals before the International Military Tribunal at Nuremberg, 14 November 1945–10 October, 1946*. 42 vols., 1947. Reprint: New York: AMS Press, 1971.

Wyman, David S., ed. *America and the Holocaust.* 13 vols. New York: Garland, 1989–1990.

5. Diaries and Memoirs

Amery, Jean. *At the Mind's Limits: Contemplations by a Survivor on Auschwitz and Its Realities.* Trans. Sidney Rosenfeld and Stella P. Rosenfeld. New York: Schocken, 1986.

Beon, Yves. *Planet Dora: A Memoir of the Holocaust and the Birth of the Space Age.* Boulder, Colo.: Westview, 1997.

Brandon, Ray, and Wendy Lower. *The Shoah in Ukraine: History, Testimony, Memorialization.* Bloomington: Indiana University Press and the U.S. Holocaust Memorial Museum, 2008.

Breitman, Richard, Barbara McDonald Stewart, and Severin Hochberg. *Refugees and Rescue: The Diaries and Papers of James G. McDonald, 1935–1945.* Bloomington: Indiana University Press and the U.S. Holocaust Memorial Museum, 2009.

Celan, Paul. *Selected Poems.* Trans. Michael Hamburger and Christopher Middleton. Harmondsworth: Penguin, 1972.

Clare, George. *Last Waltz in Vienna: The Rise and Destruction of a Family, 1842-1942.* New York: Holt, Rinehart & Winston, 1980.

Donat, Alexander. *The Holocaust Kingdom.* New York: Holt, Rinehart & Winston, 1963.

Edelman, Marek. *Shielding the Flame: An Intimate Conversation with Dr. Marek Edelman, the Last Survivor of the Warsaw Ghetto Uprising.* Trans. Joanna Stasinsk and Lawrence Wechsler. New York: Holt, 1986.

Eisner, Jack. *The Survivor.* New York: Morrow, 1980.

Fenelon, Fania. *Playing for Time: The Musicians of Auschwitz.* New York: Atheneum, 1977.

Frank, Anne. *The Diary of a Young Girl.* Trans. B. M. Mooyart. New York: Doubleday, 1967.

Frankl, Victor. *Man's Search for Meaning.* New York: Pocket Books, 1984.

Friedlander, Saul. *When Memory Comes.* New York: Farrar, Straus & Giroux, 1979.

Gay, Peter. *My German Question: Growing Up in Nazi Berlin.* New Haven, Conn.: Yale University Press, 1998.

——. *Hitler's Table Talk, 1941–1944: His Private Conversations.* 1953. Edited by Hugh Trevor-Roper. Introduction by Gerhard L.Weinberg. New updated ed. New York: Enigma, 2008.

Gilbert, Martin. *The Boys: The Story of 732 Young Concentration Camp Survivors.* New York: Henry Holt, 1997.

Graf, Malvina. *The Krakow Ghetto and the Plaszow Camp Remembered*. Tallahassee: Florida State University Press, 1989.

Hart, Kitty. *Return to Auschwitz*. New York: Atheneum, 1981.

Heppner, Ernst G. *Shanghai Refuge: A Memoir of the World War II Jewish Ghetto*. Lincoln: University of Nebraska Press, 1994.

Hilberg, Raul, Stanislaw Staron, and Josef Kermisz, eds. *The Warsaw Diary of Adam Czerniakow: Prelude to Doom*. Trans. Stanislaw Staron and the staff of Yad Vashem. New York: Stein & Day, 1979.

Hillesum, Etty. *An Interrupted Life: The Diaries of Etty Hillesum, 1941–1943*. Trans. Arno Pomerans. New York: Pantheon, 1983.

Höss, Rudolf. *Commandant of Auschwitz*. New York: World, 1960.

Kantor, Alfred. *The Book of Alfred Kantor*. New York: McGraw Hill, 1971.

Kaplan, Chaim. *The Warsaw Diary of Chaim Kaplan*. Ed. Abraham I. Katsh. New York: Collier, 1973.

Karski, Jan. *Story of a Secret State*. Boston: Houghton-Mifflin, 1944.

Klemperer, Victor. *The Language of the Third Reich: LTI-Lingua Tertii Imperii: A Philologist's Notebook*. New York: Continuum, 2006.

Kogon, Eugon. *The Theory and Practice of Hell*. New York: Berkeley Medallion Books, 1968.

Korczak, Janusz. *Ghetto Diary*. New York: Holocaust Library, 1978.

Lanzmann, Claude. *Shoah: An Oral History of the Holocaust* (The Complete Text of the Film). New York: Pantheon, 1985.

Lengyel, Olga. *Five Chimneys: The Story of Auschwitz*. Chicago: Ziff-Davis, 1947.

Levi, Primo. *The Drowned and the Saved*. New York: Summit Books, 1986.

——. *The Reawakening: A Liberated Prisoner's Long March Home through East Europe*. Trans. Stuart Woolf. Boston: Little, Brown, 1965.

——. *Survival in Auschwitz*. New York: Collier, 1973.

Lewin, Abraham. *A Cup of Tears: A Diary of the Warsaw Ghetto*. Ed. Antony Polonsky, trans. Christopher Hutton. Oxford: Basil Blackwell, 1988.

Lindeman, Yehudi, ed. *Shards of Memory: Narratives of Holocaust Survival*. Westport, Conn.: Praeger, 2007.

Niemoller, Martin. *Here Stand I!* Chicago: Willett, Clarke, 1937.

Orbuch, Sonia Shainwald, and Fred Rosenbaum. *Here There Are No Sarahs: A Woman's Courageous Fight against the Nazis and Her Bittersweet Fulfillment of the American Dream*. Muskegon, Mich.: RDR Books, 2009.

Orenstein, Henry. *I Shall Live: Surviving against All Odds, 1939–1945*. New York: Touchstone, 1989.

Paskuly, Steven, ed. *Death Dealer: The Memoirs of the SS Kommandant at Auschwitz by Rudolf Hoss*. New York: DaCapo Press, 1992.

Pomerantz, Jack, and Lyric Wallwork Winik. *Run East: Flight from the Holocaust*. Urbana: University of Illinois Press, 1997.

Redlich, Gonda. *The Terezin Diary of Gonda Redlich*. Ed. Saul S. Friedman and Laurence Kutler. Lexington: University of Kentucky Press, 1992.

Ringelblum, Emmanuel. *Notes from the Warsaw Ghetto*. Ed. and trans. Jacob Sloan. New York: McGraw-Hill, 1958.

Robinson, Jacob. *The Holocaust and After: Sources and Literature in English*. Jerusalem: Israel Universities Press, 1973.

Sachs, Nelly. *O the Chimneys!* New York: Farrar, Straus & Giroux, 1967.

Szwajger, Adina Blady. *I Remember Nothing More: The Warsaw Children's Hospital and the Jewish Resistance*. Trans. Tasja Darowska and Danusia Stak. New York: Pantheon, 1990.

Tec, Nechama. *Dry Tears*. New York: Oxford University Press, 1982.

Toll, Nelly S. *Behind the Secret Window: A Memoir of a Hidden Childhood during World War Two*. New York: Dial, 1993.

Tory, Abraham. *Surviving the Holocaust: The Kovno Ghetto Diary*. Trans. Jerzy Michalowica. Cambridge, Mass.: Harvard University Press, 1990.

Wells, Leon. *The Janowska Road*. New York: Macmillan, 1963.

Wiesel, Elie. *Night*. New York: Avon Books, 1969.

Zyskind, Sara. *Stolen Years*. Minneapolis, Minn.: Lerner, 1981.

BOOKS ON THE HOLOCAUST BY TOPIC

6. General Holocaust Histories

Aly, Götz. *The Final Solution*. New York: Arnold, 1999.

Arad, Yitzhak. *The Pictorial History of the Holocaust*. New York: Macmillan, 1993.

Bauer, Yehuda, and Nili Keren. *A History of the Holocaust*. New York: Franklin Watts, 1982.

Bergen, Doris L. *The Holocaust: A Concise History*. New York: Rowman & Littlefield, 2009.

Botwinick, Rita Steinhardt. *A History of the Holocaust*. New Jersey: Prentice Hall, 1996.

Dawidowicz, Lucy. *The War against the Jews, 1933–1945*. New York: Bantam, 1975.

Evans, Richard. *The Coming of the Third Reich*. New York: Penguin Press, 2003.

——. *The Third Reich in Power*. New York: Penguin Press, 2005.

——. *The Third Reich at War*. New York: Penguin Press, 2008.

Fischel, Jack. *The Holocaust*. Westport, Conn.: Greenwood Press, 1998.

Gilbert, Martin. *The Holocaust: A History of the Jews of Europe during the Second World War*. New York: Holt, Rinehart & Winston, 1985.

Grunfeld, Frederick V. *The Hitler File: A Social History of Germany and the Nazis, 1918–1945*. New York: Random House, 1974.

Kershaw, Ian. *Hitler, the Germans, and the Final Solution*. New Haven, Conn.: Yale University Press, 2008.

Hilberg, Raul. *The Destruction of the European Jews*. 3 vols. New York: Holmes & Meier, 1985.

Levin, Nora. *The Holocaust*. New York: Schocken Books, 1973.

Marrus, Michael. *The Holocaust in History*. Hanover, N.H.: University of New England Press, 1987.

Pauley, Bruce F. *From Prejudice to Persecution: A History of Austrian Anti-semitism*. Chapel Hill: University of North Carolina Press, 1992.

Reitlinger, Gerald. *The Final Solution: The Attempt to Exterminate the Jews of Europe*. New York: Beechhurst, 1953.

Weindling, Paul. *Health, Race and German Politics between National Unification and Nazism, 1870–1945*. New York: Cambridge University Press, 1989.

Yahil, Leni. *The Holocaust: The Fate of European Jews*. New York: Oxford University Press, 1990.

7. Traditional Anti-Semitism

Abella, Irving, and Harold Troper. *None Is Too Many: Canada and the Jews of Europe, 1933–1948*. New York: Random House, 1982.

Flannery, Edward H. *The Anguish of the Jews: Twenty-Three Centuries of Anti-Semitism Reviewed*. New York: Paulist Press, 1985.

Gager, John G. *The Origins of Anti-Semitism: Attitudes toward Judaism and Pagan Christian Antiquity*. New York: Oxford University Press, 1983.

Hay, Malcolm. *Europe and the Jews: The Pressure of Christendom over 1900 Years*. Chicago: Academy Chicago, 1992.

——. *The Roots of Christian Anti-Semitism*. New York: Freedom Library, 1981.

Niemoller, Martin. *Here Stand I!* Chicago: Willek, Clarke, 1937.

Parkes, James. *Anti-Semitism*. Chicago: Quadrangle Books, 1969.

Passelecq, Georges, and Bernard Suchecky. The Hidden Encyclical of Pius XI. New York: Harcourt, Brace, 1997.

Poliakov, Leon. *Harvest of Hate*. New York: Walden Press, 1979.

——. *The History of Anti-Semitism*. 4 vols. New York: Vanguard, 1965–1975.

Tal, Uriel. *Christians and Jews in Germany: Religion, Politics in the Second Reich, 1870–1914*. Trans. Noah Jonathan Jacobs. Ithaca, N.Y.: Cornell University Press, 1975.

Trachtenberg, Joshua. *The Devil and the Jews: The Medieval Conception of the Jew and Its Relation to Modern Antisemitism*. Philadelphia: Jewish Publication Society, 1961.

8. Ideological, Political, Social, and Racial Anti-Semitism

Baumgarten, Murray, Peter Kenez, and Bruce Thompson, eds. *Varieties of Antisemitism: History, Ideology, Discourse*. Newark: University of Delaware Press, 2009.

Berg, Scott. *Lindbergh*. New York: G. P. Putnam's Sons, 1998.

Burrin, Philippe. *Nazi Anti-Semitism: From Prejudice to the Holocaust*. New York: New Press, 2005.

Callil, Carmen. *Bad Faith: A Forgotten History of Family, Fatherland, and Vichy France*. New York: Alfred A. Knopf, 2006.

Chamberlain, Houston S. *Die Grundlagen des neunzehnfen Jahrhunderts* (The Foundation of the Nineteenth Century). Munich: Bruckmann, 1906.

Cohn, Norman. *Warrant for Genocide: The Myth of the Jewish World Conspiracy*. Chico, Calif.: Judaic Studies, 1981.

Fischer, Klaus. *The History of an Obsession: German Judeophobia and the Holocaust*. New York: Continuum, 1998.

Goodricke-Clarke, Nicholas. *The Occult Roots of Nazism: Secret Aryan Cults and Their Influence on Nazi Ideology*. New York: New York University Press, 1985.

Jochmann, Werner. "Die Ausbreitung des Antisemitismus in Deutschland, 1914–1923." In *Gesellschaftskerise und Judenfeindschaft in Deutschland, 1870–1945*, 99–112. Hamburg: Hans Christian Verlag, 1988.

Katz, Jacob. *From Prejudice to Destruction: Anti-Semitism, 1700–1933*. Cambridge, Mass.: Harvard University Press, 1980.

Langmuir, Gavin I. *History, Religion, and Anti-Semitism*. Berkeley: University of California Press, 1990.

Large, David Clay. *Nazi Games: The Olympics of 1936*. New York: W. W. Norton, 2007.

Lindemann, Albert S. *Esau's Tears: Modern Anti-Semitism and the Rise of the Jews*. New York: Cambridge University Press, 1997.

Massing, Paul W. *Rehearsal for Destruction: A Study of Political Anti-Semitism in Imperial Germany*. New York: Harper & Brothers, 1949.

Poliakov, Leon. *The Aryan Myth: A History of Racist and Nationalist Ideas in Europe*. New York: New American Library, 1977.

Spicer, Kevin P. ed. *Antisemitism, Christian Ambivalence, and the Holocaust*. Bloomington: University of Indiana Press and the U.S. Holocaust Memorial Museum, 2007.

Viereck, Peter. *Metapolitics: The Roots of the Nazi Mind*. New York: Capricon Books, 1961. Revised eds., 1961, 1965.

Weiss, John. *Ideology of Death: Why the Holocaust Happened in Germany*. Chicago: Ivan R. Dee, 1996.

Wildt, Michael. *An Uncompromising Generation: The Nazi Leadership of the Reich Security Main Office*. Trans. Thomas Lampert. Madison: University of Wisconsin Press, 2009.

Wistrich, Robert S. *Laboratory for World Destruction: Germans and Jews in Central Europe*. Lincoln: University of Nebraska Press, 2007.

Zeskind, Leonard. *Blood and Politics: The History of the White Nationalist Movement: From the Margins to the Mainstream*. New York: Farrar, Straus & Giroux, 2009.

9. Weimar Republic

Bessel, Richard. *Germany after the First World War*. New York: Oxford University Press, 1993.

Bolkosy, Sidnet M. *The Distorted Image: German Jewish Perceptions of Germans and Germany, 1918–1935*. New York: Elsevier, 1975.

Gallin, Alice. *Midwives to Nazism: University Professors in Weimar Germany, 1925–1933*. Macon, Ga.: Mercer, 1986.

Gay, Peter. *Freud, Jews, and Other Germans: Masters and Victims in Modernist Culture*. New York: Oxford University Press, 1978.

———. *Weimar Culture: The Outsider as Insider*. New York: Harper & Row, 1968.

Laqueur, Walter. *Weimar: A Cultural History, 1918–1933*. New York: G. P. Putnams's Sons, 1974.

Mosse, George. *Germans and Jews: The Right, the Left and the Search for a Third Force in Pre-Nazi Germany*. New York: Grosset & Dunlap, 1970.

Niewyk, Donald L. "The Economic and Cultural Role of Jews in the Weimar Republic." *Leo Baeck Institute Yearbook* 16 (1971): 163–73.

Stern, Fritz. *The Politics of Cultural Despair*. Berkeley: University of California Press, 1961.

Szwajger, Adina Blady. *I Remember Nothing More: The Warsaw Children's Hospital and the Jewish Resistance.* Trans. Tasja Darowska and Danusia Stak. New York: Pantheon, 1990.

10. Adolf Hitler

Aronson, Shlomo. *Hitler, the Allies, and the Jews.* New York: Cambridge University Press, 2004.

Bankier, David. "Hitler and the Policy-Making Process on the Jewish Question." *Holocaust and Genocide Studies* 3 (1988): 1–20.

Bromberg, Norbert, and Verna Volz Small. *Hitler's Psychopathology.* New York: International Universities Press, 1983.

Bullock, Alan. *Hitler: A Study in Tyranny.* New York: Harper & Row, 1962.

Burrin, Philippe. *Hitler and the Jews: The Genesis of the Holocaust.* New York: Edward Arnold, 1994.

Davidson, Eugene. *The Making of Adolf Hitler: The Birth and Rise of Nazism.* New York: Macmillan, 1977.

Fest, Joachim. *Hitler.* Trans. Richard and Clara Winston. New York: Harcourt, Brace & Jovanovich, 1973.

Fleming, Gerald. *Hitler and the Final Solution.* Los Angeles: University of California Press, 1984.

Gellately, Robert. *Lenin, Stalin, Hitler: The Age of Social Catastrophe.* New York: Vintage Books, 2007.

Hamann, Brigitte. *Hitler's Wien.* Munich: Piper, 1996.

———. *Winifred Wagner: A Life at the Heart of Hitler's Bayreuth.* New York: Harcourt, 2005.

Heiden, Konrad. *Der Fuhrer.* Boston: Houghton-Mifflin, 1944.

Himmelfarb, Martin. "No Hitler, No Holocaust." *Commentary* 76, no. 3 (March 1984): 37–43.

Hitler, Adolf. *Mein Kampf.* Trans. Ralph Manheim. Boston: Houghton-Mifflin, 1943.

Irving, David. *Hitler's War.* New York: Avon Books, 1990.

Jackel, Eberhard. *Hitler's World View: A Blueprint for Power.* Cambridge, Mass.: Harvard University Press, 1981.

Kershaw, Ian. *Hitler, 1889–1936: Hubris.* New York: W. W. Norton, 1998.

———. *Hitler, 1936–1945: Nemesis.* New York: W. W. Norton, 2000.

———. *The "Hitler" Myth.* Oxford: Clarendon Press, 1987.

Kubizek, August. *The Young Hitler I Knew.* Trans. E. V. Anderson. Boston: Houghton-Mifflin, 1955.

Langer, Walter C. *The Mind of Adolf Hitler.* New York: Basic Books, 1972.

Lee, Albert. *Henry Ford and the Jews*. New York: Stein & Day, 1980.

Lukacs, John. *The Hitler of History*. New York: Knopf, 1997.

Maser, Werner. *Hitler: Legend, Myth, and Reality*. Trans. Peter and Betty Ross. New York: Harper & Row, 1973.

Miller, Alice. "Adolf Hitler's Childhood: From Hidden to Manifest Terror." In *For Your Own Good: Hidden Cruelty in Child-Rearing and the Roots of Violence*. 3rd ed., 142–97. New York: Noonday Press, 1990.

Rosenbaum, Ron. *Explaining Hitler*. New York: Random House, 1998.

Rosenfeld, Alvin H. *Imagining Hitler*. Bloomington: Indiana University Press, 1985.

Toland, John. *Adolf Hitler*. New York: Doubleday, 1976.

Trevor-Roper, H. R. *The Last Days of Hitler*. Chicago: University of Chicago Press, 1962.

Victor, George. *Hitler: The Pathology of Evil*. Washington: Brassey's, 1998.

Waite, Robert G. L. *The Psychopathic God*. New York: Basic Books, 1977.

11. Nazi Germany

American Jewish Committee. *The Jews in Nazi Germany: A Handbook of Facts Regarding Their Precarious Situation*. New York: American Jewish Committee, 1935.

Angress, Werner T. *Between Fear and Hope: Jewish Youth in the Third Reich*. New York: Columbia University Press, 1988.

Baker, Leonard. *Days of Sorrow and Pain: Leo Baeck and the Berlin Jews*. New York: Macmillan, 1978.

Bankier, David. *The Germans and the Final Solution: Public Opinion under Nazism*. Oxford: Blackwell, 1992.

Barkai, Avraham. *From Boycott to Annihilation: The Economic Struggle of German Jews, 1933–1943*. Hanover: University Press of New England, 1989.

Bendersky, Joseph. *A History of Nazi Germany*. Chicago: Nelson Hall, 1985.

Bergen, Doris L. *Twisted Cross: The German Christian Movement in the Third Reich*. Chapel Hill: University of North Carolina Press, 1996.

Blumenthal, W. Michael. *The Invisible Wall: Germans and Jews, a Personal Exploration*. Washington, D.C.: Counterpoint, 1998.

Bolkosky, Sidney M. *The Distorted Image: German Jewish Perceptions of Germans and Germany, 1918–1935*. New York: Elsevier, 1975.

Burleigh, Michael, and Wolfgang Wippermann. *The Racial German State: 1933–1945*. New York: Cambridge University Press, 1991.

Dodd, William E. *Ambassador Dodd's Diary*. New York: Harcourt Brace, 1941.

Erickson, Robert P. *Theologians under Hitler*. New Haven, Conn.: Yale University Press, 1985.

Fischer, Klaus P. *Nazi Germany: A New History*. New York: Continuum, 1995.

Friedlander, Saul. *Nazi Germany and the Jews: The Years of Persecution, 1933–1939*. Vol. 1. New York: Harper Collins, 1997.

Gellately, Robert, and Nathan Stolzfus, eds. *Social Outsiders in Nazi Germany*. Princeton, N.J.: Princeton University Press, 2001.

Gross, Leonard. *The Last Jews in Berlin*. New York: Simon & Schuster, 1982.

Heschel, Suzanne. *The Aryan Jesus*. Princeton, N.J.: Princeton University Press, 2008.

Kamenetsky, Christa. *Children's Literature in Hitler's Germany: The Cultural Policy of National Socialism*. Athens: Ohio University Press, 1984.

Kaplan, Marion A. *Between Dignity and Despair: Jewish Life in Nazi Germany*. New York: Oxford University Press, 1998.

Kershaw, Ian. *Popular Opinion and Political and Dissent in the Third Reich: Bavaria 1933–1945*. Oxford: Clarendon Press, 1983.

Klemperer, Victor. *I Will Bear Witness: A Diary of the Nazi Years, 1933–1941*. Trans. and preface Martin Chambers. New York: Random House, 1998.

Koonz, Claudia. *The Nazi Conscience*. Cambridge, Mass.: Belknap Press, 2003.

Levi, Erik. *Music in the Third Reich*. New York: St. Martin's Press, 1996.

Lochner, Louis P., ed. *The Goebbels Diaries, 1942–1943*. Garden City, N.Y.: Doubleday, 1948.

Lozowick, Yaacov. *Hitler's Bureaucrats: The Nazi Security Police and the Banality of Evil*. New York: Continuum, 2002.

Merkl, Peter. *Political Violence under the Swastika*. Princeton, N.J.: Princeton University Press, 1975.

Miller, Richard Lawrence. *Nazi Justiz: Law of the Holocaust*. Westport, Conn.: Praeger, 1995.

Nelson, Anne. *Red Orchestra: The Story of the Berlin Underground and the Circle of Friends Who Resisted Hitler*. New York: Random House, 2009.

Paucker, Arnold, ed. *Die Juden im Nationalsozialistischen Deutschland: The Jews in Nazi Germany, 1933–1943*. New York: Leo Baeck Institute, 1986.

Pehle, Walter H., ed. *November 1938: From "Reichkristallnacht" to Genocide*. New York: Berg, 1991.

Schoenbaum, David. *Hitler's Social Revolution: Class and Status in Nazi Germany, 1933–1945*. New York: Doubleday, 1966.

Spielvogel, Jackson. *Hitler and Nazi Germany: A History.* Englewood Cliffs, N.J.: Prentice Hall, 1988.

Stern, Fritz. *The Politics of Cultural Despair.* Berkeley: University of California Press, 1961.

Trevor-Roper, Hugh, ed. *Final Entries 1945: The Diaries of Joseph Goebbels.* New York: G. P. Putnam, 1973.

Wienrich, Max. *Hitler's Professors: The Part of Scholarship in Germany's Crimes against the Jewish People.* New York: YIVO, 1946.

Wyden, Peter. *Stella.* New York: Simon & Schuster, 1992.

12. Eugenics and Euthanasia

Burleigh, Michael. *Death and Deliverance: "Euthanasia" in Germany: 1900–1945.* New York: Cambridge University Press, 1994.

Carlson, Elof Axel. *The Unfit: A History of a Bad Idea.* Cold Springs Harbor, N.Y.: Cold Springs Harbor Laboratory Press, 2001.

Friedlander, Henry. *The Origins of Nazi Genocide: From Euthanasia to the Final Solution.* Chapel Hill: University of North Carolina Press, 1995.

Glass, M. James. *Life Unworthy of Life: Racial Phobia and Mass Murder in Hitler's Germany.* New York: Basic Books, 1997.

Gotz, Aly, Peter Chroust, and Christian Pross. *Cleansing the Fatherland: Nazi Medicine and Racial Hygiene.* Trans. Belinda Cooper. Baltimore: Johns Hopkins University Press, 1994.

Hillel, Marc, and Clarissa Henry. *Of Pure Blood.* Trans. Eric Mossbacher. New York: McGraw-Hill, 1976.

Kuhl, Stefan. *The Nazi Conscience: Eugenics, American Racism, and German National Socialism.* New York: Oxford University Press, 1994.

Lifton, Robert J. *The Nazi Doctors: Medical Killing and the Psychology of Genocide.* New York: Basic Books, 1986.

Muller, Ingo. *Hitler's Justice: The Courts of the Third Reich.* Cambridge, Mass.: Harvard University Press, 1991.

Muller-Hill, Benno. *Murderous Science: Elimination by Scientific Selection of Jews, Gypsies, and Others, Germany, 1933–1945.* New York: Oxford University Press, 1988.

Proctor, Robert N. *Racial Hygiene: Medicine under the Nazis.* Cambridge, Mass.: Harvard University Press, 1988.

Weindling, Paul. *Health, Race and German Politics between National Unification and Nazism: 1870–1945.* Cambridge: Cambridge University Press, 1989.

13. The Ghettos of Occupied Europe

Arad, Yitzhak. *Ghetto in Flames: The Struggle and Destruction of the Jews in Vilna in the Holocaust.* Jerusalem: Akiva Cooperative Printing Press, 1980.

Bender, Sara. *The Jews of Bialystok: During World War II and the Holocaust.* Waltham, Mass.: Brandeis University Press, 2008.

Corni, Gustavo. "Hitler's Ghettos: Voices from a Beleaguered Society, 1939–1944." *Central European History* 37 (2004): 322–24.

Epstein, Barbara. *The Minsk Ghetto, 1941–1943.* Berkeley: University of California Press, 2008.

Graf, Malvina. *The Krakow Ghetto and the Plaszow Camp Remembered.* Tallahassee: Florida State University Press, 1989.

Gutman, Yisrael. *The Jews of Warsaw, 1939–1943: Ghetto, Underground, Revolt.* Bloomington: Indiana University Press, 1989.

Hilberg, Raul, Stanislaw Staron, and Josef Kermisz, eds. *The Warsaw Diary of Adam Czerniakow: Prelude to Doom.* Trans. Stanislaw Staron and staff of Yad Vashem. New York: Stein & Day, 1979.

Hoffman, Eva. *Shtetl: The Life and Death of a Small Town and the World of Polish Jews.* New York: Houghton-Mifflin, 1997.

Horowitz, Gordon J. *Ghettostadt: Lödz and the Making of a Nazi City.* Cambridge, Mass: Harvard University Press, 2008.

Kaplan, Chaim. *The Warsaw Diary of Chaim Kaplan.* Ed. Abraham I. Katsh. New York: Collier, 1973.

Kassow, Samuel D. *Who Will Write Our History: Emanuel Ringelblum, the Warsaw Ghetto, and the Oyneg Shabes Archive.* Bloomington: Indiana University Press, 2007.

Naimark, Norman. *Fires of Hatred: Ethnic Cleansing in Twentieth-Century Europe.* Cambridge, Mass.: Harvard University Press, 2001.

Robinson, Jacob, and Phillip Friedman. *Guide to Jewish History under Nazi Impact.* New York: YIVO, 1960.

Szwajger, Adina Blady. *I Remember Nothing More: The Warsaw Children's Hospital and the Jewish Resistance.* Trans. Tasja Darowska and Danusia Stak. New York: Pantheon, 1990.

United States Holocaust Memorial Museum. *Hidden History of the Kovno Ghetto.* New York: Bullfinch Press, 1997.

14. The Refugee Crisis, 1933–1945

Breitman, Richard, and Allen Kraut. *American Refugee Policy and European Jewry: 1933–1945.* Bloomington: Indiana University Press, 1987.

Dwork, Deborah, and Robert Jan Van Pelt. *Flight from the Reich: Refugee Jews, 1933–1946.* New York: W. W. Norton, 2009.

Feingold, Henry L. *The Politics of Rescue*. New Brunswick, N.J.: Rutgers University Press, 1970.

Friedman, Saul S. *No Haven for the Oppressed: United States Policy toward Jewish Refugees, 1938–1945*. Detroit, Mich.: Wayne State University Press, 1971.

Heppner, Ernst G. *Shanghai Refuge: A Memoir of the World War II Jewish Ghetto*. Lincoln: University of Nebraska Press, 1994.

Jarvik, Laurence, director. *Who Shall Live and Who Shall Die?* New York: Kino International, 1982. 90-minute video.

Kranzler, David. *Japanese, Nazis, Jews*. New York: Yeshiva University Press, 1976.

Marrus, Michael. *The Unwanted: European Refugees in the Twentieth Century*. New York: Oxford University Press, 1985.

Milton, Sybil. *Rescue to Switzerland: The Missy and Sally Mayer Affairs*. New York: Garland, 1982.

Robinson, Nehemiah. *The Spain of Franco and Its Policies towards the Jews*. New York: Institute of Jewish Affairs, 1944.

Ross, James R. *Escape to Shanghai: A Jewish Community in China*. New York: Free Press, 1994.

Wells, Allen. *Tropical Zion: General Trujillo, FDR, and the Jews of Sosúa*. Durham, N.C.: Duke University Press, 2009.

Wyman, David. *Paper Walls: America and the Refugee Crisis*. Amherst: University of Massachusetts Press, 1968.

15. The Consequences of the German Invasion of Poland and the Soviet Union

Bartov, Omar. *The Eastern Front, 1941–1945: German Troops and the Barbarization of Warfare*. London: Macmillan, 1985.

———. *Hitler's Army: Soldiers, Nazis, and War in the Third Reich*. New York: Oxford University Press, 1991.

———. *Mirrors of Destruction: War, Genocide, and Modern Identity*. New York: Oxford University Press, 2000.

Dallin, Alexander. *German Rule in Russia, 1941–1945: A Study of Occupation Policies*. Boulder, Colo.: Westview Press, 1981.

Dean, Martin. *Collaboration in the Holocaust: Crimes of the Local Police in Belorussia and Ukraine, 1941–1944*. New York: St. Marin's Press, 2000.

Desbois, Father Patrick. *The Holocaust by Bullets: A Priest's Journey to Uncover the Truth behind the Murder of Six Million Jews*. New York: Palgrave Macmillan, 2008.

Dobroszycki, Lucjan, and Jeffrey Gurock, eds. *The Holocaust in the Soviet Union*. Armonk, N.Y.: M. E. Sharpe, 1993.

Ehrenburg, Ilya, and Vasily Grossman, eds. *The Black Book*. Trans. John Glad and James Levine. New York: Holocaust Library, 1981.

Ezergailis, Andrew. *The Holocaust in Latvia, 1941–1944: The Missing Center*. Riga: Historical Institute of Latvia, in association with the U.S. Holocaust Memorial Museum, 1996.

Garrard, John, and Carol Garrard. *The Bones of Berdichev: The Life and Fate of Vasily Grossman*. New York: Free Press, 1996.

Grossman, Vasily. *Life and Fate*. New York: Harper & Row, 1980.

Hirschteld, Gerhard, ed. *The Politics of Genocide: Jews and Soviet Prisoners of War in Nazi Germany*. London: Allen & Unwin, 1986.

Jacobsen, Hans-Adolf. "The Kommissarbefehl and Mass Executions of Soviet Prisoners of War." In *Anatomy of the SS State*. Ed. Helmut Krausnick et al., 505–35. New York: Walker, 1968.

Kuznetzov, Anatoly. *Babi Yar*. New York: Dell, 1967.

Levin, Dov. *The Lesser of Two Evils: Eastern European Jewry under Soviet Rule, 1939–1941*. Philadelphia: Jewish Publication Society, 1995.

Mayer, Arno J. *Why Did the Heavens Not Darken?* New York: Pantheon, 1990.

Paul, Allen. *Katyn: The Untold Story of Stalin's Polish Massacre*. New York: Scribner's, 1991.

Rubinson-Ginaite, Sara. *Resistance and Survival: The Jewish Community in Kauna, 1941–1944*. Oakville, Ont.: Mosaic, 2005.

Schulte, Theo J. *The German Army and Nazi Policies in Occupied Russia*. Oxford: Berg, 1989.

Spector, Shmuel. *The Holocaust and Volhynian Jews, 1941–1944*. Jerusalem: Yad Vashem, 1990.

16. The Final Solution

Abrahamsen, Samuel. *Norway's Response to the Holocaust: A Historical Perspective*. New York: Holocaust Library, 1991.

Adam, Uwe Dietrich. "The Gas Chambers." In *Unanswered Questions: Nazi Germany and the Genocide of the Jews*. Ed. Francois Furet, 134–54. New York: Schocken Books, 1989.

Anger, Per. *With Raoul Wallenberg in Budapest*. New York: Holocaust Library, 1981.

Aronsfeld, C. C. *The Text of the Holocaust: A Study of the Nazis' Extermination Propaganda, from 1919–1945*. Marblehead, Mass.: Michah, 1985.

Bankier, David. "Hitler and the Policy-Making Process on the Jewish Question." *Holocaust and Genocide Studies* 3 (1988): 1–20.

Bar-Zohar, Michael. *Beyond Hitler's Grasp: The Heroic Rescue of Bulgaria's Jew*. Holbrook, Mass.: Adams Media, 1998.

Bauer, Yehuda. "The Death Marches, January–May, 1945." In *The Nazi Holocaust: Historical Articles on the Destruction of European Jews*. Vol. 9, ed. Michael Marrus, 491–511. Westport, Conn.: Meckler, 1989.

———. *Jews for Sale? Nazi-Jewish Negotiations, 1933–1945*. New Haven, Conn.: Yale University Press, 1994.

Ben-Tov, A. *Facing the Holocaust in Budapest: The International Committee of the Red Cross and the Jews of Hungary, 1943–1945*. Geneva: Henry Dunant Institute and Martinus Nijhoff, 1988.

Borkin, Joseph. *The Crimes and Punishment of I. G. Farben*. New York: Free Press, 1978.

Braham, Randolph L. *The Politics of Genocide: The Holocaust in Hungary*. Vol. 1. New York: Columbia University Press, 1981.

Breitrnan, Richard. *The Architect of Genocide: Himmler and the Final Solution*. New York: Knopf, 1991.

Browning, Christopher. *Fateful Months: Essays on the Emergence of the Final Solution*. New York: Holmes & Meier, 1986.

———. *The Final Solution and the German Foreign Office: A Study of Referat D III of Abteilung Deutschland, 1940–1943*. New York: Holmes & Meier, 1978.

———. *Ordinary Men: Reserve Police Battalion 101 and the Final Solution in Poland*. New York: Harper Collins, 1992.

———. *The Origins of the Final Solution: The Evolution of Nazi Jewish Policy, September 1939–March 1942*. Lincoln: University of Nebraska Press, 2004.

Cesarani, David. *Becoming Eichmann*. Cambridge, Mass.: DaCapo Press, 2006.

———. *Path to Genocide*. Cambridge: Cambridge University Press, 1992.

Fein, Helen. *Accounting for Genocide*. New York: Free Press, 1979.

Ferencz, Benjamin B. *Less Than Slaves: Jewish Forced Labor and the Quest for Compensation*. Cambridge, Mass.: Harvard University Press, 1979.

Friedlander, Henry. The Origins of Nazi Genocide: From Euthanasia to the Final Solution. Chapel Hill: University of North Carolina Press, 1995.

Friedman, Philip. *Roads to Execution: Essays on the Holocaust*. Philadelphia: Jewish Publication Society, 1980.

Friedrich, Otto. *The Kingdom of Auschwitz*. New York: Harper Perennial, 1982.

Furet, Francois. "The Gas Chambers." In *Unanswered Questions: Nazi Germany and the Genocide of the Jews*, 134–54. New York: Schocken, 1989.

Gerlach, Christian. "Die Wannsee-Konferenz, das Schicksal der Deutschen Juden und Hitlers Politische Grundsatzentscheidung, alle Juden Europas zu Ermorden." *Werkstattgeschichte* 6, no. 18 (November 1997): 7–44.

Gilbert, Martin. *Final Journey: The Fate of the Jews in Nazi Europe.* New York: Mayflower Books, 1979.

Hartog, Kristen Den, and Tracey Kasaboski. *The Occupied Garden.* Toronto, Ont.: McClelland & Stewart, 2008.

Hilberg, Raul. *The Destruction of the European Jews.* 3 vols. New York: Holmes & Meier, 1985.

Klarsfeld, Serge. *French Children of the Holocaust: A Memorial.* New York: New York University Press, 1996.

———. *La Mémorial de la Déportation des Juifs de France.* Paris: Klarsfeld Foundation, 1978. Published in English by the Klarsfeld Foundation in 1983 as *The Memorial to the Jews Deported from France.*

Koblik, Steven. *The Stones Cry Out: Sweden's Response to the Persecution of the Jews, 1933–1945.* New York: Holocaust Library, 1988.

Kogon, Eugen, Hermann Langbein, and Adalbert Ruckerl, eds. *Nazi Mass Murder: A Documentary History of the Use of Poison Gas.* New Haven, Conn.: Yale University Press, 1993.

Lang, von Jochen, ed. *Eichmann Interrogated: Transcripts from the Archives of the Israeli Police.* Trans. Ralph Manheim. New York: Vintage Books, 1984.

Langerbein, Helmut. *Hitler's Death Squads: The Logic of Mass Murder.* College Station: Texas A&M Press, 2004.

Lanzmann, Claude. *Shoah: An Oral History of the Holocaust* (The Complete Text of the Film). New York: Pantheon, 1985.

Lifton, Robert J. *The Nazi Doctors: Medical Killing and the Psychology of Genocide.* New York: Basic Books, 1986.

Marrus, Michael, and Robert O. Paxton. *Vichy France and the Jews.* New York: Schocken Books, 1981.

Michaelis, Meir. *Mussolini and the Jews.* Oxford: Clarendon Press, 1978.

Milton, Sybil. *Rescue to Switzerland: The Missy and Sally Mayer Affairs.* New York: Garland, 1982.

Mommsen, Hans. "The Realization of the Unthinkable: The 'Final Solution of the Jewish Question' in the Third Reich." In *The Policies of Genocide: Jews and Soviet Prisoners of War in Nazi Germany.* Ed. Gerhard Hirschfeld, 98–99. London: Allen & Unwin, 1986.

Moore, Bob. *Victims & Survivors: The Nazi Persecution of the Jews in the Netherlands 1940–1945.* New York: Arnold, 1997.

Presser, Jacob. *The Destruction of the Dutch Jews.* Trans. Arnold Pomerans. New York: Dutton, 1969.

Rosenbaum, Alan S. *Is the Holocaust Unique? Perspectives on Comparative Genocide*. Boulder: Colo.: Westview Press, 1996.

Rummel, R. J. *Genocide: Nazi Genocide and Mass Murder*. New Brunswick, N.J.: Transaction, 1992.

Sabrin, B. F., ed. *Alliance for Murder: The Nazi-Ukranian Nationalist Partnership in Genocide*. New York: Sarpedon, 1991.

Scheffler, Wolfgang. "The Forgotten Part of the 'Final Solution': The Liquidation of the Ghettos." *Simon Wiesenthal Center Annual* 2 (1985): 31–51.

Schneider, Gertrude. *Exile and Destruction: The Fate of Austrian Jews, 1938–1945*. Westport, Conn.: Praeger, 1995.

Sereny, Gitty. *Into That Darkness: From Mercy Killing to Mass Murder*. London: Andre Deutsch, 1974.

U.S. Holocaust Memorial Council. *Planning Guide: Fifty Years Ago: From Terror to Systematic Murder*. Washington, D.C.: U.S. Holocaust Memorial Museum, 1991.

Whittman, Rebecca. *Beyond Justice: The Auschwitz Trial*. Cambridge, Mass: Harvard University Press, 2005.

Zuccotti, Susan. *The Holocaust, the French, and the Jews*. New York: Basic Books, 1993.

———. *The Italians and the Holocaust: Persecution, Rescue, and Survival*. New York: Basic Books, 1987.

17. German Concentration and Death Camps

Adam, Uwe Dietrich. "The Gas Chambers." In *Unanswered Questions: Nazi Germany and the Genocide of the Jews*. Ed. Francois Furet, 134–54. New York: Schocken Books, 1989.

Arad, Yitzhak. *Belzec, Sobibor, and Treblinka: The Operation Reinhard Death Camps*. Bloomington: Indiana University Press, 1987.

Bartov, Omer. *Murder in Our Midst: The Holocaust, Industrial Killing and Representation*. New York: Oxford, 1996.

Berben, Paul. *Dachau, 1933–1945: The Official History*. London: Norfolk Press, 1975.

Brown, Daniel, Patrick. *The Beautiful Beast: The Life and Crimes of SS Aufseherin Irma Grese*. 2nd ed. Ventura, Calif.: Golden West Historical, 2004.

Donat, Alexander, ed. *The Death Camp Treblinka: A Documentary*. New York: Holocaust Library, 1979.

Dwork, Deborah, and Robert Jan van Pelt. *Auschwitz: 1270 to the Present*. New York: Norton, 1996.

———. *Children with a Star: Jewish Youth in Nazi Europe*. New Haven, Conn.: Yale University Press, 1991.

Feig, Konnilyn. *Hitler's Death Camps: The Sanity of Madness.* New York: Holmes & Meier, 1979.

Fenelon, Fania. *Playing for Time: The Musicians of Auschwitz.* New York: Atheneum, 1977.

Gutman, Yisrael, and Michael Berebaum, eds. *Anatomy of the Auschwitz Death Camp.* Bloomington: Indiana University Press, 1994.

Hackett, David, ed., trans. *The Buchenwald Report.* Boulder, Colo.: Westview Press, 1995.

Hill, Mavis M., and L. Norman Williams. *Auschwitz in England: A Record of a Libel Action.* New York: Stein & Day, 1965.

Kogon, Eugon. *The Theory and Practice of Hell.* New York: Berkeley Medallion Books, 1968.

Lagnado, Lucette Matalon, and Sheila Cohn Dekel. *Children of the Flames: Dr. Josef Mengele and the Untold Story of the Twins of Auschwitz.* New York: William Morrow, 1991.

Langbein, Hermann. *Menschen in Auschwitz.* Frankfurt: Ullstein, 1980.

Lengyel, Olga. *Five Chimneys: The Story of Auschwitz.* Chicago: Ziff-Davis, 1947.

Levy, Primo. *Survival in Auschwitz.* New York: Collier, 1973.

Madajcyk, Czeslaw. "Concentration Camps as Tools of Oppression in Nazi-Occupied Europe." In *The Nazi Concentration Camps: Structure and Aims, the Image of the Prisoner, the Jews in the Camps,* 55–57. Jerusalem: Yad Vashem, 1984.

Muller, Filip. *Eyewitness Auschwitz: Three Years in a Gas Chamber.* New York: Stein & Day, 1979.

Paskuly, Steven, ed. *Death Dealer: The Memoirs of the SS Kommandant at Auschwitz by Rudolf Höss.* New York: DaCapo Press, 1992.

Plant, Richard. *The Pink Triangle.* New York: Henry Holt, 1986.

Reilly, Joanne. *Belsen: The Liberation of a Concentration Camp.* New York: Routledge, 1998.

Sofsky, Wolfgang. *The Order of Terror: The Concentration Camp.* Trans. William Templer. Princeton, N.J.: Princeton University Press, 1997.

Troller, Norbert. *Theresienstadt: Hitler's Gift to the Jews.* Chapel Hill: University of North Carolina Press, 1991.

18. Judenräte

Arendt, Hannah. *Eichmann in Jerusalem.* New York: Viking, 1963.

Cohen, Yerachmiel (Richard). *The Burden of Conscience: French Jewish Leadership during the Holocaust.* Bloomington: Indiana University Press, 1987.

Epstein, Leslie. *King of the Jews.* New York: Avon, 1980.

Robinson, Jacob. *And the Crooked Shall Be Made Straight: The Eichmann Trial, the Jewish Catastrophe, and Hannah Arendt's Narrative*. Philadelphia: Jewish Publication Society, 1965.

Trunk, Isaiah. *Judenrat: The Jewish Councils in Eastern Europe under Nazi Occupation*. Lincoln: University of Nebraska Press, 1996.

19. Resistance

Ainsztein, Reuben. *Jewish Resistance in Nazi-Occupied Eastern Europe*. New York: Barnes & Noble, 1974.

———. *The Warsaw Ghetto Revolt*. New York: Schocken Books, 1979.

Cohen, Asher. *The Halutz Resistance in Hungary, 1942–1944*. New York: Columbia University Press, 1986.

Edelman, Marek. *Shielding the Flame: An Intimate Conversation with Dr. Marek Edelman, the Last Survivor of the Warsaw Ghetto Uprising*. Trans. Joanna Stasinska and Lawrence Wechsler. New York: Holt, 1986.

Fuchs, Abraham. *The Unheeded Cry: The Life of Rabbi Michael Weissmandle*. New York: Torah Umesorah, 1984.

Gutman, Yisrael. *The Jews of Warsaw, 1939–1943: Ghetto, Underground, Revolt*. Bloomington: Indiana University Press, 1989.

Hebrew University of Jerusalem and New York Times. "Contemporary Jewry Oral History Collection. Pt. 2: World War II." *The Holocaust: Resistance and Rescue*. Glen Rock, N.J.: Microfilming Corp. of America, 1975.

Krakowski, Shmuel. *The War of the Doomed: Jewish Armed Resistance in Poland, 1942–1944*. New York: Holmes & Meier, 1984.

Laska, Vera, ed. *Women in the Resistance and in the Holocaust: The Voices of Eyewitnesses*. Westport, Conn.: Greenwood Press, 1983.

Latour, Anny. *The Jewish Resistance in France (1940–1944)*. New York: Holocaust Library, 1981.

Stroop, Jurgen. *The Stroop Report: The Jewish Quarter of Warsaw Is No More!* Trans. Sybil Milton. New York: Pantheon Books, 1979.

Suhl, Yuri, ed. *They Fought Back*. New York: Crown, 1967.

Syrkin, Marie. *Blessed Is the Match: The Story of Jewish Resistance*. Philadelphia: Jewish Publication Society of America, 1947.

Tec, Nechama. *Defiance*. New York: Oxford University Press, 2009.

Trunk, Isaiah. *Jewish Responses to Nazi Persecution*. New York: Stein & Day, 1982.

20. Bystanders, the Churches, and Other Institutions

Aarons, Mark, and John Loftus. *Unholy Trinity: The Vatican, the Nazis, and Soviet Intelligence*. New York: St. Martin's Press, 1991.

Baranowski, Shelley. *The Confessing Church, Conservative Elites, and the Nazi State*. New York: Edwin Mellen Press, 1986.

Barnett, Victoria. *For the Soul of the People: Protestant Protest against Hitler*. New York: Oxford University Press, 1992.

Bergen, Doris L. "Catholics, Protestants and Anti-Semitism in Nazi Germany." *Central European History* 27 (1994): 329-48.

Conway, John S. *The Nazi Persecution of the Churches, 1933–1945*. New York: Basic Books, 1968.

Falconi, Carlo. *The Silence of Pius XII*. Boston: Little, Brown, 1970.

Friedlander, Saul. *Pius XII and the Third Reich: A Documentation*. New York: Octagon Books, 1980.

Gutteridge, Richard. *The German Evangelical Church and the Jews, 1879-1950*. New York: Harper & Row, 1976.

Helmreich, Ernst Christian. *The German Churches under Hitler: Background, Struggle, and Epilogue*. Detroit, Mich.: Wayne State University Press, 1979.

Hilberg, Raul. *Perpetrators, Victims, Bystanders: The Jewish Catastrophe, 1933–1945*. New York: Harper Collins, 1992.

Lewy, Guenter. *The Catholic Church and Nazi Germany*. New York: McGraw-Hill, 1964.

Littell, Franklin, and Hubert G. Locke, eds. *The German Church Struggle and the Holocaust*. San Francisco: Mellen Research University Press, 1990.

Morley, John F. *Vatican Diplomacy and the Jews during the Holocaust 1939–1943*. New York: Ktav, 1980.

Passelecq, Georges, and Bernard Schecky. *The Hidden Encyclical of Pius XI: The Vatican's Loss of Opportunity to Oppose Nazi Racial Policies That Led to the Holocaust*. New York: Harcourt Brace, 1997.

21. Righteous Gentiles and Other Acts of Rescue

Anger, Per. *With Raoul Wallenberg in Budapest*. New York: Holocaust Library, 1981.

Bejski, E. "The Righteous among the Nations and Their Part in the Rescue of Jews." In *Rescue Attempts during the Holocaust: Proceedings of the Second Yad Vashem International Conference, April 1974*. Ed. Y. Gutman and E. Zuroff, 627–47. Jerusalem: Yad Vashem, 1977.

Block, Gay, and Malka Drucker. *Rescuers: Portraits of Moral Courage in the Holocaust*. New York: Holmes & Meier, 1992.

Carpi, Daniel. *Between Mussolini and Hitler: The Jews and the Italian Authorities in France and Tunisia*. Hanover, Mass.: Brandeis University Press.

——. "The Rescue of Jews in the Italian Zone of Occupied Croatia." In *Rescue Attempts during the Holocaust: Proceedings of the Second Yad Vashem International Conference, April 1974.* Ed. Y. Gutman and E. Zuroff, 465–507. Jerusalem: Yad Vashem, 1977.

Flender, Harold. *Rescue in Denmark.* New York: Simon & Schuster, 1963.

Fogelman, Eva. *Conscience and Courage of Jews during the Holocaust.* New York: Anchor, 1994.

Friedman, Philip. *Their Brother's Keepers.* New York: Crown, 1957.

Hallie, Philip. *Lest Innocent Blood Be Shed.* New York: Harper Colophon Books, 1979.

Hellman, Peter. *Avenue of the Righteous.* New York: Bantam, 1980.

Keneally, Thomas. *Schindler's List.* New York: Simon & Schuster, 1982.

Levine, Hillel. *In Search of Sugihara.* New York: Free Press, 1996.

Maga, Timothy. "The Quest for a Generous America: Varian Fry and the Refugee Cause, 1940–1942." *Holocaust Studies Annual.* Vol. 1, ed. Sanford Pinsker and Jack Fischel, 69–87. Greenwood, Fla.: Penkeville Press, 1983.

Ramati, Alexander. *The Assisi Underground: The Priests Who Rescued Jews.* New York: Stein & Day, 1978.

Rosenfeld, Harvey. *Raoul Wallenberg, Angel of Rescue: Heroism and Torment in the Gulag.* Buffalo, N.Y.: Prometheus, 1982.

Ross, James R. *Escape to Shanghai: A Jewish Community in China.* New York: Free Press, 1994.

Schmitt, Hans A. *Quakers and Nazis: Inner Light in Outer Darkness.* Columbia: University of Missouri Press, 1997.

Tec, Nechama. *When Light Pierced the Darkness: Christian Rescue of Jews in Nazi-Occupied Poland.* Oxford: Oxford University Press, 1986.

Zuccotti, Susan. *The Italians and the Holocaust: Persecution, Rescue, and Survival.* New York: Basic Books, 1987.

22. Allies

Abella, Irving, and Harold Troper. *None Is Too Many: Canada and the Jews of Europe, 1933–1945.* New York: Random House, 1982.

Abzug, Robert H. *Inside the Vicious Heart: Americans and the Liberation of Nazi Concentration Camps.* New York: Oxford University Press, 1985.

Cohen, Michael J. *Churchill and the Jews.* London: Frank Cass, 1985.

——. *Truman and Israel.* Berkeley: University of California Press, 1991.

Dinnerstein, Leonard. *America and the Survivors of the Holocaust* New York: Columbia University Press, 1982.

Feingold, Henry L. *The Politics of Rescue.* New Brunswick, N.J.: Rutgers University Press, 1970.

Friedman, Saul S. *No Haven for the Oppressed: United States Policy toward Jewish Refugees, 1938–1945*. Detroit, Mich.: Wayne State University Press, 1971.

Gilbert, Martin. *Churchill and the Holocaust*. Hopkinton, N.H.: Dragonwyk, 1993.

Hamerow, Theodore S. *Why We Watched: Europe, America and the Holocaust*. New York: W. W. Norton, 2008.

23. Controversy over the Bombing of Auschwitz

Erdheim, Stuart G. "Could the Allies Have Bombed Auschwitz-Birkenau?" *Holocaust and Genocide Studies* 11, no. 2 (Fall 1997): 129–70.

Gilbert, Martin. *Auschwitz and the Allies*. New York: Holt, Rinehart & Winston, 1981.

Kitchens, James H. III. "The Bombing of Auschwitz Reconsidered." *Journal of Military History* 58 (April 1994): 233–66.

Levy, Richard H. "The Bombing of Auschwitz Revisited: A Critical Analysis." *Holocaust and Genocide Studies* 10, no. 3 (Winter 1996): 267–98.

Markusan, Eric, and David Kopf. *The Holocaust and Strategic Bombing: Genocide and Total War in the 20th Century*. Boulder, Colo.: Westview, 1995.

Newton, Verne W., ed. *FDR and the Holocaust*. New York: St. Martin's Press, 1996.

Rubinstein, William. *The Myth of Rescue: Why the Democracies Could Not Have Saved More Jews from the Nazis*. New York: Routledge, 1997.

Wyman, David S. "Why Auschwitz Was Never Bombed." *Commentary* 65 (May 1978): 37–49.

24. Response of American and Palestine Jewry to the Holocaust

Bauer, Yehuda. *American Jewry and the Holocaust: The American Joint Distribution Committee, 1939–1945*. Detroit, Mich.: Wayne State University Press, 1981.

———. "Negotiations between Sally Mayer and the S.S." *Rescue Attempts during the Holocaust: Proceedings of the Second Yad Vashem International Conference, April 1974*. Ed. Y. Gutman and E. Zuroff, 5–45. Jerusalem: Yad Vashem, 1977.

Black, Edwin. *The Transfer Agreement: The Untold Story of the Secret Pact between the Third Reich and Jewish Palestine*. New York: Macmillan, 1984.

Edelheit, Abraham J. *The Yishuv in the Shadow of the Holocaust: Zionist Politics and Rescue Aliya, 1933–1939*. Boulder, Colo.: Westview Press, 1996.

Feingold, Henry L. *Bearing Witness: How America and Its Jews Responded to the Holocaust*. New York: Syracuse University Press, 1995.

Finger, Seymour Maxwell. *American Jewry during the Holocaust*. New York: Holmes & Meier, 1984.

Gruber, Ruth. Haven: *The Unknown Story of 1000 World War II Refugees*. New York: Coward-McCann, 1983.

Lookstein, Haskal. *Were We Our Brother's Keepers? The Public Response of American Jews to the Holocaust*. New York: Hartmore House, 1985.

Porat, Dina. *The Blue and the Yellow Stars of David: The Zionist Leadership in Palestine and the Holocaust, 1939–1945*. Cambridge, Mass.: Harvard University Press, 1990.

Teveth, Shabtai. *Ben-Gurion and the Holocaust*. New York: Harcourt Brace, 1996.

25. Studies of Holocaust Survivors

Brenner, Reeve Robert. *The Faith and Doubt of Holocaust Survivors*. New York: Free Press, 1980.

Des Pres, Terrence. *The Survivor: An Anatomy of Life in the Death Camps*. New York: Oxford University Press, 1976.

Dwork, Deborah. *Children with a Star: Jewish Youth in Nazi Europe*. New Haven, Conn.: Yale University Press, 1991.

Epstein, Helen. *Children of the Holocaust*. New York: Atheneum, 1977.

Fein, Helen. *Accounting for Genocide*. New York: Free Press, 1979.

Felstiner, John. *Paul Celan: Poet, Survivor, Jew*. New Haven, Conn.: Yale University Press, 1995.

Gelissen, Rena Kornreich, with Heather Dune Macadam. *Rena's Promise: A Story of Sisters in Auschwitz*. Boston: Beacon Press, 1995.

Habe, Hans. *The Mission*. New York: Coward-McCann, 1966.

Lagnado, Lucette Matalon, and Sheila Cohn Dekel. *Children of the Flames: Dr. Josef Mengele and the Untold Story of the Twins of Auschwitz*. New York: William Morrow, 1991.

Langer, Lawrence Langer. *Admitting the Holocaust: Collected Essays*. New York: Oxford University Press, 1995.

———. *Holocaust Testimonies: The Ruins of Memory*. New Haven, Conn.: Yale University Press, 1991.

Levy, Primo. *Survival in Auschwitz*. New York: Collier, 1973.

Lore, Shelly. *Jewish Holocaust Survivors' Attitudes toward Contemporary Beliefs about Themselves*. Ann Arbor, Mich.: University of Michigan Press, 1984.

Meed, Vladka. *On Both Sides of the Wall*. Haifa: Ghetto Fighters' House, 1972.

Moskovitz, Sarah. *Love Despite Hate: Child Survivors of the Holocaust and Their Adult Lives*. New York: Schocken Books, 1983.

Niewyk, Donald L. ed. *Fresh Wounds: Early Narratives of Holocaust Survivors*. Chapel Hill: University of North Carolina Press, 1998.

Rabinowitz, Dorothy. *New Lives: Survivors of the Holocaust in America*. New York: Knopf, 1976.

Rothchild, Sylvia, ed. *Voices from the Holocaust*. New York: New American Library, 1981.

Vrba, Rudolf, and Alan Bestic. *I Cannot Forgive*. New York: Bantam, 1968.

26. The Holocaust in Art, Literature, and Similar Topics

Appelfeld, Ahron. *The Age of Wonder*. Boston: Godine, 1980.

——. *Badenheim 1939*. Trans. Dalya Bilu. New York: Pocket Books, 1980.

——. *The Iron Tracks*. Trans. Jeffrey M. Green. New York: Schocken, 1998.

Avisor, Ilan. *Screening the Holocaust: Cinema's Image of the Unimaginable*. Bloomington: Indiana University Press, 1988.

Bassani, Giorgio. *The Garden of the Finzi-Continis*. San Diego: Harcourt Brace Jovanovich, 1977.

Bellow, Saul. *Mr. Sammler's Planet*. New York: Viking, 1970.

Bicker, Jurek. *Jakob the Liar*. New York: Harcourt Brace, 1975.

Blatter, Janet, and Sybil Milton. *Art of the Holocaust*. New York: Rutledge Press, 1981.

Bor, Josef. *The Terezin Requiem*. New York: Alfred A. Knopf, 1963.

Borowski, Tadeusz. *This Way for the Gas, Ladies and Gentlemen*. New York: Viking, 1967.

Columbat, Andre Pierre. *The Holocaust in French Film*. Metuchen, N.J.: Scarecrow Press, 1993.

Costanza, Mary S. *The Living Witness: Art in the Concentration Camps and Ghettos*. New York: Free Press, 1982.

Daneson, Judith E. *The Holocaust in American Film*. Philadelphia: Jewish Publication Society, 1987.

Epstein, Leslie. *King of the Jews*. New York: Avon, 1980.

Goodrich, Frances, and Albert Hackett. *The Diary of Anne Frank*. New York: Random House, 1956.

Green, Gerald. *The Artists of Terezin*. New York: Hawthorn, 1969.

——. *Holocaust*. New York: Bantam, 1978.

Grossman, Vasily. *Life and Fate*. New York: Harper & Row, 1980.

Gurdus, Luba Krugman. *Painful Echoes: Poems of the Holocaust*. New York: Holocaust Library, 1985.

Hochhuth, Rolf. *The Deputy.* New York: Grove Press, 1964.

Hull, David. *Film in the Third Reich: A Study of the German Cinema, 1933–1945.* Berkeley: University of California Press, 1969.

Insdorf, Annette. *Indelible Shadows: Film and the Holocaust.* New York: Vintage Books, 1983, 2002.

Kaes, Anton. *From Hitler to Heimat: The Return of History as Film.* Cambridge, Mass.: Harvard University Press, 1989.

Kanink, Yoram. *Adam Resurrected.* New York: Atheneum, 1971.

Karas, Joiza. *Music in Terezin, 1941–1945.* New York: Pendragon, 1975.

Kuzentzov, Anatoly. *Babi Yar.* New York: Dell, 1967.

LaCapra, Dominick. *History and Memory after Auschwitz.* Ithaca, N.Y.: Cornell University Press, 1998.

Lanzmann, Claude. *Shoah: An Oral History of the Holocaust* (The Complete Text of the Film). New York: Pantheon, 1985.

Lask, Israel Meir. *Songs of the Ghetto.* Tel Aviv: Eked, 1976.

Lind, Jakov. *Landscape in Concrete.* New York: Grove Press, 1966.

Littell, Jonathan. *The Kindly Ones.* New York: Harper Collins, 2009.

Loshitzky, Yosefa, ed. *Spielberg's Holocaust: Critical Perspectives on "Schindler's List."* Bloomington: Indiana University Press, 1997.

Malamud, Bernard. *The Assistant.* New York: Avon, 1980.

Miller, Arthur. *Incident at Vichy.* New York: Viking, 1965.

Milton, Sybil. *The Art of Jewish Children: Germany, 1936–1941.* New York: Philosophical Society.

Morrow, Lance. "Television and the Holocaust." *Time,* May 1, 1978: 53.

Muffs, Judith. *The Holocaust in Books and Films.* New York: Anti Defamation League, 1982.

Ozick, Cynthia. *The Shawl: A Story and Novella.* New York: Knopf, 1989.

Rentschuler, Eric. *The Ministry of Illusion: Nazi Cinema and Its Afterlife.* Cambridge, Mass.: Harvard University Press, 1996.

Robinson, Jacob. *The Holocaust and After: Sources and Literature in English.* Jerusalem: Israel Universities Press, 1973.

Schwarz-Bart, Andre. *The Last of the Just.* New York: Bantam, 1961.

St. John, Robert. *The Man Who Played God.* Garden City, N.Y: Doubleday, 1962.

Steiner, George. *The Portage to San Cristobal of A. H.* New York: Simon & Schuster, 1979.

Steiner, Jean Francois. *Treblinka.* New York: Simon & Schuster, 1967.

Styron, William. *Sophie's Choice.* New York: Random House, 1979.

Stuzkever, Abraham. *Burnt Pearls: Ghetto Poems of Abraham Sutz Lever.* Trans. Seymour Mayne. Oakville, Ont.: Mosaic Press, 1981.

Thomas, D. M. *The White Hotel.* New York: Pocket Books, 1981.

Toll, Nelly. *Without Surrender: Art of the Holocaust.* Philadelphia: Running Press, 1978.

Uris, Leon. *Exodus.* Garden City, N.Y.: Doubleday 1958.

———. *Mila 18.* Garden City, N.Y.: Doubleday, 1961.

———. *QBVII.* Garden City, N.Y: Doubleday, 1970.

Veret, Paul. "Art and Music in the Shoah." In *Out of the Whirlwind: A Reader of Holocaust Literature,* 259–82. New York: Doubleday, 1968.

Volavkova, Hana, ed. *I Never Saw Another Butterfly.* Trans. Jeanne Necova. New York: McGraw-Hill, 1964.

Wiesel, Elie. "Trivializing the Holocaust: Semi-Fact and Semi-Fiction." *New York Times,* 16 April 1978, sec. 2.

Wiesenthal, Simon. *Max and Helen.* New York: Morrow, 1981.

———. *The Sunflower.* New York: Schocken Books, 1970.

Yevtushenko, Yevgeny. "Babi Yar." In *Selected Poems.* Trans. Robin Milner-Gulland and Peter Levi. Baltimore, Md.: Penguin, 1974.

Young, James. *The Texture of Memory: Holocaust Memorials and History.* New Haven, Conn.: Yale University Press, 1993.

27. Perpetrators

Bartov, Omar. *Hitler's Army: Soldiers, Nazis, and War in the Third Reich.* New York: Oxford University Press, 1991.

Black, Peter. *Ernst Kaltenbrunner: Ideological Soldier of the Third Reich.* Princeton, N.J.: Princeton University Press, 1984.

Bytwerk, Randall L. *Julius Streicher: The Man Who Persuaded a Nation to Hate Jews.* New York: Dorset Press, 1983.

Calic, Edouard. *Reinhard Heydrich: The Chilling Story of the Man Who Masterminded the Nazi Death Camps.* New York: Hippocrene, 1988.

Dmysryshyn, Basil. "The Nazis and the SS Volunteer Division 'Galicia.'" *American Slavic and East European Review,* no. 15 (1956): 1–10.

Fenyo, Mario D. *Hitler, Horthy, and Hungary.* New Haven, Conn.: Yale University Press, 1972.

Fest, Joachim C. *The Face of the Third Reich: Portraits of the Nazi Leadership.* Trans. Michael Bullock. New York: Pantheon Books, 1970.

Freiwald, Aaron, with Martin Mendelsohn. *The Last Nazi: Josef Schwammberger and the Nazi Past.* New York: W. W. Norton, 1994.

Golsan, Richard J. *Memory, the Holocaust and French Justice: The Bousquet and Touvier Affairs.* Trans. Lucy Golsan. Hanover, N.H.: University Press of New England, 1996.

Hilberg, Raul. *Perpetrators, Victims, Bystanders: The Jewish Catastrophe, 1933–1945.* New York: Harper Collins, 1992.

Hohne, Heinz. *The Order of the Death Head: The Story of Hitler's SS*. New York: Coward-McCann, 1970.

Höss, Rudolf. *Commandant of Auschwitz*. New York: World, 1960.

Kater, Michael H. *The Nazi Party: A Social Profile of Members and Leaders, 1919–1945*. Cambridge, Mass.: Harvard University Press, 1983.

Klee, Ernst, Willi Dressen, and Volker Riess, eds. "The Good Old Days." In *The Holocaust as Seen by Its Perpetrators and Bystanders*. New York: Free Press, 1988.

Krausnick, Helmut, and Martin Broszat. *Anatomy of the SS State*. Cambridge: William Collins & Sons, 1968.

Langer, Lawrence. *The Holocaust and the Literary Imagination*. New Haven, Conn.: Yale University Press, 1975.

Lemkin, Raphael. *Axis Rule in Occupied Europe, Laws of Occupation—Analysis of Government, Propositions for Redress*. Washington, D.C.: Carnegie Foundation for International Peace, 1944. Reprint, New York: Howard Fertig, 1973.

Lumans, Valdis O. *Himmler's Auxiliaries: The Volksdeutsche Mittelstelle and the German National Minorities of Europe, 1933–1945*. Chapel Hill: University of North Carolina Press, 1993.

Mattar, Philip. *The Mufti of Jerusalem*. New York: Columbia University Press, 1988.

Merkl, Peter H. *Political Violence under the Swastika: 581 Early Nazis*. Princeton, N.J.: Princeton University Press, 1975.

Michaelis, Meir. *Mussolini and the Jews*. Oxford: Clarendon Press, 1978.

Overy, R. J. *Goering, the "Iron Man."* London: Routledge & Kegan Paul, 1984.

Padfield, Peter. *Himmler*. New York: Henry Holt, 1991.

Posner, Gerald. *Mengele: The Complete Story*. New York: McGraw-Hill, 1986.

Reitlinger, Gerald. *The SS, Alibi of a Nation*. Englewood Cliffs, N.J.: Prentice-Hall, 1956. Revised ed., 1981.

Reuth, Ralf Georg. *Goebbels*. Trans. Krishna Winston. New York: Harcourt Brace, 1993.

Sabrin, B. F., ed. *Alliance for Murder: The Nazi-Ukrainian Nationalist Partnership in Genocide*. New York: Sarpedon, 1991.

Segev, Tom. *Soldiers of Evil: The Commanders of the Nazi Concentration Camps*. New York: McGraw-Hill, 1987.

Sereny, Gitta. *Albert Speer: His Battle with Truth*. New York: Knopf, 1995.

Steinberg, Jonathan. *All or Nothing: The Axis and the Holocaust, 1941–1943*. London: Routledge, 1990.

Van Der Vat, Dan. *The Good Nazi: The Life and Lies of Albert Speer*. Boston: Houghton-Mifflin, 1997.

Wegner, Bernd. *The Waffen-SS: Organization, Ideology and Function*. Oxford: Basil Blackwell, 1990.

Weisberg, Richard H. *Vichy Law and the Holocaust in France.* New York: New York University Press, 1996.

Wiesenthal, Simon. *Justice Not Vengeance.* London: Weidenfeld & Nicolson, 1989.

———. *The Murderers amongst Us.* New York: McGraw-Hill, 1967.

Wildt, Michael. *An Uncompromising Generation: The Nazi Leadership of the Reich Security Main Office.* Trans. Thomas Lampert. Madison: University of Wisconsin Press, 2009.

Ziegler, Herbert F. *Nazi Germany's New Aristocracy: The SS 27 Leadership, 1925–1939.* Princeton, N.J.: Princeton University Press, 1989.

28. Gypsy Holocaust

Bauer, Yehuda. "Gypsies." *Encyclopedia of the Holocaust.* Vol. 2, ed. Israel Gutman, 634–38. New York: Macmillan, 1990.

———. "Whose Holocaust?" *Midstream* (November 1980): 42–46.

Crowe, David M. *A History of the Gypsies of Eastern Europe and Russia.* New York: St. Martin's Griffin, 1994.

Hancock, Ian. *The Pariah Syndrome.* Ann Arbor, Mich.: Karoma, 1986.

———. "Responses to the *Porajmos*: The Romani Holocaust." *Is the Holocaust Unique? Perspectives on Comparative Genocide.* Ed. Alan S. Rosenbaum, 39–64. Boulder, Colo.: Westview Press, 1996.

———. "Uniqueness of the Victims: Gypsies, Jews and the Holocaust." *Without Prejudice: International Review of Discrimination* 1, no. 2 (1988): 45–67.

Kenrick, Donald, and Grattan Puxon. *The Destiny of Europe's Gypsies.* New York: Basic Books, 1972.

Ramati, Alexander. *And the Violins Stopped Playing.* New York: Franklin Watts, 1986.

Yates, Dora. "Hitler and the Gypsies." In *On Prejudice: A Global Perspective.* Ed. Daniela Gioseffi, 103–10. New York: Anchor Books, 1993.

29. Interpretative Works on the Holocaust

Arendt, Hannah. *Eichmann in Jerusalem.* New York: Viking, 1963.

———. *The Origins of Totalitarianism.* New York: Harcourt Brace & World, 1966.

Baldwin, Peter, ed. "A Controversy about the Historicization of National Socialism." In *Reworking the Past: Hitler, the Holocaust, and the Historian's Debate,* 102–34. Boston: Beacon Press, 1990.

Bartov, Omer. *Murder in Our Midst: The Holocaust, Industrial Killing and Representation.* New York: Oxford University Press, 1996.

Bauman, Zygmunt. *Modernity and the Holocaust.* Ithaca, N.Y.: Cornell University Press, 1989.

Berenbaum, Michael, and Abraham J. Peck, eds. *The Holocaust and History: The Known, the Unknown, the Disputed, and the Reexamined.* Bloomington: Indiana University Press and the U.S. Holocaust Memorial Museum, 1998.

Browning, Christopher. *Ordinary Men: Reserve Police Battalion 101 and the Final Solution in Poland.* New York: HarperCollins, 1992.

Dawidowicz, Lucy S. *The Holocaust and the Historians.* Cambridge, Mass.: Harvard University Press, 1981.

Fischer, Klaus P. *The History of an Obsession: Judeophobia and the Holocaust.* New York: Continuum, 1998.

Friedman, Saul, ed. *Holocaust Literature: A Handbook of Critical, Historical, and Literary Writings.* Westport, Conn.: Greenwood Press, 1993.

Fritzsche, Peter. *Germans into Nazis.* Cambridge, Mass.: Harvard University Press, 1998.

Goldhagen, Daniel Jonah. *Hitler's Willing Executioners: Ordinary Germans and the Holocaust.* New York: Knopf, 1996.

Gordon, Sarah. *Hitler, Germans, and the Jewish Question.* Princeton, N.J.: Princeton University Press, 1984.

Hartmann, Geoffrey. *The Longest Shadow: In the Aftermath of the Holocaust.* Bloomington: Indiana University Press, 1994.

Katz, Steven T. *The Holocaust in Historical* Context. Vol. 1. New York: Oxford University Press, 1994.

Lipstadt, Deborah E. *Beyond Belief: The American Press and the Coming of the Holocaust.* New York: Free Press, 1988.

Milgram, Stanley. *Obedience to Authority.* New York: Harper & Row, 1974.

Robinson, Jacob. *And the Crooked Shall Be Made Straight: The Eichmann Trial, the Jewish Catastrophe, and Hannah Arendt's Narrative.* Philadelphia: Jewish Publication Society, 1965.

Ross, Robert W. *So It Was True: The American Protestant Press and the Nazi Persecution of the Jews.* Minneapolis: University of Minnesota Press, 1980.

Rubenstein, Richard. *After Auschwitz.* Indianapolis: Bobbs-Merrill, 1966.

———. *The Cunning of History: The Holocaust and the American Future.* New York: Harper Colophon Books, 1975.

Rubenstein, William. *The Myth of Rescue: Why the Democracies Could Not Have Saved More Jews from the Nazis.* New York: Routledge, 1997.

Schleunes, Karl A. *The Twisted Road to Auschwitz: Nazi Policy toward German Jews, 1933–1939.* Chicago: University of Illinois Press, 1990.

Steiner, George. *In Bluebeard's Castle: Some Notes towards the Definition of Culture.* New Haven, Conn.: Yale University Press, 1971.

Weiss, John. *Ideology of Death: Why the Holocaust Happened in Germany.* Chicago: Ivan R. Dee, 1996.

Wyman, David, ed. *The World Reacts to the Holocaust.* Baltimore: Johns Hopkins Press, 1996.

30. Poland

Bethell, Nicholas. *The War Hitler Won: The Fall of Poland, September 1939.* New York: Holt, Rinehart & Winston, 1972.

Davies, Norman. *God's Playground: A History of Poland. Vol. 2, 1795 to the Present.* New York: Columbia University Press, 1982.

Gross, Jan Tomasz. *Polish Society under German Occupation: The General-Gouvernement, 1939–1944.* Princeton, N.J.: Princeton University Press, 1979.

Gutman, Israel. *The Jews of Warsaw, 1939–1943: Ghetto, Underground, Revolt.* Bloomington: Indiana University Press, 1989.

———. "Poland: The Jews in Poland." *Encyclopedia of the Holocaust.* Vol. 3, ed. Israel Gutman, 1151–76. New York: Macmillan, 1990.

Heller, Celia. *On the Edge of Destruction: The Jews of Poland between the Two World Wars.* New York: Columbia University Press, 1976.

Hoffman, Eva. *Shtetl: The Life and Death of a Small Town and the World of Polish Jews.* New York: Houghton-Mifflin, 1997.

Kaplan, Chaim. *The Warsaw Diary of Chaim Kaplan.* Ed. Abraham I. Katsh. New York: Collier, 1973.

Karski, Jan. *Story of a Secret State.* Boston: Houghton-Mifflin, 1944.

Krakowski, Shmuel. *The War of the Doomed: Jewish Armed Resistance in Poland, 1942–1944.* New York: Holmes & Meier, 1984.

Lanzmann, Claude. *Shoah: An Oral History of the Holocaust* (The Complete Text of the Film). New York: Pantheon, 1985.

Lukas, Richard. *Forgotten Holocaust: The Poles under German Occupation 1939–1944.* Lexington: University of Kentucky Press, 1986.

Madajczyk, Czeslaw. "Poland: General Survey." *Encyclopedia of the Holocaust.* Vol. 3, ed. Israel Gutman, 1143–51. New York: Macmillan, 1990.

Tec, Nechama. *When Light Pierced the Darkness: Christian Rescue of Jews in Nazi-Occupied Poland.* Oxford: Oxford University Press, 1986.

Vinecour, Earl. *Polish Jews: The Final Chapter.* New York: New York University Press, 1977.

Weinryb, Bernard. *The Jews of Poland: A Social and Economic History of the Jewish Community in Poland from 1100 to 1800.* Philadelphia: Jewish Publication Society, 1973.

31. Theological, Philosophical, and Ideological Responses to the Holocaust

Bauman, Zygmunt. *Modernity and the Holocaust.* Ithaca, N.Y.: Cornell University Press, 1989.

Berkovitz, Eliezer. *Faith after the Holocaust.* New York: Ktav, 1973.

———. *With God in Hell.* New York: Sanhedrin Press, 1979.

Burleigh, Michael. *Ethics and Extermination: Reflections on Nazi Genocide.* Cambridge: Cambridge University Press, 1997.

Dietrich, Donald J. *God and Humanity in Auschwitz: Jewish-Christian Relations and Sanctioned Murder.* New Brunswick, N.J.: Transaction, 1995.

Erickson, Robert P. *Theologians under Hitler: Gerhard Kittel, Paul Althouse and Emanuel Hirsch.* New Haven, Conn.: Yale University Press, 1985.

Fackenheim, Emil L. *God's Presence in History.* New York: New York University Press, 1970.

———. *The Jewish Bible after the Holocaust.* Bloomington: Indiana University Press, 1991.

Frankl, Victor. *Man's Search for Meaning.* New York: Pocket Books, 1984.

Haas, Peter J. *Morality after Auschwitz.* Philadelphia: Fortress Press, 1988.

Huberband, Shimon. *Kiddush Hashem: Jewish Religious and Cultural Life in Poland during the Holocaust.* Ed. Jeffrey Gurock and Robert Hirt, trans. David Fishman. Hoboken, N.J.: Ktav, 1987.

Low, Alfred D. *The Third Reich and the Holocaust in German Historiography: Toward the Historikerstreit of the Mid-1980s.* New York: Columbia University Press, 1994.

Maier, Charles S. *The Unmasterable Past: History, Holocaust, and German National Identity.* Cambridge, Mass.: Harvard University Press, 1988.

Melson, Robert F. *Revolution and Genocide: On the Origins of the Armenian Genocide and the Holocaust.* Chicago: University of Chicago Press, 1992.

Peck, Abraham J. *Jews and Christians after the Holocaust.* Philadelphia: Fortress Press, 1982.

Roth, John K., and Michael Berenbaum, eds. *Holocaust: Religious and Philosophical Implications.* New York: Paragon House, 1989.

Rubenstein, Richard L., and John K. Roth. *Approaches to Auschwitz.* Atlanta: John Knox Press, 1987.

32. Anne Frank

Bloom, Harold, ed. *A Scholarly Look at the Diary of Anne Frank.* Philadelphia: Chelsea House, 1999.

The Diary of Anne Frank: The Revised Critical Edition. Prepared by the Netherlands State Institute for War Documentation, David Barnouw, and B. M. Mooyaart. New York: Doubleday, 2003.

The Diary of a Young Girl: The Definitive Edition. Ed. Otto H. Frank and Mirjam Pressler. Trans. Susan Masotty. New York: Doubleday, 1995.

Lee, Carol Ann. *The Hidden Life of Otto Frank.* New York: Collins, 2002.

Levin, Meyer. *The Obsession.* New York: Simon & Schuster, 1973.

Melnick, Ralph. *The Stolen Legacy of Anne Frank.* New Haven: Yale University Press, 1997.

Mintz, Alan. *Popular Culture and the Shaping of Holocaust Memory in America.* Seattle: University of Washington Press, 2001.

Muller, Melissa. *Anne Frank: The Biography.* New York: Metropolitan Books, 1998.

Prose, Francine. *Anne Frank: The Book, the Life, the Afterlife.* New York: HarperCollins, 2009.

Robbins, Mari Lu. *A Guide for Using Anne Frank's "The Diary of a Young Girl" in the Classroom.* Westminister, Calif.: Teacher Created Resources, 2007.

Roth, Philip. *The Ghostwriter.* New York: Vintage, 1979.

Schnabel, Ernst. *Anne Frank: A Portrait in Courage.* Trans. Richard Winston and Clara Winston. New York: Harcourt, Brace & World, 1958.

33. Restitution and the Holocaust

Aly, Götz. *Hitler's Beneficiaries: Plunder, Racial War, and the Nazi Welfare State.* New York: Metropolitan Books, 2005.

Bower, Tom. *Nazi Gold: The Full Story of the Fifty-Year Conspiracy to Steal Billions from Europe's Jews and Holocaust Survivors.* New York: HarperCollins, 1997.

Dean, Martin. *Robbing the Jews: The Confiscation of Jewish Property in the Holocaust, 1933–1945.* Cambridge, Mass: Harvard University Press, 2008.

Eizanstadt, Stuart. *Report on Nazi Theft of Jewish Assets.* Washington, D.C.: Government Printing Office, 1997.

LeBor, Adam. *Hitler's Secret Bankers: The Myth of Swiss Neutrality during the Holocaust.* Secaucus, N.J.: Birch Lane Press, 1997.

Marrus, Michael R. *Some Measure of Justice: The Holocaust Era Restitution Campaign of the 1990s.* Madison: University of Wisconsin Press, 2009.

Yahil, Leni. "Switzerland." *Encyclopedia of the Holocaust.* Vol. 4, ed. Israel Gutman, 1441–44. New York: Macmillan, 1990.

Ziegler, Jean. *The Swiss, the Gold, and the Dead: How Swiss Bankers Helped Finance the Nazi War Machine.* Trans. John Brownjohn. New York: Harcourt Brace, 1998.

34. Holocaust Denial, Nazis, and Neo-Nazis

Goodrick-Clarke, Nicholas. *Hitler's Priestess: Savitri Devi, the Hindu-Aryan Myth, and Neo-Nazism.* New York: New York University Press, 1998.

Hunt, Linda. *Secret Agenda.* New York: St. Martin's Press, 1991.

Shermer, Michael, and Alex Grobman. *Denying History: Who Says the Holocaust Never Happened and Why Do They Say It?* Berkeley: University of California Press, 2000.

Stern, Kenneth S. *Holocaust Denial.* New York: American Jewish Committee, 1993.

Strum, Phillippa. *When the Nazis Came to Skokie: Freedom for Speech We Hate.* Lawrence: University of Kansas Press, 2007.

Wiesenthal, Simon. *The Murderers amongst Us.* New York: McGraw-Hill, 1967.

Zeskind, Leonard. *Blood and Politics: The History of the White Nationalist Movement from the Margins to the Mainstream.* New York: Farrar, Straus & Giroux, 2009.

35. Books on Holocaust Films

Avisar, Ilan. *Screening the Holocaust: Cinema's Images of the Unimaginable.* Bloomington: Indiana University Press, 1988.

Baron, Lawrence. *Projecting the Holocaust into the Present: The Changing Focus of Contemporary Holocaust Cinema.* Lanham, Md.: Rowman & Littlefield, 2005.

Bartov, Omer. *The "Jew" in Cinema: From the Golem to Don't Touch My Holocaust.* Bloomington: Indiana University Press, c2005.

Bernard-Donals, Michael. *Between Witness and Testimony: The Holocaust and the Limits of Representation.* Albany: State University of New York Press, 2001.

Colombat, Andre. *The Holocaust in French Film.* Metuchen, N.J.: Scarecrow Press, 1993.

Davis, Todd F., and Kenneth.Womack, eds. "The List Is Life: Schindler's List as Ethical Construct." In *Mapping the Ethical Turn: A Reader in Ethics, Culture, and Literary Theory,* 151–64. Charlottesville: University Press of Virginia, 2001.

Doneson, Judith E. *The Holocaust in American Film.* Syracuse, N.Y.: Syracuse University Press, 2002.

Erens, Patricia. *The Jew in American Cinema.* Bloomington: Indiana University Press, 1984.

Flanzbaum, Hilene, ed. *The Americanization of the Holocaust.* Baltimore: Johns Hopkins University Press, 1999.

Friedman, Murray. "Jews in American Film and Television." In *Ethnic Images in American Film and Television.* Ed. Randall M. Miller. Philadelphia: Balch Institute, 1978.

Furman, Nelly. "Called to Witness: Viewing Lanzmann's 'Shoah.'" In *Shaping Losses: Cultural Memory and the Holocaust.* Ed. Julia Epstein and Lori Hope Lefkovitz, 55–74. Urbana: University of Illinois Press, 2001.

Gabler, Neal. *An Empire of Their Own: How the Jews Invented Hollywood.* New York: Crown, 1988.

Gilman, Sander L. "'Smart Jews': From *The Caine Mutiny* to *Schindler's List* and beyond." In *Screening the Past: Film and the Representation of History.* Ed. Tony Barta, 63–81. Westport, Conn.: Praeger, 1998.

Haggith, Toby, and Joanna Newman. *Holocaust and the Moving Image: Representations in Film and Television since 1933.* New York: Wallflower, 2005.

Herzstein, Robert Edwin. "The Jew in Wartime Nazi Film: An Interpretation of Goebbels' Role in the Holocaust." *Holocaust Studies Annual* 3 (1984): 177–88.

Hirsch, Joshua Francis. *Afterimage: Film, Trauma, and the Holocaust.* Philadelphia: Temple University Press, 2004.

Insdorf, Annette. *Indelible Shadows: Films and the Holocaust.* New York: Vintage, 1983, 2002.

Shandler, Jeffrey. *While America Watches: Televising the Holocaust.* New York: Oxford University Press, 1999.

36. Selected Feature Films

Amen (Germany-France). Dir. Costa-Gavras, 2002.
Au Revoir Les Enfants (France). Dir. Louis Malle, 1987.
The Believer (USA). Dir. Henry Bean, 2001.
The Counterfeiters (Germany-Austria). Dir. Stefan Ruzowitzky, 2007.
Defiance (USA). Dir. Edward Zwick, 2008.
The Devil's Arithmetic (USA). Dir. Donna Deitch, 1999.
The Diary of Anne Frank (USA). Dir. George Stevens, 1959.
Europa Europa (Germany). Dir. Agnieszka Holland, 1990.
Everything Is Illuminated (USA). Dir. Lev Schreiber, 2005.
Fateless (Hungary). Dir. Lajos Koltai, 2005.
The Garden of the Finzi-Contini (Italy). Dir. Vittorio De Sica, 1970.
Gloomy Sunday (Germany). Dir. Rolf Schübel, 1999.
Good Afternoon, Mr. Wallenberg (Sweden). Dir. Kjell Grede, 1990.
The Great Dictator (USA). Dir. Charlie Chaplin, 1940.

The Grey Zone (USA). Dir. Tim Blake Nelson, 2001.
Jakob the Liar (USA). Dir. Peter Kassovitz, 1999.
Judgment at Nuremberg (USA). Dir. Stanley Kramer, 1961.
The Juggler (USA). Dir. Edward Dmytryk.
Korczak (Poland). Dir. Anrzej Waida, 1990.
Left Luggage (Dutch-Belgium-USA). Dir. Jeroen Krabbě, 1998.
The Man in the Glass Booth (USA). Dir. Arthur Hill, 1975.
Music Box (USA). Dir. Costa-Gavras, 1989.
Nowhere in Africa (Germany). Dir. Caroline Link, 2001.
One Day You'll Understand (France). Dir. Amos Gitai, 2008.
Out of the Ashes (Poland-USA). Dir. Joseph Sargent, 2003.
The Pawnbroker (USA). Dir. Sidney Lument, 1964.
The Pianist (France-Germany-Poland-United Kingdom). Dir. Roman Polanski, 2002.
The Reader (United Kingdom-USA). Dir. Stephan Daldry, 2008.
Schindler's List (USA). Dir. Steven Spielberg, 1993.
The Search (USA). Dir. Fred Zinnemann, 1948.
Ship of Fools (USA) Dir. Stanley Kramer, 1965.
Sophie's Choice (USA). Dir. Alan J. Pakula, 1982.
Sophie Scholl (Germany). Dir. Marc Rothemund, 2005.
The White Ribbon (Germany). Dir. Michael Haneke, 2009.

37. Television Films

Anne Frank: The Whole Story. Dir. Robert Dornhelm, 2001.
Broken Glass. Dir. David Thacker, 1996.
Conspiracy. Dir. Frank Pierson, 2001.
The Diary of Anne Frank. Dir. Alex Segal, 1967.
The Diary of Anne Frank. Dir. Boris Sagal, 1980.
Escape from Sobibor. Dir. Jack Gold, 1987.
God on Trial. Dir. John De Emmony, 2008.
Haven. Dir. John Gray, 2001.
Holocaust. Dir. Marvin J. Chomsky, 1978.
Max and Helen. Dir. Phillip Saville, 1990.
Never Forget. Dir. Joseph Sargent, 1991.
Playing for Time. Dir. Daniel Mann, 1980.
QBVII . Dir. Tom Gries, 1974.
Quarrel. Dir. Eli Cohen, 1991.
Skokie. Dir. Herbert Wise, 1981.
Uprising. Dir. John Avnet, 2001.
The Wall. Dir. Robert Markowitz, 1982.

War and Remembrance. Dir. Dan Curtis, 1988.
Winds of War. Dir. Dan Curtis, 1983.

38. Documentaries

As Seen through These Eyes (USA). Dir. Hilary Helstein, 2009.
Berga: Soldiers of Another War (USA). Dir. Charles Guggenheim, 2003.
Blood Money: Switzerland's Nazi Gold (USA). Dir. Stephen Crisman, 1997.
CANDLES: The Story of the Mengele Twins (USA). Dir. Gordon J. Murray, 1990.
Death Mill. (USA). Dir. Billy Wilder, 1945.
The Eighty-first Blow (Israel). Dir. David Bergman, Jacques Ehrlich, and Haim Gouri, 1974.
Genocide (USA). Dir. Arnold Schwartzman, 1982.
Hotel Terminus (France, USA). Dir. Marcel Ophüls, 1988.
Imaginary Witness: Hollywood and the Holocaust (USA). Dir. Donald Anker, 2004.
In the Shadow of the Reich: Nazi Medicine (USA). Dir. John Michalczyk, 1997.
Into the Arms of Strangers: Stories of the Kindertransport (UK, USA). Dir. Mark Jonathan Harris, 2000.
Jerusalem in the Woods (USA). Dir. Dean Ward, 2006.
Killing Kasztner: The Jew Who Dealt with Nazis (USA). Dir. Gaylen Ross, 2009.
Lodz Ghetto (USA). Dir. Alan Adelson and Kate Taverna, 1989.
The Long Way Home (USA). Dir. Mark Jonathan Harris, 1997.
The Memory of Justice (France, UK, USA, and West Germany). Dir. Marcel Ophüls.
Mr. Death: The Rise and Fall of Fred A. Leuchter, Jr. (USA). Dir. Errol Morris, 1999.
My Knees Were Jumping: Memories of the Kindertransport (USA). Dir. Melissa Hacker, 1996.
Nazi Concentration Camps (USA). Dir. George Stevens, 1945.
Nazi Designers of Death (USA). Dir. Nova and Robert Jan van Pelt, 1995.
Paper Clips (USA). Dir. Elliot Berlin and Joel Fab, 2004.
Paragraph 175 (USA). Dir. Rob Epstein and Jeffrey Friedman, 2000.
Partisans of Vilna (USA). Dir. Joshua Waletzky, 1986.
Prisoner of Paradise (Canada, Germany, UK, USA). Dir. Malcom Clarke and Stuart Sender, 2002.
Rape of Europa (USA). Dir. Richard Berge, Bonnie Cohen, and Nicole Newnham, 2006.

The Rise and Fall of the Third Reich (USA). Dir. Jack Kaufman, 1968.
Schindler: The Documentary (United Kingdom). Dir. Jon Blair, 1983.
Shoah (France). Dir. Claude Lanzmann, 1985.
The Sorrow and the Pity (France). Dir. Marcel Ophüls, 1969.
To Bear Witness (USA). Dir. Gavin P. Boyle, 1983.
Who Shall Live and Who Shall Die (USA), Dir. Lawrence Jarvik, 1982.

39. General Repositories for Holocaust Archival Information, Collections, Documents, Websites, and Oral History Centers

United States

Fred R. Crawford Witness to the Holocaust Project, Emory University, Atlanta, Georgia
Jewish and Slavic Divisions, New York Public Library, New York
Simon Wiesenthal Center Archives and Library, Los Angeles, California
United States Holocaust Memorial Museum, Washington, D.C.
United States Library of Congress, Washington, D.C.
Leo Baeck Institute, New York
Yivo Institute Archives and Library, New York
National Jewish Resource Center, New York
Museum of Jewish Heritage, New York
Guide to Yale University Library Holocaust Video Testimony, 2nd ed. New Haven, Conn.: Yale University
Fortunoff Video Archive for Holocaust Testimonies, Yale University Library, Geoffrey H. Hartman, Director
Survivors of the Shoah Visual History Foundation, Los Angeles, California
American Red Cross; Holocaust and War Victims Tracing Information Center, Baltimore, Maryland

Great Britain

Wiener Library, London

Israel

Histadrut Archives, Tel Aviv
Yad Vashem, Jerusalem
Ben-Gurion Research Center, Kiryat Sde-Boker

Poland

Main Commission for Investigation of Nazi Crimes in Poland, Warsaw
Institute of National Remembrance, Warsaw
Jewish Historical Institute of Warsaw

Netherlands

Netherlands State Institute for War Documentation, The Hague

Germany

Berlin Documentation Center, Berlin

France

Center of Contemporary Jewish Documentation, Paris

Italy

Center for Contemporary Jewish Documentation, Milan

40. Internet Resources

United States Holocaust Memorial Museum at www.ushmm.org. The website reconstructs the history of the Holocaust through multiple media: The meaningful arrangement of objects as well as the . . . networking sites, like Facebook.
The Holocaust Teacher Resource Center at http://www.holocaust-trc.org. The website includes numerous articles, book reviews, and lesson plans, as well as videos aboutmany aspects of the Holocaust.
About.Com at www.about.com/Holocaust. The website includes a glossary, timelines, maps, lists of the concentration camps, other information, and a weekly electronic newsletter on issues related to the Holocaust.
Anne Franks's Life at www.Annefrank.com. This is the website for the Anne Frank Center and includes a 90-minute on-site program focusing students on in-depth observation and inquiry into the life of Anne Frank. The website also includes a screening of the documentary *The Short Life of Anne Frank*, and Holocaust survivors who share their personal stories.

The H-NET List for History of the Holocaust at http://www.h-net.org/ ~holoweb/. A member of H-Net Humanities and Social Sciences On Line. H-Holocaust exists so scholars of the Holocaust can communicate with each other. This is primarily, though not exclusively, an academic list. Coverage of the list includes the Holocaust itself and closely related topics like anti-Semitism and Jewish history in the 1930s and 1940s.

The Nizkor Project at http://www.nizkor.org/index.html. The website is a response to Holocaust denial. It includes documents on most aspects of the Holocaust, including the Nuremberg Trials, the death camps, Holocaust research guides, and much more. It has a vast collection of Holocaust documents.

Yad Vashem at www.yadvashem.org. The website is the Jewish people's memorial to the murdered six million people and symbolizes the ongoing confrontation with the rupture engendered by the Holocaust. Containing the world's largest repository of information on the Holocaust, Yad Vashem is a leader in Shoah education, commemoration, research, and documentation.

The March of the Living at www.motl.org. The website is an international educational program that brings Jewish teens from all over the world to Poland on Holocaust Memorial Day, to march from Auschwitz to Birkenau, the largest concentration camp complex built during World War II, and then to Israel to observe Yom Ha Zikaron or Israel Memorial Day, and Yom Ha'Atzmaut or Israel Independence Day. The goal of the March of the Living is for these young people to learn the lessons of the Holocaust.

Remembrance and Beyond at www.un.org/holocaustremeberance. The United Nations' official website is devoted to the International Day of Commemoration in memory of the victims of the Holocaust, which was marked for the first time on 27 January 2006.

The Center for Holocaust and Genocide Studies at the University of Minnesota at www.chgs.umn.edu/webBiB/ is one of many national and international centers dedicated to the study of the Holocaust and contemporary genocide and teaching about the subjects.

About the Author

About the Author

Jack R. Fischel is emeritus professor of history at Millersville University in Pennsylvania. He is presently a visiting professor of the humanities at Messiah College in Grantham, Pennsylvania, where he teaches a course on the Holocaust. He has coedited *Jewish American History and Culture: An Encyclopedia*, which received the Association of Jewish Libraries award as the outstanding Judaica reference book of 1992, and *The Encyclopedia of Jewish American Popular Culture* (2009). He has coedited five volumes of the *Holocaust Studies Annual* and also written two books, *The Holocaust* (1998) and *The Holocaust and Its Religious Impact* (2004). Dr. Fischel has also contributed articles and reviews on the Holocaust to many publications, including *Congress Monthly*, *Forward*, *Midstream*, *Holocaust and Genocide Studies*, *Virginia Quarterly*, *The Weekly Standard*, and other periodicals. He served for five years as the editor of *Congress Monthly*, the publication of the American Jewish Congress.

Breinigsville, PA USA
05 July 2010
241148BV00001B/2/P